ALIEN INVASION

How the Harris Tories Mismanaged Ontario

ALIEN INVASION

How the Harris Tories Mismanaged Ontario

edited by Ruth Cohen

INSOMNIAC PRESS

Edited by Richard Almonte
Copy edited by Steven Beattie
Designed by Mike O'Connor

National Library of Canada Cataloguing in Publication Data

Main entry under title:

Alien invasion

Includes bibliographical references and index.
ISBN 1- 895837-08-1

1. Ontario - Politics and government - 1993- .   I. Cohen, Ruth.

FC3077.2.A44 2001   971.3'03   C2001-930392-0
F1058.A44 2001

The publisher gratefully acknowledges the support of the Canada Council, the Ontario Arts Council and Department of Canadian Heritage through the Book Publishing Industry Development Program.

Some of the essays in this book first appeared in CCPA *MONITOR*, *Canadian Dimension*, *eye magazine*, the *Globe and Mail*, *Now Magazine*, OSSTF District 7 *Minutes*, *Report on Business* magazine and the *Toronto Star*. Essays are reprinted with permission from the *Globe and Mail* and The Toronto Star Syndicate, as well as with permission of the other publications and authors.

Printed and bound in Canada

Insomniac Press, 192 Spadina Avenue, Suite 403,
Toronto, Ontario, Canada, M5T 2C2
www.insomniacpress.com

The Canada Council | Le Conseil des Arts
for the Arts | du Canada
since 1957 | depuis 1957

ONTARIO ARTS COUNCIL
CONSEIL DES ARTS DE L'ONTARIO

Table of Contents

Part Three: Essential Reading
Chapter 5: The Harris Tories In Context

Chapter 6: What Can Be Done?

Part Four: Conclusion

Acknowledgements

First of all, I must give credit to the indefatigible Susan Smethurst, a teacher in one of Toronto's most deprived elementary schools, for this book's highly appropriate title. It is perhaps more palatable than *The Rape of Ontario* which was originally running through my mind. I admit that may be tame by comparison, but the misdeeds chronicled herein are every bit as violent as the earlier title would suggest.

I would like to pay tribute to the C4LD (Citizens for Local Democracy) listserv which was started by Liz Rykert back in the days of our innocence. In the fall of 1995, then-Minister of Municipal Affairs Al Leach sent out an amazing brochure to the citizens of Metropolitan Toronto, describing an amalgamation process that would do away with the region's existing cities and boroughs. The brochure treated this momentous change to the lives of the citizens of Metropolitan Toronto as if it were a minor alteration and a fait accompli. From that opening salvo, the C4LD listserv was an important weapon in the mobilization of a citizen opposition to the lengthy list of outrages perpetrated by the Harris regime during its first term in office.

When the Harrisites were re-elected for a second term, the experience was rather like being punched in the stomach. However, opposition is not dead, the listserve is still alive, if only barely, and many activists owe an unparalleled education in politics to its continued existence. Some of them are represented in this book: Jeff Jewell, Adrian Adamson and Ann Emmett are a few of the contributors who met through the Internet or at the meetings of Citizens for Local Democracy. I pay tribute to them and to the hundreds of wonderful social activists I have met who never gave up and never will give up until social justice and democracy once again prevail in Ontario.

I am especially grateful for the detailed research on the Harris 'Days of Destruction' contributed by Ross McClellan of the Ontario Federation of Labour. This research presents the facts of the Common Sense Revolution with a clarity that no amount of vainglorious self-trumpeting can deny. And in a strange way, I thank the aliens who landed at Queen's Park for the wake-up call that more and more of us are hearing and that will teach us what we need to do to preserve democracy, if by a very circuitous route. —Ruth Cohen

Preface by Adrian Adamson

With the passage of Bills 103 and 160, despite the most concerted opposition from the people of Ontario in the history of this province, Ontario entered into a new and ominous phase in its political development. At risk is democracy itself. Democracy has always rested on two basic pillars that distinguish it from autocracy. The first is a "social contract" between government and governed. This theory, first developed by Jean-Jacques Rousseau, rests on the concept of the "general will"—the will of the people as a whole, determined by election and majority rule.

Under this social contract the people consent to obey the laws of the government that represents the general will, and the government governs with the consent of the people who have expressed their will. But the other pillar of democracy is the notion of balance and compromise. Citizens agree to obey the laws implemented by the elected government, even if they do not agree with them, and even if they had voted for another political party. Disappointed citizens have to wait until the next election. In turn, the governing party, once in power, learns it has to govern for all the people, both those who voted for it and those who voted against it, and that as a result it may have to put some of its policies on hold.

The 'mandate' of a political party to govern is not always clear even if a government is elected by a solid majority. Some of its supporters are citizens who indeed voted for the election platform, but others voted strategically against the former government's actions. Few people believe that Ontario voters really turned socialist twelve years ago when the NDP was elected, and few believe the same people became radical conservatives when the Tories were elected in 1995.

In Ontario this democratic compromise—the social contract—has been decisively destroyed. Numerous polls, published or leaked, and every huge demonstration in city after city, indicate that the majority of the people of Ontario have withdrawn their consent (despite the two successful Tory elections) and consequently that the government has lost its legitimacy. All normal and extraordinary measures to work for change have now been tried and failed. Many may wonder on what basis they are obligated to obey the laws now passed by what is, in effect, a rogue government.

On the surface everything appears normal in Ontario. But our democracy is in deep crisis.

Adrian Adamson is a retired professor of History, as well as a writer.

Introduction by Jeff Jewell

Ontario is living through the greatest turmoil in its history. Under the cross-linked and colossal forces of globalization and the Harris regime, Ontario—and the future way of life for Ontarians—is being radically transformed before our eyes. While globalization is presently a curse common to all nations and people, the Harris regime is Ontario's very own problem.

The Harris government has inflicted the most ideological and dangerous attack on democracy that Ontario has ever faced. This ideological attack can be characterized as a usurpation of power by a handful of elected members and their unelected strategists and spin doctors. How can it be—in this country that is so proud of its tradition of freedom and its way of life—that a generation is letting these cherished things slip away without finding a way to mount an effective protest?

Every sector wants only what it perceives as best for itself, with very few people willing to consider what might be best for the common good, or for future generations. This sad situation is the product of a value system that has replaced honesty, integrity and morality with the worship of money and 'the market' as arbiters of life.

Our leaders have abandoned their people and joined instead with the global elites as the architects and engineers of their neo-con revolution. Just as importantly, the people are divided into a multitude of small factions. Many have been co-opted into this new world order, while many are trying to survive under increasingly depressed conditions. Hence, in Ontario's time of greatest peril, its citizens are found wanting.

The ruling class of decision makers—those with commanding wealth and power—only want to increase their power and wealth. The mainstream political parties only want to hold on to power—and exercise it in the interests of their benefactors, for which they can count on being well rewarded. The mainstream media only wants to serve its corporate masters. The 'public' broadcaster only wants to satisfy its political master sufficiently to avoid being privatized. The middle class only wants to hold onto its jobs and pensions, and will vote for anybody who will promise a tax break, regardless of the consequences.

The working poor only want to pay the rent and have enough food for their families, and the unemployed only wish for gainful work. Activists are largely divided and frustrated, and only want the public to pay attention to their own particular special issues. Everyone in Ontario wants what's best for themselves—and for everybody else to stop being so selfish.

As a province, a nation, a world, a civilization, we are all found wanting at this critical time in history. We must all face up to this stark reality pretty soon. We must find ways to come together and remedy the damage we have done.

Jeff Jewell is a writer. He stood as a candidate in the last federal election for the Candian Action Party.

Part One
The Background to the Harris Revolution

Chapter 1: Prologue

Take Cover, the Worst Is Yet to Come
by Ruth Cohen

*What a huge irony, to choose as best manager the most incompetent
government of a Western democracy in modern times. —Guy Crittenden*

On June 4, 1999 Ontario awoke to another Tory majority. By means of
focus group exercises to find the hot button issues, by persistent
propaganda commercials funded with taxpayers' money, by sophistries
which concealed the Tories' four-year devastation of a province, by
close scripting of the premier to "soften" his naturally lupine image,
by gerrymandering riding boundaries and tampering with the electoral process in other ways, including refusing to do a proper enumeration, the Tories conned themselves into a second term.

The voters who cast their ballots for Tory candidates consisted of
the usual core Tory support of about 28% of the population, plus
enough confused voters who were not yet sure about what had been
done to them, or how to fix it. What the voters did, to the conster-
nation of about 52% of the population who did not want another
round of Harris nostrums, was to elect a dangerous regime, guided by
unscrupulous American dirty-trick experts, whose real purpose was
anything but to deliver peace, order and good government. To the
contrary, these experts helped foment crises, destroy democracy and
ultimately deliver formerly democratic, representative governments
into the hands of the private sector.

To the Harris Tories who had again grabbed the levers of power
through chicanery of a kind never before seen in this country, democratic government—government that is respectful of human rights—
is an impediment to the free movement of capital. Since the free
movement of capital was the Tories' primary concern, they set out to
systematically dismantle those institutions that formerly governed
society. This kind of objective used to be called sedition, but is now
the sole motive of the wealthy and powerful whose hegemonic belief
is that capitalism equals freedom and the free market must reign
supreme.

Were Ontarians gulled by the cheap tricks used by Harris on the hustings—the pitiful loonie jars, the labelling of the opposition leaders as "Gloom and Doom", the hallelujah chorus celebrating the second coming of "tax cuts"— because they were foolish or because they had they lost their senses as a result of having been subjected to cunning propaganda? During the first phase of the Tories' reign in Ontario, many felt that at least they would be gone in the next election. Instead, the Tories were triumphantly borne back into office by a solid mass of Tory supporters, primarily in the so-called '905 region' around Toronto. The question arises as to why seemingly normal, well educated, family-oriented suburbanites would visit this scourge on the rest of the province, particularly on their neighbours in Toronto.

Stephen Dale, author of *Lost in the Suburbs: A Political Travelogue*, addresses this very question. He writes that "evidently the region was hugely receptive to the Ontario Tories' U.S.-style platform promoting privatization, tax cuts, workfare, and deregulation, and mesmerized by its American-inspired advertising campaign attacking welfare recipients, racial and gender-based hiring targets and pay equity." According to Dale, the psychological preconditions for supporting the politics of cruelty were abundant in Southern Ontario, making the Tories' second election win virtually a done deal. These pre-conditions include the movement to the suburbs as an expression of a preference for the private over the public; the notion that suburban consumers who are used to buying their own transportation or entertainment quite naturally expect to be able to buy their own government; the propensity among suburbanites to quite happily pay user fees to cover the cost of services they themselves use, but chafe at writing a cheque for taxes to be applied to a greater but more distant public good; and finally the stress induced in suburbanites by their long commutes in heavy traffic, their heavy debt load and their lack of community involvement.

Even these preconditions, however, which were very helpful to the Tories, did not ensure their winning the election, as the next essay shows.

Ruth Cohen is a retired secondary school teacher and a writer. She is an Active Retired Member of the Ontario Secondary School Teachers' Federation, and a member of the Toronto Seniors Council.

Tories Tipped the Cards in Ontario Election by Robert MacDermid

The 1999 financial statements for Ontario's political parties as released at the end of 1999 by Elections Ontario, reveal some astonishing details about the extent of Progressive Conservative fundraising and expenditures in the year of the 1999 election. Perhaps most importantly, they continue to demonstrate how Tory changes to the campaign finance and election laws have worked dramatically in their favour and how Tory campaign strategies have undermined the effectiveness of Ontario's laws on campaign spending—laws that are designed to ensure that Ontario election campaigns do not become the orgies of spending that are the rule in America.

The most remarkable finding is that in 1999 the Progressive Conservative central party spent more money than any other Ontario central party has spent in a single year in fifteen years of record keeping and, surely, an all-time spending record. The $12.1 million was almost double the next highest annual central party expenditure figure, $7 million, which the party spent in 1998. It also meant that the party ran a deficit of $3.7 million for the year. In the same period, the NDP central party spent $3.5 million and the Liberals spent $3.0 million.

Second, we can begin to get a fairly accurate picture of what the Tories spent in the election year. To the $12.1 million reported in the set of statements released on December 3, 1999, we can add the $5.8 million the Tory central campaign spent during the campaign period, expenditures both under and outside the cap (something the Tories redefined), and all directed at their re-election bid. To these two figures, add the spending on behalf of Tory candidates in constituencies. These figures were not complete at the time of writing, but we can arrive at a reasonable and cautious estimate by supposing that all Tory candidates spent two-thirds of the riding expenditure caps. (The average will probably turn out to be higher.) The total value of all of the 103 constituency spending caps is $7.3 million dollars or, on average, about $71,000 per riding. Assume that the candidates and constituency associations spent two-thirds of that figure, $4.8 million, on re-election bids and the total spending in 1999 then becomes $22.7 million. Subtract the two or three million the party would have spent on party maintenance, and the $2.3 million the Tories spent on raising money, and that means the Tories spent something in the region of $15 million to $17 million on getting re-elected. That is an astonishing figure by Ontario standards and it does not include the money spent on what the opposition parties, the provincial auditor and the Speaker of the House all considered to be partisan government advertising in the pre-campaign period.

The third remarkable aspect of the December 3 filing is the sum that the Progressive Conservative party spent on advertising in 1999. My analysis of TV station logs, made available by the CRTC, shows that the Tory advertising campaign of April and early May 1999, just before the election was called, was in some instances more intense than their TV advertising campaign during the election period itself. For example, between April 7 and May 5, the Tories ran on CFTO 155 spots in the pre-campaign and 180 during the campaign; on CJOH they ran 256 spots in the pre-campaign and 124 in the real campaign; and on CKCO they ran 125 spots in the pre-writ period and 130 between May 12 and June 1, the legal campaign advertising period. What did those spots cost? We know that during the campaign the Tories paid MBS Retail Media, a media buying company, $3.4 million. The December 3 statement indicates that they spent almost $3.5 million on advertising during 1999, most of which must have been spent in April and May, just prior to when they called the election.

It is now even clearer why the Tories shortened the campaign period to twenty-eight days. That change brought pre-campaign advertising closer to the campaign itself, with only a week long black-out at the beginning of the campaign, and allowed them to spend completely unrestricted sums of money in the unregulated pre-campaign period. It seems reasonable to suggest that the Tories have made campaign expenditure laws almost entirely pointless.

Finally, the Tory central party took in $5.9 million in contributions during 1999. Another Ontario record. But even with the $4.9 million the party raised during the campaign period, they still went temporarily into debt. Once again, the Tories were assisted by the changes they made to the contribution limits, raising the limit a corporation or individual could give in an election year from \$14,000 to \$25,000. This change alone brought in an additional \$1 million to the 1999 Tory central campaign. When the extra giving for all other contribution periods during 1999 can be calculated, it will surely show that this change alone added an additional \$2 million to \$3 million to the Tory coffers. The changes will have benefited the Liberals by a fraction of this and the NDP hardly at all, since they, in comparison to the Tories, had very few donors wealthy enough to give the maximum donation. In 1999, the Liberal party reported taking in \$1.5 million in contributions and the NDP \$2.2 million.

More than ever, these figures show the yawning gap between the financial health of the Progressive Conservative party, flush with contributions from wealthy individual and corporate supporters, and the opposition Liberal and New Democrat parties, both deeply in debt. This can never be a good thing for the health of any democracy.

Robert MacDermid is a professor of Political Science at York University.

Ontario's 1999 Provincial Election Revisited by Gordon Garland

More than a year has passed since the 1999 Ontario provincial election. At the time, the province's Chief Election Officer called it his "day from hell." Local, regional and provincial media all reported extensively about problems with the voters list. Analysts and observers equated the overall effect to an election in a banana republic. The response was swift:

- Both opposition parties called for the resignation of the Chief Election Officer.
- The Chief Election Officer claimed "chaos on election day" was the result of organized "election terrorism" (his claim was proven groundless).
- Citizens and various groups called for an independent public inquiry into the election and Election Act changes.

Those making complaints were told to await the Chief Election Officer's Report on the election. His report is now out. It is a short twenty-seven-page study in defensive tactics. The report overwhelmingly confirms the need for a full public inquiry into the election and into the Election Act changes.

The report contains glaring errors of omission. After reading the report, one is left wondering what election the Chief Election Officer is referring to. The report makes no reference to inaccurate or incomplete voters lists. Nor is there any analysis of the voters lists—who was on the list and could vote "as of right" and who was left off the lists and had to attempt to "register." The registration process placed serious obstacles in the way of people entitled to vote. Phone lines at Elections Ontario were jammed. Their newspaper ads wrongly told people that unless they were registered before election day, they couldn't vote.

In some urban polls almost 30% of those who voted were not even on the voters lists. Potential voters came in all day to find out where they should vote. In many cases no one could answer them, and they wandered off in search of the unknown. Long lineups persisted from 4:30 P.M. onwards as potential voters tried to register. Many left in sheer frustration, denied their fundamental right to vote. The Chief Election Officer repeatedly refused to use his discretion to order "spot enumerations," even in ridings where the lists were hopelessly inaccurate. Astonishingly, the 1999 election chaos was a repeat of what the Chief Election Officer oversaw in the 1997 Toronto 'Megacity' election. After that election a *Toronto Star* editorial noted that "the provincial voters list was way out of whack, by as much as 50% in areas of high transient population... All of which could and should have been anticipated."

The most important questions raised by the election are not even asked in this report:

• How accurate were the voters lists in each riding?
•Was there a significant difference in accuracy between urban and rural ridings?
•Were people who had moved in the past year systematically left off the voters list?
•Were those left off the list disproportionately tenants, young people, immigrants, the disabled and the poor?
•Does voter registration systematically discriminate against these groups?
•Would enumeration of voters solve most problems?

The Chief Election Officer had the election data, the time, the resources and the contacts to answer these very basic questions. Yet all remain unanswered.

The cruel reality is that if we cannot learn from the problems of the past we are doomed to repeat those problems. The report offers one insight: "Elections Canada advised Elections Ontario in a Statement of Data Quality that: 'The release includes 95.7% of the eligible electors in Ontario and 86.7% of electors on the release are listed at the correct address.'" Considering that one needs a correct address to receive a voter card, this means that at least 13.3% of the voters list was wrong. This error rate rises to 17% when those who were entirely missed are added in. Was this level of inaccuracy ever checked by Elections Ontario?

Our democracy is based on one person, one vote. In a close election many ridings can be decided by less than 5% of the vote. A 13.3% or 17% level of inaccuracy for a voters list is the equivalent of disenfranchising those who would and could decide a close provincial election. This is patently unacceptable in a democracy. A door-to-door enumeration of eligible voters would have produced an up-to-date voters list that approached 100% accuracy. Yet the Chief Election Officer concludes: "A register system to produce current voters lists is practical and workable and a suitable and appropriate replacement for the enumeration process." This conclusion is not supported by even the very limited facts in his report.

Finally, the report contains glaring errors in its assertions. This includes at least two cases where the facts are not fully stated, causing the Legislature to have possibly been misled. In the first case, the Chief Election Officer explains that the government's Election Act changes (Bill 36) were based on recommendations from his 1987 and 1990 reports. A review of these reports shows that none of the major changes in Bill 36 (a move from enumeration of all eligible voters to U.S.-style voter registration, a shorter 28-day election campaign, down from 37 days and a dramatic increase in both election spending by political parties and in corporate and individual political donations) were based on the Chief Election Officer's recommendations. Bill 36 is the most radical change in election laws in the past fifty years.

How was it passed? The Chief Election Officer is silent on this issue. One might conclude that passage was normal in every way. In fact, Bill 36 was rammed through the Legislature over 15 days in June 1998. No opposition party amendments were allowed and no public hearings were permitted.

The second case is more contrived and manipulative than the first, and involves the Chief Election Officer's analysis of the costs of the 1999 election. He concludes that "this election cost Ontario taxpayers $40.9 million or $5.38 per elector, representing savings per elector of $1.04 over 1995." The fundamental problem with this assertion is that it is wrong. The cost of the 1995 election includes the enumeration of all eligible voters at a cost of $12 million, or $1.88 for each identified voter (a very small price to ensure accurate and complete preliminary voters lists). However, in his calculations for the 1999 election, the total costs of the new Register of Voters are never identified. A subsequent call to his office could not produce these costs.

Then the Chief Election Officer takes the cost of the 1999 election and divides it by the inaccurate final list of electors (inflated by at least 13.3% with wrong addresses, duplicate names, dead people and adding in those who registered on election day). While costs may be underestimated, the number of eligible voters is significantly overstated. The result is the creation of a fiction: understated costs per 'real' elector for 1999.

The Chief Election Officer concludes that solving election day problems will require more staff, more pay, better training and more computers. So much for the alleged savings from the new Register of Voters. However, the report's primary concern is that the new system of voter registration requires a fundamental shift of responsibility. "It is the responsibility of the individual elector," the report states, "to take the necessary action to have their name included on the list of electors." This change creates a key problem. People move and some people move more often (tenants) than others (homeowners). And when they move, informing Elections Ontario will be a low priority, if not the furthest thing from their mind.

In essence, the permanent voters list is anything but permanent and cannot hope to match the accuracy, completeness and fairness of an enumeration. The current legislation requires the Chief Election Officer to take whatever steps are necessary to ensure that the voters list "is as accurate as reasonably possible." What definition of "reasonable" did he use in the 1999 election, and what definition should be used, as public policy, in the next provincial election? A full public inquiry into the 1999 election, and into the Elections Act changes which have guided that election, is necessary. Leaving our democracy in the hands of those who have diminished it, and created a two-tier system, is not an option.

Gordon Garland is President of Strategic Directions Consulting.

Chapter 2: How Did We Get Here?

The Ideology Driving the Common Sense Revolution by Ruth Cohen

The Harris government prides itself on having kept its promises. It has 'stayed the course', unswayed by criticism or protest. If the polls are to be believed, some 65% of the population apparently agrees that indeed the government is 'on the right track', but has just gone a little too fast to achieve its goals. The government claims to have achieved all it set out to do — reduce taxes, reduce the welfare rolls, downsize government, merge municipal governments, restructure health care, restructure schools, manage the environmnent and create jobs. However, in view of the fact that the implementation of these goals has resulted not in savings but rather in increased costs, increased taxes and decreased services — the very opposite of what was contained in the promises—the meaning of 'on the right track' and the reason why the majority of people think the Harris government is there, is somewhat difficult to fathom.

To overcome the total discrepancy between its stated goals and its actual accomplishments, the Harris Tories employ various spin techniques. However, no amount of clever propaganda will conceal the reality that the Common Sense Revolution has been a disaster for Ontario. No amount of electioneering fixes or pie-in-the-sky propaganda will hide the fact that they have been on the wrong track all along.

The 905 voters who were given their hush money to approve the hostile takeover of the province will get their fair share of suffering eventually, as all of Ontario begins to feel the full impact of the end of education—other than business education—the end of medicare and the end of environmental regulation, not to mention shouldering the increased costs of privatization and downloading. We will see health decline as a result of air and water pollution, and poverty increase to include more of the middle class. We will see restrictive measures tightened not only against the poor but against dissidents who do not subscribe to the senseless Common Sense Revolution.

'Common Sense' Ideology

Ur-Fascism is still around us, sometimes in plainclothes. Ur-Fascism can come back under the most innocent of disguises. Our duty is to uncover it and to point our finger at any of its new instances—every day, in every part of the world... Freedom and liberation are an unending task. —Umberto Eco

The occupation of Ontario in June of 1995 by a party of right-wing revolutionaries did not come entirely as a bolt from the blue. It was preceded by an accumulation of business school pseudo-scientific jargon in the popular press by economists who saw the free market as the ultimate reality. It was also preceded by about thirty years of organized propaganda by right-wing think-tanks. Political theorists like Hobbes who saw the human condition as mirroring the life of animals in the wild—nasty, brutish and short—also paved the way for the Common Sense Revolution. In the long term the example of various tyrants from history, whose main purpose was to impose their will on the populations they sought to control in the interests of acquiring riches, power and glory for themselves, made the Tory victory acceptable.

Before the era of cuts and downsizing in the interests of "deficit reduction", Ontario governments, Liberal, Conservative and, more recently, NDP, had listened, consulted, provided social services, paid attention to real needs and in general fostered a civil society which was the envy of the world. In particular, Toronto was known for having a high quality of life, for being a city where neighborhoods flourished and local democracy was strong. It was a city where municipal governments had responded to citizens' concerns by putting neighborhoods first, making Toronto one of the few cities in North America where people lived and walked in safety downtown.

Suddenly, with the passing of Bill 26 in the fall of 1995, everything changed. The Mike Harris government had been elected with the largest majority in provincial history: eighty-two seats against a combined forty-eight for the opposition parties. Against all opposition, including a heroic thirty-six-hour filibuster by Alvin Curling, the government passed Bill 26, An Act to achieve Fiscal Savings and to promote Economic Prosperity through Public Sector Restructuring, Streamlining and Efficiency and to implement other aspects of the Government's Economic Agenda. This precursor to Bill 103, the municipal amalgamation bill, and Bill 160, the school restructuring bill, let a new sentiment loose in the land—an ugly sentiment that governments themselves must be run like a businesses and show a profit. This profit could then be returned to the 'shareholders', the new name for citizens, in the form of reduced taxes.

The voters had been so thrilled by the promises of tax reduction in the manifesto of the Common Sense Revolution that they had opened their beaks wide, like fledglings in a nest, to be fed the heady elixir of tax cuts cooked up by Harris and his merry band of revolutionaries. There were those even then who knew that these promises were empty, that the premises they were based on were false and that their outcome could only be vastly increased costs, profound shock and disorder and a chaotic, unworkable mess. Six years later, when upheaval and chaos affecting the very foundations of civil society have disrupted peace, order and good government for all to see, an important question arises. How and why did so perverse a doctrine as the belief that the public sector must be destroyed and privatized gain so much ground in Ontario?

By the time the revolutionary cadre who framed the Common Sense Revolution had sold it to a mesmerized populace, it had already taken on the character of a new religion, or more correctly, a cult. It had acquired many adherents whose worship of 'private enterprise' and 'laissez-faire capitalism' has imposed a new world order that has supplanted the ideals and goals of democracy throughout the world.

Ur-Fascism derives from individual or social frustration. That is why one of the most typical features of historical fascism was the appeal to a frustrated middle class, a class suffering from an economic crisis or feelings of political humiliation, and frightened by the pressure of lower social groups. In our time, when the old "proletarians" are becoming petty bourgeois (and the lumpen are largely excluded from the political scene), the fascism of tomorrow will find its audience in this new majority.   —Umberto Eco

An argument can be made that the Harris government is part of a particularly virulent business cult that has been working for decades to undermine democratic governments and supplant them with corporate rule. At this moment in history, this business cult has succeeded in becoming the de facto government in almost all the nations on earth. Even the Canadian federal government is hard at work achieving the decades-long goal of the voracious moneyed interests to dismantle all the social safety nets on which communities depend, in turn making governments completely subservient to corporations.

The Origins of Free Market Ideology

The term hegemony crops up in current criticism that grapples with the whys and wherefores of the new age of corporate rule. Hegemon means "leader" in Greek and hegemony has been used traditionally to refer to the influence of states over other states.

The concept was further developed in the 1920s and '30s by the Italian thinker Antonio Gramsci who used it to explain how one class could establish its leadership over others through ideological dominance. He showed how, once ideological authority or "cultural hegemony" is established, the use of violence to impose change can become superfluous. The concept of ideological hegemony has once again come into prominence in the writing of economists such as as Michel Chossudovsky of the University of Ottawa, and Susan George of the Transnational Institute.

In an article titled "How to Win the War of Ideas: Lessons from the Gramscian Right," George uses the concept of hegemony to telling effect. She writes, "Today, few would deny that we live under the virtually undisputed rule of the market-dominated, ultracompetitive, globalized society with its cortege of manifold inequities and everyday violence. Have we got the hegemony we deserve? I think we have, and by 'we' I mean the progressive movement, or what's left of it. The Rule of the Right is the result of a concerted, long-term ideological effort on the part of identifiable actors. If we recognize that a market-dominated, iniquitous world is neither natural nor inevitable, then it should be possible to build a counter-project for a different kind of world."

Exclusion and Ideology

In a revealing paragraph, Susan George demolishes the myth of the free market as a passport to freedom and democracy: "The late twentieth century can be dubbed the Age of Exclusion. It's now clear that the 'free market,' which increasingly determines political and social—as well as economic—priorities, cannot embrace everyone. The market's job is not to provide jobs, much less social cohesion. It has no place for the growing numbers of people who contribute little or nothing to production or consumption. The market operates for the benefit of a minority. The now-dominant economic doctrine, of which widespread exclusion is a necessary element, did not descend from heaven. It has, rather, been carefully nurtured over decades, through thought, action, and propaganda; bought and paid for by a closely knit fraternity (they mostly are men) who stand to gain from its application."

The cold-hearted, implacable insistence of the Harrisites on acting upon the tenets of an ideology designed to destroy democratic government is but one especially extreme and mean-spirited manifestation of this decades-long movement to dismantle all the social safety nets on which communities depend. That the Harris regime actually gets credit for 'staying the course' by behaving like a cruel, pitiless tyrant, is breathtaking in its sheer irrationality.

How can such irrational ideas have come to dominate the thinking of entire populations of Western democracies? The answer is that the ground had already been prepared by a new brand of philosophy that found Judaeo-Christian values abhorrent. Imbued with the Nietzschean philosophy of writers like Ayn Rand who worshipped the titans of big business, certain economists took up the outcry against the Keynesian economics of the mid-twentieth century and spoke out against any kind of government intervention. Even health, welfare and education were regarded as interference with the natural momentum of free enterprise and the rights of those who knew how to make money and keep it.

Friedrich Nietzsche and the Superman

In *Thus Spake Zarathustra* (1883-85), Friedrich Nietzsche introduced in eloquent, poetic prose a way of relating his concepts of the death of God, the superman, and the will to power. Vigorously attacking Christianity and democracy as moralities for the "weak herd," he argued for the "natural aristocracy" of the superman who, driven by the "will to power," celebrates life on Earth rather than sanctifying it for some heavenly reward. Such a heroic man of merit has the courage to "live dangerously" and thus rise above the masses, developing his natural capacity for the creative use of passion.

Nietzsche's later writings are particularly strident. Although more forceful than his earlier essays and books, they retain clear continuity with his earlier ideas. In a collection of essays published posthumously as *The Will to Power* (1901), Nietzsche further developed his ideas of the superman and the will to power, asserting that humans must learn to live without their gods or any other metaphysical consolations. Like Goethe's Faust, humans must incorporate their devil and evolve "beyond good and evil." Nietzsche's pronouncements, originally seen as outrageous, are now tacitly and even openly accepted by the 'realists' of the right.

Nietzsche's effect on late-twentieth century right-wing conservatism can be seen in the following quotations. Nietzsche claims that

> man is finished when he becomes altruistic. Instead of saying naively 'I am no longer worth anything,' the moral lie in the mouth of the decadent says 'Nothing is worth anything life is not worth anything.' (The reasoning here seems to be that if I do things for people less able than I to do things for themselves, I demean myself.) An "altruistic" morality—a morality in which self interest wilts away—remains a bad sign under all circumstances. This is true of individuals. It is particularly true of nations. The best is lacking when self interest begins to be lacking.

And about the sick, Nietzsche argues that "the sick man is a parasite of society. In a certain state it is indecent to live longer. To go on vegetating in cowardly dependence on physicians and machinations, after the meaning of life, after the right to life has been lost, that ought to prompt a profound contempt in society." Nietzsche despised socialism perhaps more than anything else. Some critics have even suggested that much of Nietzsche's work responds directly to the socialist doctrines of Karl Marx who was a contemporary, and whose work was much more popularly received. Of the socialists Nietzsche says:

> How ludicrous I find [them], with their nonsensical optimism concerning the "good man," who is waiting to appear from behind the scenes if only one would abolish the old "order" and set all the "natural drives" free.

Politically, Nietzsche could be best described as an 'aristocratic radical,' one who believed in the value of a rigidly stratified social order where the 'higher type' ruled. He writes:

> Every enhancement of the type called "man" has so far been the work of an aristocratic society—and it will be so again and again—a society of the type that believes in the long ladder of an order of rank and differences in value between man and man, and that needs slavery in some sense or other.

Socialism is anathema to an aristocratic society because it seeks to make everyone equal, whereas Nietzsche argues that social stratification is not only inevitable, but positively beneficial and necessary for the advancement of the species. Nietzsche's writings are a response to the political realities of Europe in the late-nineteenth century, where socialism was seen the wave of the future: "Let us stick to the facts: the people have won—or 'the slaves' or 'the mob' or 'the herd' or whatever you like to call them." Socialism, Nietzsche suggests, is a political manifestation of the slave morality that seeks to negate life because "Life itself is essentially appropriation, injury, overpowering of what is alien and weaker; suppression, hardness, imposition of one's own forms, incorporation and at least, at its mildest, exploitation."

Irrationalism is an essential ingredient in the cult of the Superman. Irrationalism depends on the cult of action for action's sake. Action being beautiful in itself, it must be taken before, or without, reflection. Thinking is a form of emasculation. Therefore culture is suspect insofar as it is identified with critical attitudes. Distrust of the intellectual world has always been a symptom of Ur-Fascism, from Hermann Goering's fondness for a phrase from a Hanns Johst play ("When I hear the word 'culture' I reach for my gun") to the frequent use of such expressions as "degenerate intellectuals," "eggheads," "effete snobs," and "universities are nests of reds." —Umberto Eco

Ayn Rand and *Ressentiment*

Altruism permits no concept of a self-respecting, self-sup-porting man—a man who supports his life by his own own effort and neither sacrifices himself nor others. When I say "capitalism", I mean a full, pure, uncontrolled, unregulated laissez-faire capitalism—with a separation of state and eco-nomics in the same way and for the same reason as the sepa-ration of church and state. A pure system of capitalism has never yet existed, not even in America; various degrees of gov-ernment control had been undercutting and distorting it from the start. Capitalism is not the system of the past; it is the sys-tem of the future—if mankind is to have a future. —Ayn Rand

Nietzsche first popularized the term *ressentiment*, which he traced back to the inception of Christianity. He argued that Christianity itself was a product of, or even the very essence of, *ressentiment*. The term is rooted in the hatred felt by the Hebrew priestly class in the Holy Land for the Romans who ruled over them. Nietzsche saw Christianity as the ultimate revenge of the powerless priests who once held the role of mediating between God and the Hebrews against the powerful, irrational and conquering Romans.

On its own, this debasement of the very concept of God is pro-foundly dark and nihilistic, yet if read another way, the notion of *ressentiment* cuts very deeply into all kinds of sociological and politcal motivations. Professor Roger Bromley, of Nottingham Trent University, has put it as follows:

In conditions of structured inequality... loss, disadvantage, and above all, powerlessness are generated to such an extent that the unsettled can only be restored by an act of *ressentiment*.

Ressentiment and the play of forces it produces is therefore part of a continuously produced narrative of inequality—it is one of the principal resources of seemingly equalizing action... Nietzsche considers it a strategy of the 'weak', the 'slave', ignoring that it is an effect of, not the cause of, enslavement... I would contend that it is derived from an ideological, cultural narrative. A graduated society curbs liberty by making spaces for the conditions of violence, by infantilizing and even maddening people: consuming them so that all their energies are engaged in a form of paranoia, with its psychical damage.

It is against such considerations that the theories of Ayn Rand on the virtues of selfishness and the glories of capitalism can be assessed.

Ayn Rand, born Alisa Rosenbaum, arrived on the shores of America in 1926. She was born in St. Petersburg in 1905. In 1917 her family's business was nationalized and their apartment building was expropriated. The Rosenbaum family fled St. Petersburg for the Crimea. In 1921, the Crimea fell to the Bolsheviks and the Rosenbaums returned to Petrograd, as St. Petersburg had been renamed. In 1926 Alisa, now Ayn, arrived in America for a visit relatives in Chicago. She moved to Hollywood, and had a fortuitous encounter with Cecil B. DeMille, which resulted in her becoming a script writer with the DeMille Studio.

Given Rand's family history, and the fact that she arrived in the U.S. at a time when the movie moguls were serving as an example of the rewards of free enterprise, it is perhaps not surprising that she became one of the most ardent defenders of capitalism, which she saw as the opposite of communism in the Soviet Union. In her novels and philosophical writings on 'objectivism' she struck a chord with many (including the redoubtable Alan Greenspan, chairman of the U.S. Federal Reserve Bank) and seems to have become a veritable beacon for the misinformed of today.

A distinct problem arises however, when a premise which is rife with false assumptions in whole and in part is offered as the only rational or objective view of the human condition. Ayn Rand created such a problem by making an absolute of the hypothesis that capitalism represents ultimate reality. She held that any denial of this fundamental reality flew in the face of reason. This completely false doctrine resonated with those who through some defect of their critical faculties or other intellectual shortcoming embraced it as 'common sense.' In combination with a strong admixture of *ressentiment*, which in the Randian case was directed against the poor and the weak, her version of objective reality enabled her to concentrate solely on personal gain and profit without regard for the well-being of fellow humans. Rand's philosophy has become the 'common sense' of the right-wing revolutionaries and their brainwashed followers of the present day.

Friedrich von Hayek

Along with the philosophy of Friedrich Nietzsche and Ayn Rand, the Harris Tories have been influenced by the work of Friedrich von Hayek. The foundations of Hayek's creed are laid out in his famous 1944 work, *The Road to Serfdom*, and further developed in his other major works, *The Constitution of Liberty* (1960) and *Law, Legislation, and Liberty* (1978). Hayek's chief pupil, Milton Friedman of the University of Chicago, has refined and popularized his mentor's teachings. According to Hayek, the largest impediment to a free economy is the presence of unions.

For Hayek, unions are special interest groups which, by securing better wages and working conditions for their members, deprive the non-organized and umemployed of resources and artificially drive up the price of goods and services. Their internal power over members ultimately depends on coercion, which they also exercise externally on the picket line. In light of all this, collective bargaining agreements, which Hayek regards as the equivalent of ransom payments to union members, should not have the same legal standing as regular business contracts, and are fair game for tearing up at any time.

At the same time, Hayek maintains that employers do not in the end have coercive power over their employees, as the latter can leave at any time. One wonders what unorganized, minimum-wage fast-food employees, or educational workers bargaining as individuals, would think of that assumption. Does Buzz Hargrove of the Canadian Auto Workers have anything approaching the same coercive power as Conrad Black?

For Hayek, government's role should be confined to national defense, local policing, and consistent enforcement of mutually agreed-upon business contracts. Everything else should properly fall within the sphere of the private sector. The theory goes that the more areas government puts within its purview, the more it plans human affairs centrally, the more inevitable the progress becomes towards totalitarianism. Hayek denies, of course, that centralizing power in the hands of large corporations can lead to the same thing.

Milton Friedman

In the mind of Milton Friedman, freedom means freedom from government interference in economic activity. Out of this single premise comes the whole web of free market ideology which has entangled the world and brought us close to extinction. According to Friedman, whose theories were put into practice in Chile under the dictatorship of Augusto Pinochet, there are many aspects of society in which the government has no business being involved. As a result, government is doing its fundamental job poorly because it devotes too much time and too many resources to business it shouldn't be involved with in the first place. His is a traditional laissez-faire liberalism, a hands-off approach to government interference in the private market.

The economic arena is the major area where Friedman feels government has no right to intrude upon the freedom of the collective or individual rights of its constituents. In Friedman's neo-liberal doctrine, "individual freedom is the ultimate social ideal. Governmental power, while necessary, must be limited and decentralized. Economic freedom, that is, capitalism, is an indispensable condition for political liberty."

All of these theorists fall into a similar intellectual trap. They believe that the entire human condition can be derived from a single proposition, that the free market is god. Nietzsche's transvaluation of values has been the gospel of these capitalist economists, who replace a reverence for life with a culture of competition. The Harrisites have succumbed to these dark doctrines. However, it is now becoming more widely understood that the interconnectedness of all life must be put forward as a replacement guiding principle of existence. This leaves us free to build a strong case against the Tories and their sad legacy.

The 'Big Lie' Is the Hallmark of Corporate Totalitarianism by John McMurtry

Classic totalitarianism is a form of political and social rule that seeks the total domination of society's members in every sphere of their lives. This includes political and economic activity, inner belief system and personal desires. It rules by sudden and disruptive decree, replacing civic debate with public scapegoating and smearing opponents as subversive or belonging to 'special interests'. Totalitarianism's hallmark characteristic is 'the big lie'—blurring fact and fiction by the saturating repetition of mind-shackling falsehoods. Its ultimate apparatus of social control is a pervasive propaganda system that appeals beneath reason to the primordial hatreds and fantasies of economically destabilized masses.

The prior social conditions required for totalitarianism to grow as a social movement are deepening unemployment and insecurity of livelihood, decay of civil infrastructures, and a corrosive cynicism about old-style government. Totalitarianism succeeds by occupying this vacuum. The social bonds of mutual concern are stripped to lay bare an atavistic selfishness whose most compelling desire is to strike out in any way that avenges the gnawing sense of anonymity, insignificance and rootlessness of its followers.

This is the leaven of any totalitarian movement, and what its opportunistic leadership always seizes upon as its vehicle to a social command which no one would have taken seriously before. Here the incapacity of both leaders and followers unite in a fury to assert themselves as the new tribunes of a society that has lost its civil bearings. Harness the resentment of faceless millions to the primitive militance of willful ignorance that links the leaders to the mob, and you have the driving force of a totalitarian movement. A demagogic mastery of the mass media then steers the undertow energy of the disaffected mass psyche from victory to victory, until the spell is finally broken by the intrusion of a collapsing reality.

It does not matter during the whole spectacle that the formless mass that supports a totalitarian movement is sold out as its leaders make deals with the wealthy and well placed in exchange for financial and inside support. This exchange takes place behind the scenes where the public interest is irrelevant. What matters, and what every demagogic twist of populist rhetoric appeals to, is that swift and decisive power is wielded to symbolize control over a deteriorating situation by aggressions against somebody the mob can hate.

In the striking conceptualization of Hannah Arendt in her classic study, *The Origins of Totalitarianism*, what propels the body politic in a totalitarian culture is "the negative solidarity of atomized masses." Arendt's 1955 study is confined to "the only two forms of totalitarianism we know"—Nazism and Stalinism. Arendt warns, however, that totalitarianism is "an ever present danger" grounded in "the endless process of capital and power accumulation" which erupts past former historical and social limits by its "alliance with classless masses."

Arendt's reference to "capital" as well as "power" accumulation has not been pursued by scholars of her work or by analysts of totalitarianism. This is myopic because the deep pattern of the totalitarian pathology is not only found in the familiar historical examples. It occurs in any industrial society where the twin conditions of insecurity and collapse of civil bonds exist.

In place of the social ties of mutual concern, the glue in a totalitarian society becomes destructive attacks on target groups. This pathology can emerge in places one would never have imagined possible. Consider as an example Ontario under Mike Harris. As in early 1980s England, an ideologically driven leadership unexpectedly assumed office in an economically depressed period with a minority of the popular vote. The new government's plans to refashion society in accordance with its ideology were put into motion immediately, and with brutal decisiveness. Those who opposed it were the people who had betrayed the hard working majority, 'stabbed them in the back.'

The Harris government thus decreed that single mothers must feed their children with 20% less income, that subsidies for universities must be cut to the lowest per student funding in North America; that public education must be restructured under direct rule; that health policies must be followed leaving 10% of the population without doctors; that the police forces must be increased even though violent crime rates are falling; that public housing must end and costs of municipal government must be downloaded; and that over 90% of the publicly owned land mass of Ontario must be turned over to big corporations and developers to exploit as private resources.

One slash of the social fabric after another would normally be political suicide for a regime that is subject to electoral recall by a widely educated population. But since less than 35% of the registered vote can garner a majority of Legislature seats, and since a saturation media campaign can convince the necessary minority of the fantasy that they are part of an historic triumph, those who prefer a civilized society can be overwhelmed.

In a society that is crumbling, civil cleansing may incite a rising popularity. Yet more and more people sense that something has gone very wrong underneath the triumphalism and repetition of slogans. So mass marketing optics must turn truth on its head. Wherever there is a policy disaster, the media must ring with new self-congratulatory messages of hard won success. Since the evidence everywhere shows a decline in the social fabric, the obliteration of the distinction between fact and fiction becomes an imperative for the regime's survival. Because once the regime is seen for what it is, it is finished. That is why a totalitarian regime always disappears without a trace once it has been exposed to its citizens. It depends on the total lie to continue from one day to the next.

This is also why the mass media must prevent any exposure of all the lies, as the corporate media has managed to do in Ontario over the last four years. What attracts massive corporate financial support for every step of the adventure is the feeding frenzy on the public sector, as it is converted to a profit-taking market on every level. And so the Harris regime has lied with impunity about every policy it has decreed:

• There are "more and more teachers in the clasroom" as thousands fewer teachers teach.

• The environment is "being protected for the future of all Ontarians" as environmental funding is stripped, millions of hectares of public lands are turned over to unregulated corporate exploitation, and air pollution is declared a public health crisis by Ontario doctors.

• Higher education is "available to all Ontario's qualified young people" as tuition fees and student debts nearly double.

• "Tax restructuring" for municipal government is "revenue-neutral" as municipalities across the province unprecedented-ly declare their budgets in the red.

• The "debt crisis is solved by tough decisions" as the debt rises by double figures.

One lie fades into the next. As long as the distinction between fact and fiction is suspended, the social destruction can continue without any consequence This is the ultimate thrill for the totalitar-ian psyche—to prescribe everything as necessary, no matter how unpleasant—and to replace reality with mass media slogans. This is the corporate agenda's final solution.

John McMurtry is a professor of Philosophy at the University of Guelph.

With a Good Deficit You Can See Forever
by Adrian Adamson

On one subject everyone will agree. The deficit is a disaster and must be lowered, through wage rollbacks if necessary. The last time so many people agreed, it was over another disaster—one so clear and obvious that anyone who disagreed was branded as lacking in mental acuity—the 1970s energy crisis. The world was going to run out of oil and we were all going to freeze in the dark. There were long line-ups at the pumps, the price of gasoline went through the roof, half the world changed its heating methods and people traded their cars in for ever smaller ones. Then, a few years later, the world was suddenly awash in a glut of oil and fortunes were made by a lot of people.

Twenty years ago the corporate class in Canada agreed on one thing: wages in Canada were outrageous, and something had to be done about them. Quite unconsciously, I am sure, the language used came right out of Karl Marx: "Greedy, bloated, unproductive, lazy workers are ripping us off. We own the capital, so we create the value, and the workers' wages are ripping off our surplus value so that a capitalist can hardly make a billion anymore. Something's got to be done! We need a revolution! Break out the blue flags. It's hard for us rich to start a revolution against the poor. But we have certain advantages: we are wealthy, and so we can buy anything; we are clever and can come up with good strategies; and, finally, we have governments and the media in our pockets. So we should be able to manage it." Successive governments have heeded the call. Their plan has included five stages.

Stage one is to secure free trade with the United States, where there are weak unions, low wages and no social programs. That should cool off wage demands, and if it doesn't, there is always free trade with Mexico, where workers earn eighty-eight cents an hour and they shoot labour leaders for breakfast. "Ha! Ha! Make our peons compete with their peons. That's competitiveness for you! That's globalization! That's free market capitalism for you!"

The second stage is tax reform. Lower the taxes on the rich and on corporations. High taxes on us lead to a lower income, which reduces our incentive to work and invest. So, make the rich richer and they'll work harder, invest more and create jobs. (Of course, as everyone knows, if you make the poor richer, they will work less. So to get the poor to work harder, cut their wages; to make the rich work harder, raise their incomes. Funny how that works, but then we aren't really the same species, are we.) So raise the taxes on the poor. Sales taxes will hit them every time they shop. And while we're at it, tax services too. Call it the GST. Don't tax services for the rich, of course, like banking, stock broking and currency speculating. Tax the workers' labour. Tax haircuts, car repairs and schoolbooks. And for the ultra-rich and their family trusts, tell them that they DON'T have to pay the $70 billion they owed in 1992 until halfway through the twenty-first century.

In the third stage the realization hits that if we continue government spending and cutting revenues, we are going to end up with a budget deficit. We can pretend total surprise: "Who would ever have predicted a budget deficit?" But with a budget deficit we will have to cut spending, which means laying off workers. This will cut tax revenues and increase spending on unemployment benefits, so the deficit gets worse, not better! "Who would have predicted it?" But, don't worry. This will produce the Golden Key: the budget crisis.

The fourth stage occurs when we finally have the Golden Key in hand, the key that will unlock every door. With a good budget crisis running we can do almost anything we want. We can savagely cut spending and roll wages back to the 1978 level—or lower. Spending too much on schools? Slash. Don't you know we have a budget crisis? Doctors making too many people well? Cut their salaries. Close half the hospitals. Don't you know we have a budget crisis? Any public service workers still working? Lay them off. Don't you know we've got a serious budget crisis? Cut! Slash! Downsize! Start with the public service. Everybody knows those teachers and hospital workers don't work. Make it easy. Start with a really vicious campaign against them and everyone will cheer. Don't forget. We've got a really serious budget crisis!

Finally, there is stage five. With a proper budget crisis and wages rolled back a decade or so, we have the final master stroke. A generalized wage collapse. Wages in Canada will fall to the bare subsistence level, where they were in the 1930s. And we will make as much money as they do in Third World dictatorships. It's that simple!

Manufacturing Consent, Canadian-Style
by Ruth Cohen

Free market propaganda flows in torrents from the propaganda mills of the business cult. Their products are everywhere in the media, including the CBC, disguised as genuine reporting or 'objective' analysis. David Langille and Asad Ismi of the Jesuit Centre for Social Faith and Justice compiled the following profiles of the most notorious propaganda mills.

Business Council on National Issues (BCNI)

The BCNI was formed in 1976 by corporate leaders anxious to exert more influence over a state that they felt had grown too large and interventionist. They organized 150 chief executive officers from the major transnational corporations so as to be able to contribute personally to the development of public policy and the shaping of national priorities. The fact that these companies have combined assets of $1.5 trillion, earn annual revenues of $400 billion, and employ about 1.3 million Canadians, helps explain why they have become the most powerful and influential interest group in the country. Their chief spokesperson, Tom d'Aquino, manages a fourteen-person staff in their Ottawa headquarters.

The Council now claims to be the senior voice of Canadian business on public policy issues in Canada and abroad, with a focus on helping to build a strong economy, 'progressive' social policies, and 'healthy' political institutions. Guided by its primary objective of curbing the role and size of the state, the BCNI has helped to maintain the fight against inflation, cut back public spending, and bolster corporate profits.

C.D. Howe Institute (CDHI)

The Institute is named after the prominent Canadian industrialist who became "Minister of Everything" in post-war Ottawa, and was most noted for using American investment to develop Canadian industry. Although it claims to be an independent think tank, the Institute consistently represents the views of the business elite. It is funded almost exclusively from Bay Street and its board is drawn from

Canada's biggest corporations, including Sun Life Assurance, Noranda and Alcan.

CDHI's main focus is on economic issues, but it has recently helped lead the attack on Canada's social programs. The Institute played a major role in generating hysteria over the deficit by insisting that the problem was government spending rather than high interest rates. The CDHI's current president and CEO, Tom Kierans, commands an annual budget of nearly $2 million and a great deal of respect at the national newspapers.

The Fraser Institute

The Fraser Institute is based on the free market theories of Milton Friedman. For many years after it was established in Vancouver in 1974, it was considered to be a radically right-wing think-tank on the fringes of the policy community. However, since the political terrain has shifted to the right, the Institute has opened a Toronto office, and the organization has become far more central in public policy debates. According to its founder and prominent spokesperson, Michael Walker, the Fraser Institute is devoted to "researching the use of markets, how markets work and how markets fail."

The Institute is involved in economic and social research, publishes books and newsletters, monitors television news to ensure "balanced" reporting, and is particularly effective in involving high school and university students in its market economics programs. Besides its own staff of twenty-two, it hires academics from around the world to develop right-wing positions on free trade, taxation, government spending, health care and Aboriginal rights. The Institute is supported by tax-deductible donations from more than 2,500 individuals, corporations and charitable foundations, giving it an annual budget of $2.35 million.

The Alliance of Manufacturers and Exporters of Canada (AMEC)

AMEC is the result of the merging of the former Canadian Manufacturers Association with the Canadian Exporters Association. The Alliance now represents 3,000 manufacturers, service companies and exporters of every size. President Stephen Houtens presents their views to the public and to governments with the aid of a $6.5 million operating budget.

The origial CMA, the Canadian Manufacturers Association, espoused tariff protectionism during its first one hundred years of existence. Since the 1980s, this group has avidly supported free marketeers in the global economy, favouring policies to increase its members' competitiveness by bringing down wages and benefits to Canadian workers.

The View from Fraser Peak: Reflections on a Fraser Institute Conference
by Ann Emmett

It has been said that there are those who make change happen, those who watch change happen and those who never know what hit them. How can we make change happen?

We're up against a powerful ideology that has informed change since the mid 1970s, when the technological revolution and the global marketplace made change imperative and inescapable. Those interest groups now labeled 'the new right'—the special interest groups who are always complaining about the undue influence of special interest groups on government—have seized the moment to vigorously market their view and promote their agenda. This is the agenda that we've come to know so well: limiting government interference, downsizing, de-regulating and privatizing.

Well-planned, well-funded organizations exist all over the world, dedicated to the propagation of this ideology and the implementation of this agenda—organizations like the Thomas Jefferson Centre Foundation in the U.S., the Adam Smith Institute in Great Britain and in Canada the Fraser Institute. The Fraser Institute opened in the same year as the Trilateral Commission, a privately financed think-tank with the explicit objective of devising strategies for managing global trade. Two of the Commissions's favourite subjects are what it calls 'excess democracy' and alerting us to the fact that we already have too many well educated people. For its part, the Fraser Institte was started with a fundraising drive headed by a former vice president of Macmillan Bloedel; annual funding was obtained from, among others, IBM, Cadillac-Fairview, and various Canadian banks.

From November 30 to December 1, 1998, John Hotson and I attended an international conference, organized by the Fraser Institute, on the implications of severe government debt. Entitled "Hitting the Wall: Is Canada Bankrupt?" the conference was a continuing part of the debt-fright campaign to batter Canadians into accepting the destruction of the social programs and the assault on the public sector—an example of how the new right makes change happen.

The Institute has tremendous resources. Thanks to the financial contributions of such companies as Loblaws, Sun Life Assurance, Macmillan Bloedel and the Toronto Dominion Bank, to name a few, the Fraser was able to bring in speakers from New Zealand, Europe and the U.S.

The seriousness of Canada's debt problem, the fact that a large fraction of this debt is held by foreigners and the fiscal threat implicit in the possibility of Québec separation, are all sober truths about which much useful information emerged as speakers explored variations on the conference theme. For example, by 2030 Canada will be the 'oldest' society ever seen in the 'developed countries.' According to an Economics Council study entitled *One in Three*, at a fixed retirement age of sixty-five, there will be one retired person for every two workers by 2031. Canadians should be weighing their options in the light of such information. The Fraser Institute is doing the right thing by drawing attention to such problems.

Alas, the conference had a pre-ordained conclusion: that the only solution to Canada's emerging debt problem is to cut government spending. Views that couldn't be bent to this way of thinking, never made it onto the conference schedule. None of the three hundred or so attendees challenged the creed that taxes cannot be raised, tax loopholes closed, nor interest rates lowered. It was rather like a revival meeting, as speaker after speaker chanted the familiar cant: privatization, cutbacks, competition.

With evangelical zeal, Thomas Donlan, editorial page editor of *Barron's Weekly* gushed:

> If Canada...lightens taxation, regulation and business mandates, it will reinforce the prosperity that changing economic and financial circles are about to deliver anyway. If it goes further, selling off public property to pay debt on debt, to put it into the hands of private managers, it's going to touch off a boom!

A boom for whom? No one asked. With the sort of common sense that would inspire a hungry castaway to eat a hole in the bottom of his raft, Fraser Institute logic pounded out the old refrain: 'Just keep following our advice and everything will be splendid!' Its solution to the debt is just more of the same old policies that got us into this mess in the first place.

From such a lofty perspective, money, to quote Thomas Donlan, "is the measure of all things." None of the charts and graphs, numbers and tables, ratios and records, measured costs in human terms. The human factor scarcely entered into these equations. The closest anyone came to a compassionate remark was the observation that, under the structural adjustment programs imposed by the International Monetary Fund, "domestic economies contracted and citizens suffered." Most of the infrequent references to people had to do with their shortcomings—the nuisance of having to win their support for weaning away from the welfare state.

One of the many ironies that gave the conference zest was the underlying preoccupation with power on the one hand, and the retreat behind inevitability and helplessness on the other. The former was reflected in jokes like, "We've put a chemical in the coffee and if you're not back in three minutes, it will render you impotent," in imagery like, "We call this chart the ball breaker" and in assertions like, "We have to change the way we govern this country!" To me, the most offensive note at the conference was struck by speakers from south of the border. One of these spewed scorn on our "self satisfied civil servants" and "the large unemployed substance-abusing underclass periodically pulled into fake trading schemes and make work projects." This speaker said there was no need to redistribute wealth and that the Canadian national character did not depend on transfer payments and civil service staffing levels.

The tirade against our public health care system was also astonishing. Americans hate it! They gloated over their success in foiling an attempt to implement one in the U.S. Their contempt and their indignation can only be appreciated in the context of the corporate campaign to privatize health care in Canada, and in the dim light of their world view. In an article that appeared in the *Canadian Forum*, Joyce Nelson exposes this campaign, and traces the connections between Canadian trilateralists, insurance companies and banks. She also notes that a significant number of hospital boards, especially in Toronto and Montreal, are peopled with trilateralists. For example, Nelson points out that Trevor Eyton is director of the Sunnybrook

Health Sciences Centre, and trade minister Roy Maclaren is a governor for the Etobicoke General Hospital. Tom Long, one of the authors of the Common Sense Revolution, is on the board of the Toronto General Hospital. The list goes on.

I'm almost embarrassed to use the word democracy any more; it has been sucked so dry of meaning. Like many other words usurped or subverted in the new-right takeover of the language, it must be recovered. The need to restore it to life and respect was chillingly clear at the conference. Bo Lundgren, former minister for fiscal and financial affairs in the Swedish government, explained: "By reforming the systems we thought it would be easier to tell people that it was necessary—a good thing to do." He boasted that his government had shown that it is possible to do things it "had heard were not possible." Lundgren was honest enough to admit, however, that " we lost the things...You tend to lose elections when you do these things...We're going one step back—but we got two steps forward."

John Fund, editorial writer for the *Wall Street Journal*, the 'hidden talent' behind Rush Limbaugh, observed that "We are in the midst of a global revolution that is changing the landscape... but like all quiet revolutions, you don't realize how much the revolution is reshaping things until it's all over." He deplored people who "think that those who are irresponsible or foolish should be subsidized by others." He did acknowledge the need for compassion, and predicted that the U.S. would not get rid of social programs— just freeze them over several generations.

The difficulty of manufacturing consent was a common theme and the consequences of the dramatic changes being advocated were not underestimated. "It used to be a question of the haves sharing with the have-nots," said one conference speaker, "In the future, I expect we'll see the have-nots struggling to keep anything through political action. Weapons are cheap and justice is poor—an economic underclass might elect to take rather than be disadvantaged." Paul McCrossan, a partner in Ekler Partners Ltd., went on to suggest that part of the solution might be to shift after-tax income away from double-income families. He warned however, that "these double-income families may become very active politically" to hang on to what they regard as the fruits of their personal labour. McCrossan argued tha-such families would not recognize any "obligation to make sure the system remains functional and equitable" adding that "political consensus on social program changes will be very hard to achieve." McCrossan concluded with another popular theme at the conference: "Almost none of the hard decisions needed to be taken by the federal government have yet been taken."

On my way home, as the bus crawled up Ossington Avenue, I looked at the modest little houses that crowd both sides of the street. Most of the front lawns had already been sacrificed to someone else's idea of progress. I thought, "Sure, these folk are going to look after themselves. They'll provide for their own old age. They'll buy their own health insurance. They'll save for their children's university education." I used to fret over how much blame to attach to the people who are running things—you don't want to judge people unfairly. What I know clearly from the Fraser experience is that it doesn't matter. Whether they do what they do out of a stunted world view, or from a demonic, unparalleled arrogance and greed, the 'collateral damage' is the same in either case.

What matters is that we understand what they're about. What matters is that we are as passionate about our vision as they are about theirs. I went to the conference despising the people who run things. I came away fearing them. They are so sure they are right! They want it all. And they want it now. And if we don't make change happen, they will get it all.

Ann Emmett is a retired secondary school teacher. For two years, she was Principal and Acting Area Administrator in the Department of Northern Affairs, Igloolik, NWT. She served as Toronto co-chair of the Council of Canadians and has fought vigorously against the Megacity and the Harris agenda.

Part Two
Re-engineering Ontario

Chapter 3: The True Believers

The True Believers by William Kennedy

The authors and promoters of the Common Sense Revolution include a number of unsavoury characters. All of them come to you courtesy of an unelected cadre of young neo-conservatives, old Tory party hacks, and business-hustling public relations flacks. These people are the bane of many of the elected Tory backbenchers, who learned some time ago that the dictates of the free market do not necessarily govern all areas of life (i.e., the Legislature) and that government by decree does not satisfy all Ontarians. The following people move effortlessly back and forth among Queen's Park, Ottawa, various Ontario municipalities, and the private sector:

•A bankrupt—Bill Young, CEO of Consumers' Distributing. Young was an important contributor to the Common Sense Revolution manifesto. A rugged individualist whose company took advantage of a government social program known as bankruptcy protection, Young high-tailed it over the border after Consumers' went belly up. He was last seen working as a consultant in Cambridge, Massachussetts. As one journalistic wag commented: "Apparently, there was not enough 'dynamic growth and new jobs' in Harris' Ontario to keep him here."

•A cheque forger—Jamie Watt, advertising whiz and former press liaison for Mike Harris. In his younger days, Watt was caught trying to shore up his Oakville-based clothing business with forged cheques amounting to $16,000. Fortunately, this occurred before the establishment of boot camps in Ontario. Lucky Jamie served out his time in relative comfort and brevity—twenty nights in jail, with freedom during the days—at a minimum security penal institution.

•A legal lackey—Guy Giorno is a legal and policy advisor to Mike Harris and a former lawyer with Hicks, Morley, a law firm specializing in, among other things, taking management's part against labour. The firm's halcyon days were during the Bill Davis era, when it had a lock on the job of conducting labour negotiations for the Conservative government. When this function was put out for proper tender under the Peterson and Rae governments, the firm was left out in the cold. Soon after Mike Harris' election victory Hicks, Morley was securely back in its former saddle. The Harris administration, without a formal tendering process, awarded the firm a $15,000-a-month contract to head up negotiations with the Ontario Public Sector Employees Union (OPSEU) that eventually culminated in a bitter strike. Allegations of patronage swirled around Giorno, who had been given a paid leave of absence by Hicks, Morley to work on Harris' campaign. Finally, he was the one put in charge of assembling the odious Omnibus Bill 26.

•A 'silent witness'—Deb Hutton, "issues management" advisor to Mike Harris. Hutton is a central figure in events leading to the fatal shooting of Dudley George, during an Ontario Provincial Police (OPP) light-brigade-style charge on unarmed Aboriginal occupiers of sacred burial grounds at Ipperwash Provincial Park in 1995. According to official minutes—the existence of which the province at first denied—the OPP were instructed at a crucial government meeting, where Hutton was present as representative of the Premier's Office, to remove the natives from Ipperwash quickly and in the best way they knew how. Until legally compelled to produce the minutes, Queen's Park also denied that any OPP action regarding Ipperwash was discussed at the meeting. Despite all this, and despite the fact that the OPP officer who killed George was subsequently charged with criminal negligence, calls for a public inquiry into the Ipperwash affair and Hutton's specific role in it—about which she has been silent—have so far been denied.

When you are next called upon to bend your neck under the yoke of Common Sense Revolution's laws and decrees, remember these folks, the special interest groups they represent, and their very real fallibility. However, notwithstanding the influence they wield, they are by no means the biggest fish in the Harris administration's sea. That honour belongs to two people:

•Leslie Noble—'The Consensus Builder'. Noble campaigned in 1978 for New York Congressman Jack Kemp, an ardent free-marketeer and eventual vice-presidential candidate on the Bob Dole ticket in the 1996 American federal election. The self-employed co-owner of Strategy Corporation, a private public relations company located in the Ernst and Young Tower in downtown Toronto, Noble played a major role in drafting the Common Sense Revolution document. She helped run Mike Harris' successful 1995 provincial election campaign and is regarded as the conciliator of the Harris election team. Noble also headed Jean Charest's 1997 provincial election campaign, imparting to it a right-wing spin stressing tax cuts and less government, a strategy that eventually helped his campaign to fizzle.

•Tom Long—'The Spiritual Leader'. Long campaigned in 1976 for Ronald Reagan in Reagan's unsuccessful attempt to take the presidential nomination away from Gerald Ford. He worked in the Prime Minister's Office for that master of fiscal and social responsibility, Brian Mulroney. In 1989, Long was hired by Conrad Black (whose first noteworthy entrepreneurial act was the selling of stolen examinations at Upper Canada College) to work for the Dominion Stores division of Black's empire. Long then ran for and became president of the Ontario Conservative party; part of his platform was his wish to abolish the party name 'Progressive Conservative'. Long was a front-runner for the Ontario Conservative party leadership but dropped out before the leadership convention at which Mike Harris was elected leader. He wrote an initial draft of the Common Sense Revolution document and played a major role in its final editing. With Leslie Noble, Long ran Harris' successful 1995 provincial election campaign. His private-sector headquarters located at First Canadian Place, across the street from Leslie Noble's Strategy Corporation, is at Egon Zehnder, a Swiss-based executive headhunting firm. Long was temporarily brought out of 'retirement' at Egon Zehnder to serve as Harris administration spokesperson against the Toronto Days of Action protests. Most recently, Long ran an unsuccessful campaign for the leadership of the federal Canadian Reform Conservative Alliance Party. Long is on record as saying a central element in the shaping of his ideology was the economic philosophy of the free-market Austrian economist, Friedrich A. von Hayek.

Within the Harris administration, conflict exists between the Tom Long element—which, like Hayek, has great contempt for traditional conservative values such as respect for democracy, benevolence toward the poor and maintaining existing institutions as much as possible—and a number of backbench MPs of a moderate or 'Red Tory' stamp.

William Kennedy is a secondary school teacher and a writer.

The Harris Kremlin: Inside Ontario's Revolutionary Politburo by Guy Crittenden

Immediately after his resounding win in the June 1995 election, Mike Harris got down to business. The new Ontario premier sacked nine NDP-appointed deputy ministers, then called in the rest to remind them that their first obligation, legally speaking, is to serve the premier's office. This pronouncement set the tone and groundwork for what was to come.

Ontario has endured an amazing shake-up since the election. The Tories have seized control of education, chopped school boards and tried to remove their taxation powers. They've amalgamated cities, slashed funds to social agencies and reduced welfare benefits. Now they're re-jigging every aspect of how the province and municipalities deliver services. They're even taking such extreme steps as closing hospitals, downsizing the environment ministry, charging drug fees to seniors and staring down the unions (particularly the teachers).

To do all this in such a short time, Mr. Harris has played fast and loose with the democratic process. He has surrounded himself with a cadre of young, fervently ideological advisors to do his bidding. Grassroots supporters who thought the party would emphasize democratic debate, plebiscites and local decision-making have been shocked. In the Harris Kremlin, power flows from the centre. (Indeed, the term, 'the centre' is now an ominous fixture of party newspeak, as in the oft-repeated phrase, "No one knows what the centre is thinking.")

Over the years it has been customary for deputy ministers and political staff to develop initiatives for their ministers, who then bring them to cabinet. Mr. Harris has altered the process. Believing the most important public consultation took place before the election, and fearing that ministers would be sandbagged by bureaucrats, the premier requested that deputies report to his office directly.

Thus, ministers are often kept in the dark, making them little more than salespeople for initiatives cobbled together in the premier's office. Stories abound of ministers caught in the crossfire of Mr. Harris' flash temper, his staff's meddling and pressures from their own portfolios. Staff have been fired for even appearing to question Mr. Harris' orders. Others, such as Catherine Steele, aide to former Health Minister Jim Wilson, and Brian Patterson, aide to former Economic Development Minister Bill Saunderson, were let go without the usual parachutes into other positions. Senior staff who have departed for private-sector jobs include Mitch Patten, a former member of the premier's staff, and Mac Penny, one-time executive assistant to Health Minister Dave Johnson when he was chair of cabinet's management board. When Environment Minister Norm Sterling was tardy in bringing forward a mandatory vehicle emissions testing program he learned how with Harris' crew you can be damned if you do and damned if you don't. It was not an item on the Common Sense Revolution agenda, and the premier's staff had the issue on the back burner. Mr. Harris gave the cautious environment minister a dressing down in front of his cabinet colleagues, then criticized Mr. Sterling on television for inaction on a program Mr. Harris had been "requesting for months."

Mr. Sterling's caution was understandable. His predecessor, Brenda Elliot, lost her job in part because she kept promoting an agenda that wasn't part of the Common Sense Revolution, including a bill that would have compelled manufacturers to subsidize curbside recycling programs. When the initiative collapsed, Mr. Harris' treatment of Ms. Elliot in front of her cabinet colleagues reduced the woman to tears. The story has become a legend around Queen's Park. The lesson from these and similar episodes was clear. Staff who claim to speak for Mr. Harris are not reliable: worse, they sometimes advance their own agendas in his name. Nevertheless, all new initiatives must receive their blessing.

So who are the behind-the-scene advisors, what are their roles and what is the process for developing and implementing policies in Mike Harris' Kremlin?

The Players

Named after the Toronto hotel where they held their meetings, The Bradgate Group is the group of advisors who wrote the Common Sense Revolution. Among others, they include:

•Tom Long: A corporate headhunter whose preppie appearance belies a strong ideology and keen intuition for the pulse of the middle-class electorate.

•Tony Clement: A long-serving party member who has risen from passing out leaflets (once while dressed in a penguin costume) to being named transportation minister in Mr. Harris' shuffled cabinet. Mr. Clement is now Minister of Health and Long-term Care.

•Alister Campbell: A young insurance executive whose bearded and bespectacled visage personifies his role as the academic brain trust of the group.

•Leslie Noble: A tough and intelligent woman who elbowed her way into the Tory boys' club to become one of its top strategists.

In typical revolutionary style, the four took over the party's youth wing in the 1980s and used it to gain control of the party itself. Fans of Margaret Thatcher and Ronald Reagan, they programmed the homespun Mike Harris with their Ivy League free market ideas, then ran the successful 1995 election campaign. They continue to guide the party to this day. Of this group, an otherwise loyal politico says, "These bright people led the party out of a decade in the political wilderness. However, with the possible exception of Mr. Clement, these chateau generals are largely oblivious to the games being played by senior officers in the field."

The Premier's Staff

These are the 'senior officers'. As a group they have been criticized as being heavy on theory and light on real-world experience. Their preternatural youth has earned them the *Frank* magazine epithet The Little Shits™.

•David Lindsay: As Mr. Harris' former principal secretary, David Lindsay has been the most important staff member. Despite his recent move to the new Ontario Jobs and

Investment Board, he will remain key advisor. He is reputedly hard at work on "Project 21," a codename for the Tories' next election platform. A former campaign aide says: "I feel most of the blame for what's happening at the centre rests with Mr. Lindsay. He was pretty much an absentee principal secretary. When he lost touch with the day to day affairs of the office, the power vacuum was created. The void has been filled by people who are in way over their heads."

•Ron McLaughlin: Formerly Mr. Lindsay's assistant, he has replaced him as a top staff aide, in the renamed post of chief of staff. Mr. McLaughlin is said to bring much-needed management skills to the premier's office.

•Guy Giorno: Any discussion with insiders about control from the centre quickly turns into a debate over the relative strengths and weaknesses of director of policy Guy Giorno, who was all of twenty-nine when the Tories came to power. Nicknamed "Rasputin" by *Frank* magazine, he is, some say, the ultimate insider right-wing "true believer" who sidelines any ministerial move that doesn't jibe with his ideology. Insiders praise his quirky brilliance, but gripe at his aversion to anything to do with central planning (a bit ironic, given his position). Mr. Giorno rejects allegations that he is a meddler: "I find it difficult to conceive how someone whose role is strictly advisory could micromanage anything. My role is advisory, not managerial," he says.

•John Toogood: The premier's economic policy advisor, he was recently promoted to assistant director of policy. The Tory Youth graduate and Giorno protegé still looks too young to shave. Says former Deputy Press Secretary Don Hogarth, now with Bell Canada, "John gives the impression of being aloof, but I think it's because he's shy. He's really wise beyond his years."

•Bill King: He holds the office of caucus liaison. A lifer who's been with Harris since the early years in North Bay, Mr. King gained fame by throwing himself into bushes at Queen's Park during a government union strike in 1995. (The suggestion of picket-line brutality was deflated when TV camera shots revealed Mr. King hadn't been shoved.) He isn't regarded as a very important player these days, but his job of keeping an eye on restless backbenchers seems secure.

•Debbie Hutton: As director of issues management and tours, Ms. Hutton preps the Premier for Legislature appearances and has become the unofficial boss of all political staff inside and outside her office. Says one political staffer, "Anyone doing Deb's job successfully has to be tough and I'll credit her with being fair most of the time." Others are less kind. Legislative assistants are terrified of her, and her reputation for yelling at people deemed disobedient has earned her the nickname 'Jabba the Hut'. Says a staffer who's been on the receiving end of one of her tirades: "She's a one-person Blitzkreig against party morale. She guards her access to Harris jealously, and frequently speaks on his behalf. She's isolated Mike from caucus. He relies too much on her filtered information and is losing touch."

•Ab Campion: He is the premier's new director of communications, a role he performed to mixed reviews at the Ministry of Consumer and Commercial Relations. Revolutions depend on good propaganda, yet Mr. Harris' spin-doctoring team has been in trouble since day one. The first communications director, Jamie Watt, resigned over a minor fraud scandal, and subsequent directors have come and gone, sometimes hired back on contract. These have included former Brian Mulroney aide Ed Arundel and outspoken media guru Paul Rhodes, who left in 1996 to form his own company. The position has been vacant for most of the year, and the opposition has exploited the weakness. Asked why the communications post remained vacant for so long, one ministry observer answers, "Sheer incompetence, that's all."

•Stewart Braddick: Newly hired, he will assume responsibility for "the important outreach function" across the province as the government implements its legislative program. As cabinet secretary, he is the province's top civil servant. Appointed by the premier, he in turn, appoints the deputy ministers and is the obedient conduit through which they report to Mr. Harris.

Two newcomers: the premier's office recently hired lawyer Paul Paton as justice and social-policy advisor and gave special assistant Rob Nicol responsibility for social and municipal policy.

The Structure and Process

Mr. Harris' cabinet has remained small at about twenty ministers (as opposed to Bob Rae's twenty-six). Only minimal staff has been allowed for each minister. Mr. Rae's many cabinet policy committees have been dispensed with. Instead Mr. Harris' cabinet has only three subcommittees: Legislation and Regulations, Management Board and Priorities and Planning (or P&P).

The normal avenue is to lobby ministers and their staff. But with this government, lobbying ministers is a fruitless exercise since the centre makes most decisions. So everyone competes for the attention of the mandarins in the premier's office. Bright as they may be, these folks can't be experts in every field, and are usually overwhelmed. Inevitably, crucial decisions are made on-the-fly. While both cabinet and the bureaucracy have had their wings clipped, the parliamentary process and the opposition parties have not been immune. The Legislature has had its powers curtailed, its debates shortened and its committees truncated.

According to Doug Prendergast of the lobbying firm Corporation House, "The Tories have made it possible, in theory, to introduce a bill on Monday and have it pass third reading on Thursday." Hearings by legislative committees—which usually contain representatives of all three parties—normally provide an opportunity to fine-tune bills. Now the hearings are frequently cut short and are sometimes farcical.

The committee dealing with Bill 136 was expected to study amendments to the proposed labour legislation without being allowed to see the text of the bill itself. The Ontario Hydro hearings have been assigned an impossibly short time frame, given the complexity and importance of the issues. The hearings have been conducted without the release of an important white paper on energy reform that has been held up by the centre for almost a year. Hearings by the committee studying Bill 160—reforms to the education system—have been dominated by presentations from government supporters, not by teachers or parents. The list of irregularities goes on and on.

The first example of the curtailment of democratic debate was Bill 26, the Savings and Restructuring Act. Bill 26 (proclaimed in November, 1995) was hefty omnibus legislation into which the government rolled amendments to forty-seven laws, allowing the Tories to proceed with ambitious downsizing plans. The legislation empowered municipalities and other groups to replace money transfers from the province with funds raised through user fees and licenses, and it empowered the province to amalgamate cities. Rather than deal with these issues through many pieces of legislation, the government cleverly planned to overwhelm the opposition with this legal Hydra. Less clever was its overwhelming of itself. In the drafting of Bill 26, deputy ministers dutifully sent every conceivable saving and restructuring they could think of to the premier's office, which pasted them up and sent them over to the finance department where the final bill was drafted.

Because the legislation was to be introduced by Finance Minister Ernie Eves along with a sensitive economic statement, the whole complicated procedure was shrouded in secrecy. The premier's staff and the ministers were barred from seeing the actual wording until the night before its introduction in the Legislature.

The discovery of numerous errors precipitated a flurry of last-minute edits, but the document was still highly flawed when it was introduced. Ministers who hadn't been involved in drafting the bill were expected to defend their respective sections, yet were given no guidance. This led to humiliating moments in the Legislature when ministers, challenged by opposition critics, offered only bumbling explanations of laws they clearly didn't understand. The bill was subjected to an astonishing 160 amendments.

Awful as the experience was, the fly-by-the-seat-of-your-pants pattern has repeated itself over and over. As polls show, the public (even Tory supporters) is increasingly uneasy about the government's haste and apparent carelessness. Former Community and Social Services minister David Tsubouchi had to amend welfare regulations that cut welfare payments to 115,000 disabled people.

When former Labour Minister Elizabeth Witmer gutted Bill 136, even the Conservatives' most loyal supporters began to wonder aloud which policies were to be taken seriously and which were a charade. Meanwhile, although legislative and ministry staff have been fired (sometimes for minor transgressions) the young overseers of these grand debacles in the premier's office have remained unscathed.

The granddaddy of all policy and communications screwups remains the forced amalgamation of cities (especially the six municipalities of Metro Toronto). Challenged in the Legislature to provide evidence the schemes will save money, Municipal Affairs Minister Al Leach was reduced to saying he had a "gut feeling." City dwellers afraid of property-tax hikes and suburbanites resistant to tax pooling were shocked and they have yet to hear a convincing argument that these dramatic changes will work. And the Ontario Court's General Division ruled that the government broke the law by appointing trustees to oversee amalgamation before legislation came into force.

Amalgamations across the province have not been accompanied by promised detailed financial information. In 2000, mayors, reeves and councilors faced a municipal election with no certainty that disentanglement would be a revenue-neutral exercise. Government-relations expert Graham Murky of Toronto-based G.P. Murray Research Ltd. says, "There's a school of thought that the Tory win in 1995 did not, in fact, really derive from a deep shift to the right in the Ontario electorate. Rather, voters looked at the three candidates and decided that Mike Harris looked like a better manager than the other two. They were voting for good management more than anything else."

What a huge irony, to choose as best manager the most incompetent government of a Western democracy in modern times.

Guy Crittenden is a freelance writer. His work has appeared in the Globe and Mail *and in* Report on Business *magazine.*

Moving and Shaking the Tory Powerbase
by Ian Urquhart

Cabinet ministers get the headlines and the TV coverage. But in the heavily centralized government of Mike Harris, the premier and his office set the policy and the bureaucrats implement it. Ministers, with rare exceptions, are mere figureheads, cutting ribbons and reading speeches. So while Harris' 1999 shuffle of cabinet ministers attracted far more attention, concurrent changes in the ranks of the senior bureaucracy and the premier's office are more significant.

Start with the deputies: Veronica Lacey is out as deputy minister of education. A former teacher and principal, she moved to Queen's Park three years ago from North York, where she was director of education. While Harris recruited her, she has spent much of her time at Queen's Park fighting the premier's office on a wide range of issues, from budget cuts to curriculum changes, and it was widely expected she would get the chop after the election.

Lacey is being replaced by Suzanne Herbert, a professional bureaucrat who was deputy minister of community and social services, where she developed a good working relationship with Janet Ecker, the new minister of education. Herbert is viewed internally as thoughtful and capable, but she will be at a disadvantage in education, where she has little experience. "In a tough, two-way discussion with the premier's office over education, she's not sombody who, through her personality or her knowledge of the field, will stand her ground," says one insider.

The situation is similar in the labour ministry, where Tony Dean is moving out of the deputy's chair to be associate secretary of the cabinet. A progressive bureaucrat with an encyclopedic knowledge of labour, Dean is being replaced by Jill Hutcheon, an assistant deputy minister in transportation. Her reputation is as a solid manager, not a policy person. "They've now got a deputy in labour who will take notes and do what she is told," opines the insider.

Other significant changes include the appointment of Kevin Costante, a career bureaucrat, as deputy minister of community and social services (replacing Herbert). His views are considered left-of-centre, which should make for interesting times in that portfolio as the new minister, John Baird, is decidedly right-wing. And Robert Christie moves from intergovernmental affairs to be deputy minister of training and post-secondary education. There he will rejoin Dianne Cunningham, who was named the minister last week. They will make a comfortable fit as they try to launch the new ministry. But policy in the training and post-secondary field is expected to be driven from 'the centre,' as the premier's office is euphemistically known at Queen's Park, and Christie is very much trusted there.

As for the premier's office itself, Ron McLaughlin, a Tom Long acquaintance who came to Queen's Park from the TTC, will remain as chief of staff. But there are major changes below him. Line Maheux is out as director of communications. Recruited from Ottawa, where she worked for Reform leader Preston Manning, Maheux never really fit in with the "whiz kids" around Harris. She is being replaced by Guy Giorno, one of the original whiz kids, who will also keep his position as Harris' chief political strategist.

John Weir, a step-grandson of John Diefenbaker who was in charge of caucus liaison, is taking over from Deb Hutton as director of "issues management." (Basically, this involves prepping the premier for question period, media scrums and any other surprises.) Hutton, who began working for Harris during the wilderness years in opposition, remains as a senior advisor for now but is on her way out. Replacing Weir as caucus liaison is Perry Martin, who was executive assistant to Health Minister Elizabeth Witmer.

Rounding out the inner circle are John Toogood, a Giorno protégé, as director of policy, and Stewart Braddick, who used to work for the provincial Liberals in British Columbia, as director of outreach. The big winner here is Giorno, whose power base expands and who now has one less rival for the premier's ear, with Hutton moving on. At the ripe age of thirty-four, this policy wonk and former labour lawyer has emerged as a major player in the Harris government.

What's it all mean? If there is a central theme it is that, in the Harris government's second term, control remains firmly planted in the centre.

Ian Urquhart is provincial affairs columnist for the Toronto Star. *This article was first published in the* Toronto Star *on June 25, 1999.*

The Man Behind Mike by Ted Schmidt

I spot him first. Tall and slightly ungainly, he is making his way north on Bay St. with his head down, talking animatedly into his cell phone. The December wind that flaps at his overcoat muffles my greeting so I find myself suddenly bellowing his name—"Guy Giorno!"

Stopping abruptly, he wheels and extends his hand, his dark eyes settling uneasily on my face. We've never met before, although that seems more the result of a cosmic error than anything else. As we negotiate for an amiable tone and a decent restaurant, I watch him closely—this eccentric young man who is one of the most important backroom guys in the Mike Harris revolution, the architect of the much-hated Omnibus Bill and a strategist for Bill 160.

We approach St. Joseph Street and, almost before I realize it, we are passing St. Michael's College, where both Giorno and I graduated, a generation apart, and from where we both honed careers of Catholic activism that would take us to very different places.

Giorno's name was bandied about quite a lot in the mid-1980s in the circles I moved in, long before he became the premier's director of policy planning. That's because the precocious twenty-year-old was a columnist for the reactionary *Catholic Register*, a veritable house organ for the then-Cardinal Carter, mired as it was it in Cold War politics, slavish pro-Rome obeisance and one-note social activism—the anti-abortion movement.

I, on the other hand, had a column in the *Catholic New Times*, the voice of progressive Catholics who could no longer abide the *Register*. Reading Giorno's neo-con rants, I used to wince—Nelson Mandela was espousing violence, unions have too much power, doctors should have the right to double bill, the list went on. "How could they give a guy like this space in a Catholic paper?" I remember thinking. Twelve years later, I am still a columnist for the *Catholic New Times* and Giorno is one of the most powerful insiders in the Ontario Tory government. Most Ontarians have never heard Giorno's name, but everyone's life is going to be irrevocably changed by what he has in his head. Slowly, journalists are twigging to his favoured place in the Tory constellation.

Frank magazine lists Giorno among the young Tory true believers—the "Little Shits"—along with Tom Long, Leslie Noble, Deb Hutton, Tony Clement, all of them ideologues long on free market dogmatism and desperately short on life experience. John Ibbitson's Promised Land: Inside the Harris Revolution situates Giorno right in the thick of things, virtually blaming him for the fiasco around the Omnibus Bill. And Tory-intimate Guy Crittenden's much quoted article "The Harris Kremlin" places Giorno in the very centre of the Tory boiler room, commenting that he "sidelines any ministerial move that doesn't jibe with his ideology."

With this increasing recognition of his influence, I figured it was time for a journalistic foray and I started calling my contacts in the Catholic community. I talked to my old teachers, schoolmates, union negotiators and ex-colleagues at the Register, one of whom called him "the most right-wing twenty-year-old" he had ever met, and "devoid of any idealism."

A profile was emerging: bright, quirky, aloof, narrow, arrogant. Then, miraculously, Guy Giorno called me. I laughed to myself and remembered the old Paul Robeson spiritual, "There's A Man Goin' Round Taking Names". I am that man. Obviously, somebody from his *Register* days has alerted him.

"I hear you're looking for me," he says on the phone.

"Indeed, I am."

"Well, why?"

"Well, Guy, I find you fascinating."

"Why?"

"Well, you're a Catholic and I am, too, and we seem to be singing out of a different hymnal."

Now we're sitting at a table at Mr. Greek, trying to stay on safe neutral ground. As long as we stay on the biographical plane, he's quite forthcoming. He's impressed that I know he's a reader in his west-end parish. I ask him about his background. Father a delegate at the Liberal convention that nominated Pierre Trudeau. One sibling married. Himself a bachelor. Born and raised in Etobicoke, high school at Michael Power-St. Joe's, where he was known more for sports than anything else. He spent five years in the debating club, then went off to St. Mike's for general arts. I ask him about Ibbitson's contention that his politics took a strong right-wing turn after he heard Peter

Worthington on a talk show.

"Well, it wasn't really like that. I had become increasingly disenchanted with Trudeau's arrogance. At that time, the Liberals had railroaded metric down our throats, and I wondered, what next? In the summer between grade twelve and thirteen, I had won a four-day holiday at Camp Enterprise, a pro-business initiative sponsored by the Rotary Club. Up until then, I had bought the Liberal idea that big business is bad. My attitude was starting to change."

Then came the Worthington moment, a quasi-Damascus experience. "I think this took place in the Christmas break of my grade thirteen year," Giorno explains. "I was home listening to a phone-in show on CKEY and I got on the air, claiming to Mr. Worthington that the Liberals had become socialists. I'll never forget his answer: 'That young man speaks for millions of Canadians.'"

It appears the Rubicon had been crossed. Matter of factly, Giorno outlines the next decade for me. Tory club at U of T, supports Harris in the 1990 leadership convention, joins Hicks, Morley, a law firm specializing in negotiating with unions, paid leave to work again for Harris in the 1995 election. Harris apparently likes him, because he is moved from writing speeches to director of policy planning.

Giorno's mood changes when I ask him about his role in Bill 160. He quickly disavows any hands-on role. My information is different. Teacher leaders say he was always at Harris' side in those days, when they were still able to see him. Giorno was, they say, obsessed with the adjective "rigorous" and had no use for "media literacy," saying that corporations are not happy with courses attempting to decipher mediaspeak. But today he goes to great lengths to downplay his role on the bill, insisting, "There are hundreds who have input on bills."

As he reaches for the first of several handouts he has brought for me, his eyes light up and he gets increasingly animated. With the use of flow charts, he takes me through the legislative process, the consultation, writing and rewriting, trying to convince me that it is impossible for one person to have so much power. Ironically, one policy statement will wind up a week later in Christina Blizzard's column in the *Toronto Sun*, reprinted almost verbatim.

Though often interrupting me, Giorno is polite to a fault and calls me "Mr. Schmidt" throughout. With Bill 160 in mind, I ask him if he has any expertise in the area of education. He admits he doesn't. Things get tense when I question the role of deputy minister Veronica Lacey, the ex-North York education director whose performance contract said she'd get a $40,000 bonus if she cut $667 million out of the system. If I don't change the subject soon, I know I'll lose it, so I get personal and confessional with Giorno.

How does Giorno square the gospel he reads on Sunday with Tory policies that attack the most vulnerable? This seems to make him nervous, and he stammers before answering, that it's more germane to question policies rather than motives. When I ask him about his familiarity with Catholic social teaching, he says he knows little about it. I ask him if he as a Christian sees any role for advocacy for the poor.

"Absolutely," he answers.

"How about solidarity with the poor?"

"Yes, they are our brothers and sisters."

"And the role of government?"

"That we have a healthy, competitive economy where jobs exist. A solution to welfare is jobs, so people can break out of welfare." Many Ontarians, he says, would argue that Bob Rae's policies caused suffering and hurt, but nobody questioned his motives. Why were they questioning the motives of Tories?

I point out that the religious leaders of the province never attacked the Rae government on the grounds of social cruelty and that Rae never refused to meet with them. Even more edgy when I ask him about the source of his religious inspiration, he doodles furiously on paper before answering. Finally, he tells me his favourite religious reading is John's Gospel. As a teacher of scripture to Catholic educators for twenty years, I find the answer quite revealing. John's Gospel is the most other-worldly book in the Christian canon. In this Gospel, Jesus hardly touches the earth, appearing as one who gives long, windy speeches in an abstract philosophical manner. There are literally no poor people in John's Gospel, no widows, no children, no women followers, no fishers or prostitutes or lepers.

When I leave Giorno, I cross the road to St. Mike's, where I have parked. This is where my brothers and I were educated in the 1960s and where my dad met my mom. This is where we were initiated into the Catholic story and vision. My mother had worked with the poor in the 1930s and raised all of us to use our education to make a difference. But Giorno, coming of age in the decade of excess, never felt the powerful wave of reform in the church that I had, the radical turn to the world that was the hallmark of Vatican II, and he never learned about the strong social teachings and Catholicism's essential communitarian nature.

I couldn't help but wonder, as well, what he thought about some of his former teachers at Power—the St. Joseph sisters. Last November 4, they wrote to the premier in language Jeremiah would have been proud of: "We objected to the dismantling of Ontario's safety net to no avail. We have protested and watched in horror as our history of excellence in health care has been reduced to minimal and inadequate levels. We cry out once again as this unresponsive government rides roughshod over the will of the people and the future of children."

My conclusion is that the sisters of St. Joseph who have dedicated 150 years of their order's life to health care and education are closer to the truth than the powerful Guy Giorno.

Ted Schmidt writes for the Catholic New Times. *This essay was first published in* Now Magazine, *January 8-15, 1998.*

Queen of the Park by Kevin Donovan and Moira Welsh

When Mike Harris was elected premier, Leslie Noble became the hottest power broker in Ontario. The thirty-seven-year-old is one of Harris' closest advisors and runs the leading lobbying firm dealing with the Ontario government. No other lobbyist has Noble's access to Harris. And no other top political advisor to Harris is a lobbyist.

Noble helped write the Common Sense Revolution, and ran Harris' successful election campaigns in 1995 and 1999. She has no official job with government but regularly briefs Harris, his cabinet ministers and Tory MPPs on what needs to be done politically to stay in power. In corporate circles, Noble is the lobbyist Ontario business executives hire when they want the Harris government's ear.

"There's really no one in the lobbying business that can offset her," said Jim Devlin, president of the Trentway-Wagar bus company. Devlin's company backed the Harris government's plan to open all Ontario bus routes to competition. Noble's client, Greyhound bus lines, did not. Greyhound won at Queen's Park. Devlin looked for a lobbyist to take on Noble but was told by people close to the government to forget it.

"I was told that I would be wasting my money because... she's got the ear of the premier or his senior officials," Devlin said.

Noble charges fees for helping her clients lobby cabinet ministers, their influential political aides, and senior bureaucrats. She has helped her clients broker deals with the Harris government, change government rules and regulations to their benefit, and even undo elements of the Common Sense Revolution.

Here are some other clients who have hired Noble to help them deal with the Ontario government:

• Highway 407 builder Canadian Highways International, which bid to buy and operate the toll road, the construction of which was financed by taxpayers' money.

• Drug company Glaxo-Wellcome, which employed Noble on several matters, including its successful efforts last summer to kill a government regulation that would have limited the amount of taxpayers' money drug companies receive.

• Computer consulting firm SHL Systemhouse and consultants Coopers and Lybrand are among clients who boosted their business with the Ontario government during the time they used Noble.

• Ontario Hydro, which has used Noble to protect it from various government attempts to weaken the giant electrical utility's monopoly.

• Four special interest groups pushing for their members' issues at Queen's Park: Brewers of Ontario, Alliance for Community Care (which represents nursing homes and home care firms), the Ontario Forest Industries Association, and the Ontario Provincial Police Association. The interests of Noble's clients reach into all ministries of the government—health, finance, economic development, solicitor-general, transportation, justice, energy and more.

Noble sees nothing wrong with her dual role as top Harris advisor and lobbyist. Her position is that she avoids conflicts of interest by dividing Harris into two people—leader of Ontario's Progressive Conservative party, and premier of Ontario. And Noble insists she only talks to the party leader—not the premier.

Noble declined repeated requests for an interview for this story. She did, however, accept nineteen written questions. Many questions—including all queries about what she did for clients—were left unanswered. Regarding her dual role, Noble says she provides only "political advice" to Harris, not governmental advice. She said she has never lobbied Harris or any government ministers on client issues. "I have offered political advice to the premier in his capacity as leader of the Progressive Conservative party of Ontario when asked," Noble responded. "Furthermore, he does consult with me in my capacity as campaign manager as to issues of election planning and readiness, however I have never allowed myself to be in a position of conflict between a client interest and giving advice to my party leader."

That's not the way some senior bureaucrats view Noble's role. "When dealing with [Noble] the message is clear—straight from the Premier's office," one government official said.

Noble's dual role raises this question: is a conflict of interest created when a close advisor to Harris makes her living lobbying the Harris government?

The *Toronto Star* repeatedly requested interviews for this story with Harris, five of his aides, two cabinet ministers (Finance Minister Ernie Eves, Economic Development Minister Al Palladini) and their aides. So far, none have responded. Tom Long, PC party campaign chair, told the *Star* yesterday in an interview that Noble polices herself when giving "political" advice.

"[Noble] absents herself from any discussion where there might be a conflict. I understand that is her practice."

Who makes the decision on whether there is a conflict?

"I would imagine she's making that," Long said.

On June 8, 1995, Leslie Noble attained a goal set seven years before, when the Tories ranked third in the polls. Mike Harris was elected premier. Much of the credit went to campaign manager Noble. For that, Tory party insiders say, Harris is eternally grateful.

Noble is described as a tough, hard-working and a savvy election strategist. As campaign manager, she was involved in every detail. Long (a partner in Egon Zehnder, a head hunting firm) was the master strategist.

A Kitchener native, Noble studied political science at the University of Toronto. Fresh out of school, she was an aide to former provincial Tory leader Larry Grossman, then consulted on several Tory campaigns in eastern Canada. In 1989, she saw in Nipissing MPP Mike Harris a future premier. Noble worked on his successful 1990 leadership campaign, and was Tory campaign secretary in the 1990 election won by the New Democratic Party's Bob Rae. The fact Noble fishes and golfs—both passions of Harris— helped her break into the Tories' male-dominated power elite.

"I am not, and since [Harris was elected] I have never been, a member of any regular group that meets to advise the premier on government issues. I strongly object to your suggestion that I am, in any way, in a decision-making capacity in government."

The Common Sense Revolution was born in a Toronto bar. In the early days of 1994, Noble and other young Tories met in the Bradgate Arms on Avenue Rd. The Bradgate Group included: Noble, Long, Mitch Patten (a gas company executive), Alister Campbell (an insurance company executive), and David Lindsay (Harris' principal secretary at the time).

The Common Sense Revolution document Noble helped write promised a thirty percent tax cut, less government through deregulation, no more provincially-funded public housing projects, and privatization of some government assets. At the time the document was written, Noble lived in a Cityhome housing project on The Esplanade in Toronto. The project was a mix of subsidized and fair market value renters. Noble paid fair market rent, but living in Cityhome was a curious choice for someone whose political manifesto railed at such buildings, calling them "the public housing boondoggle" and criticizing such "inefficiencies" for wasting taxpayer dollars. The Common Sense Revolution said government should house the poor by paying "shelter subsidies" to private landlords.

With the 1995 election won, a Tory slogan was coined: "Ontario is open for business." Leslie Noble was one of the first to cash in. Other members of the Harris election team (such as Long) returned to their private-sector jobs or took political posts in the premier's office (Patten, Lindsay and Harris aides Deb Hutton and Guy Giorno). Noble was going to be a lobbyist.

Working, at first, out of her Cityhome apartment, she set up two companies. The first was Political and Communication Strategies. It did some lobbying, and also performed work for the PC party. In 1997, for example, the PC party paid it $51,928 for "research and polling." Noble explained: "On three occasions I have purchased services for the PC party through a company I own. That company has been reimbursed on a cost-past-through basis without any markup or fee whatsoever." Noble would not say who provided these services.

In November, 1995, Noble set up a second company, StrategyCorp Inc., which was to be her main lobbying firm. She was in partnership with Liberal John Duffy. Also in November, Noble purchased a penthouse condominium on Front St. and moved out of Cityhome. As her business grew, she acquired possessions, most recently a $75,000 BMW.

The province was Noble's domain; Duffy would lobby the federal Liberals. The duo moved into offices on the thirty-ninth floor of the Toronto Dominion Bank Tower. StrategyCorp's Web site touts the firm as: "Canada's leading government relations consultants" and boasts: "StrategyCorp exists because it adds value for its clients. Whether it is tackling a regulatory matter, bidding to privatize a government asset, or levering an entire new policy commitment, StrategyCorp gets results." Among the first clients of StrategyCorp was Greyhound bus lines.

The Common Sense Revolution promised less government and less red tape. Al Palladini, transportation minister in the new Tory government, tried to keep that promise. In August, just after the June 1995, election, Palladini said he would end the route monopolies created by government regulation. Previously, even if another company could provide better service at cheaper rates, it was not allowed to compete. Palladini was going to end all that. Seeking consensus, he met with the Ontario Motor Coach Association, which then included Greyhound, Trentway-Wagar, and others. In September 1995, at an association meeting, transportation ministry official Frank D'Onofrio announced they had no option.

"Read the Common Sense Revolution," D'Onofrio said. "This is what we are doing."

Reluctantly, the association agreed. In anticipation of the new competitive regime, association president Brian Crow said his members purchased new buses, at $500,000 each. Palladini said deregulation would begin Jan. 1, 1998. Standing in the Legislature on April 4, 1996, he introduced the deregulation bill, saying it would do away with an unfair barrier to business development.

"Government has no business telling bus companies how to run their businesses," Palladini said to applause from other Tory MPPs.

Greyhound broke from the pro-deregulation motor coach association. Dick Huisman, Greyhound's chief executive officer at the time, said Greyhound was not ready.

"We had a major concern that the regulation as proposed and the timing of it would be far too fast for us to be able to react," Huisman said.

Huisman hired Leslie Noble in early 1996.

"We asked [Noble] if she was able to help us make our position known to the powers that be," said Huisman.

Noble won't talk about Greyhound. Generally, Noble said, she does not get clients in to see cabinet ministers.

"Our clients set up their own meetings. We are not retained for this purpose; indeed it is our view that any client would be wasting their money if they retained a consultant simply for the purpose of setting up meetings with ministers," Noble told the *Star*. Noble says what she does is give clients business advice.

But Huisman says Noble was not hired for her advisory abilities: "No, no, no," he said, "that was not her competency." He had another consultant, Don Haire, arguably Canada's top bus expert. Huisman hired Noble to get access to Palladini and other decision-makers.

"It was in my interest to have somebody on short notice to set up meetings where I am able to meet with these people," said Huisman.

He said Noble got him in to see Palladini and several transportation bureaucrats before he left Greyhound in the fall of 1997. All told, Huisman said he attended about ten meetings. (Current Greyhound vice-president Dan Squigna earlier told the *Star* Noble did not work on deregulation).

Said Huisman: "[Noble] would facilitate whatever we needed to do to get our story known. Also, she met and circulated within the governing circles, whether with the governing party, the opposition... so that whatever is being said with regard to transportation, that would be fed back to us," said Huisman.

Meanwhile, a government-initiated report gave a green light for deregulation, saying competition would mean lower fares and better service. Then the move toward deregulation stopped. Today, several small bus companies, which leased new buses, are facing financial difficulty because the new routes never materialized, the motor coach association says. Trentway-Wagar's Devlin believes the brakes were applied at the highest levels.

"The only way this could have been stopped was by the premier himself," Devlin said. He's disappointed in Harris.

"I have a letter from Mike Harris dated Oct. 30, 1998, that they sent out to a whole bunch of business people," Devlin recalled. "He wanted me to send him ideas. He said, 'I'm writing for two reasons. The first is to congratulate you on your key contribution as a hard working small-business person in helping to turn Ontario around.'"

"Well, when I read that line, I threw it over in the corner. I thought, who the hell does this guy think he is? He has created more hardships in the Ontario bus industry than any leader we've ever had."

The Motor Coach Association's Brian Crow now looks on the Harris government with cynicism.

"Bus companies who believed the government was going to open the market to competition went out and bought new buses, invested in their business. They got set. Now, they've lost faith."

Greyhound, like many of Noble's clients, is a significant contributor to the Ontario PC party. Between 1995 and 1997, Greyhound donated $27,666, compared with $3,600 to the Liberals.

There is nothing wrong with lobbying. It is generally understood that companies and special interest groups who deal with government use consultants to connect with politicians and bureaucrats. What's unique about Noble is that she is both lobbyist and a top advisor to Harris and former Finance Minister Ernie Eves. Over the past four years, her advice has been given over breakfast at the Albany Club on King St. in Toronto, at Bigliardi's restaurant on Church St., and at other locations, including on the golf greens. A favourite course is the Red Tail club near London. Other Harris advisors include Ontario Hydro Chairman Bill Farlinger and David Lindsay, formerly of the premier's office, now Ontario Jobs and Investment Board chairman.

Noble also occupies a powerful position in the PC party of Ontario. For campaign manager work that ran from January, 1994, to July, 1995, Noble was paid $181,940. PC party records say this was for "consulting" and "travel." By contrast, campaign chair Long's PC Party payments totalled $29,214 for the same period.

As campaign director in 1995, Noble was the field marshall for Tory troops who went on to run the offices of the premier and key Tory ministers. As campaign manager for the 1999 election, Noble was again the boss. For a year, she had been giving regular briefings to Harris and all Tory MPPs on pre-election issues. Some, even those outside politics, perceive Noble as part of the Tory government. For example, World Wildlife Fund president Monte Hummel went to

Noble in 1997 to see what the Tory government would do for the environment.

"We were interested in her own thinking because she was obviously a key advisor to the government," said Hummel.

Noble met Hummel for ninety minutes—at no charge.

"Given who she is and the role she plays in the government, it was like an hour and half of gold for us, getting access to her," Hummel said.

He recalls Noble saying the environment doesn't have a lot of political payoff because people don't expect Tories to do much for the environment. At the same time, Noble had a client—the Ontario Forest Industries Association—whose views often collide with environmentalists. Noble's client, an association of major logging and pulp and paper corporations, is a powerful force in the Tory government's controversial Lands for Life process, which will soon decide how much of Ontario's forests will be opened up to logging, and for how long.

One pipeline Noble has to influence government decision-makers is the unelected cadre of political aides in the offices of the premier and his top ministers. These aides, many of whom report to Noble during the election campaign, wield tremendous power in government, a reality acknowledged by some Tory MPPs. Tory backbencher Bill Murdoch says they openly flaunt their power.

"They say, 'Hey Murdoch, we didn't even have to go through an election and we're running the place.'" Queen's Park Speaker Chris Stockwell, a Tory MPP, calls them a "cabal" and says they make decisions without input from elected politicians. Noble's own correspondence to clients demonstrates a familiar, routine relationship with this unelected cadre. To a client, Noble explains she is contacting Giorno (Harris' director of policy), Hutton (Harris' director of issues management), Lindsay (Harris' former chief of staff), Brian Patterson (former Economic Development Minister Bill Saunderson's executive assistant, and assistant to former Transportation Minister Tony Clement), Peter Clute (former Finance Minister Eves' executive assistant), and John Guthrie (he was Consumer Minister David Tsubouchi's executive assistant).

In her correspondence, Noble also describes how she contacts members of "P & P"—Priorities and Planning—the inner cabinet that makes most government decisions. In addition, Noble's correspondence confirms that, as numerous sources told the Star, Harris and his then-right-hand man, Eves, make the key decisions. In one example, on whether the Ontario government would place video lottery terminals in bars or charity casinos, she tells one client that (former) Economic Development Minister Bill Saunderson is powerless, though the matter involved his ministry.

"The decision will be made between the premier and the treasurer [Eves], not by the minister," Noble writes to a client.

Noble told the Star she has no sway over the Harris government. As for her lobby business, Noble downplayed it.

"Much of our company's work is related to monitoring and analyzing public policy and providing information to clients on government direction and attitudes," Noble said in her response to the Star. Two clients of Noble's confirmed this, saying she has a great ability to tell them what government is thinking.

"I was told that I would be wasting my money because . . . [Noble's] got the ear of the premier or his senior officials," said Jim Devlin.

But generally, the Star found a reluctance to talk among Noble's clients. Dr. Robert Gordon, president of Humber College, is an exception.

"I know who she is, I know who she knows, she's a political operator," said Gordon, who hired Noble to help change government regulations so his college can run businesses in partnership with private companies. StrategyCorp's website stresses Noble's Tory ties. Gordon said he hired her for those ties. Other clients would only confirm they used Noble and her firm.

The Toronto office of Coopers and Lybrand (now Price Waterhouse Coopers) hired Noble in late 1995 seeking more government business. Coopers had $1.4 million annual business with the government before hiring Noble. After, the consulting firm's government contracts more than doubled.

SHL Systemhouse, an Ottawa-based computer consulting firm, hired Noble in early 1996 and retains her services to this day. SHL spokesperson Mary Keating would only say Noble's firm provides SHL with "information and consulting services"—not lobbying.

During the course of Noble's retainer, SHL's government business has grown by leaps and bounds. Before Noble, $8 million; after one year with Noble, $32 million; after two years with Noble, $41 million. Neither Noble, nor her clients, would reveal her role, if any, in boosting government business.

Drug company Glaxo-Wellcome says it retained Noble in June, 1998. That was a few weeks after the government said it would curb the rising cost of the Ontario Drug Benefit Plan (ODB), which pays about $953 million annually to cover prescriptions for seniors and welfare recipients. Government bureaucrats wanted to establish maximum ODB payouts for each new drug listed. A drug industry source says government bureaucrats believed that drug companies low-balled the expected usage of new drugs to get them listed on the plan.

Under the proposed regulation, if a new drug exceeded the maximum, the drug company would have to reimburse the government for the extra amount. Such penalties could have been in the millions of dollars. Glaxo and other drug companies did not like the plan. A Glaxo spokesperson confirmed that Noble was hired to work on this and other issues, but would not say what she did.

Some light on the activities of StrategyCorp is shed by John Perenack, a StrategyCorp consultant. Perenack says that, as a StrategyCorp consultant, he does the following: "Advise structuring of client bids on privatizations and outsourcing including TV Ontario; Highway 407; water and waste water treatment; and prisons." Perenack explains that his job is to "represent client interests and develop strategies to sell client initiatives to political and bureaucratic staff in the provincial and federal governments."

Noble maintains she does not get her clients in to see ministers. Yet when Bank of Nova Scotia chair Peter Godsoe wanted to bend Eves' ear on Eves' opposition to the recent flurry of proposed bank mergers, StrategyCorp set it up. Noble's lobbying contract with Ontario Hydro states she will "organize interventions with key decision-makers in the Ontario government."

From April, 1997, to May, 1998, Noble was the lobbyist for Ontario Hydro. The Common Sense Revolution said that a Mike Harris government "will sell off some (government) assets" and Ontario Hydro might very well be one of them. When Noble was hired by Ontario Hydro, government plans for the debt-ridden utility were up in the air. Ontario Hydro did not want to be broken up and sold off. That never happened. The government agreed to maintain Ontario Hydro as a public utility, but allow competition by other firms. During Noble's time on Hydro's payroll, Ontario Hydro had pressed hard to maintain a strong market share for the new competitive environment.

Noble's contract, which was not tendered by Ontario Hydro, states: "Specifically, StrategyCorp would work with Hydro to ensure positive outcomes in three Government of Ontario processes: 1) the development of cabinet submissions, 2) the completion and issuance of the Ministry of Environment and Energy's White Paper, 3) the drafting of legislation and subsequent parliamentary debate thereon." Noble's fee was $14,000 for the first six weeks, then $7,000 per month plus expenses. Ontario Hydro records show total payments of $162,215 were authorized to Noble's company, but only $91,000 was paid out because she stopped working for Hydro six months before her contract was to end.

Jobnet, an Internet employment site for Ontario's proposed work-fare scheme, used Noble in 1996 to get meetings with then-Social Services Minister Tsubouchi, Tsubouchi's aides and, following a cabinet shuffle, a meeting with newly appointed minister Janet Ecker's top advisor. Jobnet's Jim Towse said he paid Noble about $50,000. While Noble got him in the door, the Harris government did not support his project. While many of Noble's clients are significant donors to the Ontario PC party, Towse was not.

He said Noble suggested several times, in writing, that his company attend fundraisers, including the gala Premier's Dinner in the spring of 1997.

Noble said she tells clients to donate to all three political parties.

"Like most firms that practise government relations, we encourage our clients to support the democratic process by financially supporting the major political parties," Noble wrote to the *Star*.

"StrategyCorp and its principals often pass on to clients solicitations for funds from all three major parties. Sometimes a donation to the party results."

Towse recalls: "She never suggested we go to any Liberal or NDP fundraisers."

Towse sent an employee to a Tory fundraiser, but decided against any others.

"I'm not into these dinners," Towse said.

The *Star* found a pattern of top Tory donors employing Noble. An example is Canadian Highways International (CHIC), the company that built Highway 407, the government-owned toll road between Markham and Mississauga. Ontario taxpayers paid $930 million to build the road in a deal struck under the NDP government. The plan at the time was for taxpayers to own the road. In early 1997, CHIC hired Leslie Noble. CHIC spokesperson Mitch Patten (a former Harris aide) would not discuss specifics of Noble's efforts. In general, Patten said of Noble:

"One of the things that Leslie helps us with is understanding where various governments are at . . . and helps us to sort of understand where they're at, what kind of approaches are likely to mesh with their priorities and sometimes there's some advocacy work (lobbying) involved with that or some talking to staff, gathering information, helping us figure it out."

Four months after Noble was hired, the Harris government said it might sell the highway. When the bidding opened. CHIC submitted a bid. The buyer must complete two other sections of the road at no cost to taxpayers and in return, will be allowed to collect tolls on the private road. Election finance records show CHIC's Tory donations were $54,557 in 1995-97. Adding the donations of CHIC's four consortium members raises the total Tory donation to $157,000.

Kevin Donovan and Moira Welsh are staff reporters for the Toronto Star. *This essay was first published in the* Toronto Star *on March 13, 1999.*

Mr. Fix-it by Judy Steed

David Lindsay, an accountant in his forties, has synthesized ideas, written speeches and created language that has defined the agenda of the Harris Tories using concepts borrowed partly from U.S. corporate restructuring shakedowns. In a speech in December, 1997, from his new post as president of the Ontario Jobs and Investment Board, Lindsay spoke about the "paradoxes of transformation." Lifted liberally from a 1994 article titled "How to Lead a Revolution" in the U.S. business magazine *Fortune*, Lindsay's speech was remarkable for its tone of self-pity.

"Want a tough job?" asks the *Fortune* article. "Try leading an organization through major change—a merger, say, or re-engineering or a devolution of power from a hierarchy to teams. Almost without exception, executives claim it's the hardest work they've ever done."

Having helped his leader "bear the trials of transformation," as *Fortune* puts it, Lindsay is focused on defining the government's new vision. Or, as he summed it up during an interview in the marble-walled Whitney block, a short walk from the cabinet office, "Where do we go from here?"

The focus of the Tories' mission was defined in 1992, on a sunny summer day at the Guild Inn in Scarborough. There, Lindsay and about fifteen other people boiled down the broad expressions of what he terms the party's "visioning exercise." They created a strategic direction that resulted, two years later, in the Common Sense Revolution—the renovation that required the sledgehammer, which was supposed to lay the foundation for rebuilding.

Old ways die off, Lindsay says. New technologies come on stream. Such as? "Instead of the government building all the roads, the hospitals, the infrastructure, you contract it out," he answers, "the way we did the new Highway 407." In fact the previous New Democrat government contracted out the building of Highway 407.

Buzz Hargrove remembers meeting twice with Lindsay, and wasn't impressed with the vision. "It's a justification for a mean-spirited transfer of wealth and power from the have-nots to the haves," Hargrove says. "We raised issues with Lindsay and there was no response, no follow-up." The teachers have a similar lament. "Their idea of dialogue is to tell you what they're going to do, and if you don't like it, too bad," says the Ontario Secondary School Teachers' Federations's Jim McQueen. Ross McClellan, a former New Democrat House leader and special policy advisor to NDP Premier Bob Rae, scoffs at Lindsay's "revolutionary" rhetoric. "It's short-sighted, tunnel vision."

McClellan, the legislative director for the Ontario Federation of Labour, says "their's is a revolution with no content. It's about one thing: cutting $6 billion in government spending and cutting taxes by $6 billion. There's nothing else."

Judy Steed writes for the Toronto Star. *This essay is an extract from a longer article that first appeared in the* Toronto Star *on April 18, 1998.*

Chapter 4: The Harris Record

The Omnibus Bill by the Caledon Institute

In 1995, the Ontario government introduced Bill 26, the Savings and Restructuring Act (known as The Omnibus Bill). This legislative package was far-reaching in that it affected forty-seven acts of the Ontario Legislature. The Omnibus Bill is more than two thousand pages long.

This legislation lays the foundation for subsequent bills, such as the Megacity Bill (Bill 104). It covers such areas as health care, pay equity, municipal affairs, public employee contracts, environmental laws and freedom of information laws. Bill 26 gives the minister of health the authority to close or force mergers in Ontario's community hospitals. The government is authorized to set up the Health Services Restructuring Commission, composed of eight appointed members. The minister of health can eliminate hospital boards, take over hospitals in order to shut them down, merge hospitals and decide on what services will be provided to the public.

Additionally, Bill 26 gives huge powers to the minister of municipal affairs to abolish local governments and to force mergers and amalgamations of local municipalities. The range of public life which the legislation affects is extraordinary. Nevertheless, the government first introduced the bill in the Legislature just before the 1995 Christmas break when most MPPs were in their ridings. Further, the government made no provision for public hearings. It was only after opposition members staged a sit-in to protest the lack of consultation that the government agreed to hold three weeks of public hearings on the Bill. This behaviour, which came early in the mandate of the Conservative government, left some Ontarians uneasy about the commitment of the Harris government to well-established democratic procedures.

What has not been much talked about in the public forum is the very notion of an Omnibus Bill in the context of our British style of parliamentary government. Our system is one in which a determined government has considerable power as long as it can keep a majority caucus on side. One of the only real checks on the power of the government is the legislative process itself, supposedly requiring even the most ruthless government to submit to parliamentary debate on each legislative initiative (most publicly during daily Question Period). To ensure that parliamentary debate happens, the tradition of parliamentary procedure is that each Bill must deal with a single, coherent theme. While many Canadian governments introduce omnibus bills, they are careful to ensure that only 'housekeeping' matters are dealt with in such a bill, and that nothing substantial is included. This kind of legislation is typically used by governments as an administrative mechanism to efficiently make a large number of small adjustments without policy implications in a variety of areas. (A common example is the correction of spelling errors accidentally inserted into a piece of legislation).

By the traditional rules of the Legislature, the Omnibus Bill should have been ruled inadmissible by the Speaker. The government should have been required to break the bill up into individual components and pass each one separately. The requirement to deal with issues individually is a vital restraint on the powers of any government. This requirement is meant to stop a government from just stapling together many different bills, calling them a single bill, and passing the whole thing as a way of railroading the Legislature and minimizing debate. But the Speaker of the Legislature has unfettered powers to make a ruling. The Speaker at the time, the Honourable Allan McLean, ruled in the government's favour.

The Caledon Institute is a progressive policy think-tank which advocates a new charter for Toronto. This essay was first published on the Institute's website in 1996.

How the Whiz Kids Screwed Up
by John Ibbitson

In September 1995, Mike Harris, Principal Secretary David Lindsay and Rita Burak, the cabinet secretary, hosted a one-day brainstorming session to discuss cutting government costs and restructuring in Ontario. Everybody hashed through the numbers, how much needed to be cut, how much each ministry should be expected to contribute, where the cuts might come from in each ministry. After the meeting, ministry staff contacted such "stakeholders" as the Ontario Hospital Association, the major universities and the Association of Municipalities of Ontario.

If you found yourself losing this much money from us, they were asked, what new powers would you need from us to make up the difference. The ministers then fed the information they received back to the premier's office. It was clear by now that so many changes from so many ministries would pose a formidable logistical challenge. Pushing through the various pieces of enabling legislation could tie up the legislative calendar for months. But what if it were passed all at once? Not only would it speed up the timetable, but the entire herd of opposition oxen could be gored at once, reducing the political fallout. Thus the Omnibus Bill was born.

The actual package was assembled by Guy Giorno, Harris' long-term policy adviser. He co-ordinated the material funnelled to him from the ministry bureaucracies through the cabinet office. As pieces of the package were assembled, Giorno shipped them over to the finance ministry. Since the bill would accompany the economic statement, it would have to be presented to the Legislature by then-Finance Minister Ernie Eves. And here the process broke down. Perhaps the largest bill ever put before the Legislature of any province was being assembled in incredible haste. Ministers had little time or opportunity to veto the recommendations coming from their bureaucracies. Instead, the recommendations were often simply shovelled up by the deputy ministers straight to cabinet office and Giorno. But Giorno, though widely respected for his intelligence, had little experience in government and none with the bureaucracy. He didn't perceive that many of the recommendations were simply wish lists of new powers that senior bureaucrats had longed for but never been given. Worse, once the legislative provisions were sent over to finance, they disappeared into a black hole of secrecy.

The Omnibus Bill would accompany a financial statement, and finance officials are justifiably paranoid about leaks. They can cost a minister his job. So Eves' officials drafted the bill without letting anyone outside the ministry see its actual wording.

Lindsay, Giorno and cabinet ministers all appealed in vain to see what the legislation would look like. And then, at the critical period of preparation, just six weeks before the economic statement and the new Omnibus Bill were due, Eves confronted a personal crisis (his son was killed in a car crash) that forced the government's most powerful minister to temporarily abandon his post. Eves' absence and the secrecy surrounding the new bill left the Tories ill-prepared to introduce their massive legislation. Only on the eve of its presentation were staff in the premier's office shown the first copies of the text.

At such a critical time, the government desperately needed a coherent communications strategy. The bill's "message track"—the rationale to be offered by ministers and advisors—should have been carefully worked out and drilled into the appropriate people's heads. The hope was that the bill's size and scope would make it so difficult to absorb that reporters and opposition politicians would give up and move on to something else.

For the first few days, the Tories' strategy of downplaying the bill appeared to work. The press gallery at first attempted to ignore the new legislation and concentrate on the seismic cuts contained in the economic statement instead. To most journalists, including this writer, Bill 26 looked like a "process bill"—legislation that changes the way decisions are made, without actually coming to any decisions.

Slowly, it penetrated the media's skulls that the new omnibus bill was about more than closings. It was even about more than user fees for prescriptions. The bill amended no fewer than forty-seven existing laws.

Tony Clement (now minister of health and long-term care) was on one of the committees examining the bill. It quickly became clear to him and others on the committee that the government had been shafted by the bureaucrats. "The bureaucracy tended to put in every item that had been on the shelf for the past five years," he believes.

Bill 26 set a precedent that would become a pattern with the Harris government. Time after time, staff from the premier's office would seize control of an issue and try to manage it, only to be slapped in the face by public reaction. Then, other elements within the government, or allies outside it, would come to the rescue. Undaunted, the premier's staff would launch the next big crisis.

John Ibbitson is a columnist for the Globe and Mail.

1,460 Days of Destruction by Ross McClellan

Since its election on June 8, 1995, the Harris government has followed a single-minded and senseless objective. It promised to make a 30% reduction in the provincial income tax rate, and balance the provincial budget at one and the same time. The goal is to shrink the size of the public sector and reduce the role of government itself. The purpose is to replace the public provision of programs and services with privatized services sold on the "free market" for whatever the traffic will bear.

Tax breaks for the rich

The lion's share of the tax cut (57%) will go to the wealthiest tax filers, that is, to the top ten percent. To pay for the tax cut, the Harris government has borrowed so much money that it will add $25 billion to Ontario's public debt. And at the same time, it is slashing public spending. By the end of 1999 Ontario's net spending on programs and capital works had been cut from 15% of GDP to 12%, a drop of twenty percent.

The Four Tory Budgets

1. Economic Statements, July and November 1995

Ernie Eves announced the first round of Common Sense Revolution cuts on July 21, 1995, adding up to $2 billion. This cutback package included $500 million in service and staff cuts to ministries and a 22% cut in social assistance rates. The Tories brought down the second and more devastating hit in November 1995 when another $3.5 billion was cut from the base of Ontario's annual spending on public programs. Added to the July cuts, this first round totalled $5.5 billion in cutbacks announced to the end of the fiscal year 1995-96.

Mike Harris did not actually cut the full $5.5 billion. Between 1995 and 1998 he cut about $4.5 billion from health, education and community programs. But he made it clear that he was prepared to cut as much as $8.2 billion if that was necessary to carry out the Common Sense Revolution. The return of growth to Ontario's economy has protected us from the full effect of the cuts needed to pay for the tax cut. The full price tag will show up whenever the next business downturn comes around again.

As the first big round of budget cuts began to sink in, it had a profound effect on the Ontario economy. It knocked Ontario back into a made-in-Ontario recession in 1996 and delayed the recovery that arrived in the rest of Canada, as a result of lower interest rates and the boom in the U.S. Between August 1996 and March 1997 Ontario actually lost 37,000 jobs.

2. First Budget, May 1996

The first full Harris budget re-announced the tax cut and confirmed the total cutback plan of $8.2 billion. Figures released under freedom of information showed clearly that the tax cut would only benefit the top 10% of taxpayers. Everybody else would see their tiny "tax break" eaten up by new user fees and charges. The economy continued to stall throughout 1996, thanks to the damage of deep spending cuts.

3. Second Budget, May 1997

The Tory budget for 1997-98 came down on May 6, 1997. By now it was crystal clear that Ontario's fiscal crisis had mysteriously disappeared. But the great jobs recovery did not happen. The government admitted that it had underestimated the previous year's revenue by nearly $2 billion. And for the coming year, 1997-98, the government deliberately understated its revenue by over $2 billion in income tax alone.

The sole reason that Ontario still had a fiscal problem was entirely due to the $6 billion tax cut! By the end of 1997-98, close to $4 billion of the $5.5 billion of announced spending cuts were scheduled to take place. And on the jobs front, after two full years Ontario had created only 137,000 new jobs, the majority in the part-time or self-employment categories.

4. Third Budget, May 1998

As the Tories came within a year of the next election, they tried to put a kinder, gentler face on their government. To do this, they cooked the books. Spending appeared to be up, but on closer examination, there was much less than met the eye. For example, $9 billion was 'provided' for millennium scholarships, and another $9.5 billion was 'added' for training. But both these announcements were fake.

They gave new names to money already in the system, combining federal and provincial funding and totalling it over ten years.

The government's budget claimed to increase spending dramatically, even above the level of the previous NDP government. That too turned out to be false. A full $2.3 billion was shown as provincial spending when in fact it represented services which were transferred to the municipal governments as part of the 'Who Does What' downloading exercise. Local government was really bearing the cost. Another $1.4 billion of spending was one-time 'contingency' funding which served to pad spending but was not part of the permanent budget base. In fact, it may never be spent at all. Since 1995-96, the Tories have allocated a total of $6.4 billion for the one-time costs of restructuring and other purposes. Of this, $5.3 billion was not spent. It was spread around as election candy, but since these were one-time, one-off expenditures, they did nothing to restore permanent services and programs.

Education spending was trumpeted as a priority, but when all the financial changes from education restructuring are taken into account, overall education spending was reduced by about one billion dollars since the 1997-98 budget.

5. Fourth Budget, May 1999

The fourth Tory budget is the culmination of four years of budgetary deception. As the Harris Government gets closer to another election, it has been less and less honest about the extent of its spending cuts. The latest budget is deliberately distorted by adding $2.7 billion in one-time contingency and restructuring costs to the permanent base budget for programs and capital spending. When these once-off items are removed, the Tory spending plan has been reduced from $49.4 billion in 1995-96 to $46.7 billion in 1998-99.

The final absurdity was former Finance Minister Ernie Eves' claim in the budget that the tax cut did not cost Ontario anything at all, and that the government has actually increased spending on health and education. The truth is exactly the opposite. While the budget promised to increase health spending by 20% over five years, it does not even keep up with population growth and inflation. The end result will leave real per capita health spending lower than it was before

Harris was elected. In 1994-95 real per capita spending was $1609; in 2003-04 it will be $1558. The Harris health care crisis will last another five years.

Education spending is also drastically lower than it was before the Harris cuts. The new education funding formula reduces real education dollars by $987 million a year, and that's on top of the $525 million the government cut from schools during its first two years in office. That represents a $1.5 billion reduction in real spending on schools.

The 1999 budget promises another round of tax cuts, totaling $4 billion. This will lead to another round of slash and burn cuts as soon as the economy begins the next cyclical downturn. And it raises the total annual revenue loss from the Harris tax cuts to $10 billion a year! The dirty little secret, of course, is that Harris has had to borrow every penny needed to pay for the tax cut. By the end of 2000-01, the total borrowed to finance the tax cut will be $25 billion, and the annual carrying cost for that debt will be $1.4 billion.

The New Off-Load

Beginning on January 13, 1997 the Harris government announced the next phase of its Revolution. This time it threatened to completely destroy Ontario's traditions of local government. And to complete its program of cutbacks to pay for the tax cut, it announced a plan to off-load over $6.5 billion in new costs to municipal governments.

The province proposed to take education finance off the residential property tax and to pay this $5.4 billion cost itself. In exchange, Harris dumped over $6 billion in costs onto municipalities. Ontario saved over $1 billion in the deal. The outcry was so ferocious the government was forced to revise its plan. The Tories backed down, but the net effect remains severe. At least $800 million in new expenses have been dumped onto the shoulders of the property taxpayer.

The Tory Megacity Bill amalgamated all locally elected municipal governments within Metro Toronto into one, as of January 1998. Elected mayors and councillors were put under the authoritarian control of a Tory-appointed Board of Trustees. In effect, Toronto and the other local governments were put into receivership by Harris. Harris ignored an overwhelming referendum vote against the Megacity.

The Megadump

Major items dumped into the laps of local property tax payers include a significant part of the costs of welfare, all of the expense for social housing and public transit.

1. Welfare, or, The Poor Have No Rights

After thirty years of provincial funding support under national standards, Ontario is scrapping its social assistance laws which give all persons in need the legal entitlement to financial aid. Local government will have to pick up new costs for these harsh new laws.

2. Social Housing

Responsibility for Ontario's 275,000 units of social housing was downloaded to municipalities, at an added cost of $890 million per year.

3. Public Transit

Responsibility for public transit was completely dumped onto municipal governments at an added annual cost of $395 million. A sleeper was the transfer of 4,000 kilometres of road maintenance to local government.

Harris claims that any inequities in this huge restructuring will be smoothed over with cash from one of three new provincial funds: the Community Re-Investment Fund ($500 million), the Municipal Capital and Operating Restructuring Fund ($800 million) and a $70 million special needs fund. Meanwhile, the old Municipal Support Fund of $600 million was scrapped. On top of all this, Ernie Eves announced a new system of municipal property tax based on a variant of market value assessment. Winners and losers are split evenly under the new scheme.

In 1995, Harris started his cuts with an incredible 48% reduction in provincial grants to municipal government. Ontario's financial support to municipal government was instantly cut in half. The total cut was $658 million over two years. A new block grant replaced the traditional municipal roads grants and unconditional grants, but at a level reduced by forty-three percent. Transit grants were slashed 21% over two years; $24 million in 1996 and $28 million in 1997-98. Libraries were cut by $12 million over two years. Blue Box funding was completely wiped out. Conservation authority budgets were cut by 70% over two years.

Megadump '97

The above cuts were simply the prelude to the megadump announcements of January 1997. Full costs for social housing and public transit, and new costs for welfare, were dumped onto the property tax. Municipalities got at least $1 billion in off-loaded new costs.

1. Police Tax

Rural Ontarians are now required to pay up to $220 per household as a special tax for Ontario Provincial Police services.

2. Bill 26

The Savings and Restructuring Act, which will be discussed in detail below, gives Mike Harris and his gang dictatorial powers to abolish municipalities at will, or to force municipal mergers and amalgamations. It allows for the massive introduction of user fees, without approval by the Legislature, for services which have always been free, like libraries and public recreation facilities. Under this bill, cancellation of 390 already approved co-op and non-profit housing projects is authorized, resulting in the loss of more than 17,000 units of affordable housing, 37,000 person-years of employment and more than $750 million in tax revenues.

Under the 1997 megadump, all 275,000 units of social housing in Ontario become the sole responsibility of local government, at a cost of $890 million. The shelter allowance portion of welfare cheques was cut by 21.6%, forcing low-income tenants to use food money for rent. Tenant protection laws were put on the chopping block, with basement apartments once more illegal. Rent control is being dismantled.

Rent Decontrol

Hearings began in August 1996 for the Tory Consultation Paper on Rent Control. For the first time since 1975, rent is decontrolled in

Ontario. All new apartments will be permanently exempt from rent control. Moreover, every apartment unit will have a window of escape from rent control whenever a given unit becomes vacant. Within four years thousands of vulnerable tenants have been exposed to eviction as their apartments were converted to condominiums. The chair of Ontario's Human Rights Commission testified that the new tenant laws violate basic human rights.

Environment

In the 1996 Tory business plan statement, the ministry of the environment was decimated; its budget was slashed by 36% and 752 positions were axed. The ministry is no longer able to protect the environment. Cuts to the ministry of the environment spell the end for recycling programs, as well as an end to enforcement of anti-pollution laws. During the toxic fire at Plastimet in Hamilton, the ministry was rendered useless. The Interim Waste Authority has been abolished, together with all its work to find three permanent waste disposal sites. Toronto and the Greater Toronto Area will now be free to use the rest of Ontario as a garbage dump.

1. Incinerators Allowed
The NDP ban on municipal garbage incineration is repealed. Deadly incineration is now promoted as official government policy.

2. Blue Box
Provincial funding to the blue box program is eliminated. The Tories have also killed funding for other 3-Rs programs (reduction, reuse, recycle) to municipalities.

3. Planning
The Sewell reforms to the Planning Act in Bill 163 have been watered down to allow environmentally irresponsible development. Ontario's new planning principle is private greed. Laws requiring mine owners to clean up behind them are repealed. Restrictions on the development of Ontario's precious wetlands are weakened. Funding for sustainable forestry is cut by $20 million for 1995-96, and government gives over responsibility for tree planting to the forest industry. Clear

cutting and tree stripping will replace sustainable forestry.

All provincial funding for building and repairing water and sewer treatment systems have been eliminated The eighty Ontario regulations covering toxic pollution were reviewed as the first step in their repeal. Funding for Ontario's conservation authorities was cut by 70% over two years. Ontario's Green Communities program was scrapped one day after the minister boasts of its effectiveness. Fish harvesting rights for First Nations peoples in Georgian Bay were abrogated.

Bill 136

This bill was designed to put free collective bargaining for over half a million Ontario public service workers into deep freeze and to strip public sector workers of the right to strike. The bill would have created two new bodies, the Labour Relations Transition Commission and the Disputes Resolution Commission, with enormous arbitrary powers over public service workers and their collective bargaining rights. These two bodies would have usurped the authority of the Ontario Labour Relations Board.

The Labour Relations Transition Commission was to be a temporary body, made up of Tory patronage appointments. It would have had the power to deal with mergers and amalgamations as the Harris revolution hit local government and school boards. This commission would have had the power to determine the size and shape of the new bargaining units, decide which union will represent workers as the bargaining agent, rule on how seniority rules would apply and to whom and set the terms and conditions of employment during the "transition" period.

The Disputes Resolution Commission was also going to be an exclusive group of Tory patronage appointees, but it was to be a permanent Commission with the power to hear and decide all collective bargaining issues for public service workers who would not have the right to strike— i.e. police, firefighters and hospital workers—and for all other public service workers, if collective bargaining should not be successful, this commission would write the collective agreement for the first contract following merger or amalgamation, at the request of either the employee or the employer.

Under the threat of this unprecedented assault on free collective bargaining, Ontario's labour movement mobilized as never before. Votes were held all across Ontario, local by local, to give a democratic mandate for strike action against Bill 136. A province-wide lobby campaign directed at municipal politicians was so effective that AMO passed an anti-Bill 136 resolution at its convention.

At the end of the day, the Harris government blinked. Bill 136 was completely gutted. All its restrictions on the right to strike were removed. The two proposed Commissions were eliminated entirely, and the existing system of independent arbitration under the jurisdiction of the Ontario Labour Relations Board was maintained. Labour continues to be vigilant to ensure that essential service workers who do not have the right to strike really do get fair and impartial arbitration. Further attempts to weaken the OLRB with Tory political hack appointments have been resisted.

Bill 84 Hits Fire Fighters

Ontario's fire fighters were stripped of collective bargaining rights—even though there has never been a strike in this sector. Bill 84 opened the door to privatize Ontario's fire departments. If that wasn't enough, Bill 136 tried to take away the firefighters' right to a fair and impartial arbitration system. As seen above, though, Harris was forced to back down.

Bill 98, Development Charges Act

From now on the costs of serviced land—including water and sewer—are switched from developers to property taxpayers.

Bill 7

The NDP labour law reforms were totally wiped out by Bill 7 which allows scabs to steal workers' jobs again in this province. The card-majority system of union certification which had been in place since 1950 were replaced by mandatory certification votes. This permits the employer to organize an anti-union election campaign every time workers try to form a union. In addition, employers are permitted to instigate petitions for a decertification vote.

Successor rights were stripped from Crown employees. This means that when the Harris gang wants to privatize public services, workers lose both their collective agreement and their bargaining rights whenever a department is sold. Workers in the contract service sector, like building cleaners, lose successor rights and their jobs whenever a contract changes hands, pounding wages back to minimum wage levels. Already the workers who clean the Tories' Queen's Park offices have lost their jobs.

This draconian legislation was introduced on October 4, and rammed through the Legislature on October 31 without a single day of hearings.

Labour Relations and Workers' Rights

The ministry of labour sustained a 46% cut in its budget, effectively cutting it in half. A total of 457 ministry staff are 'surplused'. A third of the employment standards inspectors are laid off, and support for health and safety inspectors is virtually eliminated. This means that the enforcement of employment standards is a thing of the past, and employers will be under less pressure to maintain safe workplaces. The result is found to be more workers injured or killed.

The chair of the Ontario Labour Relations Board, Judith McCormick, was dismissed in 1996 in an unprecedented act of political vindictiveness. The OLRB vice-chairs and members who the Tories dislike were also fired in mid-term, without cause. The courts have forced Harris to back down from his attempt to crush the independence of the OLRB.

On August 23, 1995 the Workplace Health and Safety Agency is disbanded. The labour directors are fired. The Agency is taken over by the Workers' Compensation Board, removing any input from workers from this vital area. The funding of the Workers Health and Safety Centre was reduced and the hours required for certification training were cut in half. The Workplace Health and Safety Agency had been set up in 1991. During the next four years the Agency trained 33,000 certified health and safety committee members resulting in a reduction of 30% in workplace accidents. Mandatory inquests when workers are killed on the job have been abolished.

The Tory Red Tape Commission calls for changes to the right to refuse work, and the new business plan for the ministry of labour demands a review of the Occupational Health and Safety Act while cutting $8.2 million out of its workplace health and safety budget.

Ontario's minimum wage is frozen, and won't be raised until the American border states catch up to our level. The Wage Protection Program, which guarantees wages, benefits, severance and termination pay to laid-off workers, was chopped back to wages and benefits only, and the maximum was cut from $5,000 to $2,000. Under Bill 136 this program was terminated entirely.

Ontario's pay equity program is slashed by $50 million, cutting payments to the lowest paid women. Pay equity payments are placed under a cap, pay equity proxy is abolished in the broader public sector and Ontario's Employment Equity Program is scrapped, the Act is repealed, the Commission abolished and the employees fired.

Bill 31, The Economic Development and Workplace Democracy Act

In June 1998 the Harris gang continued its assault on worker protection law with Bill 31. This bill completes the dirty work of Bill 7 by taking away the only effective penalty protecting workers from intimidation and harassment during a union organizing drive. Until now, the OLRB could punish an employer found guilty of misconduct under the Act by awarding automatic union certification, as in the Wal-Mart case, where the Board ruled that the employer had so poisoned the workplace that a fair election was impossible. This deterrent against employer retaliation is now gone.

There's more. Bill 31 eliminated access to interim orders from the OLRB, to get speedy protection from employer harassment in a certification contest. The employer was also given the power to dispute the union estimate for the number of persons in a proposed bargaining unit.

The construction unions were dealt a particularly heavy blow by provisions which exempt "non-construction employers" from the requirement to abide by the terms of construction industry collective agreements. This means that thousands of construction workers who have had union protection for decades will be stripped of their bargaining rights at the "declaration" of the employer, with massive losses in wages, benefits and job security.

Bill 99

Following the proposals to gut workers' compensation made in the Jackson Report, Bill 99 was introduced. The bill

- took $6 billion in benefits from injured workers and gave it to employers;
- allowed employers to force injured workers back to work prematurely;
- removed the independence of the Workers' Compensation Appeal Tribunal;
- gave workers' private medical records to employers;
- eroded inflation protection for Workers' Compensation Board benefits;
- terminated the Occupational Disease Panel;
- forced injured workers to get their accident claim forms from the employer assuring that many accidents would be covered up;
- returned Ontario to the days when the burden of proof was on the worker in an injury dispute and the benefit of the doubt went to the employer; and
- outlawed compensation for chronic stress and limited benefits for chronic pain.

Privatization

Whole sections of the Workers' Compensation Board have been privatized. Vocational rehabilitation, claims and benefit management and medical management will all become profit centres for business. Hundreds of WCB employees lost their jobs. Under Bill 15, passed in 1996, the WCB's bi-partite board of directors, consisting of equal representation from labour and management, was replaced by a Board of bosses. The independent Royal Commission on Workers' Compensation was disbanded.

Bill 49 Gutting the Employment Standards Act

After promising "minor housekeeping amendments" to the Employment Standards Act, then Minister of Labour Elizabeth Witmer introduced Bill 49. Among its reactionary provisions, Bill 49 would:

•strip union workers of the minimum floor of rights by allowing "flexible standards" for hours of work, public holidays,
overtime pay and severance pay;
•shorten time for claims and investigations against employers;
•impose a limit of $10,000 on the amount of money workers
can claim from the employer, no matter how much is owed;
•allow the ministry of labour to weasel out of enforcement,
because unionized workers cannot make a claim to the ministry, but must instead use the grievance/arbitration provision
of their collective agreement (non-union workers must choose
between a claim to the ministry or a court action); and
•turn collection of money owed to workers over to private collection agencies, while the ministry washes its hands of
responsibility.

Under pressure from labour, social action groups and the NDP,
the minister removed the "flexible standards" provision from the proposed Bill.

The Omnibus Bill
Bill 26 gave the Harris government the powers it needed to carry
out its agenda. It was introduced on November 29, 1995 with no warning and at a time when most members of the opposition were still in
the budget lock-up. The bill amended a total of 44 statutes, as well as
creating three new Acts and repealing two others entirely. It took a
sit-in by opposition MPPs to force the Harris government to even
hold public hearings on the bill. The bill itself was 211 pages thick, and
the compendium of background explanation was over two thousand
pages long. There has never been anything like Bill 26 in Ontario's history. Here is some of what it does.

1. Health
Bill 26 gives the minister of health dictatorial powers over Ontario's
community hospitals, with the authority to depose hospital boards
and to take over hospitals directly, to run them, shut them down, or
force mergers. The minister can dictate what medical services a given
hospital can or cannot provide.

The bill deregulates drug prices and introduces user fees and deductibles for seniors. It also paves the way for the privatization of medicare, invalidates the government's agreement with the Ontario Medical Association, strips doctors of collective bargaining rights and gives the minister the power to decide where a doctor can work. Finally, Bill 26 gives the government the power to set up the Health Services Restructuring Commission to do the government's dirty work of closing public hospitals all across Ontario. The slashing and shutdowns from the Hospital Restructuring Commission are on top of the $800 million cutbacks to Ontario's overall hospital budget. The total cost of hospital restructuring is estimated at $2.3 billion by CIBC.

2. Municipalities

Bill 26 gives enormous arbitrary power to the minister of municipal affairs to abolish local government by decree and to force mergers and amalgamations of local municipalities. It allows for privatization and new forms of local taxation, including new user fees, forms of direct taxation like gasoline tax and even a head tax, also known as the hated poll tax. At the same time it takes away traditional democratic checks and balances, such as the municipal referendum and accountability to the Legislature.

3. Public Employees

Arbitration for workers in the public sector, such as police, fire fighters, teachers and hospital workers is severely fettered and constrained. The ability of the employer to pay, the possibility of service reductions and the economic situation of the government are among the new legal fetters placed upon arbitrators.

Bill 26 permits the legalized theft by the government of up to $400 million in pension benefits from public sector employees who are facing a mass lay-off, by exempting them from the wind-up provisions of the Pension Benefits Act.

4. Other

Bill 26 scraps environmental laws governing the clean-up of abandoned mines and forest protection. It also changes freedom of information lawssuch that it is much harder for citizens to gain access to their own personal files, or to information about the government. At the same time, the minister of health is given unprecedented power to see and distribute the confidential health records of individual citizens.

Bill 26 was rammed through the Legislature on January 29, 1996 after a scant three weeks of hearings.

Health

In November 1995 Ontario's health budget was cut by an incredible $1.5 billion. This makes a lie out of the Harris election promises that medicare funding will not be touched.

1. Hospitals

Ontario's hospitals bore the brunt of the attack, with a cut of 18% over three years, as follows: $365 million cut in 1996-97, $435 million in 1997-98 and $507 million in a postponed third installment, for a total of $1.3 billion. The actual cuts by 1999 totalled $800 million.

Thirty-five hospitals were slated to be closed. The first twelve hospitals were put on the chopping block in Metro Toronto on September 29, 1997. Despite the election promise of a 20% increase in the health budget over five years, real per capita spending for medicare will be lower in 2003-04 than it was in 1994-95.

2. Seniors Get User Fees

User fees were imposed on the Ontario Drug Benefit plan for seniors, breaking the second major Harris election promise of "no user fees." This tax on the sick will save the Tories $225 million. All seniors eligible for OAS-GIS will pay $2 for each prescription. All other seniors will be charged a $100 deductible for their essential medicines.

3. Long-term Care Cut

The "Neighbours" homecare and home support agencies for seniors and the disabled are abolished and $33 million is cut out of long-term care in 1996.

4. Other

All community health centres funded by the ministry of community and social services have been hit by budget cuts, including agencies providing services to ethno-cultural and immigrant groups. Toronto's only francophone health centre lost all its social workers on October 31, 1996.

The home oxygen program was cut by $10 million. Five birthing centres, which were intended to provide a low-cost alternative to hospital-based obstetrics, were scrapped. $3 million to fund new abortion clinics was eliminated. Hearing aid assistance was slashed by $5 million. Community mental health programs were chopped by $2 million and even AIDS prevention programs were cut. A total of $20 million is cut from the 1995-96 Health Capital Budget.

The following page is a summary of the Commission's recommendations and the real impacts, city by city.

Education

The former minister of education and training, John Snobelen, told his bureaucrats to "invent an education crisis." The Harris government did exactly that. The November 1995 budget cut grants to school boards horrendously. A cut of $400 million turned out to be for only part of the year. The deputy minister's employment contract called for her to cut of another $687 million. The new grant formula reduced real overall funding by a further $987 million for a total schools cut of $1.5 billion.

Another $400 million was lopped off the core budgets for community colleges (cut $120 million) and universities (cut $280 million)—a 15% cut overall. The shortfall had to be made up by huge increases in tuition fees. Effective September 1996, college fees rose 15% and university fees were hiked up by between 10% and twenty percent. The day after the 1998 budget, tuition fees were totally deregulated. Medical school tuition fees are now over $8,000 per year.

A new student aid program promised in the first budget turns out to be a major cutback to the Ontario Student Assistance Plan. Graduating students can now be sure of one thing... a huge loan debt.

Junior kindergarten has been made optional, which means that many school boards wiped it out. There are more than 100,000 children enrolled in junior kindergarten.

As a result of the cutbacks, the new college of teachers downloaded the costs of licensing to teachers and will impose user fees. On October 6, 1995, the Ontario Training and Adjustment Board had its 1995-96 training budget cut by $20 million and the board itself was then disbanded. Sick leave benefits for teachers were stripped from the Education Act as of August 31, 1998.

Child Care

Child care subsidies have been cut. Metro Toronto alone lost more than 4,000 subsidy spaces. The huge cuts to municipal grants will surely devastate child care. The NDP program to make all child care centres non-profit is also cut. A Child Care Review paper released in August 1996 will lead to deregulation of child care in Ontario, lower standards, lower child care workers' wages and a switch from a non-profit system to private for-profit child care.

Social Assistance

Welfare rates were cut by 22% on October 1, 1995, thus taking food off the table for 500,000 children across Ontario. Then-Minister David Tsubouchi issued a welfare diet for a single person that came out to $90 per month for food, or $3 per day, a level of funding that would constitute a crime under the Geneva Convention if it represented rations for a prisoner of war. Special relief to municipalities with extra-high welfare caseloads is terminated, shifting the full load on to the property tax, and despite Harris' promise not to cut funding for the disabled, newspapers were full of stories about welfare cuts to single moms caring for disabled children.

Further, the spouse-in-the-house rule was reinstated to cut single moms off family benefits. Welfare workers could also cut off separated women if there is deemed to be a "possibility" of a reconciliation. Millions of dollars worth of child support payments go unpaid as a result of the Tory destruction of the Family Support Plan, and over two hundred FSP workers are fired, leaving the program a total shambles. Youth welfare was restricted, throwing young people onto the street, and "fraud" snitch lines were set up to scapegoat the poor .

A $2.6 million cut to the budgets of Ontario's shelters for battered women put abused women at risk of being stalked, injured or killed, and eliminating counselling services for perpetrators of domestic assault saved the government another $1.1 million. Funding for the Ontario Association of Internal and Transition Houses—the womens' shelters—was terminated on the first day of Wife Assault Prevention month, 1995.

Job Link training funds of $46 million for young people were cut from the community and social service ministry's budget. The 13,000 social service agencies that depend on the Ministry for funding, have their grants cut by 5% in October 1995 — a hit of $44 million. This affects children's aid, child abuse services, ESL programs for new Canadians, job training, and thousands of other services across the province. A three-month wait for welfare is imposed as a penalty for quitting a job or being fired.

Workfare was introduced for all able-bodied welfare recipients, even single moms, raising the question of whose jobs will now be done for welfare-level wages. Anyone refusing a workfare job is severely penalized: three months loss of benefits for the first refusal; six months for subsequent refusals. The first workfare projects started in the fall of 1996. Some municipalities refused to participate because—surprise—there are no jobs!

In 1998, a special law was rammed through the Legislature to make it illegal for workfare workers to join a union. In July of that year, the minister announced that workfare would be extended to the private sector later in the year. Instead of providing the unemployed with decent work through jobs creation, the Harris gang seemed determined to create a new class of slave labour that it can serve up to any employer interested in untrammelled exploitation.

Public sector workers were singled out for special punishment. A minimum of 13,000 employees were to be fired from the Ontario public service and Harris said that up to 22,000 jobs were at risk. The first installment of 10,600 layoffs was announced on April 11, 1996, with the release of the so-called 'business plans'. Some ministries—like natural resources with 2,170 job cuts; transportation with 1,239 job cuts; agriculture with 954 job cuts; and environment with 752 job cuts are literally chopped to shreds. While planning for these massive layoffs, the government was also dismantling the job security and adjustment measures put in place by the NDP government.

The real reason for the business plan exercise was to prepare for the privatization of billions of dollars of public assets, which the government planned to sell to Harris business supporters. The list already includes Ontario Hydro, the LCBO, provincial parks, and billions of dollars worth of service contracts. Road maintenance and building maintenance for hospitals and schools would generate hundreds of millions of dollars worth of profit for Conservative entrepreneurs. This is why successor rights have been taken away from both Ontario government employees and contract service workers—when their jobs are privatized, wages shoot down and profits shoot up.

The huge cuts to Ontario's transfer payments to municipalities, schools, colleges, universities, and hospitals announced in the November 1995 budget statement, threaten tens of thousands of jobs in the broader public sector. The megadump off-loads another $1 billion in new local costs. Over 100,000 jobs are now at risk.

Hydro

Ontario Hydro came under the privatization gun, once Tory hack Bill Farlinger, an avowed advocate of privatization, was appointed chair. To smooth the path to what could be the biggest giveaway of public assets in any country, the Hydro Board was cut from twenty-two to fourteen members, and five board members were unilaterally dismissed, including union President John Murphy. Fortunately, the Courts ruled that this action was unlawful, and ordered the government to reinstate the people it hads dismissed.

In 1998 a new Energy Act, Bill 35, was passed. Thanks to a vigorous public campaign, the hydro workers were able to fully protect their collective bargaining rights. But Bill 35 could be the Trojan Horse for the dismemberment and privatization of Hydro, which remains the Harris goal.

The Disabled

Harris broke his promise not to cut services to the disabled by chopping transit grants to Wheel-Trans and by shutting down the advocacy commission. Thousands of disabled people on general welfare assistance received a 22% rate cut, breaking the Harris election promise to exempt the disabled. The Tories' Bill 142 threatens their total impoverishment. The Harris promise of a Disabled Persons

Rights Act has not been kept, and a totally secretive consultation process has kept everybody in the dark about the government's intentions in this regard.

Bill 142, The Social Assistance Reform Act

On June 12, 1997, the government introduced Bill 142, one of the most reactionary pieces of legislation ever to see the light of day in Ontario. Prior to Bill 142, the legal right to a subsistence for persons in need allowance was enshrined in the welfare laws. This right has now been taken away. The legal obligation of society to provide for the poor has been abolished. Bill 142 imposes forced labour (workfare) as a condition of eligibility for assistance, even for single mothers of dependent children. Workfare victims are excluded from employment protection laws.

It also changes the definition of 'disabled person' so that only the most severely disabled will qualify for benefits under the Ontario Disability Support Program. Many disabled people fall to a new low in benefits from their current GAINS rate. The impact of disability upon a person's ability to obtain work is ignored.

Jobs

On the job creation front, the Harris government has put up a 'going out of business' sign. Harris killed all the job creation programs of the previous NDP government. Jobs Ontario Homes was cut, and 390 approved co-op and non-profit housing projects were cancelled. Jobs Ontario training, which had taken 60,000 unemployed people off welfare or UI and put them back on a payroll, has been scrapped. Jobs Ontario Community Action is gone too. Ontario's industrial strategy, based on support for key economic sectors, is gone, replaced by... nothing. Jumpstart, the NDP jobs program for young people, was killed, and with it first-time job-support for 66,000 young people. Jobs Ontario capital has been cut by $2 billion so far. Cancellation of the Eglinton subway alone costs 36,000 direct and indirect jobs.

Transportation paid the heaviest price, as $500 million was slashed out of rapid transit, roads, highways and Go Transit projects. Cuts of $16 million in municipal operating subsidies leave the Wheel-Trans service for the disabled on the chopping block. The Canada-

Ontario Infrastructure jobs creation program was cut by $287 million.

As can be seen from this spine-chilling account of the destructive policies inflicted on a once-flourishing province, the Harris Tories are essentially a rogue government acting without thought for the future.

Ross McClellan was an MPP in the Ontario NDP government between 1990 and 1995. He is currently Communications Director at the Ontario Federation of Labour. This essay first appeared on the OFL's website.

Jobs ! Jobs ! Jobs! by Ian Connerty

Ontario Tories line up at the trough while Premier Mike Harris preaches restraint and rails against waste. His government spent almost $1 million on spin doctors and public opinion polls alone during its first nine months of its first term in office. Many of the people who were hired had close ties to the Tories. These embarrassing revelations came in response to questions asked by the opposition Liberals. The answers were released by the Harris government only after the legal time limit for answering them had passed.

The ministry of health was the big spender, writing cheques for more than $100,000 to wordsmiths and spin doctors. Among well-known Tories getting money from health were long-time supporter Carole Kerbel ($24,000) and former Brian Mulroney chief of staff David McLaughlin, who got $12,900 for "editorial services." Ironically, Health Minister Jim Wilson is the same guy who was extremely critical of the former NDP government when they gave fat communications contracts to their political friends.

Other Tories at the trough include Gord Haugh, who was part of the Harris election team. He and his firm Perceptus Communications, got more than $23,000 from the ministries of finance and the attorney general for "communications services." Haugh is now executive assistant to Cam Jackson, the junior minister in charge of the Workers' Compensation Board. Former Tory candidate in Ottawa and long-time backroom boy David Small got $29,800 from Management Board Chair Dave Johnson for "communication planning" during the OPSEU strike.

Long-time Tory campaign worker and former minister's aide Jan Dymond of ZED Communications, got $24,900 to keep the accident-prone David Tsubouchi from talking to anyone about dented tins of tuna. Another veteran of many election campaigns, Michael Daniher, got $14,500 from the attorney general for "communications" and long-time Tory Doug Reid got $2,000 from the ministry of labour for "editorial services."

The big winner at the Tory trough among the pollsters was Angus Reid, whose Toronto office got six contracts totalling $136,000 for work called "Ontario government issues," "OPSEU tracking" and

"Pre-budget survey." Angus Reid's Toronto office is run by long-time Tory John Wright. Ten other firms got one contract each, and Decima Research, where Harris' deputy principal secretary Mitch Patten used to work, got two. Liberal MPP Joe Cordiano told *eye*: "Mike Harris obviously told his cabinet to go out and hire the best Tories that taxpayers' money could buy."

Ian Connerty was a columnist for eye *magazine. This piece first ran in* eye magazine *on August 8, 1996.*

Monopoly Man: Beyond the Free-Market Rhetoric, is Mike Harris Really a Central Planner? by Guy Crittenden

Despite their *laissez-faire* rhetoric, Mike Harris and his closest aides have chosen central planning over the messy marketplace time and again. Forget individual freedom and consumer choice. These guys just want the trains to run on time! Harris is no Margaret Thatcher or Ronald Reagan. With the exception of a tree nursery, the Ortech research facility, and toll Highway 407, Rob Sampson's hamstrung Privatization Secretariat has privatized, well, nothing. Not TV Ontario. Not the Liquor Control Board of Ontario (LCBO). Not the Ontario Clean Water Agency (OCWA). Not Ontario Hydro, cash-strapped Ontario Place or even the lowly Metro Toronto Convention Centre.

And the about-face on this issue has been harmful to many businesses. The failure to privatize the Liquor Control Board of Ontario, which was explicitly promised in the Common Sense Revolution, is a good example. Cosmetic changes like longer store hours (which are visible to voters) are apparently enough change for Harris and his advisors. The fact that the Crown corporation stifles retail competition and wholesale efficiency doesn't appear to bother them at all.

John Swan is a wine importer and president of the Ontario Imported Wine, Spirits and Beer Association (OIWSBA). The association's members represent about half of all alcohol beverage sales in the province, and Swan says they took the LCBO privatization pledge seriously. "The LCBO is not a monopoly in the strict sense, since certain vintners and the brewers may sell their wares through separate stores," Swan says. "But for liquor producers it is a retail monopoly since you have no options if the LCBO chooses not to list your product."

The LCBO's propensity to deny shelf space to certain brands is well known. Over the years, Ontario wine producers have fought pitched battles to get their products listed. Eventually, some—such as Magnotta Wines—have opened their own stores out of frustration. The conflicted LCBO, which both issues licences and competes with wine and beer retailers, has turned down every application the Brewers of Ontario have made since January, 1996, to open a new Beer Store in rural areas already served by an LCBO 'combo' store. The LCBO says such requests "have been shared with the government before decisions have been communicated to Brewers Retail."

At the same time, the LCBO has tripled its own beer sales and opened new outlets while Beer Store sales have declined. Encouraged by the Tories, the importers developed a policy paper entitled Project Harmony. Project Harmony was hardly earth-shattering. According to Swan, "The goal was not to tear down LCBO outlets. Rather, it was to gradually introduce competition by allowing private ownership of stores that might, for instance, specialize in wines of a certain country." Consumers have been the real losers, since the number of available brands could have increased threefold. But the government rejected every tentative free market idea, including the privatization of liquor warehouses--an uncontroversial step that has even been taken by the NDP in British Columbia.

According to Swan, "Importers would like to ship wine and beer directly to restaurants and bars. The red tape associated with having all our consignments managed through the LCBO's warehouse system adds months of needless delay to shipments of products that the LCBO isn't even selling."

Usman Valiante is principal at Toronto-based consultant General Science Works, whose clients include independent vintners and brewers. "Because it both licenses and competes with alcohol beverage producers," Valiante says, "the LCBO can give itself a competitive advantage through manipulation of the regulatory environment." LCBO president Andy Brandt, a former interim leader of the Progressive Conservative Party, successfully lobbied staff at the premier's office and consumer and commercial relations minister David Tsubouchi's office to preserve the LCBO's status as regulator and market bully. Harris, satisfied that the LCBO generates upward of $730 million in profit each year and $200 million in sales tax revenue, never acted on the suggestion that, at a minimum, the province's Alcohol and Gaming Commission should issue licenses, not the LCBO.

Another example of private sector business being thwarted by the Harris government's abandonment of its free enterprise commitments is municipal waterworks. The Common Sense Revolution document never explicitly stated that the government would privatize the Ontario Clean Water Agency (OCWA), but it did indicate that private investment would be encouraged in what were once state enterprises. OCWA has been reviewed by Rob Sampson's Secretariat, but nothing has been done. When the province cancelled millions of dollars worth of grants to municipalities that used to help them maintain and upgrade Ontario's old and crumbling infrastructure of underground pipes and water and sewage treatment plants, independent companies assumed that their willingness to invest billions in improvements would be encouraged. However, the presence of an 800-pound government-subsidized gorilla has sent their plans, so to speak, down the drain.

Paul Boucher is a manager with Allied Water/Agra, one of several engineering and water management firms that have faced tax-favoured competition from OCWA. The Crown agency operates about 400 water and sewage systems in the province. According to Boucher, OCWA stifles competition. Says Boucher, "A good example is the recent 10-year, $215-million contract that Peel Region awarded to OCWA to manage its water and sewage plants. OCWA and three private-sector bidders were short-listed: my company, a partnership between Philip Utilities and Northwest Water, and United Water [Lyonnaise des Eaux]." Most of the private consortia have successful long-standing records operating treatment plants in France, Britain and the United States where private water management is commonplace. OCWA was able to offer the lowest price, but for troubling reasons.

"OCWA's bid was low," says Boucher, "in large part because it doesn't pay income tax. It also provided the Region with a 10-year guarantee against inflation that was more aggressive than any private company would offer. OCWA takes on this risk—assuming inflation will not rise above 1.5%—only because the province backstops it. OCWA sweetened the deal with $4 million in plant upgrades for much the same reason." Boucher says his company would be happy to compete against a truly privatized OCWA, but complains that OCWA describes itself as public or private depending on whose lunch it's trying to eat. "When OCWA bid on the Peel contract, it didn't ask for approval from the province. Yet when Peel asked OCWA if it was binding the Crown, it answered 'yes'. So here you have the CEO of a corporation with the power to bind the Crown, but there's no governance, no review and no approval."

Boucher believes that such situations are common and it's ratepayers who ultimately lose. "When competition occurs, the average savings realized by a municipality is 23%," Boucher says. A California study that compared private and public waterworks operations supports Boucher's contention. "But OCWA's loss-leader pricing is killing competition. United Water and Northwest Water have disbanded their offices in Ontario and gone home to France and England," Boucher says. OCWA's Fausto Saponara acknowledges that the Crown corporation is exempt from corporate income tax, but denies that the Peel Region tender process was unfair. "Our inflation assumptions were based on estimates from the Conference Board of Canada," Saponara states. "Also, half the contract risk was taken on by the Region which agreed to absorb any fluctuation in electricity and gas prices. Power is roughly half the cost of running these systems."

OCWA controls about 30% of Ontario's waterworks systems; the rest are owned and operated by municipalities (except for Hamilton which is now managed by Enron Corporation). OCWA may consider the tendering process fair, but it's worth noting that the Crown agency has won 43 out of the 50 municipal contracts that have come on the market during its five-year existence, including a large bid to operate 11 plants for the Region of Waterloo. Like the LCBO, OCWA also has an uncomfortably close relationship with its regulator, the ministry of environment. Minister Norm Sterling is aware that many OCWA plants release pollutants above regulated levels, yet he cancelled $140 million in annual funds that used to go for treatment plant improvement, and there have been few fines or prosecutions. Sterling he hasn't used his position as a member of Cabinet's important Planning and Priorities Committee to move OCWA toward privatization or break it into smaller competing units. This is a shame, since overwhelming evidence from the United Kingdom and elsewhere shows that privatized waterworks operators, fearing prosecution, make massive investments in pollution prevention upgrades.

In the absence of true competition, ratepayers will continue to face closed beaches in the summer and subsidize contract risk with every flush. Sadly, there's one area of service the Harris government has privatized that perhaps it ought not. The semi-privatization of former government analytical laboratories is creating potential hardship for existing private sector labs and is not providing a public benefit. Tanya Stirtzinger, Ph.D., a manager with Markham-based Vita-tech Canada Laboratory Services, says there's lots to be concerned about. Vita-tech was established in 1984 and performs small animal tests for veterinarians as well as work in the lucrative field of pharmaceutical research, agricultural monitoring and food safety testing.

"Two years ago, government labs at the Ontario Ministry of Agriculture, Food and Rural Affairs (OMAFRA) withdrew from offering services to vets. This gave our company an opportunity to expand," Stirtzinger says. But the company, which now employs 100 people, finds government-subsidized labs are reentering those markets and are poised to steal away bread-and-butter contracts. Like other testing professionals, Stirtzinger was unfazed by the government's announcement in early 1996 that its labs would be privatized and given a year to succeed or fail on their own. She believed her company could compete successfully on a level playing field.

But the government altered its decision. Instead of having to fend for itself, OMAFRA's lab services division, for instance, was grafted onto the University of Guelph and given millions of dollars worth of state-of-the-art analytical equipment that Stirtzinger says could easily have been sold to private companies. "These labs can now compete directly with us," Stirtzinger says, "but don't have to finance their equipment, which is one of the greatest expenses for private labs." The government's former Animal Health Laboratory was moved from an old ministry building into new digs at the Ontario Veterinary College and given $2.5 million for renovations. It was then given back the mandate to do small animal testing—precisely the work that allowed Vita-tech's expansion—and was awarded the OMAFRA contract for disease surveillance. After one year, the untendered contract (worth $4.5 million per year) was extended for another five years.

Stirtzinger wonders why the government is setting these former civil servants up in business while ignoring well-established companies like hers. Vita-tech initially resisted any assault on its core business by offering superior customer service, but Stirtzinger says the well-heeled public servants are learning fast. "Our customers appreciate our exclusive internal courier service for test samples and our extended business hours," she says. "However, at a recent trade show the Animal Health Lab staff began telling our clients they're introducing a courier service and extended hours too. They've also opened a DNA diagnostics division that duplicates ours. Their advertising trumpets that they're leaders in the field and that there's no such service available anywhere. Yet we've been offering it for two years!"

Vita-tech believes it recently lost a key pharmaceutical contract because of low prices that Stirtzinger feels the former public sector lab could only offer because of the government's equipment and contract handouts. The Animal Health Lab's Grant Maxie denies that his organization will duplicate the work of the private sector. "We only conduct a fringe number of tests on small animal samples when these are components of large animal work," he says. Instead, Maxie argues, the Animal Health Lab will continue to focus on much-needed public health services such as performing autopsies on dead pigs, cows and other large animals to keep Ontario livestock free of dangerous viruses and disease. He stipulates that much of this work isn't profitable and farmers are often charged less than a quarter of the real cost of the tests. When asked why the government privatized the lab in the first place if its main purpose is to continue to provide an important public service that's not profitable, Maxie replies, "I suppose that's a fair question."

If lab testing seems like an overly esoteric example of the Harris government's mistreatment of the private sector, its handling of private sector casino operators should not. The manner in which Harris dealt with the establishment of permanent charity casinos in Ontario speaks volumes about his real attitudes toward the private sector.

Before the 1995 election, a network of three-day charity casinos roved the province. The system was ad hoc and the charities were very junior partners, receiving only about $10 million from revenues estimated at more than ten times that amount. The challenge was to get more money into the hands of charities in a credible system managed by efficient market competitors.

So, in his May 1996 budget, Harris proposed to establish permanent charity casinos and put video lottery terminals in bars, restaurants and racetracks. The charity casinos were to be part of a program completely separate from the commercial casinos in Niagara, Windsor and Orillia that are operated by Ontario Casino Corporation. Forty-four charity casinos were to be established, thirty-six of them full-time facilities and eight seasonal. A request for proposals was circulated in February, 1997, and more than forty organizations responded. The contract tenders were packaged into market clusters to ensure that no single company would dominate the market.

In September 1997, the province's Alcohol and Gaming Commission of Ontario (AGCO) selected seven bidders. Each would control 150 slot machines or VLTs and about forty tables for traditional casino games. Casino Windsor bid. RPC Anchor Gaming bid and won, as did Trillium Gaming (which won five casinos) and Carnival (which operates the commercial Casino Rama casino in Orillia and won the largest award: 11 casinos). Canadian entrepreneur Michael Mandel formed Win Gaming with a firm owned by Australian tycoon Kerry Packer, took it public, bid and won six casinos. Mandel was the only former operator of a roving charity casino to be awarded a market cluster. The casino companies were to sign eight-year contracts and put up all the capital for the projects. They would receive 10% of gross slot machine revenue and a similar share of the tables.

It looked like Harris was about to prove himself a fan of competitive markets after all. But it turned out the dice were loaded. First, the municipalities wanted a piece of the action. Second, the government changed its mind again and again about its revenue-sharing formula. The province appeared to want between 50 and 80% of the final take (on top of its 20% tax on all winnings). The optics of this weren't good—in political terms—since the casinos were supposed to raise funds for charities.

In March 1998, the provincial government transferred responsibility for the casinos from the AGCO to the most central of all government entities, the Management Board of Cabinet chaired by Chris Hodgson, a Harris confidant. At this point, insiders say, the whole process became very politicized. The installation of VLTs in bars and restaurants was cancelled, along with casinos for communities such as Kitchener-Waterloo and Cambridge that were opposed. At first blush, this was still acceptable to the private casino operators. But then they were told they were to report to a Crown entity, the Ontario Lottery Corporation, chaired at the time by Tom Reid. The Corporation was still smarting from the cancellation of video lottery terminals in bars and restaurants that it was to oversee. Suddenly, negotiations with the private contractors ground to a halt, despite the fact that many such as Michael Mandel had received municipal zoning variances and building permits in cities like Hamilton and Windsor and were quietly encouraged, they say, to start construction.

On June 26 (the last day the House sat) the government, without notice or discussion, cancelled the contracts and handed them to the Ontario Lottery Corp. Money from the casinos, it subsequently emerged, will be distributed to non-profit groups via regional boards administered by the Trillium Foundation, a granting agency whose application rules and senior management the Tories replaced. The government has since guaranteed $100 million to the charities, but will proceed with only four "pilot program" charity casinos in the province. "We lost millions from the cancellation," says Mandel. "Our share price fell from $4.50 to 15 cents overnight. We'd begun demolition and remodelling of thousands of square feet of commercial space. The landlords suddenly found themselves with neither a tenant nor a space that could be leased."

Though they were shattered by the news, the private casino operators know when to hold 'em and when to fold 'em. Most left the province for good and are negotiating cash settlements with the province. Again, Harris replaced what promised to be an efficient, competitive and privately operated system with one controlled by the central government and its Crown agencies. Sadly, taxpayers rather than gamblers will guarantee the $100 million in Trillium charity funds and no one will ever know how much more money could have been generated for good causes by the privately operated system.

It remains to be seen whether the Tories, who have now been re-elected, will understand the importance of fulfilling any new commitments they might make to privatize Crown corporations, deregulate certain industries, or encourage fair and open market competition. Unfortunately, recent history does not provide encouragement.

This essay first appeared in a longer version in the June 1999 issue of Report on Business *magazine, and was one of three finalists in the "Politics" category at the National Magazine Awards that year.*

Contamination: The Poisonous Legacy of Ontario's Environmental Cutbacks

by Ulli Diemer

This is a story about fanaticism and death. The dead are buried in fresh graves in the cemeteries of Walkerton, Ontario. The fanatics are very much alive, going about their daily business in the premier's office and the cabinet room in Queen's Park, the seat of Ontario's government. Investigators are still working to determine exactly how deadly E. coli 0157 bacteria found their way into Walkerton's water, causing at least seven and perhaps eleven deaths, and leaving hundreds seriously ill.

The story of the Walkerton tragedy is not primarily a story about Walkerton at all. This was no unforeseen accident. It was the predictable—and predicted—result of deliberate policy decisions that gravely compromised the safety of Ontario's drinking water. The broader story of Walkerton is the story of repeated warnings, from many different experts, officials, and agencies, that the Harris government's environmental cutbacks were putting public health in jeopardy. And it is also the story of how those warnings were dismissed or ignored. Step by step, a disaster was being prepared. The only question was where, and when, it would happen. Unluckily for Walkerton's citizens, it was in their town that the system broke down, with fatal results.

To understand how a government could utterly ignore, over a period of five years, the warnings of its own environmental experts, it is necessary to know the mentality of the Harris government, a highly centralized administration where all important decisions are made by Premier Mike Harris and a small group of militantly ideological advisors, and where all outside input is scorned. This is a government which prides itself on "making unpopular decisions," on never compromising, on never changing course. The man in charge, Mike Harris, is as determined as the captain of the *Titanic*, disdainfully brushing off ridiculous warnings and giving orders to push on, full steam ahead. The chain of events begins in June 1995, when Harris' Progressive Conservatives take office, and start ramming through their "Common Sense Revolution."

The phrase was concocted by the party's election strategists, but it captures perfectly the attitudes of Harris and his inner circle: the private sector can do everything better. That's a fact. That's common sense. Obviously, then, anything that interferes with the private sector—environmental regulations enforced by busy-body inspectors, for example—is nonsense and needs to be dismantled. You don't need public input or so-called 'expert' advice to figure that out.

Armed with these certainties, the Tories set out to slash Ontario's "bloated" public services and "red tape." Environmental programs and agencies are attacked with particular savagery. The ministry of the environment loses 42% of its budget. Front-line staff, charged with monitoring, testing, inspection, enforcement, and research, are decimated: 900 of 2,400 front-line staff are laid off. Regional offices are closed. Environmental agencies set up over the years to respond to complex environmental problems are dismantled in days.

What remains of the ministry is in total disarray. Similar cuts hit other ministries, including natural resources and agriculture. A number of industries formerly regulated by the government are told they can now regulate their own environmental performance. The act establishing "self-regulation" for the aggregates industry is a model. "Monitoring" consists of general questions on checklist-style forms which companies are asked to fill in every now and then and mail to the government. Just in case the message—nudge, nudge, wink, wink—isn't clear enough yet, compliance is based on the "honour system." Under the legislation, it is not an offence for a company to submit false information.

Not content with the environmental chaos it has already succeeded in bringing about, the government quickly turns its attention to water quality issues, an area still burdened by excessive red tape. Ontario's contribution to the Great Lakes clean-up effort is cancelled. The Water and Sewage Services Improvement Act is passed. (No piece of legislation is allowed to leave the cabinet office before it has acquired a suitably Orwellian title.) The "improvement" consists of shutting down the provincial government's water testing labs, downloading control of provincially-owned water and sewage plants to the municipalities, eliminating funding for municipal water utilities, and ending the provincial Drinking Water Surveillance Program, under which the ministry of the environment had monitored drinking water across the province.

The act also serves to pave the way for the privatization of municipal water systems by making the municipalities responsible for future capital costs which many will not have the resources to assume, thus making them takeover targets for private corporations. Increasing the pressure on municipalities to privatize their water systems, David Lindsay, a senior Harris advisor who now heads the province's SuperBuild fund for infrastructure projects, makes it clear that infrastructure money will only be spent on projects to aid "economic development," not to renew and repair water and sewage systems. The Tories' model is the United Kingdom, where the Thatcher Tories privatized water services in 1989. Water-related illnesses soared (hepatitis A by 200%, dysentery by 600%), but, more importantly, company profits and their executives' remuneration increased even more spectacularly. The mantra of the privatization fanatics is the same on both sides of the ocean: you can't make omelettes without breaking a few eggs.

In the midst of the upheaval, there are many voices trying to warn the government of the dangers of what it is doing. Environmental organizations prepare earnest briefs arguing against the cutbacks. Their concerns are dismissed out of hand. For the leaders of the Common Sense Revolution, arguments in favour of clean water or environmental preservation are the pleadings of 'special interest groups'. The provincial ombudsman issues an urgent report saying that cutbacks have been so damaging that the government is no longer capable of providing the services which it is mandated to provide. The provincial auditor, in his annual reports, criticizes the ministry of the environment for deficient monitoring of groundwater resources and for failing to audit small water plants across the province. The International Joint Commission states its concern about Ontario's neglect of water quality issues. The environmental commissioner of Ontario (an arms-length environmental ombudsman) says that the government is compromising environmental protection, pointing specifically to the testing of drinking water as an area of concern.

Other events underscore these warnings. In the spring of 1996, hundreds of people in Collingwood, an hour's drive from Walkerton, become ill after cryptosporidium, a parasite linked to animal feces, contaminates the drinking water. No one dies, but it is a clear signal that Ontario's water monitoring system is faltering. In Japan, also in 1996, thirteen children die and 20,000 fall ill with E. coli after eating sprouts grown in water contaminated by cattle manure. It is a stark warning of the dangerous link between livestock and water contamination.

The livestock-E. coli-water contamination link is being looked at with increasing concern by scientists. Studies show that cattle manure is responsible for E. coli contamination of water and food in the United States, the United Kingdom, and Argentina. A Health Canada study says that the cattle counties of southwestern Ontario, where Walkerton is located, are high-risk areas for E. coli infections. It shows that there is a direct link between cattle density and E. coli infection. The report also shows that 32% of the wells in rural Ontario show fecal contamination. The Harris government takes its own action on the E. coli problem in 1996. It decides to snip another piece of useless red tape, and drops E. coli testing from its Drinking Water Surveillance Program.

The following year, the government shuts down the Drinking Water Surveillance Program entirely. It further directs ministry staff not to enforce dozens of environmental laws and regulations still on the books. Farm operators, in particular, are to be treated with understanding if they are discovered to be in violation of livestock and waste-water regulations. Environment ministry officials, deeply concerned, warn the government again in 1997 that closing the water testing program will endanger public health. Their concerns are dismissed as the self-interested exaggerations of empire-building civil servants.

Also in 1997, senior officials in the environment ministry draft another memo which the government does heed. This memo warns that cutbacks have impaired the ministry's ability to enforce environmental regulations to the point that the ministry could be exposed to lawsuits for negligence if and when things go wrong. The government's response is two-fold. It holds a meeting of ministry staff to discuss how to protect itself from liability if and when an environmental catastrophe occurs. And it passes Bill 57, The Environmental Approvals Improvement Act, which, among other improvements, prohibits legal action against the government by anyone adversely affected by the environment minister's failure to apply environmental regulations.

Walkerton sits in the heart of Ontario's Bruce County, where environmental regulations—or the lack of them—governing livestock production have a very direct impact. The county, with a population of only 60,000 people, is home to 163,000 beef cattle and 100,000 hogs. The animal population produces as much waste as 1.6 million people. But whereas even two people living on a farm are required to have a functioning septic system, there are no comparable requirements for factory farms, where a single 1,200-head hog operation can produce as much waste as 60,000 people. All of this waste is spread on the adjacent fields, a practice that was perhaps sustainable when farms typically produced fifty or sixty animals at a time, but is utterly unsustainable when feedlots hold ten or twenty times that number. The fields can't absorb such massive quantities of manure, so inevitably serious contamination of the groundwater and surrounding watercourses results. The associated health risks are well known.

Dr. Murray McQuigge, the medical officer of health for Bruce-Grey-Owen Sound raises the issue forcefully in September 1999. He warns in a memo to local authorities that "in large farm productions that require large use of antibiotics, there are increasing concerns about the production of antibiotic-resistant bacteria. Studies have shown that such antibiotic-resistant bacteria spread into the immediate farm family and from there into the community." He adds that locally there is increasing concern "that poor nutrient management on farms is leading to degradation of the quality of ground water, streams and lakes."

As time goes on, staff at the environment ministry's water policy branch become more and more concerned about the safety of Ontario's drinking water. In January 2000, they submit another report to the government, warning that "not monitoring drinking-water quality is a serious concern for the ministry in view of its mandate to protect public health." The report states that a number of smaller municipalities are not up to the job of monitoring the quality of their drinking water. It further warns that because of the privatization of the testing labs, there is no longer a mechanism to ensure that the ministry, and the local medical officer of health, are informed if problems are detected in local water systems. The Harris government ignores the report.

Walkerton is the place where the system finally falls apart. Walkerton's drinking water system receives its last ministry inspection in February 1998. The inspection shows that there have been problems with the water supply for years, including the detection of E. coli in the system. The ministry outlines improvements that should be made, but, desperately short of inspection staff, and faced with small water systems across the province which aren't meeting standards, it never schedules a follow-up inspection to see if the improvements are in fact being carried out. Between January and April of 2000, the lab which tests Walkerton's water repeatedly detects coliform bacteria— an indication that surface water is getting into the water supply. The lab notifies the ministry of the environment about its findings on five separate occasions. The ministry phones the Walkerton public utilities commission, is assured the problems are being fixed, and lets it go at that. The ministry fails to inform the medical officer of health, as by law it is required to do. In early May, Walkerton starts using a new lab, A&L Canada Laboratories East, to test its water. This is the lab which discovers the E. coli 0157 contamination on May 16. It communicates its findings to the Walkerton public utilities commission, but does not inform the environment ministry, though provincial guidelines state it must do so. Asked why the lab failed to report the E. coli contamination to the Ministry, lab spokesman Gabriel Farkas said that the lab considers test results confidential intellectual property. "To send them to anyone other than the client would violate the basic principle of confidentiality" said Mr. Farkas.

Apparently unaware of how serious the problem is, the manager of the Walkerton utility covers up the fact that the water is contaminated, and tries to fix the problem himself. Several days go by before Dr. Murray McQuigge, the medical officer of health, discovers the truth and blows the whistle. By that time, hundreds of people have been exposed to the deadly contamination.

The Walkerton story is the story of how systems which were

established to protect public health were deliberately dismantled by a government driven by a fanatical hatred of the public sector. In the name of eliminating "environmental red tape," a water protection system designed with multiple safeguards to protect against a failure at any one point or by any one person was undermined until it could no longer function, despite the clearest possible warnings of the foreseeable consequences. The Walkerton story is the logical result of the "Common Sense Revolution." It may also yet be the story of the undoing of the government responsible.

Ulli Diemer is a landowner in the Walkerton area. This essay first appeared in the July-August 2000 issue of Canadian Dimension. *For more information about Walkerton and water saftey visit www.connexions.org/walkerton.*

Of Caterpillars and Butterflies: Reading John Snobelen's Infamous "Caterpillar" Speech by Ruth Cohen and Bill Greaves

John Snobelen, former minister of education and training, has clearly embraced irrationalism as a method of effecting change. "We need to invent a crisis in order to bring about change in the educational system." This statement has been making the rounds ever since he threw it out in his first address to senior bureaucrats at Queen's Park after taking over his portfolio. Fortunately, someone had taped a video of the occasion and a verbatim transcript is reprinted for the first time in this book.

The spectacle of John Snobelen, the first neo-conservative minister of education waxing eloquent in a motivational session for civil servants, was initially not understood by then-deputy minister, Charles Pascal, who had introduced Snobelen to the gathering. Once Pascal realized the full import of what the new minister was saying, he promptly resigned and began speaking against what now passed for education policy.

In the speech, Snobelen reveals how he proposes to effect "transformational change." "There are two theories of change management," he enthuses:

> One is this: shortening down the survival period or... bankrupting the organization... that's kind of ugly because that means putting your foot right down to the floor and saying, 'Oh boy, there's a wall coming' and stepping on the gas—it's not intuitive... Transformation is that stage between caterpillar and butterfly. I keep having to work with caterpillars... occasionally, just plain running over them works... If you don't bankrupt it, if you don't create a great crisis, you'll improve to death.

Quite a few educators' jaws have dropped since the full transcript of this remarkable speech has made the rounds. It seems to be time to resurrect it, since some still believe they can negotiate changes to the neo-conservative agenda.

Snobelen's remarks are so outrageous that they are difficult to take seriously, but Snobelen was perfectly serious when he made them and they remain Harris government policy to this day. Given this kind of public policy, it should surprise no one that no notice is taken of those who bitterly opposed the transformations, or of those adversely affected by them.

Just after Snobelen gave this speech, at the time of the first teachers' strike, Bill Greaves wrote, in his capacity as president of the Brown School Parent Teacher Association, to the Brown School parents and teachers and other members of the Brown School community, the following letter:

> As a former President of Brown Home and School... I would like to urge teachers at Brown and the parents of Brown children to support the teachers' strike. I would also urge you to read, reproduce and pass on the attached transcript of the speech by John Snobelen to civil servants in the ministry of education and training, July 6, 1995. These were senior bureaucrats with whom Snobelen obviously felt comfortable. It was a candid talk, occasionally a bit incoherent, but chillingly clear in its message. We are hugely indebted to whoever videotaped it. The word for word transcription makes absolutely clear the purposes and morality of the cabinet and senior MET bureaucrats—the clique that is in the process of legislating the control of our children's education from parents, teachers and locally elected school boards into its own hands. Part of the speech has already become widely known, especially Snobelen's statement that "we need to invent a crisis" in order to bring in the change he envisions. But what hasn't yet emerged is just how keen he is on the notion. He doesn't just say it once... he says it six separate times: "if you don't bankrupt it well, if you don't create a great crisis," "Inventing a crisis is something we're not... intuitvely good at," "they couldn't make the thing change, because we were late with the declared crisis," "how to bankrupt it... I like to think of it as 'creating a useful crisis'," "'Creating a useful crisis' is part of what it will be about" and finally, "But, yeah, we need to invent a crisis."

Related to inventing a crisis are the words "declare" and "bankrupt." Circle them every time they appear. You'll be astounded when you see what they come to mean. Here's a sample: "Now, occasionally someone makes a declaration... someone makes a declaration that's heard powerfully enough that it causes a bankruptcy." In Snobelen and Common Sense Revolution-speak, causing a bankruptcy is a specific way to 'create a useful crisis' and it is done by "declaration." In this speech "declare" essentially means to state without a basis of evidence. According to Snobelen, this kind of declaration is an effective tool. He contrasts declaration with "assertion." "An assertion is a statement for which you are willing to give back evidence," claims Snobelen. In his view, "assertion," or basing your claims on evidence, is bad. "Bankruptcy" also gets re-defined. It isn't something financial, rather it's a matter of rep-utation. You "declare" your intention to destroy an organiza-tion's reputation and then people will accept your stepping in with a radical change. This of course is exactly what the cur-rent government is trying to do with education in Ontario. But don't take my word for it. Read Snobelen's speech care-fully and see if you don't come to exactly the same conclusion as I do.

Snobelen implies that it isn't just any sort of person who can "declare" rather than "assert." The cabinet and senior bureaucrats are clearly a species of supermen. Ordinary peo-ple are like caterpillars. "When we're looking at transforma-tional change, an ordinary person is always the caterpillar," says Snobelen. And the superman has to regretfully deal with these ordinary people: "So convincing and prodding caterpil-lars is part of the function." Sometimes this can get a bit vio-lent: "Occasionally just plain running over them works," he states matter-of-factly.

The superman is tough. "How brave you have to be," remarks Snobelen describing "the power of the declaration." In order to "make that kind of enormous change happen, to actually kill the caterpillar" you must be strong. "It's very brave work. It requires an enormous amount of courage, nastiness, and all that stuff," he claims, addding, "It is ugly." But the bureaucrats Snobelen is talking to are up this challenge. "You are on a rather brave voyage," he says, "and I honour you deeply for the kind of tenacity you have that I've seen in that voyage." Furthermore, the strong leader may at times be unreasonable, "and the unreasonable man expects circumstances to bend to his will."

Another key Snobelen concept is vision. Vision comes from "alignment of intentions." Alignment of intention is what happens when members of the ruling clique talk to themselves and pay no attention to the world of fact. This alignment of intention supposedly gives these special people their unique vision. Ordinary people live in a world where argument from evidence is valued, rather than "vision." Ordinary people work with what they have and try to improve it. But "improvement is the enemy of change," according to Snobelen, and is not fast enough for the superman. The superman must "act powerfully," and by powerfully, Snobelen means "the rate at which your intentions become reality." So the rational world of collecting evidence, working constructively with what one has, and making it better, is out. Rather we have a messianic world in which a vision divorced from the bother of consulting voters and teachers and parents and ordinary folk is simply imposed by strong leaders from above.

My last point is that it is important to realize that all this is not just a reflection of Snobelen's private world. "My job inside of cabinet is to be brilliantly led," he says clearly. The pack who are trying to take over education are all in it together. In Snobelen's words, they have a wonderful "alignment of intention" in which they are being "brilliantly led" by their strong leader, Mike Harris. Read Snobelen's speech for yourself and try to enjoy it. But then reflect that the only thing keeping your children from the clutches of this group is the determination of the province's teachers. Let's give them our full support and heartfelt thanks.

Bill Greaves is a professor of English at York University.

The "Caterpillar" Speech by John Snobelen

Published here for the first time, this is a verbatim transcript of a speech given by John Snobelen, then minister of education and training, to senior bureaucrats in his department. —R.C.

I would be remiss in not starting out by thanking those folks, many of whom are in this room, some of whom are not, who have been of great assistance to me over the last five days, or six days that we worked together, as you've added to your list of responsibilities the daunting task of bringing me up to speed. I greatly appreciate your energy in that, and your competence in it. Whatever failings we have in the briefing process will be mine, not yours. And I deeply appreciate how quickly you've brought me in here, made me feel at home, and attempted to bring me up to speed on the issues. [...]

There's a couple of things I want to start with, and this will be very brief... A long time ago—or what seems like a long time ago, with the compressed air around here—I personally took on a commitment to doing whatever it was that I could do to enable people to act powerfully. There was some possibility of our province, and country and world working a different way if people would all act powerfully. And by 'powerfully', I mean the rate at which your intentions become reality. So that, if you will, is the context in which I've been working for the last decade or so.

And you'll probably appreciate fairly quickly what a great honour it was to have the privilege of serving in this ministry when I have that commitment. Because there could be no more perfect place to do that work [...]

Today, what I would like to do this morning, and I want to be real clear about this, is not kind of jump into your process. I have read some of what you've been up to, read a little of the e-mail—and that's dangerous stuff, that e-mail—and had a look at some of the kind of research work you've been working with, some of which is familiar to me, some of which is not. And I don't want to get involved in your process, in the sense of faltering, at all.

I just want to do two things this morning. One, try to find out where you are in the process, and to have you get some sense of my background so that [we] can communicate in some real way very quickly. As Charles pointed out earlier, I'm somewhat dangerous in this field, because I actually think I know something about it. That always is a dangerous place to come from. I'll try to avoid it whenever possible, but you should be cautioned in that way.

So what I'd like you to do, is to sort of locate me, if you would, in this process, and I think that will make our relationship much easier. I also should warn you that anything I'm going to talk about, or show you, or visit with about this morning is all really old stuff.

Most of the technology and most of the information on leadership is at least twenty years old [...] that stuff shouldn't be thought of as being new. For the most part, it's just more cleverly said, sometimes better phrased, old information. So it you are listening for something new today, you're in the wrong room. This is all old stuff.

It seems to me that there are three useful places to look. One of those is in the nature of organization and one of those is in the whole area of change. The last is leadership. Those run through the work you're doing and I'd like to just visit a little bit about each of those for a moment or two this morning.

The first is organization, and we all mean something different when we say that. So that's one of the places communication breaks down pretty fast. To me, an organization is an aligned network of conversations, and the quality of the organization has to do with the alignment and the ability to speak and listen in the organization. We could go through a very long piece on that, but you'll be pleased to know that we're not going to.

So, when we talk about quality organizations, that's where I look, is alignment of intention and the way people speak and listen inside the organization, internally and externally.

There's a lot of talk, and you are probably guilty of it, about the difference between public sector and private sector. Much has been written, lots has been speculated, all of which I disagree with. There has been, recently, some interesting works on this, that may or may not be useful, but for my purposes, private sector and public sector tend to act more alike than different. There are differences, but they are more alike than different. [...]

So that's again, a little different thinking than some have thought recently. I think the public sector, much of it is overdone in terms of its slowness, stodginess. I think it resembles Procter & Gamble quite a bit, don't you? It's probably useful to think from there.

The goal of an organization, an aligned network of conversations, is normally to do... especially if it's an older organization and the time frames are different for different tasks, but an older organization generally moves into designing itself around survival. That's not bad thinking, because the alternative to survival is not always pretty.

And that's what you'll find at the core of most structures and processes in most large, relatively old organizations, is that there'll be a real key of survival in everything they do. Again, that's not bad. It makes good sense sometimes.

What it costs, though, is accomplishment. Because survival in my experience, is always the enemy of accomplishment. And if you think about that in almost any human endeavour, I think that's what you'll find.

In order to accomplish, you have to put something at risk, and often your own survival in terms of your identity and all of those other things that you hold close to you. The same is true for an organization.

Now for those who are teleconferencing, this is the part where you are actually going to be better than the people here because I'm going to draw a picture on a flipchart. It's really not essential, but it's just that I feel the need to use a flipchart because we're in one of those meetings.

This is going to look like an upside-down checkmark. That's actually not a very good way of describing it, but that's how I'll describe it. Organizations go through periods of—like this [Minister Snobelen draws a downward bumpy line], and the time period in which they go through these periods has a lot do with what they're up to, their age, their size. The older and bigger they are, the slower they go through this process.

They go through brief bursts of accomplishment. Very quick. Typically when an organization is in that frame, they'll have lots of vitality, they'll have a lot of uncertainty. Just to dispel the press rumours, I can spell 'cat'. [LAUGHTER]

They have limited resources, and lots and lots of change happens, so...

Let me give you an example of an organization that went through that. There's lots and lots of examples of it. A good friend of mine at Reebok who's president of Reebok, and he describes the time when a very small group of those people took that company from being what was sixty-seventh in the world in athletic footwear to number one for a brief period of time. And they went from... I don't know, tens of millions of dollars in sales into billions of dollars in sales.

And he describes that brief period when that company made that huge jump in terms that would talk to you about the vitality of the organization. I mean, it was place where people were very alive. They had a lot at stake.

The uncertainty, they had absolutely no idea what they were doing. Firestone and Parkes had absolutely no idea what they were up to. They had to go in in the morning at six o'clock and make decisions like, "Do we ship or receive today?" Because they didn't have the technology to do both at once. Now, that is how they grew that business.

Limited resources is obvious. They were way ahead of themselves in terms of their funding, in terms of their structure, information, technology, all of that stuff. In an article in *Harvard Business Review*, the president or the CEO of Nike suggested that the most technologically advanced piece of equipment at Reebok was the photocopier. And Parkes said, "That's probably right. That's probably accurate."

So they were way ahead of themselves and they changed a lot. The background of change in the organization... I mean, change was a daily thing. I mean, who knew what to wear at that place? When you were getting dressed in the morning, you had no idea what your job would be by the end of the day. It was that quality of organization.

Now that's Reebok. Lots and lots and lots and lots and lots of organizations have gone through some similar period—we call lots of those, in my view wrongly, entrepreneurial. [...]

Then, all organizations go through this period, which what I call the survival phase. And accomplishment shifts to survival about the time you win at anything. You know, nothing fails like success; they can pretty well write that on a rock.

I call this the paper clip phase, because this is when all of that vitality and energy is turned into... conversation about who should authorize the purchase of paper clips, how should we process the authorization for the purchases of paper clips; how many paper clips do we use, and what do other people... what's the benchmark for paper clips. [LAUGHTER]

I call it the paper clip phase, and it's fairly easily identifiable. There is, you will note, not a steady progression downward, and no ways do organizations go downward; the rest of the world sometimes just goes by them. In any event, it looks like this. [INDICATING]

This time period can be generations in some organizations; in some, it's a matter of months. If you were in the PC business four or five years ago—I guess longer than that now; it's more like seven or eight years ago—this might have been a matter of weeks.

If you're in the digital telephone business right now, this might be a function of about six months, organization skills of wow, through yuck, and back into wow pretty rapidly in that technology.

Most organizations have prolonged periods of survival. Here's what it looks like. It's very low energy, or at least relative to this low energy. [INDICATING] This is the time when people actually work hard in the sense of dragging themselves through something. It's sort of a forced energy level. There's a lot of certainty.

There are a lot of rules in this phase. There aren't such rules over here. In this phase you've got lots and lots and lots of rules and regulations and changes and all that kind of stuff, in any organization, which allow a certain amount of certainty. Now you kind of know what to wear to work in the morning.

And it is also very busy. Organizations in this area are very busy doing something called improvement. Improvement is the enemy of change. I think that's sometimes startling for organizations, but you can't change if you're improving. The background of improvement is hope. I hope this will work out. Change is much different than that.

This is the area where management occurs. Management is the act of getting where you're already going, smoothly. There's degrees often in that, and you're usually judged by the rate of smoothness. [NOISE] A helicopter? They only gave us a car. You obviously haven't read the premier's briefing notes. [LAUGHTER]

It's about survival: managing. It's a great art. Listen, I'm not telling you what's right and wrong here. Organizations should try to survive, I think. I think it makes good sense to me. Managing is an art, it's wonderful, it produces certain things. An amount of certainty is not a bad thing. It just doesn't get some places. You know, it's not good for some things.

You know, if you go play football, and you take your bat with you, I don't think that would work too well with football. Forget that analogy. Call the Department of Acronyms and get me one.

You just don't want to use this tool for what it's not good for. There's a lot... it's about agreement. Agreement is real important in the area of survival.

When organizations are in this stage, they consult with each other, and other people, and they have these things called stakeholders, and stuff. You probably haven't used that term 'stuff'.

And that's the game. You know, it's about agreement... Management is the game of plans and assertion. So an assertion is a statement for which you are willing to give back evidence.

So that's survival, and you can kind of tell when you are there by measuring how much of those things you're doing or what's valued in the organization.

In this accomplishment phase you're in the, what I would think to be the whole area of leadership. It mostly accidentally occurs here. Leadership is distinct. Leadership is the act of getting where you're already going smoothly. You lead to get where you're already going.

Now what's important or valuable when organizations are going... there's a lot of conversation going on through these periods. This is alignment. Agreement is absolutely not important.

To use Reebok again. Firestone and Parkes argued to the point of fisticuffs every day while they built that million dollar... I mean, they didn't have agreement to talk, but they had a high degree of alignment. So alignment is way more important to folks over here [INDICATING] than is agreement.

The speech action of leadership is declaration. I love doing this work in the United States, because they were founded on this declaration, and they think it is an assertion. "We hold that all people are created equal." What a ludicrous statement. In the time it was written, it was absolutely wrong. Can you imagine an assertion of that kind? That assertion today wouldn't hold water. A couple of hundred years, it was ludicrous. That was a time when... one thing people were for certain about was, folks weren't created equal. And yet, that declaration led to something.

So we don't have any tolerance in our culture for declarations: statements for which there [are] no facts. Mere statements.

If you look at great acts of leadership, there's usually a quality of declaration about them. When Ghandi said, "The British will leave India," Her [sic] Majesty's troops didn't pack up. It was a ridiculous declaration. There was no evidence.

There was this guy in the United States called Kennedy, who one day uttered this statement about putting a man on the moon by the end of the decade. Absolutely without evidence. The scientific [community] unanimously declared him insane. There were a lot of physical problems and mechanical problems that had to be overcome in order to have that happen, that were not doable in that time period.

And as soon as they got past the grumbling state, they went through... the American space industry went through one of these [INDICATING] for about nine years. And you can clear see the point of demarcation in that declaration. You can clearly see the alignment, you can clearly see the lack of agreement, and then you can get what's happened to NASA in the time period after that, as they went through the survival phase.

It is a classic. It started with a very bizarre declaration. We could go through a whole lot more examples of that but I think there's not much point in that.

This kind of change [INDICATING]... here's what happened in organizations. They also—this is not the ending point, although a lot on the private sector sides, the name change of the company is about here someplace [INDICATING]... but whatever its purpose or mission was, carries on under some new name. And usually they go through a crisis, and then back through the accomplishments, and that will lead to survival.

There are two theories, broad theories of change management. One is this: shortening down the survival period, or—and this is all theory—bankrupting the organization here [INDICATING]. Those are the two possibilities of causing change in an organization.

Shortening down the survival phase. And that's kind of ugly, because that means putting your foot right to the floor when the orga-

nization's about here [INDICATING] and saying, "Oh boy, there's a wall coming, and stepping on the gas." It's not intuitive.
[LAUGHTER]

The alternative to that is to bankrupt the organization at the point of its highest accomplishment. This has not yet... there are examples where this may have happened, but very few. This is kind of brave stuff. This also is brave stuff [INDICATING]. And when you take on leadership in an organization, you are saying: I am willing to take on one of these two things, both of which are counterintuitive, both of which are difficult to survive.

Let's talk about why that is. You can tell I'm not yet comfortable with y'all, because I've brought a note. When you have a note it's a little bit distracting, but I thought there might be something important I have to say, and I want to make sure I haven't missed it.

This whole change versus improvement... we've talked about transformational changes. Transformation is putting at risk the success you've been for the possibility you are; that's the personal definition of 'transformation'.

You talk about metamorphosis. Often transformation is described as that stage between caterpillar and butterfly. That's the way folks talk about it. Those who like transformation, talk about it nicely, but I keep having to work with caterpillars and I have yet to find a caterpillar that wanted to be a butterfly. That caterpillar says: "Thanks, but I'll just keep crawling." So it's not really a pretty sight.

When we're looking at transformational change, we are always the caterpillar. It's an important thing to remember, because otherwise we get thinking that we'll be other than human in the process, and that's always a set up for disaster, in my view.

So convincing and prodding caterpillars is part of that function and occasionally just plain running over them works. [LAUGHTER]

The only time a caterpillar wants to be a butterfly is when the survival of the caterpillar is threatened, which is why transformational qualities of change are only available during bankruptcy. Only when survival is threatened will the caterpillar go: "Okay, let's try to fly." Otherwise the caterpillar ain't buying this. You know, they'll nod nicely and stuff, and do that kind of thing, but unless you threaten the survival of the organization, and in doing so something about the identity of the individual—because after all, we're nothing but than aligned network of conversations—then change is not real change, core change, transformational change.

That kind of change, that quality of change, isn't available until you bankrupt how it is. Really bankrupt how it is. If you don't bankrupt it well, if you don't create a great crisis, you'll improve to death, which you'll probably be glad to know brings me closer to the conclusion of my remarks.

When you bankrupt an organization, not a lot of folks know much about that. It's well avoided, but not well studied. Inventing crisis is something we're not, again, intuitively good at. [...]

Now occasionally, someone makes a declaration—and there are only a very few who are internally in an organization or in a network of conversations, someone makes a declaration that's heard powerfully enough that it causes a bankruptcy. People realize they can't get to there [INDICATING] from here [INDICATING] by doing what they're doing, and that getting to there is worthwhile. Usually very reluctantly.

So welcome. When I read about what you're doing... the purpose of this, by the way, is to do two things: One is to let you know what it is that I'm doing here, which is trying to figure out where we are here [INDICATING] as an organization.

What's complicated about this in a big organization, is that you'll have different departments that are at different places in this chart, and you can get blind, departmentally blind, as to where the organization is. So that's a real function of where you're looking from.

So I want to locate where we are. That's part of what I'm doing, walking around and listening with that sort of dazed look on my face. I'm occasionally contemplating this, or wondering when it is I'm actually going to get to use my golf clubs. It's the only two thoughts I have. [LAUGHTER]

Now one thing you should know, I think, about this is that... and I've read about what you're doing. What's not underscored often enough, in my experience, is how brave you have to be. You know, the elements of making these changes are a real crisis, or one that's perceived as real in an organization , is the ability of the organization, or the core resources available to it. [...]

And the power of the declaration, the power of where you want to get to. Is there something for the organization to do, the doing of which is worth your life? Really worth your life? And it takes those three elements to make that kind of enormous change happen, to actually kill the caterpillar.

It's very brave work. It requires an enormous amount of courage. You have to go through all sorts of false starts, and mess and morass, and nastiness and not walking your talk, and all that stuff.

You just have to go through all that. It is ugly. The only thing uglier than this, in my personal experience, is living your life in the survival phase. The only thing I hate worse than change, is living in that of stuckedness.

So when you look into these declarations, they need to be powerful enough that people can actually see their future, and maybe the future of their children, in the declaration. There has to be some possibility there that's worth investing without giving your life in.

So your are on a rather brave voyage, and I honour you deeply for the kind of tenacity you have that I've seen in that voyage. And really, I want to acknowledge you for the importance of it not selling out on this organization, and what its intentions are.

However poorly said they may be, the future that you're investing in, and that you've invested in, is worthwhile. Don't give up on it because it's not yet well said, or you're not all the way through, or it looks like we're not going anywhere. It's important in a lot of ways. Things are up to you. That concludes this piece.

I'd be more than happy to talk to you about any or all of this ad nauseam. After all, I got paid for a long time to talk about this ad nauseam... But I would love to entertain a few of your questions or comments; probably more your comments than your questions. If you'd like to, we can go into some long dissertation about my academic accreditations, and that won't take a very long time and from the floor we could discuss that very briefly. [LAUGHTER]... which seems to be what most of the media would like to talk about...

From the floor: Given your remarks about organizational change what would you say are the characteristics of the leadership you envision for the next little while?

Snobelen: Ask me the back half of that just to make sure I got it.

From the floor: Given what you have said about organizational development and change, you did tread very lightly on what the leadership requirements would be in the next little while. I just wanted you to elaborate on that.

Snobelen: OK, the question, if I can paraphrase it—by the way, it's a wonderful stall, I haven't yet thought up a great answer. Given that I've talked, what's the nature of leadership and what do I see in the nature of leadership over here in the next period of time, it's a great question. I don't know that I've got a great answer.

Front again, back again, with leadership is followership. You know, I can speak to either one of those if you'd like me to this morning. I've got this fellow who I work for and I guess lady that I work for, named Elizabeth, I'm not exactly sure about how our relationship goes.

My job inside of cabinet is to be brilliantly led. Now that's a tough job some days. I mean not in that cabinet it's very easy to do that. [LAUGHTER] It's not easy for an organization to take on a responsibility and actually be held to account for being brilliantly led. It's called, not letting whoever he is you've got leading you off the hook.

It's called 'talking'. I hate the word 'empowerment' so bad that I'm going to use it. I've been to places where people are empowered. It's really ugly. Empowered people are nasty. They are not happy. They are mean and miserable. They do not want to hear one more program. [LAUGHTER]

So I think that what we need to do is... I'm not really comfortable enough in the organization to talk to you about the organization. You know more about it than I do. And everything I've said about it right now, would be a very callous, quick observation and it wouldn't do either one of us very much good. So I can't speak about its future very well at the moment. I intend to be able to soon.

I would suggest the work you're doing has two components at the moment. In terms of leadership: one, being able to take the brave grounds of leadership, understanding the values of leadership, not just the practices of it and designing the organization so that it can value you those things. Vision, unreasonableness. We didn't do that, did we?

Vision. I like to call it dreaming. It's got a connotation for me. I can often tell you what I'm meaning with my eyes closed.

Unreasonableness and tenacity. Einstein described how he came up with relativity. We did quantum mechanics this morning. That was grade eleven and I didn't quite make it through... I quit before quantum mechanics. Einstein described what happened to him and he said, if you remember, that it occurred to him in a dream that he was riding on a beam of light and then it bent. It's not a very accurate description of his dream but that's where it occurred for him.

Walt Disney, when he built Disney, I love this story, what's the one out in California the first one. Disneyland? When Walt built Disneyland, he had already gone broke. With a company that was based on a bad picture of a mouse, twice. His brother, Roy Disney, must have been the most patient man on earth.

Walt decided he was going to build a theme park. The problem: there's no such thing as a theme park. But, however, this is the interesting part of the story to me, there were vision, unreasonableness. We didn't do that, did we?

The experts at the Disney corporation—at that time it's a very small organization—spent $8.5 million expecting a reasonable return on their investment. So Walt did what any rational person would do, who made his money with a bad picture of a mouse. He spent $31 million on the place. That's pretty close to $8 million which was all borrowed and most desperately.

When the theme park was ready to open, almost, and the investors were ready go get some small return on that enormous investment, [Walt] looked at Main Street U.S.A. and it was different from the mental image he had of the theme park. It was on an angle that he envisaged, dreamed.

So he did what any sane person would do, he had them rip it up and put [it] together the way he wanted it so there would be something, and I forget what it was, in the background, when people took pictures of the kids. That cost $6 million, but that's how powerful his dream was, his picture was. This guy had it sorted out.

If you look at any of those leadership things you'll see real people who spent a lot of time and attention to dreams and the value of them. This organization is in Toronto and if it values vision, albeit one piece at a time—I have not run into an organization in North America that values vision really as a core value.

Unreasonableness. George Bernard Shaw said this great thing.

This is going to be a horrible rendition, he said that: a reasonable man bends to circumstance and the unreasonable man expects circumstances to bend to his will. All progress depends on the unreasonable man. Of course that was written a long time ago and I'm not sure he was speaking that way. Knowing Shaw, I'm sure he wasn't but... [LAUGHTER]

So there's a quality of unreasonableness about reasonableness that's of value in the organization. You know, if your organization says to you, let's be reasonable twelve times a day, you can bet you're not going to build great leadership there. So get familiar with the values of leadership and alter the organization consciously to where it holds those values, really as part of its culture. That's the work that has to be done, at least in part.

You've already done lots of it. You're already in the face of it. As near as I can tell. And remember, I'm not here to tell you what you should do. I'm here to tell you what it is that I've been fooling around with, so that you'll know when I say weird things that they probably are weird. Does that kind of get you partly there?

From the floor: Yes it does.

Snobelen: I mean, you've got to have the value thing before you can build on it. And this idea of let's just declare something, isn't responsible either. You know, that's a function of doing a lot of other work.

I'm sorry. Another question. I promise not to be so long. My apologies to those who are still sleeping on the telephone.

From the floor: My question: given this prophecy of change, I can understand how you can do some of this stuff internally. My question would be: How do you bring your clients along with you. Is it just a vision, or is—

Snobelen: Great question. It's beautiful because it's also inter-organizational. I mean all the way down to... the organization is two or more people yes? So whenever there's two of you, you've got an organization.

How big an organization can evolve. Aren't your clients... boy... the language around clients and customers is unfamiliar to me. And I apologize for my awkwardness here. It's mine, not yours. Your stakeholders, your clients, those client groups, the folks who work with who are, yes, committed to the same outcome you are, you are all an organization. [...]

The question is the alignment. And if you go back and keep working on the alignment, or from the alignment, the cut is a 'slash us' cut. I suppose someone is going to tell me that a flat tire is not a problem. Where you'll tend to look is what's the difference between my organization and that organization and that's ok that's fine; you know. [...]

It seems to me an organization... if you can't get to work on... what is the alignment. What are we aligned at? Or are we? Because if you're not, then quit having a conversation. It's not hard to do. As a married person I learned that a long time ago. [LAUGHTER] I've survived ten consecutive years of marriage which is a record in my family. Are you guys still there? For the guys on the teleconference you don't know this but I've sat on your lap. [LAUGHTER] Does that help out? Going in there, and conceptually getting how big the alignment is, it's real tough for people to hold responsibility for that which they're not response-able. And it's an awkwardness we have [in] the language. Things can mean the same or not.

From the Floor: We have this thing in public service that's called ministerial accountability. And the way the public supports that is by [demanding] error-free behaviour. What's your tolerance for error?

Snobelen: I'm going to give you a good guess on that. A lot higher than my boss's. What you said is accurate. But it's a manifestation of something else, which is a refusal to honour failure... The only thing I can tell you [if] the organization has gone through great, wonderful periods in its accomplishment [...] they have [also] had enormous failures on a daily basis. When the most technologically advanced piece of equipment in a$2 billion company is the photocopier, you are going to have failures a lot.

What they could do with it is move off it quickly. Actually, I go: "Oh boy, that's failure." Culturally, we're not designed that way... I'll be talking to [the] media or through [the] media to a bunch of stakeholders and the media will all be listening for: What's the plan? And failure we've not acknowledged as some brave, brave attempt.

So we'll have to be cautious about how we language... let me say that differently... let me say that differently. We'll have to be responsible for educating the people, the people who are listening to us—and that's underlined—the people who are listening, as we go through this process. It's different than being cautious, I think. We have to take into account the listening that people have for failure at this point.

Moderator: I think we'll have probably time for, I think for one question for the minister. The minister can stay about another five minutes...

Participant on telephone: Here's my question. Do we need to bankrupt [the ministry of education and training] before change can take place?

Snobelen: In my opinion...

Participant on telephone: I'm waiting. [LAUGHTER]

Snobelen: So am I. In my opinion, yes, in a way that's responsible for what we want to accomplish, and that is to [...] bankrupt those actions and activities that aren't consistent with the future that we're committed to.

There's a couple of things that we need to get done, probably along the way. One of those... and we've already made great attempts at this... I don't think it's a complete process... in my view... and that is declaring a future.

One of the problems with that is there's a tendency to want to wait for others to prepare it for you. And it's not a very collaborative process. So that needs to done before what needs bankrupting, and how to bankrupt it, occurs.

Like to think of it as creating a useful crisis. The word bankrupt might conjure up other images. Creating a useful crisis is what part of this will be about. [...]

In my term, we need to probably move fairly in that area. And so the first bunch of communications that the public might hear, might be more negative than I would be inclined to talk about [and might emphasize] the need for change [rather] than talking about what the changes might be.

Let me give you an example of the politics of this, and then I'll get out of your way, and you can go on doing something really productive. There was this federal government. That prime minister—I can't remember his name... and they brought in this tax called the GST which you may or may not have heard of.

One of the things that they failed to do—whether or not there was a good process or not is really important—but they failed to bankrupt the manufacturer's sales tax.

In the broad public sector, there was neither an understanding of the MST, where it applied, how people were paying for it and what was wrong with it. I suggest to you, or submit to you for your consideration, that if the federal government had spent three months getting it so people could identify where the manufacturers sales tax lived in their lives... [TAPE CUTS OUT]

Charter Schools: Charting a Course for Social Division by Murray Dobbin

Charter schools—something the Harris Tories are itching to introduce into Ontario— represent the application of free market principles to education; they are the Trojan horse of those who would privatize education. Privately run but publicly funded, they are administered by committees of parents and teachers outside the jurisdiction of the elected school board. Most have a special focus—academic, music, arts, teaching method—but all adhere to established curricula and testing methods. Most exist outside the terms of collective agreements. Although the majority of charter schools have a formal open-door policy, many are able to pick their students.

Ideologically motivated attacks propagating myths about the lack of performance of public schools have prepared the way for charter schools. These attacks are supported and sometimes generated by neo-conservative institutions like the Fraser Institute, and by business groups, including the Business Council on National Issues. They promise an increase in diversity, in direct parental involvement in the substance of their child's education, and a decrease in school board and teacher union bureaucratic barriers.

However, in the cases studied so far, there is no saving of public money and no lessening of bureaucracy when charter schools are compared to public schools. Charter schools provide few enhanced opportunities for parents to be meaningfully involved. Often, in fact, parents are frustrated, as the schools choose students, not the other way around. Stimulated by incentive grants, over 1,100 public schools in England and Wales have become a version of charter schools called grant-maintained schools. Many schools ear-marked for closure have applied for GM status, thus frustrating planning and innovation. Parental 'choice' has not increased, as many GM schools are traditionalist or status quo. They hand-pick their students, and in one district of London, almost one-fifth of local students could not get the school of their choice as they were filled with out-of-district students. Principals have accumulated more power at the expense of staff and parental involvement in planning and decision-making. At the same time, principals spend increasing amounts of time on budgetary and entrepreneurial activities, and dealing with the new bureaucracies that have sprung up to administer the GM schools. Schools serving the middle class have benefited; those serving disadvantaged areas have lost resources and numbers.

New Zealand has mandated charter schools to replace regular public schools. A two-tier system based on social class has been the result. Poor schools have top-up user fees averaging $48 NZ, richer area schools benefit from fees that average $200 NZ. Middle class parents have pulled their students out of 'bad' neighbourhood schools, leaving a disproportionate number of disabled or high needs students for teachers to deal with, at the same time as parental support is diminished. Hundreds of teachers, unable to cope with the stress, have resigned. In 1995 and 1996, the New Zealand government has had to advertise abroad for one thousand new teachers. Meaningful parental involvement, one of the key goals of charters, has not been achieved. As the New Zealand government controls curriculum and testing, parents have seen their role reduced to that of fundraising. The result has been high parent turnover.

Although twenty-two states in the U.S. have legislation approving them, only ten states are running charters. There are about 240 schools in operation, with another 320 approved. Almost fifteen years of cuts to education funding have created a climate favourable to charters: an increasing percentage of high school teachers are unqualified (40% in math) and 30% of teachers quit within the first three years. Charters are seen as a last hope for education in disadvantaged inner cities. The National Education Administration has developed guidelines for such charters to assure the accountability of these schools. Although charters skim off funds earmarked for reform of public schools, their small size (average 240 students) and lack of financing may make them unviable in the long run. Of schools surveyed, 55% percent said they used uncertified staff, including 'parent instructors'. Furthermore, even when charters are established to help disadvantaged neighbourhoods, it is primarily middle class families who benefit from moving to the new school; the subsequent exodus of middle class students from abandoned local schools has meant the loss of human resources, financial support and role models.

Canada does not have the same inner-city crisis as has existed in the U.S. Charter school proponents must therefore convince citizens that the whole public system here is a failure. Like John Snobelen, they have to "create a crisis" to attempt to create a climate favourable to charters. Alberta, whose government is ideologically supportive, now has eight such schools in operation out of the provincial total of 2,000 schools. Two serve disadvantaged students, six are conservative and elitist. These schools adhere to provincial guidelines and receive regular per-pupil funding, which can be topped up by voluntary fees. No formal evaluation of these schools has been conducted as yet.

As in other parts of Canada, free-market ideology is the main driving force for charter schools in British Columbia. They are promoted by Teachers for Excellence (TFE), an anti-union group financially supported by right-wing special interest lobbies like the National Citizens' Coalition and the Donner Foundation. Alberta's prime lobbyist for charters, Joe Freedman, facilitated the grant from the Donner Foundation. The TFE has a two-pronged strategy: a relentless attack on the public system and its allegedly poor record, and the promotion of charter schools as an alternative, using highly selective examples, primarily from the U.S. inner-city experience.

The by-product of charter schools in both England and New Zealand has been social division. Parents identify more with their class than with their neighbourhoods, communities or more broadly, with democracy. When education becomes a product and students customers prepared to toil for a corporation, the ideal of community is impoverished. The argument for charter schools in Canada is largely based on myths: that our schools offer no choice, that education is deteriorating, that we cannot compete with Asia and Europe, that our students cannot read. Although these myths are refuted by study after study and by the experience of hundreds of thousands of parents, teachers and administrators, many Canadians have been affected by them. Supporters of public schools must actively defend them by debunking the myths, by showing the choices available and the willingness to embrace progressive change. Otherwise, the attraction of private alternatives like charters will persist.

Murray Dobbin is a political analyst who has written extensively on Ontario government policy. This essay was originally published in the Canadian Centre for Policy Alternatives MONITOR.

A Lesson From the Protest by Charles E. Pascal

You and your students are back in the classroom and the win/lose rhetoric is boisterous. Former Education Minister David Johnson clearly wins the fiction award for his spin, claiming there were no winners or losers. This kind of claim is usually the cant of the real winner trying to calm the waters with transparent false humility. Mr. Harris and Mr. Johnson actually think they have won. After all, they rammed their virtually untouched Bill 160 through the Legislature. I truly hope you understand that apart from a few members of cabinet and some influential unelected political advisors who likely told the premier to stick it to you and your very able union leaders, that the majority of Ontario citizens know otherwise. As the kids would say, you won big-time!

With the government's poll numbers plummeting as a result of your efforts, Mr. Johnson will begin to spin out the notion that they have always had reinvestment in mind. He will incorrectly assume the public is dumb enough to believe that their admission about an additional $667 million cut during your protest never happened. The finance minister will likely rise in the Legislature for his early 1998 budget and with a straight face, announce plans to reinvest in education, probably something to do with the early years or class size. And an angry public will cause their numbers to drop even further.

I think you have accomplished far more than you know. You may have unmasked a real bona fide conspiracy to eliminate publicly funded education. Pretty heady stuff when you were simply out to show that Bill 160 is an undemocratic and anti-education reform bill. Sure you got some help from others, including the premier, to expose that this bill was designed to remove cash from the system to fuel a prematurely balanced budget to shore up a less than successful tax cut prior to the next election.

But what about this conspiracy nonsense? It is important to note that conspiracies are not the stuff of large groups like caucuses or cabinets. They are born out of the minds of a few ideologues who score high on influence. Conspiracies are not linear either. They do not have a clear beginning, middle and end. They are the results of the confluence of a very clear and narrow philosophy, power and opportunity. Here's my take on the context in which Bill 160 was tabled. Imagine if you were part of a small group of folks who could influence a government to destabilize and discredit publicly funded education in Ontario so badly, that people of means would clamour for something different and better. What might you do, if you were one of the conspirators? Here's a list for starters:

•Create a crisis by maligning and demoralizing teachers, describing them as overpaid and under-worked. Use lots of numbers and comparisons regardless of their validity to portray how lousy the system is.

•Start bankrupting the system by ripping up the foundation. For example, get rid of junior kindergarten and good not-for-profit childcare. Start taking money out of the system and remove democratic structures, all of this too quickly for the system to adapt.

•Do not reinvest savings for reform initiatives, not even for a transition period. Use reform as a smokescreen but ensure reforms don't work, that they are strangled by an absence of time and money.

•Create a bill and ensure that the process for discussing it is so undemocratic that it forces teachers' unions to put up or shut up. Take a page from Ronald Reagan's handbook, noting the section on the air traffic controllers, and force teachers into a work stoppage. Tough it out so your poll numbers will rise.

•Once you have teachers out on the bricks, find the most sincere person you can to act as minister and tell him to do his nice guy bit publicly while he privately tells his negotiators to put their feet up on the table and to do everything but negotiate.

•Spend over $1 million on commercials urging teachers to cross school picket lines. This is a coup if successful, because every publicly funded school in the province becomes a battle ground for years to come, with teachers fighting other teachers.

•Lie about your intent to take $667 million more out of the education budget, and when the lie is exposed, trot out your finance minister to throw in totally misleading teacher pension information and to lie again and say that you haven't really taken any money out of the system.

•Pit principals and vice-principals against teachers.

•Fuel the fears of parents that our system of education isn't competitive and that their students won't get jobs unless the system is overhauled. Ensure that the school system remains the scapegoat for Generation X students' chances by avoiding saying anything about the private sector's high profit/high lay-off record.

•Finally, appoint someone as chairperson of the Ontario Parents' Council who just happens to be the chairperson of last year's conference on charter schools, and say it's just a coincidence.

While it is likely that most of the Harris cabinet and caucus would be surprised by the notion that the real endgame for education and health care reform in Ontario is a have/have not, two-tiered model, those faceless disciples of survival of the fittest neo-conservatism who call the shots in the government may be squirming a tad because you, the teachers of Ontario, have provided all Canadians with the most telling example in recent memory of what pure laissez-faire marketeers have in mind and how they operate. The signals have been clear from the first:

•There was Ontario Conservative leader Mike Harris, before he became premier, calling early childhood education "the stupidest single idea" he'd ever heard, as if Big Government was plotting to brainwash the minds of young Ontario. In fact, the experts agree that universal junior kindergarten enhances students' learning infinitely more than any imaginable curriculum change.

•There was the order, personally delivered by one of the new premier's senior aides, that the ministry of education must immediately stop all work related to equity and antiracism. That's why the latest elementary curriculum is conspicuously silent on these important, value-forming issues.

•There was Education Minister John Snobelen explaining that "unless you threaten the survival of the organization... if you don't bankrupt it... if you don't create a great crisis... then real change isn't available."

•There was the unprecedented occasion that Snobelen actually turned over a ministerial press conference to the Coalition for Education Reform. This small lobby group—really the Reform party in education, advocate simplistic policies, rooted in ideology, for a public education system it mostly loathes—gives Ontario schools a D+ rating. These back-to-basic champions yearn for the good old days when passive kids wrote standardized exams where they regurgitated back the memorized factoids pumped into them by authoritarian teachers.

•There is the continuing extraordinary influence of this same special interest group, as reflected in the final outcome of the elementary curriculum. Typical of this government, the work of dedicated, knowledgeable educators in the ministry of education is repeatedly ignored by the political appointees in Mike Harris' office, quietly coached by the right-wing ideologues of the Coalition for Education Reform who hold most trained educators in contempt.

In short, American-style neo-conservative values are determining our children's futures. Just as Harris has adopted so much of his strategy and policies from the U.S.—"common sense revolution" itself comes from New Jersey Republicans—so his views on education come directly from the American conservative movement.

First, all public institutions, including schools, are automatically suspect; as Ronald Reagan explained, government's part of the problem, not the solution. Beyond that, teachers and schools are seen to reflect the same mushy liberalism that created welfare dependency. Neo-cons consider teachers to be underworked and overpaid, just another selfish interest group, while they're sure schools have been dumbed-down by a flabby do-goodism that obsesses about kids' self-esteem and advances students who ought to be failed. It is no accident that recent Republican presidential nominee Bob Dole liked to single out teachers' unions as one of America's malevolent forces. Snobelen and Harris have learned the lesson well.

The real agenda of American neo-cons is no great secret. Here's David Frum, a reliable conveyor belt into Canada of politically correct American right-wing recipes for ever-greater inequality: "parents need an exit from the public (school) system when things go wrong." Or neo-con guru William Kristol: vouchers are a fine way "to help young people at risk to escape from dreadful government schools." Harris isn't ready to go this far yet. But he's setting the groundwork. Just look at the calculated strategy, systematically and relentlessly executed, to destabilize the education system by undermining public confidence in schools while scapegoating and demoralizing teachers, without whose active support no reform initiatives can work. The propaganda barrage unleashed by this government has been endless:

•Amalgamating school boards will save $1 billion.
•Ontario spends more on schooling than any other province in Canada.
•Non-classroom administrative costs represent 47% of schools' budgets.
•More testing leads magically to better schools. Ontario, to quote the ministry publication *Our Schools*, "is the last jurisdiction in Canada to launch a reform of its education system."
•Elementary teachers boycotted the pathetic "orientation sessions" the ministry held for the revised elementary curriculum.

Not one of these statements is true. Whatever else they are, Harris and his team are shrewd, disciplined politicians. Once they concoct their spin, they stick to it. Their latest line is that they're introducing a first-rate education system at the least possible cost. In fact, common sense tells us the government can't cut yet another billion dollars from our schools and provoke fights with teachers without increasing the serious damage it's already caused. Our children deserve and need the best schools that money and dedicated teachers can provide, and Ontarians will not settle for less. That's the message we must send to Queen's Park.

Charles E. Pascal was the former Deputy Minister of Education and Training in the government of Ontario. He is currently a director of the Atkinson Foundation.

Re-engineering and the Harris Agenda
by Bruce Allen

I would like to start by noting some very illuminating things that Ontario Premier Mike Harris said during a speech to the right-wing Fraser Institute concerning the formulation, implementation and goals of the Ontario Tories' "Common Sense Revolution". Harris' speech to the Fraser Institute was very important. He made a number of key points concerning his party's agenda about which the main forces on the Left in this province (the Ontario New Democratic Party, the Ontario Federation of Labour and the social movement that has mobilized against the Harris government) have been noticeably and consistently silent.

Specifically, Mike Harris spoke about "re-inventing government" in essentially the same way that today's gurus of the business community commonly speak about 'reinventing a corporation'. He also said that his government sought to bring "common sense business principles to the public service." Now, these statements caught my attention. They made it immediately apparent to me that Mike Harris and his government equate currently fashionable business strategies like re-engineering with common sense and this, by implication, reveals that he and his party equate these business strategies with his party's Common Sense Revolution platform.

Harris' comments challenge us to understand exactly what reeengineering is and what the implications of it are for workers. Michael Hammer and James Champy's bestselling book *Reengineering the Corporation: Manifesto for Business Revolution* is arguably the defining work to date regarding business re-engineering. I base my understanding of re-engineering upon their analysis of it. This leads me to view re-engineering as a process-oriented (meaning it is oriented around a production process) and customer-focused (meaning that it is focused upon the wholesale subordination of everything and everyone involved in a production process to the demands of the market it serves) strategy for "reinventing corporations." This applies equally to public and private sector corporations.

In practical terms re-engineering involves simplifying the way in which a production process is organized and doing so in a manner designed to maximize its efficiency and capacity utilization. In other words, re-engineering involves radically restructuring and 'rightsizing' a business organization's operations and making corresponding reductions in its workforce through 'new ways of working'. These 'new ways of working' invariably require annihilating job classifications, and traditional seniority and departmental structures, and replacing them with practices like multi-skilling or multi-tasking and the use of team-based structures organized around the achievement of outcomes rather than the performance of specific tasks. Re-engineering is a fast-track strategy for achieving the lean system's ostensible primary objective of restructuring to do better with less.

Indeed, Mike Harris explicitly stated that his government sought to work with those public institutions he referred to as "our partners" in order to "restructure to do better with less." So, which public institutions did he cite as his government's "partners?" Harris said they are our school boards, colleges, universities, hospitals and municipalities. These are the very institutions that are directly under the re-engineering axe. Furthermore, these comments are of no small significance in light of the passage of legislation like the Harris government's infamous Bill 136.

The point I am making is simple. Mike Harris' speech to the Fraser Institute plainly revealed that his government has consciously deployed, in a very fundamental way, some of the principal tactics and methodologies for reorganizing the way work is done that major corporations have been employing for a decade or more in the private sector. Recent events in Ontario have further demonstrated that his government has 'optimal capacity utilization', or the biggest bang for its buck.

One may ask, are these really common sense business principles? I believe the answer to that question depends upon whether you are benefiting from their implementation or whether you are one of the countless victims of this government's neo-conservative agenda. Consequently, I believe it is critically important for opponents of the Harris government to fully appreciate and emphasize the fact that the employment of re-engineering in the public sector is a central feature of its neo-conservative agenda. I also believe that it is critical to recognize that this has not been adequately noted let alone understood in any meaningful way by those people who have been directing the fight against the Harris government and its neo-conservative agenda. Indeed, at times, one suspects that Harris' opponents haven't got a clue as to exactly what they are up against. The leaders of the labour movement are notable in this respect. But the same can be said of the ineffectual leadership of the Ontario New Democratic Party and, with one or two notable exceptions, of prominent activists in the social movement that has been mobilizing against the Harris government.

Public sector management has been promoting work re organization methodologies such as 'total quality management' and 'patient focused care' in this province for years. Total quality management is a methodology based on the use of 'kaizen,' or continuous improvement, and it is intimately associated with the lean system of production and the guiding ideas of the late Dr. W. Edwards Deming. Patient focused care is closely akin to re-engineering. But its focus is specifically on health care delivery and the health care workforce.

The leaders of the labour movement in this province should have clearly understood by now that the widespread, ongoing and methodical use of these work reorganization strategies clearly shows that public and private sector workers are facing one and the same onslaught by capital and its representatives at Queen's Park. But they have not. They should also have seen that a serious fight against the Harris government's neo-conservative agenda demands a common, pervasive and very coherent strategy. This would entail a strategy based on an understanding of the fact that public and private sector workers face a common challenge rooted in what is taking place every day on the shop and office floor. And it would explicitly recognize that this challenge is clearly expressed in both the form and content of these lethal, anti-labour strategies. But it has not. Finally, Ontario's labour leaders should have recognized that insofar as all workers are faced with these work reorganization strategies, they have become unwitting accomplices in bridging the gulf that all too often keeps public and private sector workers apart. But, once again, the forces of the Left have not and, perhaps, they really don't want to.

Understanding that re-engineering the way work is done in the public sector is central to the Harris government's neo-conservative agenda makes it easier to comprehend more fully that legislation like

Bill 136 exists for no other reason than to facilitate precisely the kind of restructuring intrinsic to re-engineering. Understanding this also makes it easy to recognize that former Labour Minister Elizabeth Witmer's claims that she is open to alternative suggestions concerning how to expedite her government's efforts to restructure or re-engineer the public sector are genuine. Elizabeth Witmer and Mike Harris don't particularly care about the details of how they get where they want to go in terms of public sector re-engineering, as long as they get there.

It follows that the union bureaucracy's response to Bill 136 basically misses the mark. They justifiably decry the government's plan to strip public sector workers of the right to strike. They justifiably decry the fact that public sector unions will lose the ability to have a say in who will arbitrate labour/management disputes and that these disputes will be settled by Tory appointees loyal to the government's agenda. They justifiably decry the prospect of government tribunals eliminating seniority provisions in public sector collective agreements and taking away the democratic rights of workers to determine who will represent them. But you absolutely do not hear these union leaders challenging the right of the government to re-engineer the public sector in the first place. Nor do they address the fact that the government would withdraw the anti-democratic measures in Bill 136 if there were other measures that would enable it to re-engineer and radically downsize the public sector and, I might add, slash the dues base of public sector unions.

This betrays a clear lack of willingness on the part of the Left to seriously question, let alone challenge, public sector management's contractual and legal right to engage in re-engineering. They did not do it during the Ontario Public Service Employees Union's (OPSEU) massive strike and they are not doing it now. Furthermore, I submit that until the leadership of the Ontario labour movement is prepared to do exactly this, they will limit us to waging a fight that is purely defensive in nature, like the OPSEU strike, and focusing on damage control rather than on terminating the Ontario government's neo-conservative agenda. Indeed, it is painfully clear that the 1996 OPSEU strike was a victory only insofar as it stopped the government from putting its plans to massively eliminate the jobs of OPSEU members

on a fast-track. In other words, OPSEU effectively succeeded in negotiating the best terms of surrender possible under the circumstances.

In view of all this, it is no wonder that the leadership of the
Ontario NDP is no more committed to a truly comprehensive and
effective fight than the union bureaucracy. Nor could it be otherwise,
because social democracy has repeatedly proven—here and elsewhere—to be quite receptive to public sector reengineering.

The criticisms of the Harris government's neo-conservative agenda by the Ontario NDP are essentially in line with the union bureaucracy's criticisms. You have not and will not hear Ontario NDP leader
Howard Hampton question the right of public sector management to
re-engineer the public sector in this province. He and his caucus carefully limit themselves to questioning particular aspects of how it is
being done. Meanwhile, Howard Hampton's counterparts in
Saskatchewan and British Columbia have been overseeing health care
re-engineering in their respective jurisdictions. Nor can we forget that
the Ontario NDP are the same people who were the architects of a
massive public sector restructuring effort called the Social Contract.
Nor should it be forgotten that union-busting methodologies like
total quality management were being promoted in the public sector in
Ontario while the Ontario NDP was still in power. The Ontario
Nurses' Association also found itself fighting against the effects of
health care re-engineering prior to the Ontario NDP government's
defeat and tried to make these an issue in the 1995 Ontario provincial
election campaign.

The current NDP leadership effectively stands for a kinder, gentler approach to public sector re-engineering in Ontario. Yet these are
the people who the union bureaucracy would like to see back in
power. Putting them back in power is the ultimate goal of their agenda. Furthermore, the union bureaucracy's consistent promotion of an
essentially defensive strategy against the Harris government is in fact
tailored to its more long term goal of returning the NDP to power in
Ontario.

So what does this mean for the social movement in Ontario? As
far as I can tell almost none of the Ontario social movement's leading
activists have given any real thought to the meaning and implications
of the re-engineering process taking place throughout the public sec-

tor in this province. Not one of them addressed this matter in any meaningful way at the Days of Action rallies. They apparently just don't grasp how central it is to the neo-conservative agenda being advanced by the Harris government. There is every reason why they should. Tackling this issue would necessitate recognition of the fact that only an agenda that challenges capital's control of the economic system (public and private) will enable us to go beyond limiting ourselves to damage control and to effectively turn back the Harris government's neo-conservative attack on our institutions.

To summarize, activists in both the labour and social movements, including those in the NDP, need to develop an analysis of the Harris government's neo-conservative agenda that grasps the real significance of its re-engineering efforts in the public sector. Furthermore, this analysis needs to fully appreciate the significance of the fact that exactly the same management strategies are being deployed by capital in both the public and private sectors of the economy. Such an analysis will then have to be translated into a program of action that fully appreciates the need to challenge the current legal and contractual right of public and private sector management to deploy strategies like re-engineering.

This will ultimately demand that we pose two fundamental questions. First, who should exercise control over the means of production? And second, are we prepared to mount a challenge to the continued rule of capital itself?

Bruce Allen is a researcher for the Canadian Automobile Workers.

Regina v. Harris: The Case Against the Tories by Greg McGillis and John McEwen

In Ontario, a succession of provincial administrations have built a tradition of responsible government. For well over a century, the citizens of this largest and richest province have not felt the need to depose a government by rough strife. Not that we have never deposed a government. A case could be made that Ontarians, in the last decade and a half, have begun not to vote for governments but instead against previous governments. To go a step further, recent elections have become judgments against those politicians who have propagated bad government in one of its many forms. Yet, people wonder whether defeating the present conservative government would achieve anything.

On what grounds can we call for a judgment against this defendant, the Harris government, at the ballot box? The case against this government is quite appalling in its range and severity. Previous governments, such as the Miller government, were ousted for such minor infractions as blandness and sincere mismanagement. The case against the current administration, on the contrary, is based on the most compelling reasons in our history to end the reign of any government.

In violation of several promises, Mike Harris and the Tories have brought our institutions of social and economic justice to the brink of destruction by restructuring on an unprecedented scale and by inflicting funding cuts with reckless disregard for the public good. Specifically, education, health, legal services, children's aid, the public service as a whole, social housing and other services, have been wracked by restructuring and cuts to funding.

This government has abused the power of its office in the following ways:

• Undermining our tradition of parliamentary democracy by passing legislation designed to render the Legislative Assembly, the legislative committee system and access to the Legislature either inoperable or irrelevant.

• Purchasing with taxpayer money approximately $87 million in partisan advertising directed against teachers and health care workers.

• Passing legislation using closure and omnibus bills to limit debate and dissent on far-reaching changes to municipal and provincial government operations, including health care and education.

• Modifying the rules of the Legislature so that laws can be passed without any real scrutiny and little protest.

• Passing legislation that increases the danger in the workplace by depriving workers of some of the few protections they had in the Occupational Health and Safety Act.

• Silencing legitimate dissent by ordering police actions which ended in at least one death.

• Passing legislation changing provincial electoral boundaries and increasing the amounts parties can raise to increase the likelihood of their own re-election.

• Passing legislation, without due process, to force striking teachers back to work before the Education Relations Commission had ruled on jeopardy and in such a way as to create a wholesale vitiation of the collective bargaining rights of every teacher in the province.

• Passing legislation that deprives citizens of several basic rights in local government, including the right of school boards to determine education taxes locally.

• Forcing Ontario's teachers to accept changes to their pension partnership that had one primary purpose: pulling the equivalent of $30 billion in future assets out of the pension plan. The consequences to this will be of interest to anyone in the Teachers' Pension Plan. We can expect continuing relatively high contribution rates and surprisingly low benefit rates. The plan has once again become the slush fund of a Tory government, but there is no pretense of propriety.

A team of media consultants and public relations practitioners awaits Mike Harris' every call, not to ensure that the public has sufficient knowledge of government programs, but to obscure the truth about the real effects of government initiatives with over-simplified sound-bites, homilies and aphorisms. These consultants are also on hand at election time, to ensure that this government is the most heavily advised party in Ontario's history vis a vis the crafting of its election propaganda.

In addition to its impeccable media relations, the list of Harris Tory 'successes' also includes:

• Vesting commissions with vast powers to act in an arbitrary fashion without recourse to judicial review. These powers have been used to close hospitals across the province, over the objections of the affected communities.

• Demonizing the young and the powerless in order to eliminate programs shown to have been successful at reducing crime and poverty, paving the way to cut welfare, introduce workfare (while preventing participants from unionizing) and erecting boot camps. These measures have done nothing to cope with the causes of poverty and crime.

• Giving itself the power to levy and apportion property taxes without the consent of the Legislature as well as the ability to keep from the Legislature the amount raised or its disposition. For nearly five hundred years, the government's prerogative to levy taxes has entailed that it tender its proposed taxation and expenditure measures for approval. The ability to hold the Crown accountable for how money was raised and spent was the means by which Parliament controlled the Crown. In its new unprecedented ability to raise and spend property taxes unilateraly, the Harris government has become an extra-parliamentary government.

• Passing legislation creating forced amalgamations of hundreds of public organizations which then, according to one ruling by the Labour Board, had the effect of depriving affected workers of their rights.

• Lifting from local governments the burden of accountability to the ratepayers of those governments. The Harris government has accomplished this through several measures:

• The provincial government can now require a municipal government to adhere to certain standards of service, and thus require that local revenues be directed to those purposes, despite the wishes of the local electorate.

• As part of its downloading exercise, the provincial government can now invoice local governments for certain services. The local government has no option but to pay the amounts demanded from local revenues.

• School boards and municipalities have been amalgamated into larger, more entities, more distant from their electorates.

• As a result of Bill 160, school boards—and ultimately the municipalities—must levy taxes in the amounts ordered by the government. The same legislation requires that trustees obey the dictates of the minister of education rather than the wishes of the local electorate. In short, local governments are accountable to Mike Harris, not to their ratepayers.

• Creating the College of Teachers which has limited accountability to its members and whose primary aim seems to be to search for those it alone deems unworthy to teach using unnaturally far-reaching powers of search and seizure not normally granted to government bodies.

• At a time when educational achievement has assumed paramount importance in the future success of the next generation, limiting access to education and restricting the amount of education to be provided by:

• Restricting the provision of junior kindergarten and kindergarten programs that provide essential learning tools to children.

• Creating a rigid model for special education which may deny appropriate services to those who need them.

• Denying students access to regular secondary school education on the basis of age.

• Erecting significant, almost insurmountable, economic barriers that bar students of modest or even middle class means, from post-secondary education.

• To ensure public and private employees are more powerless against its financial supporters in the big business lobby than at any time in our history, limiting the right of employees to organize into trade unions and imposing arbitrary restrictions on the power of unions to represent workers fairly.

•Enacting legislation intended to facilitate privatization of public services. In this way, the Harris Tories deprived workers of their collective rights to be represented and to bargain fairly with their employers.

The evidence is damning. Our rights have been trampled on. We are in the grips of a government that is no longer responsible or accountable to its citizens. In the coming months, you will hear the government attempt to explain away these measures. They will say that they have made the tough decisions. They will claim that they did what they said they would do. This government did not have a mandate to make these changes. No one voted for a tyranny that rams through irreversible measures without sober consideration of their effects or consultation with stakeholders. What have we profited if the trains run on time, but we have lost our right to ride on those trains? The greatest fear for our province, and the greatest hope, is that we will, as Thomas Jefferson prophesied, get the government we deserve.

Greg McGillis and John McEwen are secondary school teachers. This essay was first published in the OSSTF District 7 (Niagara South) Minutes, September 1997, Volume 25, Number 1.

Part 3
Essential Reading

Chapter 5: The Harris Tories in Context

Welcome to the Brave New World
by Ian O. Angell

Welcome to the future. Welcome to a world as different from today, as today is from the pre-industrial age. Welcome to SPECTRE: We are NOT Ian Fleming's notorious Special Executive for Counter-Espionage, Terrorism, Revenge and Extortion. The James Bond myth, that the state is good and global corporations (we in SPECTRE) are bad, is blatant propaganda on behalf of the nation-state; a morality tale told by tax collectors.

We're merely global capitalists, and we are tired of the vicious lies pouring out of the nation-state; lies that categorize global business as criminal, just because we refuse to kow-tow to mere politicians. The nation-state is dead. James Bond, the patron saint of civil servants, the thug of state, is now just another dirty old man. Welcome to our Brave New World.

But why new? New, because new technology is forcing new order upon an unsuspecting world. The future is being born on the so-called information superhighways, where everyone in the world (at least those who can afford it) can talk to everyone else. Anyone bypassed faces ruin. We're on the verge of a new revolution, an Information Revolution, that is taking us out of the Machine Age into a Brave New World.

Why brave? This is not a world for the timid. None but the brave will win here. The certainties of the twentieth century are collapsing. The twentieth century is over. It ended at the Berlin Wall in 1989. Everything is changing, and I really do mean everything: politics, economics, society as a whole. And I really do mean change; not the nice neat change that snake-oil salesmen peddle in their change management seminars; not nice tidy transition, but severe and total dislocation with the past.

Organizations like SPECTRE do not identify with, are indifferent to, any particular country, and relocate (physically, fiscally or electronically) to where the profit is greatest and the regulation least. We think globally, because we communicate globally and because our shareholders, our executive and our employees are spread out across the globe!

We are virtual enterprises at the hub of loosely knit alliances, all linked together by global networks: electronic, transport and human. We assemble to take advantage of any temporary business opportunity; and then we separate, each company moving on to its next major deal. We are project-based, and developed around complex information systems.

The information system is the virtual enterprise; it is the headquarters; and it can be based virtually anywhere in cyberspace. And while in cyberspace the apparent size of the firm can be amplified far beyond the physical reality. You are what you claim to be; you are what you can deliver via telecommunication networks.

Companies will shed office space. Offices can be hired on short time scales perhaps within even just a few hours. Hotels, railway stations and airports are already supplying temporary office space. We in SPECTRE don't pay any rent at all. We hold our meetings in the lobby of the best hotel in town, and all for the price of afternoon tea.

The demand for space is a tiny fraction of the supply: the value of commercial real estate will enter free-fall. There are going to be very bad times ahead for the owners of office blocks. So don't get tied into long-term office leases; there are bargains galore around the corner. Sell your property shares quickly before the meltdown.

No office means: no rent, heat and light, no insurance. The number of support jobs can be slashed: tea ladies, security men, cleaners, receptionists, canteen staff, porters, electricians, plumbers, carpenters, janitors. All the jobs that supported the workplace of the Machine Age are now endangered species in the Information Age.

Companies will use fewer workers to cover the same work load. Those lucky enough to be in work will have to work harder, for more hours each week, for less pay, in less secure jobs. And they had damn well better be grateful for it. No longer tied to a single location, we are free to exploit workers. Management can finally get its revenge and kill off those damn trade unions. We can really shaft troublesome workers. In SPECTRE we don't even look them in the eye. We fire them by e-mail. For humanity is polarizing into two employment categories: the financial, intellectual, cultural and business elite (the knowledge workers)—otherwise known as the Alphas—and the rest (the service workers). It is time to rid ourselves of the backward looking idea that work involves physical effort. Of course labour is needed, but there is a world full of labourers out there. It is that rare commodity—human intellect—that is the stuff of work in tomorrow's world.

No company can survive without its Alphas, but it can replace service workers with robots, or export the jobs anywhere on the globe. Offices, factories and headquarters will move from high cost areas to low cost. British Telecom directory enquiries for London is based in Scotland. Companies can just as easily move abroad. ICL, the British computer company, runs its mainframe help line from Poona in India. Courage, a British institution, makes all its toys in China. A host of countries are out there making you an offer you can't refuse.

Meanwhile, money, which is merely a means of facilitating economic transactions, has itself become electronic information. What constitutes money can no longer be monopolized by the state. Money does not have to be created legal tender by governments. Like law, language and morals, it can emerge spontaneously. Such private money has often been preferred to government money, but government has usually soon suppressed it. In the age of the Internet can government keep suppressing it? Friedrich von Hayek's vision of the denationalization of money can now become a reality.

The real issue is not dollar bills, but Bill Gates' dollars. Every corporation will issue its own electronic money. Such trends make taxation of profits and regulation of the process almost impossible. But a real competitive advantage is gained by those who are willing to trade their expertise in this electronic market. We Alphas are the real generators of wealth. Our income will increase substantially. We will be made welcome anywhere in the world. Foreign entrepreneurial investors with $1 million at their disposal can bypass the usual entry rules into the U.K.

However, service workers are a net loss. There are a billion new workers in the global marketplace. It is no accident that most Western companies are instigating major downsizing, delayering and outsourcing programs. The motto for everyone is "add value or perish!"

There is no room for sentimentality in this Brave New World. Companies must ask, and answer, some very brutal questions concerning which workers are resources and which are liabilities. Acting in this way they are not being callous, unscrupulous, unprincipled or immoral. "Nature is not immoral," Nietzsche wrote, "when it has no pity for the degenerate."

States must learn that they are now just a form of commercial enterprise and they will have to be run like corporations. Governments, like all other organizations will have to survive economically on the efforts of an elite few, and no nation-state has an automatic right to exist. Now the Alpha chooses to give his loyalty freely and voluntarily; loyalty is no longer an accident of birth. It is individual, not tribal; contractual not judicial; it is made consciously on the basis of unashamed rational self-interest. If the state can't produce quality people products, in sufficient quantities, then it must buy them from abroad.

Each state must scour the globe for elite knowledge workers, no matter what their age, sex, religion or race. Drag them off the planes if necessary. These entrepreneurs, who can flee, will be immune to taxation. Tax credits and tax holidays will be the name of the game everywhere.

Governments have no choice. They must submit to the will of global enterprise. The British government recently had to bribe the Chung Hwa Picture Tube Company with $80 million to open a factory in Scotland. In order to attract the elite with their knowledge and money to enliven the economy, Alphas will be expected to be less taxed and not more! Arbitrage pressures, exploitation of price/tax/regulation differentials mean the end of progressive taxation. Companies can demand that senior executives be given diplomatic status: no income tax! When Leona Helmsley said only the little people pay taxes she was making a prediction. Strapped for cash, governments will tax anything in solid form: we will see taxes on fuel, food and clothes. Property taxes will rise: in 1913 60% of U.S. tax revenues came from property; today it is 10%; in 2013 will it be back at 60%?

Nobody wants more service workers; each state has a surplus of its own to support. Barriers will be thrown up everywhere to keep out alien service workers. It is already happening. In California,

Proposition 187 bars nearly two million illegal immigrants from schools, welfare services, and all but emergency health care. How long before there are differential rights for differentiated citizens, identified in a database, and policed by smart cards? How long before the notion of human rights is as outdated as the Divine Right of Kings?

The fact is, many too many are born. The state was devised for the superfluous ones. Mass-production methods needed an oversupply of humanity. The Machine Age spawned the nation-state, but with its demise what is to be done with the population glut as we enter the Information Age? Not only will state be pitted against state, but also area against area, town against town, even suburb against suburb.

And what will replace the nation-state? We Alphas, tired of supporting the ungrateful masses, are on the move to hot spots modeled along the lines of Hong Kong, Singapore, Liechtenstein. We are reinventing the medieval city-state as the Smart City at the hub of global electronic and transport networks. An independent cosmopolitan city state of London makes real economic sense. Think of it! Home rule for London inside the M25 orbital motorway. The Free City of London can be a tiger economy attracting in global corporations, but only if we chop off the dead hand of the Mother of Parliaments, the sleaze-machine of Westminster. If the House of Commons really wants to help London, then they should move to Birmingham.

The lights are going out for wide sectors of society, and for whole categories of employment. Involvement in the underground economy, in essence an alternative economy, is the only option open to the losers who are surplus to requirements in the legitimate economy. We are entering a new Dark Age: an age of hopelessness, an age of resentment, an age of rage. Redundancy rage is appearing among the unemployed. Newly redundant workers attack senior management and their ex-colleagues in the workplace, on the street and in their homes. A certain Los Angeles company has had five senior executives murdered in the past two years. Grudge terror, whether the grudge is real or imagined, is reality. Just think of the Unabomber in the U.S. and the Mardi Gras bombers' attacks on Barclays Bank in the U.K.

Societies are stratifying; new elites are appearing. The rich are getting richer, and the poor, poorer. We are already witnessing the emergence of a rapidly expanding underclass. The streets of London are again littered with beggars. In the transition we can expect massive civil unrest and disorder. The soon-to-be-have-nots have nothing to lose and will riot. This is what happened in France in the winter of 1995, when workers and students took to the streets in defense of their cradle-to-grave welfare system.

Don't look to the police for help. With the lack of government resources, the main role for state police, perhaps the only role, will be the maintenance of civil order. Governments are control freaks, they will never give up pushing the population round. But because of the lack of revenue, other police duties, such as solving crime, which today you take for granted, will increasingly be outsourced. Today in the U.S. there are nearly three times as many private security guards as there are public police—even in the U.K. the figure is two to one. The eleventh biggest police force in the U.S. is the New York Schools Authority.

The natural order is reasserting itself: the police are not there to protect the masses, they are there to protect the property of the rich from the masses. Lack of government funding may mean the end of the welfare state, but the rich will always find money for security. The security of Alphas is going to be big business, perhaps the only growth business in the Information Age. Whenever anyone asks me for career advice I always say: if you can't be a knowledge worker... be a policeman.

So this is not a time for despair, quite the opposite. It is a time of great opportunity for the few, a great opportunity for you. It is in such times that new empires are made — today that means new global business empires. For a few companies the future looks very bright.

Information technology has liberated the elite few from the mindset and the moralities of the tribe. We ignore tribal loyalties. There are enormous opportunities for those who have the vigour and vitality, the nerve, to break free of the limitations of tribal boundaries drawn from the past, and who have the vision to redraw their own orders, their own future.

It isn't going to be easy, and it isn't going to be nice. "I have often laughed at the weaklings who thought themselves good because they had no claws" (Nietzsche). Societal evolution is not benign. Evolution is by nature red in tooth and claw; it spawns carnivores as well as herbivores. The carnivores of SPECTRE care nothing for democracy or the rules of parliament, that are representative of herbivores. Grass eaters beware, the jackals are circling, the hyenas are laughing. SPECTRE's time has come. Why not join us?

In this brutal and brutish world remember Baudelaire's words: "one is punished for being weak, not for being cruel." From your expressions I seem to have shocked many of you. It's discouraging to think how many people are shocked by honesty and how few by deceit. I'm discouraged, but not surprised. But whether you like it on not, you are faced with a very simple choice: create your own future, or fall into somebody else's; take control of your own destiny, or be at the mercy of another's whim.

SPECTRE is the government in waiting. We will create our own new world order. Don't think you can deny global business. For remember, those who are not with us are against us. Take the advice of Niccolo Machiavelli. On his deathbed, a priest asked him : do you renounce the devil and all his works? To which Machiavelli replied: "This is no time to be making enemies."

Don't make an enemy of global business. Why not join us? The choice is yours.

Where will you fit in? Will you fit in?

Ian O. Angell is a professor of Information Systems at the London School of Economics. Professor Angell has no involvement with the editor of this book, or with the other opinions stated herein.

Is This For Real? by Victor Milne

Ian O. Angell really does exist. He is a professor of Information Systems at the London School of Economics. You can find a page devoted to him on the LSE website at http://www.lse.ac.uk/experts /information/angelli.htm. It gives a picture of him and a list of some of his papers. I once heard him interviewed on CBC radio expressing the same ideas contained in this talk.

Is this some kind of satire? Because of the reference to Ernst Stavro Blofeld, the archvillain of numerous James Bond movies, many members of a listserv believed that Angell must be a satirist whose deepest convictions run counter to his surface argument. Just as Jonathan Swift in A *Modest Proposal* satirized the greed and heartlessness of the wealthy Irish landlords by suggesting that they raise the children of the poor as meat animals, so, many people concluded, Professor Angell must be on the side of the progressive angels and is attacking those who are moving us towards a world with a few fantastically rich and masses of poor people.

I am skeptical of this viewpoint. It is not the impression that I received from Angell's radio interview. It is not the impression that I get from reading half a dozen of his papers which you can find online at http://www.csrc.lse.ac.uk/Academic_Papers/List_of_Papers.htm. The papers express the same themes as this talk but without the irony and the whimsical James Bond references.

Angell frequently quotes Nietzsche, the nineteenth-century German philosopher, whose central tenet was that might defines what is right in the course of evolution. No one, as far as I know, ever thought that Nietzsche was kidding. The Nazis understandably hailed him as their intellectual progenitor.

There is unquestionably satire in Angell's speech to the Association of Manufacturers and Exporters of Canada. I think the satire is just what it professes to be, ridicule of those who are shocked by the brave new world or pretend it is not coming into being: the techno-peasants who think they can roll it back; the politicians, both knaves and naive, who promise that the global business agenda will soon produce lots of good jobs; and the would-be Blofelds who want to have wealth and power but lack the courage to step into the

Nietzschean moral vacuum that lies beyond good and evil.

Angell's main reason for the satire and the outrageous statements is probably simple self-promotion. He is, after all, an academic. To succeed beyond the common run, academics must get themselves noticed, and outrageous pronouncements are often an excellent strategy. The little boys, the members of the Canadian Federation of Independent Business, react as Angell says: "I seem to have shocked many of you." I suspect that the big boys, the members of the the Business Council on National Issues, wish that Angell would stop letting the cat out of the bag. They understand well enough that they are moving us toward a world of haves and have-nots. Sincere right-wingers, the big boys really believe in Ronald Reagan's trickle-down economics, or as John Kenneth Galbraith called it the horse-and-sparrow theory: if you feed the horse lots of oats, some will pass through and fall on the street to feed the sparrows.

Is this scenario very likely? Professor Angell's vision of the near future is very close to the cyberpunk genre exemplified in the writings of Bruce Sterling and William Gibson: a high-tech world run by transnational corporations with private armies while the bulk of the population are reduced to the status of impoverished techno-peasants. It therefore behooves us to take this vision seriously as a highly probable future. Major science fiction writers have a good track record of foreseeing, not so much the details of the gadgetry, but rather the social structures that will be implemented by technological change.

Another notable convergence is that right-winger Angell agrees with liberal American futurologist Jeremy Rifkin that technological advances will soon result in massive unemployment. Rifkin entitled his most famous book *The End of Work*. The only difference is that Angell is unconcerned with the fate of the displaced workers while Rifkin is searching for ways to make a decent provision for them. In one of his papers Angell commented that Rifkin should have entitled his book *The End of Workers*.

From my very different perspective I personally would agree with Angell that "many too many are born." Population reduction would be the greatest boon for the working class. If their numbers were few, then the value of labour would rise. There is also the matter of the environment. World population is far too high to allow the biosphere to repair the damage we do as a species. However, I doubt that Professor Angell loses any sleep over that. I give Angell full credit for possessing a very formidable intellect. He is telling it like it is based on the current trends. His brave new world is a highly probable future. However, it does not have to happen, and if it does, it will be such an unstable social order that it will self-destruct in a relatively short time.

It does not have to happen. If humanity takes the rational course, we will realize that we are all in a lifeboat together. There is enough material wealth to feed and support the entire current population of the world. This wealth is being sucked into the black hole of corporate and individual greed. Once everyone has a decent standard of living, the birthrate will begin to fall, and the environment can start to restore itself.

Professor Angell imagines that the new economy will be totally based on information technology. This is intellectual myopia. The information technology economy can only exist by piggybacking on the real world economy. No matter how many intermediate stages there are, information has economic value only insofar as it ultimately produces goods and services that people want to buy — large numbers of people. Angell has forgotten what Henry Ford well understood, that if you want to sell millions of automobiles, the workers who produce them must be paid well enough to buy them.

We are at the midpoint of a corporate pyramid scheme. A number of corporations have become highly profitable by relocating to low-wage nations, downsizing, replacing workers with robots, and lowering the wages of workers in industrialized countries. As long as a substantial number of corporations have not completed the transition, their relatively well-paid workers provide a consumer base for the Grinch corporations. As soon as the process nears completion, the corporations will perish. They need a world of mass consumerism where most people earn $20 an hour, but they are creating a world where the masses earn $5 an hour at best.

Angell mentions the appearance of cyber-crime but seems to think that the wealthy can contain it. Not likely. In his other statements it is clear that he regards computer programmers as techno-peasants, and this is how many corporations do treat them with programming outsourced to low-wage countries like India. Read a few Dilbert books to get an idea of what technologically-savvy peons can do to their bosses just for fun. Imagine when they turn ugly. Professor Angell, or his heirs, may also find that in the brave new world being an IT Alpha does not guarantee a place in the sun. Many specialists in the information technology field believe that it will become almost completely automated so that the CEOs will no longer need to offer big remuneration to their trusted IT toadies.

Finally, if humanity does not rise up and stop this nasty future, the environment will. Corporate executives by nature refuse to spend money on anything that does not make more money or provide them with personal status symbols. They will not do anything to even slow down environmental degradation. If this is not done in the next few decades, we will have runaway global warming, and the biosphere will wipe itself clean of most of humanity without making any distinction between the winners and the losers.

Victor Milne is a horse ranch operator, pastor and writer.

A Short History of Neo-Liberalism
by Susan George

Between 1945 and 1950, if you had seriously proposed any of the ideas and policies in today's standard neo-liberal toolkit, you would have been laughed off the stage. At least in the Western countries, everyone was a Keynesian, a social democrat or a social-Christian democrat or some shade of Marxist. The idea that the market should be allowed to make major social and political decisions, the idea that the state should voluntarily reduce its role in the economy, or that corporations should be given total freedom, that trade unions should be curbed and citizens given much less rather than more social protectio—such ideas were utterly foreign to the spirit of the time. With the possible exception of Ayn Rand, even if someone actually agreed with these ideas, he or she would have hesitated to take such a position in public and would have had a hard time finding an audience.

The first order of business in the post-War world was to put social programs back in place. The other major item on the agenda was to get world trade moving—this was accomplished through the Marshall Plan which established Europe once again as the major trading partner for the U.S., the most powerful economy in the world. And it was at this time that the strong winds of decolonization also began to blow, whether freedom was obtained by grant as in India or through armed struggle as in Kenya, Vietnam and other nations.

On the whole, the world had signed on for an extremely progressive agenda. The scholar Karl Polanyi published his masterwork, *The Great Transformation*, in 1944; it is a fierce critique of nineteenth-century industrial, market-based society. Over fifty years ago Polanyi made this amazingly prophetic and modern statement: "To allow the market mechanism to be sole director of the fate of human beings and their natural environment... would result in the demolition of society." However, Polanyi was convinced that such a demolition could no longer happen in the post-war world because, as he writes, "Within the nations we are witnessing a development under which the economic system ceases to lay down the law to society and the primacy of society over that system is secured."

Alas, Polanyi's optimism was misplaced—the whole point of neo-liberalism is that the market mechanism should be allowed to direct the fate of human beings. The economy should dictate its rules to society, not the other way around. And just as Polanyi foresaw, this doctrine is leading us directly towards the "demolition of society."

So what happened? Why have we reached this point half a century after the end of the Second World War? The question really worth asking is, "How did neo-liberalism ever emerge from its ultra-minoritarian ghetto to become the dominant doctrine in the world today?" Why can the International Monetary Fund and the World Bank intervene at will and force countries to participate in the world economy on basically unfavourable terms. Why is the welfare state under threat in all countries where it was established? Why is the environment on the edge of collapse and why are there so many poor people in both rich and poor countries at a time when never before has there existed such great wealth? Those are the questions that need to be answered from an historical perspective.

As I've argued in detail elsewhere, one explanation for this triumph of neo-liberalism and the economic, political, social and ecological disasters that go with it is that neo-liberals have bought and paid for their own vicious and regressive "Great Transformation". They have understood, as progressives have not, that ideas have consequences. Starting from a tiny embryo at the University of Chicago with the philosopher-economist Friedrich von Hayek, and his students like Milton Friedman, at its nucleus, the neo-liberals and their funders have created a huge international network of foundations, institutes, research centres, publications, scholars, writers and public relations hacks to develop, package and push their ideas and doctrine relentlessly.

They have built this highly efficient ideological cadre because they understand what the Italian Marxist thinker Antonio Gramsci was talking about when he developed the concept of cultural hegemony. If you can occupy peoples' heads, their hearts and their hands will follow. I do not have time to give you details here, but believe me, the ideological and promotional work of the Right has been absolutely brilliant. They have spent hundreds of millions of dollars, but the result has been worth every penny to them because they have made neo-liberalism seem as if it were the natural and normal condition of humankind. No matter how many disasters of all kinds the neo-liberal system has visibly created, no matter what financial crises it may engender, no matter how many losers and outcasts it may create, it is still made to seem inevitable, like an act of God, the only possible economic and social order available to us.

Let me stress how important it is to understand that this vast neo-liberal experiment we are all being forced to live under has been created by people with a purpose. Once you grasp this, once you understand that neo-liberalism is not a force like gravity but a totally artificial construct, you can also understand that what some people have created, other people can change. But they cannot change it without recognizing the importance of ideas. I'm all for grassroots projects, but I also warn that these will collapse if the overall ideological climate is hostile to their goals.

So, from a small, unpopular sect with virtually no influence, neo-liberalism has become the major world religion with its dogmatic doctrine, its priesthood, its law-giving institutions and perhaps most important of all, its hell for heathen and sinners who dare to contest the revealed truth. Oskar Lafontaine, the ex-German finance minister whom the *Financial Times* called an "unreconstructed Keynesian" has been consigned to that hell because he dared to propose higher taxes on corporations and tax cuts for ordinary and less well-off families.

Having set the ideological stage and the context, now let me fast-forward to 1979, the year Margaret Thatcher came to power and undertook the neo-liberal revolution in Britain. The Iron Lady was herself a disciple of Friedrich von Hayek, she was a social Darwinist and had no qualms about expressing her convictions. She was well known for justifying her programme with the single word TINA, short for There Is No Alternative. The central value of Thatcher's doctrine and of neo-liberalism itself is the notion of competition—competition between nations, regions, firms and of course between individuals. Competition is central because it separates the sheep from the goats, the men from the boys, the fit from the unfit. It is supposed to allocate all resources, whether physical, natural, human or financial with the greatest possible efficiency.

In sharp contrast, the great Chinese philosopher Lao Tzu ended his *Tao-te Ching* with these words: "Above all, do not compete." The only actors in the neo-liberal world who seem to have taken his advice are the largest actors of all, the transnational corporations. The principle of competition scarcely applies to them; they prefer to practice what we could call 'alliance capitalism'. It is no accident that, depending on the year, two-thirds to three-quarters of all the money labelled 'foreign direct investment' is not devoted to new, job-creating investment but to mergers and acquisitions that almost invariably result in job losses.

Because competition is always a virtue, the argument goes its results cannot be bad. For the neo-liberal, the market is so wise and so good that like God, the Invisible Hand can bring good out of apparent evil. Thus Thatcher once said in a speech, "It is our job to glory in inequality and see that talents and abilities are given vent and expression for the benefit of us all." In other words, don't worry about those who might be left behind in the competitive struggle. People are unequal by nature, but this is good because the contributions of the well-born, the best-educated, the toughest, will eventually benefit everyone. Nothing in particular is owed to the weak, the poorly educated, what happens to them is their own fault, never the fault of society. If the competitive system is "given vent" as Thatcher says, society will be the better for it. Unfortunately, the history of the past twenty years teaches us that exactly the opposite is the case.

In pre-Thatcher Britain, about one person in ten was classed as living below the poverty line, not a brilliant result, but honourable as nations go and a lot better than in the pre-War period. Now one person in four, and one child in three, is officially poor. This is the meaning of survival of the fittest: people who cannot heat their houses in winter, who must put a coin in the metre before they can have electricity or water, who do not own a warm waterproof coat. I am taking these examples from the 1996 report of the British Child Poverty Action Group. I will illustrate the result of the Thatcher-Major "tax reforms" with a single example. During the 1980s, 1% of taxpayers received 29% of all the tax reduction benefits, such that a single person earning half the average salary found his or her taxes had gone up by seven percent, whereas a single person earning ten times the average salary got a reduction of twenty-one percent.

Another implication of competition as the central value of neo-liberalism is that the public sector must be brutally downsized because it does not and cannot obey the basic law of competing for profits or for market share. Privatization is one of the major economic transformations of the past twenty years. The trend began in Britain and has spread throughout the world.

Let me start by asking why capitalist countries, particularly in Europe, had public services to begin with, and why many still do. In reality, nearly all public services constitute what economists call 'natural monopolies'. A natural monopoly exists when the minimum size to guarantee maximum economic efficiency is equal to the actual size of the market. In other words, a company has to be a certain size to realize economies of scale and thus provide the best possible service at the lowest possible cost to the consumer. Public services also require very large investment outlays at the beginning—like railroad tracks or power grids—which does not encourage competition either. That's why public monopolies were the obvious optimum solution. In any event, Margaret Thatcher set out to change all that. As an added bonus, she could also use privatization to break the power of the trade unions. By destroying the public sector where unions were strongest, she was able to weaken them drastically. Thus between 1979 and 1994, the number of jobs in the public sector in Britain was reduced from over seven million to five million, a drop of twenty-nine percent. Virtually all the jobs eliminated were unionized jobs. Since private sector employment was stagnant during those fifteen years, the overall reduction in the number of jobs came to 1.7 million, a drop of 7% compared to 1979. To neo-liberals, fewer workers is always better than more, because workers impinge on shareholder value.

As for other effects of privatization, they were predictable and predicted. The managers of the newly privatized enterprises, often exactly the same people as before, doubled or tripled their own salaries. The government used taxpayer money to wipe out debts and recapitalize firms before putting them on the market—for example, the water authority got £5 billion of debt relief plus £1.6 billion called the "green dowry" to make the bride more attractive to prospective buyers. A lot of public relations fuss was made about how small stockholders would have a stake in these companies—and in fact nine million did buy shares—but half of them invested less than £1,000 pounds and most of them sold their shares rather quickly, as soon as they could cash in on the instant profits.

From the results, one can easily see that the whole point of privatization is neither economic efficiency nor improved services to the consumer but simply to transfer wealth from the public purse—which could redistribute it to even out social inequalities — to private hands. In Britain and elsewhere, the overwhelming majority of privatized company shares are now in the hands of financial institutions and very large investors. The employees of British Telecom bought only 1% of the shares, those of British Aerospace 1.3 percent. Prior to Thatcher's onslaught, a lot of the public sector in Britain was profitable. Consequently, in 1984, public companies contributed over £7 billion to the treasury. All that money is now going to private shareholders. Service in the privatized industries is now often disastrous—the *Financial Times* reported an invasion of rats in the Yorkshire Water system and anyone who has survived taking Thames Trains in Britain deserves a medal.

Exactly the same mechanisms have been at work throughout the world. In Britain, the Adam Smith Institute was the intellectual partner for creating the privatization ideology. U.S. Agency for International Development and the World Bank have also used Adam Smith experts and have pushed the privatization doctrine in the Southern Hempisphere. By 1991 the Bank had already made 114 loans to speed the process, and every year its Global Development Finance report lists hundreds of privatizations carried out in the Bank's borrowing countries. I submit that we should stop talking about privatization and use words that tell the truth: we are talking about alienation and surrender of the product of decades of work by thousands of people to a tiny minority of large investors. This is one of the greatest hold-ups of ours or any generation.

Another structural feature of neo-liberalism consists in remunerating capital to the detriment of labour and thus moving wealth from the bottom of society to the top. If you are, roughly, in the top 20% of the income scale, you are likely to gain something from neo-liberalism, and the higher you are up the ladder, the more you gain. Conversely, the bottom 80% lose and the lower they are to begin with, the more they lose proportionally.

Lest you thought I had forgotten Ronald Reagan, let me illustrate this point with the observations of Kevin Phillips, a Republican analyst and former aid to President Nixon, who published a book in 1990 entitled *The Politics of Rich and Poor*. He charts the way Reagan's neo-liberal doctrine and policies changed American income distribution between 1977 and 1988. These policies were largely elaborated by the conservative Heritage Foundation, the principle think-tank of the Reagan administration and still an important force in American politics. Over the decade of the 1980s, the top 10% of American families increased their average family income by sixteen percent, the top 5% increased theirs by twenty-three percent, but the extremely lucky top 1% of American families could thank Reagan for a 50% increase. Their revenues went from an affluent $270,000 to a heady $405,000. As for poorer Americans, the bottom 80% all lost something. True to the rule, the lower they were on the scale, the more they lost. The bottom 10% of Americans reached the nadir. According to Phillip's figures, they lost 15% of their already meagre incomes: from an already rock-bottom average of $4,113 annually, they dropped to an inhuman $3,504. In 1977, the top 1% of American families had average incomes sixty-five times as great as those of the bottom ten percent. A decade later, the top 1% was 115 times as well off as the bottom decile.

America is one of the most unequal societies on Earth, but virtually all countries have seen inequalities increase over the past twenty years because of neo-liberal policies. The United Nations Conference on Trade and Development published some damning evidence to this effect in its 1997 Trade and Development Report, based on some 2,600 separate studies of income inequalities, impoverishment and the hollowing out of the middle classes. The UNCTAD team documents these trends in dozens of widely differing societies, including China, Russia and other formerly socialist countries.

There is nothing mysterious about this trend towards greater inequality. Policies are specifically designed to give the already rich more disposable income, particularly through tax cuts and by pushing down wages. The theory and ideological justification for such measures is that higher incomes for the rich and higher profits will lead to more investment, better allocation of resources and therefore more jobs and welfare for everyone. In reality, as was perfectly predictable, moving money up the economic ladder has led to stock market bubbles, untold paper wealth for the few and numerous financial crises. If income is redistributed towards the bottom 80% of society, it will be used for consumption and consequently benefit employment. If wealth is redistributed towards the top, where people already have most of the things they need, it will go not into the local or national economy but to international stockmarkets.

As you are aware, the same policies have been carried out throughout the South and East under the guise of structural adjustment, which is merely another name for neo-liberalism. I've used Thatcher and Reagan to illustrate the policies at the national level. At the international level, neo-liberals have concentrated all their efforts on three fundamental points: free trade in goods and services, free circulation of capital and freedom of investment. Over the past twenty years, the IMF has been strengthened enormously. Thanks to the debt crisis and the mechanism of conditionality, it has moved from balance of payments support to being quasi-universal dictator of so-called "sound" economic policies, meaning of course neo-liberal ones. The World Trade Organization was put in place in January 1995 after long and laborious negotiations, often rammed through parliaments which had little idea what they were ratifying. Thankfully, one recent effort to make binding and universal neo-liberal rules, the Multilateral Agreement on Investment, has failed, at least temporarily. It would have given all rights to corporations, all obligations to governments and no rights at all to citizens.

The common denominator of these institutions is their lack of transparency and democratic accountability. This is the essence of neo-liberalism. It claims that the economy should dictate its rules to society, not the other way around. Democracy is an encumbrance, neo-liberalism is designed for winners, not for voters, who necessarily encompass the categories of both winners and losers.

I'd like to conclude by asking you to take very seriously the neo-liberal definition of the loser, to whom nothing in particular is owed. Anyone can be ejected from the system at any time—because of illness, age, pregnancy, perceived failure or simply because economic circumstances and the relentless transfer of wealth from top to bottom demand it. Shareholder value is all. The *International Herald Tribune* reported that foreign investors are "snapping up" Thai and Korean companies and banks. Not surprisingly, these purchases are expected to result in "heavy layoffs."

In other words, the results of years of work by thousands of Thais and Koreans is being transferred into foreign corporate hands. Many of those who laboured to create that wealth have already been, or soon will be, left on the pavement. Under the principles of competition and maximizing shareholder value, such behaviour is seen not as criminally unjust but as normal and indeed virtuous. I submit that neo-liberalism has changed the fundamental nature of politics. Politics used to be primarily about who ruled whom and who got what share of the pie. Aspects of both these central questions remain, of course, but the great new central question of politics is, in my view, who has a right to live and who does not? Radical exclusion is now the order of the day, I mean this deadly seriously.

A lot is already happening to counter these life-threatening trends and there is enormous scope for further action. It's time we set the agenda instead of letting the Masters of the Universe have their way. Let me repeat what I said earlier: neo-liberalism is not the natural human condition, it is not supernatural, it can be challenged and replaced because its own failures will require this. We have to be ready with replacement policies which restore power to communities and democratic states while working to institute democracy, the rule of law and fair distribution at the international level. Business and the market have their place, but this place cannot occupy the entire sphere of human existence.

Further good news is that there is plenty of money sloshing around out there and a tiny fraction, a ridiculous, infinitesimal proportion of it would be enough to provide a decent life to every person on earth, to supply universal health and education, to clean up the environment and prevent further destruction to the planet, to close the North-South gap—at least according to the United Nations Development Programme, which calls for a paltry $40 billion a year. That, frankly, is peanuts.

Finally, please remember that neo-liberalism may be insatiable but it is not invulnerable. A coalition of international activists obliged them to abandon, at least temporarily, their project to liberalize all investment through the MAI. The surprise victory of its opponents infuriated the supporters of corporate rule and demonstrates that well organized network guerillas can win battles. Now we have to regroup our forces and keep at them so that they cannot transfer the MAI to the WTO.

Look at it this way. We have the numbers on our side, because there are far more losers than winners in the neo-liberal game. We have the ideas, whereas theirs are finally coming into question because of repeated crises. What we lack, so far, is the organization and the unity which in this age of advanced technology we can overcome. The threat is clearly transnational so the response must also be transnational. Solidarity no longer means aid, or not just aid, but finding the hidden synergies in each other's struggles so that our numerical force and the power of our ideas become overwhelming.

Susan George has written widely on development and world issues. She is Associate Director of the Transnational Institute and is the author of several works including How the Other Half Dies, A Fate Worse than Debt, The Debt Boomerang *and* The Lugano Report *(Pluto Press).*

Financial Warfare by Michel Chossudovsky

Practices of the unscrupulous money changers stand indicted in the court of public opinion, rejected by the hearts and minds of men.
—Franklin D. Roosevelt

Humanity is undergoing in the post-Cold War era an economic crisis of unprecedented scale leading to the rapid impoverishment of large sectors of the World population. The plunge of national currencies in virtually all major regions of the World has contributed to destabilizing national economies while precipitating entire countries into abysmal poverty.

The crisis is not limited to Southeast Asia or the former Soviet Union. The collapse in the standard of living is taking place abruptly and simultaneously in a large number of countries. This worldwide crisis of the late-twentieth century is more devastating than the Great Depression of the 1930s. It has farreaching geopolitical implications. Economic dislocation has also been accompanied by the outbreak of regional conflicts, the fracturing of national societies and in some cases the destruction of entire countries. This is by far the most serious economic crisis in modern history.

The existence of a 'global financial crisis' is casually denied by the Western media, its social impacts are downplayed or distorted. International institutions including the United Nations deny the mounting tide of World poverty: 'the progress in reducing poverty over the [late] 20th century is remarkable and unprecedented..."[1]. The 'consensus' is that the Western economy is 'healthy' and that 'market corrections' on Wall Street are largely attributable to the 'Asian flu' and to Russia's troubled 'transition to a free market economy'.

Evolution of the Global Financial Crisis

The plunge of Asia's currency markets (initiated in mid-1997) was followed in October 1997 by the dramatic meltdown of major bourses around the World. In the uncertain wake of Wall Street's temporary recovery in early 1998—largely spurred by panic flight out of Japanese stocks—financial markets backslided a few months later to reach a new dramatic turning-point in August with the spectacular nose-dive of the Russian ruble. The Dow Jones plunged by 554 points on August 31st (the second largest decline in the history of the New York stock exchange) leading in the course of September to the dramatic melt-down of stock markets around the World. In a matter of a few weeks (from the Dow's 9337 peak in mid-July), $2,300 billion in 'paper prof-its' had evaporated from the U.S. stock market.[2]

The ruble's free-fall had spurred Moscow's largest commercial banks into bankruptcy, leading to the potential takeover of Russia's financial system by a handful of Western banks and brokerage houses. In turn, the crisis has created the danger of massive debt default to Moscow's Western creditors including the Deutsche and Dresdner banks. Since the outset of Russia's macro-economic reforms, follow-ing the first injection of IMF 'shock therapy' in 1992, some $500 bil-lion worth of Russian assets—including plants of the military indus-trial complex, infrastructure and natural resources—have been confis-cated (through the privatization programs and forced bankruptcies) and transferred into the hands of Western capitalists.[3] In the brutal aftermath of the Cold War, an entire economic and social system is being dismantled.

'Financial Warfare'

The worldwide scramble to appropriate wealth through 'financial manipulation' is the driving force behind this crisis. It is also the source of economic turmoil and social devastation. In the words of renowned currency speculator and billionaire George Soros (who made $1.6 billion of speculative gains in the dramatic crash of the British pound in 1992) "extending the market mechanism to all domains has the potential of destroying society."[4]

This manipulation of market forces by powerful actors constitutes a form of financial and economic warfare. No need to recolonize lost territory or send in invading armies. In the late twentieth century, the outright 'conquest of nations' meaning the control over productive assets, labour, natural resources and institutions can be carried out in an impersonal fashion from the corporate boardroom: commands are dispatched from a computer terminal or a cell phone. The relevant data are instantly relayed to major financial markets—often resulting in immediate disruptions in the functioning of national economies.

'Financial warfare' also applies complex speculative instruments including the gamut of derivative trade, forward foreign exchange transactions, currency options, hedge funds, index funds etc. Speculative instruments have been used with the ultimate purpose of capturing financial wealth and acquiring control over productive assets. In the words of Malaysia's Prime Minister Mahathir Mohamad: "This deliberate devaluation of the currency of a country by currency traders purely for profit is a serious denial of the rights of independent nations."[5]

The appropriation of global wealth through this manipulation of market forces is routinely supported by the IMF's lethal macroeconomic interventions which act almost concurrently in ruthlessly disrupting national economies all over the World. 'Financial warfare' knows no territorial boundaries; it does not limit its actions to besieging former enemies of the Cold War era. In Korea, Indonesia and Thailand, the vaults of the central banks were pillaged by institutional speculators while the monetary authorities sought in vain to prop up their ailing currencies. In 1997, more than $100 billion of Asia's hard currency reserves had been confiscated and transferred (in a matter of months) into private financial hands. In the wake of the currency devaluations, real earnings and employment plummeted virtually overnight leading to mass poverty in countries which had in the post-War period registered significant economic and social progress.

The financial scam in the foreign exchange market had destabilized national economies, thereby creating the preconditions for the subsequent plunder of the Asian countries' productive assets by so-called 'vulture foreign investors'.[6] In Thailand, fifty-six domestic banks and financial institutions were closed down on orders of the IMF; unemployment virtually doubled overnight.[7] Similarly in Korea, the IMF 'rescue operation' has unleashed a lethal chain of bankruptcies leading to the outright liquidation of so-called 'troubled merchant banks'. In the wake of the IMF's 'mediation' (put in place in December 1997 after high-level consultations with the World's largest commercial and merchant banks), "an average of more than 200 companies [were] shut down per day [...] 4,000 workers every day were driven out onto streets as unemployed."[8] Resulting from the credit freeze and "the instantaneous bank shut-down," some 15,000 bankruptcies are expected in 1998 including 90% of Korea's construction companies (with combined debts of $20 billion to domestic financial institutions).[9] South Korea's Parliament has been transformed into a 'rubber stamp'. Enabling legislation is enforced through 'financial blackmail': if the legislation is not speedily enacted according to IMF's deadlines, the disbursements under the bail-out will be suspended with the danger of renewed currency speculation.

In turn, the IMF sponsored 'exit program' (i.e., forced bankruptcy) has deliberately contributed to fracturing the chaebols which are now invited to establish "strategic alliances with foreign firms" (meaning their eventual control by Western capital). With the devaluation, the cost of Korean labour had also tumbled: "It's now cheaper to buy one of these [high tech] companies than buy a factory—and you get all the distribution, brand-name recognition and trained labour force free in the bargain..."[10]

The Demise of Central Banking

In many regards, this worldwide crisis marks the demise of central banking, meaning the derogation of national economic sovereignty and the inability of the national state to control money creation on behalf of society. In other words, privately held money reserves in the hands of 'institutional speculators' far exceed the limited capabilities of the world's central banks. The latter, acting individually or collectively are no longer able to fight the tide of speculative activity. Monetary policy is in the hands of private creditors who have the ability to freeze state budgets, paralyze the payments process, thwart the regular disbursement of wages to millions of workers (as in the former Soviet Union) and precipitate the collapse of production and social programs. As the crisis deepens, speculative raids on central banks are extending into China, Latin America and the Middle East with devastating economic and social consequences.

This ongoing pillage of central bank reserves, however, is by no means limited to developing countries. It has also hit several Western countries including Canada and Australia where the monetary authorities have been incapable of stemming the slide of their national currencies. In Canada, billions of dollars were borrowed from private financiers to prop up central bank reserves in the wake of speculative assaults. In Japan—where the yen has tumbled to new lows—"the Korean scenario" is viewed (according to economist Michael Hudson), as a "dress rehearsal" for the take over of Japan's financial sector by a handful of Western investment banks. The big players are Goldman Sachs, Morgan Stanley, Deutsche Morgan Gruenfell, among others, who are buying up Japan's bad bank loans at less than ten percent of their face value. In recent months both former U.S. Secretary of the Treasury Robert Rubin and former Secretary of State Madeleine Albright have exerted political pressure on Tokyo insisting "on nothing less than an immediate disposal of Japan's bad bank loans—preferably to U.S. and other foreign 'vulture investors' at distress prices. To achieve their objectives they are even pressuring Japan to rewrite its constitution, restructure its political system and cabinet and redesign its financial system... Once foreign investors gain control of Japanese banks, these banks will move to take over Japanese industry..."[11]

Creditors and Speculators

The World's largest banks and brokerage houses are both creditors and institutional speculators. In the present context, they contribute (through their speculative assaults) to destabilizing national currencies, thereby boosting the volume of dollar-denominated debts. They then reappear as creditors with a view to collecting these debts. Finally, they are called in as 'policy advisors' or consultants in the IMF-World Bank sponsored 'bankruptcy programs' of which they are the ultimate beneficiaries. In Indonesia, for instance, amidst street rioting and in the wake of Suharto's resignation, the privatization of key sectors of the Indonesian economy ordered by the IMF was entrusted to eight of the World's largest merchant banks including Lehman Brothers, Credit Suisse-First Boston, Goldman Sachs and UBS/SBC Warburg Dillon Read.[12] The World's largest money managers set countries on fire and are then called in as firemen (under the IMF 'rescue plan') to extinguish the blaze. They ultimately decide which enterprises are to be closed down and which are to be auctioned off to foreign investors at bargain prices.

Who Funds the IMF Bailouts?

Under repeated speculative assaults, Asian central banks entered into multi-billion dollar contracts (in the forward foreign exchange market) in a vain attempt to protect their currencies. With the total depletion of their hard currency reserves, the monetary authorities were forced to borrow large amounts of money under the IMF bailout agreement. Following a scheme devised during the Mexican crisis of 1994-95, the bailout money, however, is not intended "to rescue the country;" in fact the money never entered Korea, Thailand or Indonesia. It was earmarked to reimburse the 'institutional speculators', to ensure that they would be able to collect their multi-billion dollar loot. In turn, the Asian tigers have been tamed by their financial masters. Transformed into lame ducks, they have been 'locked up' into servicing these massive dollar-denominated debts well into the third millennium.

But where did the money come from to finance these multi-billion dollar operations? Only a small portion of the money comes from IMF resources: starting with the Mexican 1995 bailout, G7 countries including the U.S. were called upon to make large lump-sum contributions to these IMF-sponsored rescue operations leading to significant hikes in the levels of public debt.[13] Yet in an ironic twist, the issuing of U.S. public debt to finance the bailouts is underwritten and guaranteed by the same group of Wall Street merchant banks involved in the speculative assaults.

In other words, those who guarantee the issuing of public debt (to finance the bailout) are those who will ultimately appropriate the loot (e.g. as creditors of Korea or Thailand). They are the ultimate recipients of the bailout money (which essentially constitutes a 'safety net' for the institutional speculator). The vast amounts of money granted under the rescue packages are intended to enable the Asian countries to meet their debt obligations with those same financial institutions which contributed to precipitating the breakdown of their national currencies in the first place. As a result of this vicious circle, a handful of commercial banks and brokerage houses have enriched themselves beyond bounds; they have also increased their stranglehold over governments and politicians around the World.

Strong Economic Medicine

Since the 1994-95 Mexican crisis, the IMF has played a crucial role in shaping the 'financial environment' in which the global banks and money managers wage their speculative raids. The global banks are craving access to inside information. Successful speculative attacks require the concurrent implementation on their behalf of 'strong economic medicine' under the IMF bail-out agreements. The 'big six' Wall Street commercial banks (including Chase, Bank America, Citicorp and J. P. Morgan) and the 'big five' merchant banks (Goldman Sachs, Lehman Brothers, Morgan Stanley and Salomon Smith Barney) were consulted on the clauses to be included in the bailout agreements. In the case of Korea's short-term debt, Wall Street's largest financial institutions were called in on Christmas Eve of 1997, for high level talks at the Federal Reserve Bank of New York.[14]

The global banks have a direct stake in the decline of national currencies. In April 1997 barely two months before the onslaught of the Asian currency crisis, the Institute of International Finance (IIF), a Washington based think-tank representing the interests of some 290 global banks and brokerage houses had "urged authorities in emerging markets to counter upward exchange rate pressures where needed..."[15] This request (communicated in a formal letter to the IMF) hints in no uncertain terms that the IMF should advocate an environment in which national currencies are allowed to slide.[16] Indonesia was ordered by the IMF to unpeg its currency barely three months before the rupiah's dramatic plunge. In the words of American billionaire and ex-presidential candidate Steve Forbes: "Did the IMF help precipitate the crisis? This agency advocates openness and transparency for national economies, yet it rivals the CIA in cloaking its own operations. Did it, for instance, have secret conversations with Thailand, advocating the devaluation that instantly set off the catastrophic chain of events? Did IMF prescriptions exacerbate the illness? These countries' moneys were knocked down to absurdly low levels."[17]

Deregulating Capital Movements

The international rules regulating the movements of money and capital (across international borders) contribute to shaping the 'financial battlefields' on which banks and speculators wage their deadly assaults. In their worldwide quest to appropriate economic and financial wealth, global banks and multinational corporations have actively pressured for the outright deregulation of international capital flows including the movement of 'hot' and 'dirty' money.[18] Caving in to these demands (after hasty consultations with G7 finance ministers), a formal verdict to deregulate capital movements was taken by the IMF Interim Committee in Washington in April 1998. The official communiqué stated that the IMF will proceed with the amendment of its Articles with a view to "making the liberalization of capital movements one of the purposes of the Fund and extending, as needed, the Fund's jurisdiction for this purpose."[19] The IMF managing director, Mr. Michel Camdessus, nonetheless conceded in a dispassionate tone that "a number of developing countries may come under speculative attacks after opening their capital account" while reiterating (ad nauseam) that this can be avoided by the adoption of "sound macroeconomic policies and strong financial systems in member countries" (i.e. the IMF's standard 'economic cure for disaster').[20]

The IMF's resolve to deregulate capital movements was taken behind closed doors (conveniently removed from the public eye and with very little press coverage) barely two weeks before citizens' groups from around the World gathered in late April 1998 in mass demonstrations in Paris opposing the controversial Multilateral Agreement on Investment (MAI) under OECD auspices. This agreement would have granted entrenched rights to banks and multinational corporations overriding national laws on foreign investment as well derogating the fundamental rights of citizens. The MAI constitutes an act of capitulation by democratic governments to banks and multinational corporations. The timing was right on course: while the approval of the MAI had been temporarily stalled, the proposed deregulation of foreign investment through a more expedient avenue had been officially launched: the amendment of the Articles would for all practical purposes derogate the powers of national governments to regulate foreign investment. It would also nullify the efforts of the worldwide citizens' campaign against the MAI: the deregulation of foreign investment would be achieved ('with a stroke of a pen') without the need for a cumbersome multilateral agreement under OECD or WTO auspices and without the legal hassle of a global investment treaty entrenched in international law.

Creating a Global Financial Watchdog

As the aggressive scramble for global wealth unfolds and the financial crisis reaches dangerous heights, international banks and speculators are anxious to play a more direct role in shaping financial structures to their advantage as well as 'policing' country-level economic reforms. Free market conservatives in the United States (associated with the Republican Party) have blamed the IMF for its reckless behaviour. Disregarding the IMF's intergovernmental status, they are demanding greater U.S. control over the IMF. They have also hinted that the IMF should henceforth perform a more placid role (similar to that of the bond rate agencies such as Moody's or Standard and Poor's) while consigning the financing of the multi-billion dollar bailouts to the private banking sector.[21]

Discussed behind closed doors in April 1998, a more perceptive initiative (couched in softer language) was put forth by the World's largest banks and investment houses through their Washington mouthpiece (the Institute of International Finance). The banks' proposal consists in the creation of a 'Financial Watchdog'—a so-called 'Private Sector Advisory Council'—with a view to routinely supervising the activities of the IMF. "The Institute [of International Finance], with its nearly universal membership of leading private financial firms, stands ready to work with the official community to advance this process."[22] Responding to the global banks' initiative, the IMF has called for concrete "steps to strengthen private sector involvement" in crisis management—what might be interpreted as a 'power sharing arrangement' between the IMF and the global banks.[23] The international banking community has also set up its own high-level "Steering Committee on Emerging Markets Finance" integrated by some of the World's most powerful financiers including William Rhodes, vice chairman of Citibank, and Sir David Walker, chairman of Morgan Stanley.

The hidden agenda behind these various initiatives is to gradually transform the IMF—from its present status as an inter-governmental body—into a full-fledged bureaucracy which more effectively serves the interests of the global banks. More importantly, the banks and speculators want access to the details of IMF negotiations with member governments which will enable them to carefully position their assaults in financial markets both prior to and in the wake of an IMF bailout agreement. The global banks (pointing to the need for 'transparency') have called upon "the IMF to provide valuable insights [on its dealings with national governments] without revealing confidential information..." But what they really want is privileged inside information.[24]

The ongoing financial crisis is not only conducive to the demise of national state institutions all over the World, it also consists in the step by step dismantling (and possible privatization) of the post-war institutions established by the founding fathers at the Bretton Woods Conference in 1944. In striking contrast with the IMF's present-day destructive role, these institutions were intended by their architects to safeguard the stability of national economies. In the words of Henry Morgenthau, U.S. Secretary of the Treasury in his closing statement to the Conference (22 July 1944): "We came here to work out methods which would do away with economic evils—the competitive currency devaluation and destructive impediments to trade—which preceded the present war. We have succeeded in this effort."[25]

Notes

[1] United Nations Development Program, *Human Development Report*, 1997, p. 2.

[2] Robert O'Harrow Jr., "Dow Dives 513 Points, or 6.4," *Washington Post*, 1 September 1998, page A.

[3] Bob Djurdjevic, "Return Looted Russian Assets, Aug. 30," *Truth in Media's Global Watch*, Phoenix, 30 August 1998.

[4] "Society under Threat—Soros", *The Guardian*, London, 31 October 1997.

[5] Statement at the Meeting of the Group of 15, Malacca, Malaysia, 3 November 1997, quoted in the *South China Morning Post*, Hong Kong, 3 November 1997.

[6] Michael Hudson and Bill Totten, "Vulture speculators," *Our World*, No. 197, Kawasaki, 12 August 1998.

[7] Nicola Bullard, Walden Bello and Kamal Malhotra, "Taming the Tigers: the IMF and the Asian Crisis," Special Issue on the IMF, *Focus on Trade No. 23, Focus on the Global South*, Bangkok, March 1998.

[8] Korean Federation of Trade Unions, "Unbridled Freedom to Sack Workers Is No Solution At All," Seoul, 13 January 1998.

[9] Song Jung Tae, "Insolvency of Construction Firms Rises in 1998," *Korea Herald*, 24 December 1997. Legislation (following IMF directives) was approved which dismantles the extensive powers of the ministry of finance while also stripping the ministry of its regulatory and supervisory functions. The financial sector having been opened up, a Financial Supervisory Council under the advice of Western merchant banks would arbitrarily decide the fate of Korean banks. Selected banks (the lucky ones) are to be "made more attractive" by earmarking a significant chunk of the bailout money to finance (subsidize) their acquisition at depressed prices by foreign buyers—ie. the shopping-spree by Western financiers is funded by the government on borrowed money from Western financiers.

[10] Michael Hudson, *Our World*, Kawasaki, 23 December, 1997.

[11] Michael Hudson, "Big Bang is Culprit Behind Yen's Fall," *Our World*, No. 187, Kawasaki, 28 July 1998. See also Secretary of State Madeleine Albright and Japanese Foreign Minister Keizo Obuchi, Joint Press Conference, Ikura House, Tokyo, 4 July, 1998, contained in Official Press Release, U.S. Department of State, Washington, 7 July 1998.

[12] See Nicola Bullard, Walden Bello and Kamal Malhotra, op cit.

[13] On 15 July 1998, the Republican dominated House of Representatives slashed the Clinton Administration's request of $18 billion in additional U.S. funding to the IMF to $3.5 billion. Part of the U.S. contribution to the bailouts would be financed under the Foreign Exchange Stabilization Fund of the Treasury.

[14] *Financial Times*, London, 27-28 December 1997, p. 3.

[15] Institute of International Finance, "Report of the Multilateral Agencies Group," *IIF Annual Report*, Washington, 1997.

[16] Letter addressed by the managing director of the Institute of International Finance ,Mr. Charles Dallara to Mr. Philip Maystadt, Chairman of the IMF Interim Committee, April 1997, quoted in *Institute of International Finance, 1997 Annual Report*, 1997.

[17] Steven Forbes, "Why Reward Bad Behaviour," *Forbes* , 4 May 1998.

[18] 'Hot money' is speculative capital, 'dirty money' is the proceeds of organized crime which are routinely laundered in the international financial system.

[19] International Monetary Fund, Communiqué of the Interim Committee of the Board of Governors of the International Monetary

Fund, Press Release No. 98/14 Washington, 16 April 1998. The controversial proposal to amend its articles on "capital account liberalization" had initially been put forth in April 1997.

[20] See Communiqué of the IMF Interim Committee, Hong Kong, 21 September 1997.

[21] See Steven Forbes, op cit.

[22] Institute of International Finance, East Asian Crises Calls for New International Measures, Say Financial Leaders, Press Release, 18 April 1998.

[23] IMF, Communiqué of the Interim Committee of the Board of Governors, 16 April, 1998.

[24] The IIF proposes that global banks and brokerage houses could for this purpose "be rotated and selected through a neutral process [to ensure confidentiality], and a regular exchange of views [which] is unlikely to reveal dramatic surprises that turn markets abruptly [...]. In this era of globalization, both market participants and multilateral institutions have crucial roles to play; the more they understand each other, the greater the prospects for better functioning of markets and financial stability..." See letter of Charles Dallara, Managing Director of the IIF to Mr. Philip Maystadt, Chairman of IMF Interim Committee, IIF, Washington, 8 April 1998.

[25] Closing Address, Bretton Woods Conference, New Hampshire, 22 July 1944. The IMF's present role is in violation of its Articles of Agreement.

Michel Chossudovsky is a professor of Economics at the University of Ottawa. He is the author of The Globalisation of Poverty: Impacts of IMF and World Bank Reforms *(Penang and Zed Books, London, 1997.) He is also the author of "Dismantling Yugoslavia, Colonizing Bosnia,"* Covert Action Quarterly, *Washington, D.C., Spring 1996, Number 56 and "The Business of Crime and the Crimes of Business: Globalization and the Criminalization of Economic Activity,"Covert Action* Quarterly, *Washington, D.C., Fall 1996, Number 58.*

The Global Economy: Can It Be Fixed?
by David C. Korten

Economic globalization is one of the most important issues of our time. In my own case, I've spent most of my adult life in Third World countries as a development worker. This included fifteen years in Southeast Asia—until recently considered one of the world's development success stories. I saw the reality behind the modern airports, express highways, luxury hotels and air-conditioned shopping malls stocked with the latest imported consumer goods, long before the recent financial collapse revealed the shallow roots of much of Asia's development. I witnessed the deepening misery of people who were displaced from their homes and lands in the name of progress for the few, the environmental devastation, and the disintegration of once vibrant cultures. My dismay turned to horror when I realized that the same trends toward declining living standards, increasing inequality, environmental destruction, and social disintegration were being played out in the industrial nations around the world including in my own country, the United States. It all suggested institutional failure at a deeply systemic level.

It is my position that an unregulated global economy dominated by corporations that recognize money as their only value is inherently unstable, egregiously unequal and destructive of markets, democracy and life. Further, such a global economy impoverishes humanity in real terms even as it enriches a few individuals in financial terms. We face very basic questions as to the goals and values we want our economies to serve. The issues go far beyond tinkering with trade rules at the margin.

An Unstable System of Winners and Losers
On February 1, 1996 the *International Herald Tribune* published an opinion piece by Klaus Schwab and Claude Smadja, respectively president and managing director of the World Economic Forum. In their piece they noted: "Economic globalization is causing severe economic dislocation and social instability. The technological changes of the past few years have eliminated more jobs than they have created." The competition "that is part and parcel of globalization leads to winner-

take-all situations; those who come out on top win big, and the losers lose even bigger." Higher profits no longer mean more job security and better wages. "Globalization tends to delink the fate of the corporation from the fate of its employees." Schwab and Smadja go on to warn that unless serious corrective action is taken soon, the backlash could turn into open political revolt and destabilize the Western democracies. If this assessment had come from some anti-globalization environmental organization it might be dismissed as hyperbole; the same cannot be said when it comes from the club of the world's thousand largest global corporations. What I found most problematic was the authors' call to the world's political and economic leaders to demonstrate how the new global capitalism can be made to work to the benefit of the majority and not only for corporate managers and investors. This raises a basic question: can the new global capitalism be made to work for the benefit of the majority, or are the problems with it more fundamental?

In their article, Schwab and Smadja recommended increases in public expenditures on training and education, upgrading telecommunications and transportation infrastructure, providing incentives to investors and reforming social policies to increase international competitiveness. Here we confront a troubling dilemma. Increasing the global competitiveness of one country by using public subsidies to boost private profit—to the extent that it works—simply draws investment away from others and creates new losers. If indeed we are to have a world that works for everyone, we must come to terms with the dark side of global capitalism's competitive dynamic.

Fortunes change quickly in a global capitalist economy that is characterized by excess productive capacity, massive unemployment, an unconscionable gap between rich and poor and large amounts of speculative money thrown out by investors looking for quick profits. Not long ago it seemed that Japan had become the invincible world economic power, eclipsing the fading fortunes of the United States and Europe. Then Japan's financial and real estate bubbles burst and countries such as South Korea, Thailand, Malaysia and Indonesia became touted as models of the opportunities available to those who embraced neo-liberal policies. Then their bubbles burst and now we find the United States being touted as the neo-liberal success story.

And when the U.S. bubble bursts, perhaps Europe will be the speculators' next haven.

There are many telling statistics illustrating the unconscionable extremes of inequality under the new global capitalism. I want to share only one. In 1997, Bill Gates, already the richest person in the world, doubled his net worth to a total of $36.4 billion—roughly equivalent to the entire gross domestic product of Bangladesh, a country of 120 million people.

As an American citizen I find it appalling that our political and economic leaders are touting the United States as a model of economic success. Yes, profits are at a forty-year high, the stock market sets new records by the week, and productivity since 1979 has increased 24%. But real earnings for workers have actually fallen by 12% during the same period. All of the benefit of our supposed success has gone to the richest 20% of Americans. The biggest declines are for the poorest twenty percent.

Capitalism Against the Market

The underlying belief that global capitalism can be made to work for everyone is based on a deep faith in the theory that markets necessarily allocate society's resources equitably and efficiently. Unfortunately, a market economy and the new global capitalism are not the same thing. To the contrary, the new global capitalism systematically violates nearly every assumption on which market theory is based—including the key assumptions about competition and cost internalization. Let me elaborate on this point.

A combination of economic globalization, deregulation and financial concentration has moved the new capitalist economy ever further away from the characteristics that make a market economy socially efficient. This combination has also shifted economic and political power away from people and democratically elected governments, and toward an unstable and predatory system of global finance. Beginning with Adam Smith, market theory has been quite explicit that market efficiency is a consequence of small, locally owned enterprises competing for consumer favour on the basis of price and quality in local markets. for consumer favor. By contrast, what we know as the global capitalist economy is dominated by a handful of gigantic corporations and financial speculators with billions of dollars at their disposal which are used to reshape markets and manipulate prices. Furthermore, the megacorporations and financial houses continue to concentrate and consolidate their power over markets, technology and capital through mergers, acquisitions, and strategic alliances— even as they shed their responsibility for people by downsizing and contracting out. The statistics are sobering.

Of the world's one hundred largest economies, fifty-one are economies internal to corporations. Only forty-nine are national economies. The total sales of Mitsubishi Trading Corporation are greater than the GDP of Indonesia, the world's fourth most populous country and a land of enormous natural wealth. The combined sales of the world's top two hundred corporations are equal to 28% of total world GDP. These same two hundred corporations employ only 18.8 million people, less than one third of 1% of the world's population— even as the downsizing continues.

Consider the fact that the economy internal to a corporation is not a market economy. It is centrally planned by corporate managers to maximize financial returns to themselves and their shareholders. No matter what authority a CEO may delegate, he can withdraw it with a snap of his fingers. In the U.S. system, which is rapidly infecting Europe, Japan and the rest of the world, the corporate CEO can hire and fire virtually any worker, open and close any plant, change transfer prices, create and drop product lines almost at will, with no meaningful recourse by the persons or communities affected.

Ironically, the global victory of capitalism is not a victory for the market so much as it is a victory for central planning. Capitalism has simply shifted the planning function from governments—which in theory are accountable to all their citizens—to corporations, which even in theory are accountable only to their shareholders. We are moving very quickly toward ever greater consolidation of this unaccountable corporate power. In the United States the total value of corporate mergers and acquisitions has increased at a rate of nearly 50% a year in every year save one since 1992. Most of these mergers and acquisitions are accompanied by large scale layoffs. The greatest concentration is taking place in the financial and telecommunications sectors—with deeply ominous implications for the future of democracy.

Merger mania is spreading. Mergers worldwide had a total value of $1.6 trillion in 1997—up 48% over 1996. European mergers and acquisitions set a record of $400 billion in 1996—double the level of just two years earlier. American investment banks, which are moving into Europe with a vengeance, were involved as advisors in two thirds of the deals. Do not for a moment think that because Europeans believe in stakeholder capitalism that what I am talking about cannot happen there. It is happening at this very moment. Stakeholder capitalism is being purged from European economies as inefficient and a violation of exclusive shareholder rights.

The primary accountability of global corporations and investment houses is to the global financial markets in which each day nearly $2 trillion in foreign exchange changes hands. The goal of these transactions is a realization of speculative profits wholly unrelated to any exchange of real goods or services. Whose interests are represented by the ruling financial markets? In the United States 77% of shareholder wealth is owned by a mere 5% of households. Globally the share of the world's population that has a consequential participation in corporate ownership is most certainly less than one percent. This concentration of power denies the most basic principles of both market economics and democratic governance.

The Myth of Corporate Efficiency

Another critical assumption of market theory is that the full cost of each good and service is internalized by producers and reflected in the prices of their products. By contrast, the success of global capitalism has been in large measure dependent on its ability to privatize the gains of economic activity for its managers and shareholders while passing the costs on to society at large. Global corporations now routinely insist that governments provide direct subsidies and tax breaks in return for jobs. Similarly, they expect many workers to accept less than a living wage. They expect communities to bear the economic and health costs of their waste discharge. And they expect consumers to bear the consequences of dangerous and defective products.

The conservative Cato Institute, based in Washington D.C., estimates that direct corporate subsidies and tax breaks in the United States now total $135 billion a year. Paul Hawken has compiled preliminary data suggesting that corporations in the United States currently receive more in direct public subsidies than they pay in total taxes. Ralph Estes, a CPA with a distinguished academic and research career has compiled an inventory of studies estimating various costs externalized onto the U.S. society by unsafe and defective corporate products and practices. Added together, the total comes to $2.6 trillion a year—roughly five times the amount of reported corporate profits in the United States and 23% of the U.S. gross domestic product for 1994. In short, the data suggest that from a societal perspective corporations are grossly inefficient institutions and that their profitability has come at an enormous cost to society.

Those familiar with market theory know that a market can function efficiently only within a framework of rules that maintain the necessary conditions. There must be rules and incentives to limit the growth and power of individual firms, encourage local ownership and require firms to internalize their costs. Therefore, our goal should not be to eliminate necessary regulation, but rather to make such regulation sensible and effective.

It is here that we experience the new global capitalism at its most perverse. NAFTA, GATT, the World Trade Organization, and the Multilateral Agreement on Investment now being negotiated under the OECD, all turn the necessary practice of market regulation on its head. To restore market efficiency and the equity essential to the legitimacy of its institutions, we must police global corporations to insure their adherence to essential market principles. Yet the international agreements and institutions in place and under negotiation not only fail to serve this need, they do exactly the opposite. They install corporate-dominated mechanisms to police democratically elected national and local governments to prevent them from requiring the corporations and financial institutions that cloak themselves in market rhetoric to actually play by market rules. This is the real impetus behind formation of the WTO. Contrary to the claims of some WTO supporters, a burning desire to protect the interests of the Third World's poor was not the driving motivation.

Privatizing Gains, Socializing Losses

Another aspect of the new global capitalism's dark side is its confusion of money with wealth. Wealth is something that has real value in meeting our needs and fulfilling our wants. It takes many forms, including human skills, technology, land, trees, functioning ecosystems, factories, buildings, food, clothing—even friendship and love. Our most important forms of wealth consist of living capital—the productive-regenerative capacities and systems of life that are the primary sources of our existence and well-being and the foundation of our civilization. These include natural, human, social, and institutional capital. Healthy living capital is the most valuable of all resources because it has the ability to continuously renew itself—to regenerate —and to evolve in its capacities through self-directed learning. Money, on the other hand, is nothing but a number on a piece of paper or a coin, or an electronic trace in a computer file. Aside from the metal in the coin, it has no intrinsic value or productive utility. We covet it only because by social convention others will accept it in exchange for things of real value. Thus, while money is not itself real wealth, it gives us a claim on the wealth of others.

One reason we fail to recognize the seriousness of our current predicament is because we are so obsessed with global capitalism's ability to make money, that we fail to recognize that it is rapidly destroying the world's real wealth. A passion for money destroys natural living capital when it strip mines forests, fisheries and mineral deposits, aggressively markets toxic chemicals and dumps hazardous wastes that turn once productive lands and waters into zones of death. It destroys human capital with substandard working conditions in places like the Mexican maquiladoras where vital and productive young women are employed for three to four years until failed eyesight, allergies, kidney problems and repetitive stress injuries leave them permanently handicapped. It destroys social capital when it breaks up unions, bids down wages and treats workers as expendable commodities, leaving it to society to absorb the family and community breakdown and violence that are inevitable consequences. It destroys institutional capital when it undermines the necessary function and credibility of governments and democratic governance by buying politicians, financing anti-government political movements, weakening environmental, health and labor standards essential to the long-term viability of society and extracting public subsidies, bailouts, and tax exemptions that inflate corporate

profits while passing the burdens of risk and public finance to governments and the working poor.

We are just barely beginning to wake up to the fact that the industrial era has in a mere century consumed a consequential portion of
the natural capital it took evolution millions of years to create. It is
now drawing down our social, institutional and human capital as well.
A few years ago during a visit to Malaysia, I had a brief conversation
with the minister responsible for Malaysia's forests. He explained to
me in all seriousness that since money grows faster than trees,
Malaysia will be better off once it has cut down all its trees and put
the money in the bank to earn interest. The image flashed through my
mind of a barren and lifeless landscape populated only by banks—
their computers faithfully recording interest payments on each of the
accounts on their hard drives.

Making Money, Growing Poor

I'd now like to summarize in fairly stark fashion what we are doing
to ourselves. A study by McKinsey and Company found that since 1980,
the financial assets of the OECD countries have been growing at two
to three times the rate of GDP. This means that potential claims on
economic output are growing from two to three times faster than the
growth in output of the things that money might be used to buy.

The distortions go far deeper, however, because an important portion of the output that GDP currently measures represents a decrease,
rather than an increase, in our well-being. When children buy guns and
cigarettes, the purchases contribute to GDP, though no sane person
would argue that this increases our well-being. When a married couple
gets divorced, it is good for GDP, because divorce action generates
lawyers fees and requires at least one of the parties to buy or rent and
furnish a new home. Other portions of GDP represent defensive
expenditures that attempt to offset the consequences of the social and
environmental breakdown caused by harmful growth. Examples include
expenditures for security devices and environmental clean-up. GDP
further distorts our reality by the fact that it is a measure of gross,
rather than net, domestic product. The depreciation or depletion of
natural, social, human, institutional and even human-made capital is
not deducted. So when we cut down our forests or allow our physical

infrastructure to deteriorate, there is no accounting for the loss of productive function. We count only the gain.

Economists in the United States, the U.K., Germany, the Netherlands and Australia have adjusted reported GDP for their countries to arrive at figures for net beneficial economic output. In each instance they have concluded that the economy's net contribution to well-being has actually been declining over the past fifteen to twenty years. Yet even the indices of net beneficial output are misleading as they do not reveal the extent to which we are depleting the underlying base of living capital on which all future productive activity depends. I know of no systematic effort to create a unified index giving us an overall measure of the state of our living capital. Obviously, this would involve significant technical difficulties. However, what measures we do have relating to the depletion of our forests, soils, fresh water, fisheries, the disruption of our climatic systems, the unraveling of our social fabric, the decline in educational standards, the loss of legitimacy of our major institutions and the breakdown of family structures give us reason to believe that the rate of depletion of our living capital is even greater than the rate of decline in net beneficial output.

The indicators of stock market performance and GDP our leaders rely on to assess the state of the economy create the illusion that their policies are making us richer, when in fact they are making us poorer. Governments do not compile the indicators that reveal the truth of what is happening to our wealth and well-being. And the power holders, whose financial assets are growing, experience no problem. In a global economy their money gives them ready access to the best of whatever real wealth remains. Those who experience the reality of the dark side have neither power nor voice.

To Create a Market Economy

The challenge before us is to replace the global capitalist economy with a properly regulated and locally rooted market economy that invests in the regeneration of living capital, increases net beneficial economic output, distributes that output justly and equitably to meet the basic needs of everyone, strengthens the institutions of democracy and the market and returns money to its proper role as the servant of productive activity. Such a market economy should favor smaller local enterprises over global corporations, encourage local ownership, penalize financial speculation and give priority to meeting the basic needs of the many over providing luxuries and diversions for the wealthy few. In most aspects it should do exactly the opposite of what the global capitalist economy is doing.

Most of the responsibility and initiative must come from local and national levels. Supporting nations and localities in this task should become the core agenda of the United Nations, as the protection of people and communities from predatory global corporations and finance is arguably the central security issue of our time. A positive first step would be to dismantle the World Trade Organization on the ground that there is no legitimate need for a global police force to protect global corporations from the actions of democratically elected national and local governments so that the richest one percent of humanity can become even richer at the expense of the rest. And while the removal of trade barriers may be a priority concern of global corporations eager to increase profits and market share, it falls far down on the list of human priorities in a world that finds itself in potentially terminal social and economic crisis. Indeed, where the trading interests of global corporations conflict with the social and environmental goals of people, social and environmental interests should trump the trade goals in nearly every instance.

The WTO is a powerful, but illegitimate and democratically unaccountable, institution, put in place through largely secret negotiations and with little or no public debate, to serve purposes largely contrary to the public interest. The 99% of the world's people whose interests it does not serve have every right to eliminate it. Addressing the real need to police the global economy requires an organization very different from the WTO. This requires an open and democratic organization with the mandate and power to set and enforce rules holding those corporations that operate across national borders democratically accountable to the people and priorities of the nations where they operate. It should also have the power to regulate and tax international financial flows and institutions. And it should have a mandate to make speculation unprofitable and to help protect the integrity of domestic financial institutions from the instability of international financial markets and the predatory practices of international financial speculators. Call it the World Organization for Corporate and Financial Accountability.

There are obvious questions as to whether such proposals are politically feasible given the stranglehold of corporations and big money over our political processes. Yet we could use this same reasoning to conclude that human survival itself is not politically feasible. I believe global corporations and financial institutions are more vulnerable than they may at first appear. They are all populated by human beings like you and me, many of us with children, all of us with human sensibilities and a stake in the future. They are our collective creations. And we have both the right and the means to change or replace them if they do not serve. For this reason, I suggest we set about defining what is necessary to the future security and prosperity of humanity and to the realization of widely shared human values. We can then turn our attention to the question of how to make feasible that which is both necessary and desirable.

David Korten is a former professor at the Harvard School of Business. He was the longtime director of USAID in Southeast Asia and is the author of When Corporations Rule the World *(Kumarian Press, 1995).*

Chapter 6: What Can Be Done?

Tips On How to Oppose Corporate Rule
by Jane Kelsey

• Be skeptical about fiscal and other "crises." Examine the real nature of the problem, find out who defines it as a crisis and who stands to gain. Demand to know the range of possible solutions, and the costs and benefits of each. If the answers are not forthcoming, burn the midnight oil to produce the answers for yourselves.

• Don't cling to a political party that has been converted to neo-conservatism. Fighting to prevent a social democratic party's capture by Right-wing zealots is important. But once the party has been taken over, maintaining solidarity on the outside while seeking change from within merely gives them more time. When the spirit of the party is dead, shed the old skin and create something new.

• Take economics seriously. Neo-liberal economic fundamentalism pervades everything. There is no boundary between economic, social, environmental or other policies. Those who focus on narrow sectoral concerns and ignore the pervasive economic agenda will lose their own battles and weaken the collective ability to resist. Leaving economics to economists is fatal.

• Expose the weaknesses of the opposing theory. Neo-liberal theories are riddled with dubious assumptions and internal inconsistencies, and often lack empirical support. These Right-wing theories need to be exposed as self-serving rationalizations which operate in the interests of the elites whom the policies empower.

• Challenge hypocrisy. Ask who is promoting a strategy as being in the "national interest," and who stands to benefit most. Document cases where self-interest is disguised as public good.

• Expose the masterminds. Name the key corporate players behind the scenes, document their interlocking roles and allegiances and expose the personal and corporate benefits they receive.

• Maximize every obstacle. Federal systems of government, written constitutions, legal requirements and regulations, supra-national institutions like the International Labour Organization and the UN and strong local governments can provide barriers that slow down the pace of the corporate takeover.

• Work hard to maintain solidarity. Avoid the trap of divide and rule. Sectoral in-fighting is self-indulgent and everyone risks losing in the end.

• Do not compromise the labour movement. Build awareness of the corporate agenda at union local and workplace levels. Resist concessions that tend to deepen co-optation and weaken the unions' ability to fight back.

• Maintain the concept of an efficient public service. Resist attempts to discredit and dismantle the public sector by admitting deficiencies and promoting constructive models for change. Build support among client groups and the public which stresses the need for public services and the risks of cutting or privatizing them.

• Encourage community leaders to speak out. Public criticism from civic and church leaders, folk heroes and other prominent 'names' makes corporate and political leaders uncomfortable. It also makes people think. Remind community leaders of their social obligations, and the need to preserve their own self-respect.

• Avoid anti-intellectualism. A pool of academics and other intellectuals who can document and expose the fallacies and failures of the corporate agenda, and develop viable alternatives in partnership with community and sectoral groups, is absolutely vital. They need to be supported when they come under attack, and challenged when they fail to speak out, or are co-opted or seduced.

• Establish an alternative think-tank. If one already exists, make sure it is adequately funded. Neo-liberal and neo-conservative think-tanks have shown how well-resourced institutes on the Right can rationalize and legitimize the corporate agenda. The need is obvious for one or more equally well-supported think-tank on the Left. Uncoordinated research by isolated critics will not suffice.

• Invest in the future. Provide financial, human and moral support to sustain alternative analysis, publications, think-tanks and people's projects that work actively to resist the corporate agenda andpromote progressive change.

• Support those who speak out. The harassment and intimidation of critics of the corporate takeover works only if those targeted for attacks lack personal, popular and institutional support. Withdrawing from public debate leaves those who remain more exposed.

• Promote ethical investment. Support investors who genuinely respond to social and ecological concerns. Expose unethical investors who don't. Boycotts have proved a powerful force in environmental, anti-nuclear and safe product campaigns. Companies that ignore social and environmental concerns can be embarrassed and called to account.
• Think globally, act locally. Develop an understanding of the

global nature of economic power, and those forces which are driving current trends. Draw the links between these global forces and local events. Target local representatives, meetings and activities which feed into the global economic machine.

• Think locally, act globally. Actively support international strategies for change, such as people's tribunals, non-governmental forums and codes of conduct and action campaigns against unethical companies and corporate practices. Recognize that international action is essential to counter the collaboration of states and corporations, and to empower civil society to take back control.

• Develop alternative media outlets. Once mainstream media are captured by the Right, it is difficult for critics to enter the debate, and impossible to lead it. Alternative media and innovative strategies must be put in place. Effective communication and exchange of information between sectoral groups and activists are essential, despite the time and resources involved.

• Raise the levels of popular economic literacy. Familiarize people with the basic themes, assumptions and goals of economic fundamentalism. Convince them that economic policy affects everyone, that everyone has a right to participate, and that alternatives to the corporate agenda do exist.

• Resist marketspeak. Maintain control of the language, challenge its capture by the Right, and refuse to convert your discourse to theirs. Insist on using hard specific terms that convey the hard realities of what is going on.

• Be realistic. Recognize that the world has changed, in some ways irreversibly, and that the past was far from perfect. Avoid being trapped solely into reacting and defending the status quo. Defending the past for its own sake adds credibility to the claims of the Right and wastes opportunities to work for genuine change.

• Be proactive. Start rethinking visions, strategies and models of development for the future. Show that there are workable, preferable alternatives from the start. This becomes progressively more difficult the longer you wait to respond to the corporate agenda.

• Challenge the TINA ("there is no alternative") claim. Convince people—individually and collectively—that there are real and workable alternatives. Present options that combine realism with the prospect of meaningful change. Actively promote these alternatives and have them ready to be implemented when the corporate agenda fails.

• Promote participatory democracy. Build a constituency for change through alternative information networks and media. Use community, workplace, women's, church, union, First Nations and other outlets to encourage people to take back control. Empower them with the knowledge they need to understand the Right-wing forces affecting them and how they can fight back most effectively.

• Hold the line. The corporate takeover is not yet complete. Social programs have not yet been entirely dismantled. Unions have not yet been destroyed. Not all environmental protections have been eliminated. There is still time, through sustained and co-ordinated action, to hold the line.

Jane Kelsey is a professor of Law at Auckland University. She is the author of A Question of Honour? *and* Rolling Back the State, *both challenging examinations of New Zealand's social and political life. Her best-selling books* The New Zealand Experiment *(1994) and* Reclaiming the Future *(1999) are commentaries on the neo-liberal changes wrought on New Zealand in the last decade.*

BASIC Democracy by Ken Ranney

The only thing necessary for the triumph of evil is for good men to do nothing. —Edmund Burke

One of these days people are going to wake up and begin to think. They are going to realize that they do not have to be pushed around by the kind of governments we have had: governments, which, while claiming to represent the people, have, in fact, represented only the rich elite.[1] And when the people wake up, they will seek an alternative to this political system called democracy, which is simply a device to maintain the power of the rich elite.

The idea of BASIC Democracy is to make a move towards genuine democracy, democracy with the potential to eliminate interference by the rich elite in political affairs.[2] The rich own the newspapers and they own or control radio and TV.[3] The vital information we need to make political decisions comes to us through the biased news media of the rich. And there is evidence that even what is taught in some of the world's churches has been heavily influenced by the rich.[4] The money of the rich is crucial in determining electoral outcomes. In the words of columnist Nicholas Van Hoffman, "if money drives politics, then we are as equal as we are equally rich. If 3% of the people control the money available for political parties and elections, they run the country."[5] The electoral process gives us only the illusion of democracy, not the real thing. It is not democracy when you mark an X on a ballot every four or five years.[6] We have to appreciate this before we are able to recognize that a reliance on reforming the system or simply electing another party will not free us from domination by the rich. What follows is offered after considerable reflection and with much hope for a world of fairness and peace. It may be the best we can do.

There is growing dissatisfaction with democracy. It is time our representatives in Parliament represented us. Photo-opportunistic bulletins sent out by MPs to their constituents a couple of times each year tell us nothing. In the U.S., voter turnout has declined significantly over the years. In Canada, voting numbers are higher than those in the U.S. but are also declining. In June 1997, Canadian voters cynically returned to power, with the lowest turnout since 1925, a Liberal government which they clearly knew had lied to them on an issue close to life and death—taxes. When first elected in 1994, the Liberals promised solemnly, vociferously and repeatedly to eliminate a highly unpopular sales tax instituted by their Conservative predecessors. Once in power, however, the Liberals refused to honour their promise. That people feel fatalistic about elections is obvious enough. "I never vote. It only encourages them."[7] This classic statement, attributed to a "little old lady in Maine" pretty much sums up the attitude many people have toward the electoral process.

BASIC democracy cannot promise to be a pure democracy. There never has been such a thing. It will, however, accomplish three important goals in the short term:

1. The creation of a system of community-based advisors to governments at all levels. The agenda of the rich elite that now comes to us largely through the news media would be set by ordinary people. MPs, MPPs, MLAs and municipal representatives could be encouraged, with the possibility of defeat at the next election, to address issues of interest to ordinary people.
2. Dissemination of information not now available in the news media of the rich.
3. An escape, before it is too late, from world domination by the rich elite.

In the long term, the proposed BASIC non-party system would replace the arguably obsolete and often destructive party system. Few are aware that the party system is as old as the Roman Empire, and just as corrupt. The party system allows the election of governments that lack the support of the majority of voters. Both the 1990 Ontario New Democratic government of Bob Rae and the 1997 Canadian federal government of Jean Chrétien were elected with 38% of the popular vote. The party system places power, not in the hands of the people but in the hands of the few who control the party. The party hierarchy gets to control the issues presented by the party and is often influential in determining the candidates for election.

How does BASIC democracy work?

BASIC democracy is a multi-level system with direct democracy at the bottom and delegated democracy at every level above that. Direct democracy starts at the neighbourhood level—actual face-to-face discussion and decision by consensus or majority, and election of a council that makes up the next level. The delegates would have to be sufficiently instructed by, and accountable to, those who elected them, to make the decisions at the council level reasonably democratic. So it goes on up to the top level, which would be made up of a national council for matters of national concern and local and regional councils for matters of less than national concern. What is needed, to make the system democratic, is that the decision-makers and issue-formulators elected from below be held responsible to those below by being subject to re-election or even recall.[8]

BASIC democracy consists of small groups electing, with no expenses, delegates to higher levels of small groups who in turn elect delegates to still higher groups. Supplementing the bottom-up process would be the top-down dissemination of minutes created from information supplied to the higher levels both from the bottom and from advisory groups made up of scientists, physicians, teachers and other specialists. In this way information suppressed by the rich-owned news media may be acted upon by the grassroots. Without information free of the bias of the rich elite, BASIC democracy will be severely handicapped.

BASIC democracy has a powerful potential. It could have a much bigger impact than the invention of the printing press. It seeks to eliminate the influence of the rich elite by gradually transforming phoney democracy through its informative and decision-making processes. At the very least, it will greatly improve the present democracy. If successful, it will convert the world to a society of compassion, fairness, reason and truth.

Apathy is the enemy of BASIC democracy. But apathy is simply a reflection of powerlessness. When people find that there is a way for them to control their own lives, this new form of democracy will generate unprecedented interest and a ferment of new ideas. As Noam Chomsky argues, people who have the ability to acquire and marshal detailed information about sports events have quite sufficient ability to take part in making decisions affecting their own lives.

People who wish to participate are divided into small groups. I have used groups of 10 in the structure proposed below. Any agreed-upon group size may be used, but the group should be small enough that there can be discussion with minimal intimidation. The groups may be as large as fifty, and this larger number greatly reduces the number of levels between the grassroots and the national council. Both ten and fifty are used below as bases for demonstration purposes.

There were 18,753,094 voters registered at the June 2, 1997 federal Canadian election. Using ten as the base group size, there would be two million groups of ten in a Canadian BASIC democracy. Following discussion of their issues, each first-level group would select one of its members to represent it at the next level. This second level would also be divided into tens; each of these second-level groups would elect a representative to the third level and so on for five levels. The fifth level would constitute a National Council for Canada, made up of 188 people whose decisions would initiate laws and be ratified by the grassroots levels groups. The structure would look something like this:

BASIC Democracy Structure Canada (groups of 10)
1,875,309 groups of ten people (1,875,309 x 10 = approx. 18,753,094 voters).
187,531 groups of ten first level representatives.
18,753 groups of ten second level representatives.
1,875 groups of ten third level representatives.
188 groups of ten fourth level representatives.
188 people acting as advisors to national council of Canada.
(Five steps to national council level.)

BASIC Democracy Structure Canada (groups of 50)
375,062 groups of fifty people (375,062 x 50 = approx. 18,753,094 voters).
7,501 groups of fifty first level representatives.
150 groups of fifty second level representatives.
150 people acting as a national council for Canada.
(Three steps to national council level.)

BASIC Democracy in Ward Three, Bowmanville (groups of ten)

Total Population = 10,100

Total Registered Voters = 6,290

629 groups of ten.

63 groups of ten first-level representatives.

63 people to advise councillor for Ward Three.

Advantages of BASIC Democracy

1. Elimination of election financing by the rich.
2. Face-to-face discussions of issues; much more direct democracy.
3. Elimination of personality cult; shift of responsibility to the people instead of hoping for the best from career politicians.
4. Initiation of discussions about issues of concern to people.
5. Greatly reduced dependence on the news media owned and/or controlled by the rich for information; minutes of meetings will be a more direct and more reliable source of facts.
6. Small groups allow for intimate discussion and readily detect power-hungry status-seeking individuals.
7. Municipal, provincial, federal and international governments could be lobbied or created.

Suggested Rules of BASIC Democracy

1. Instant recall of representatives, when indicated.
2. Representatives beyond the first level subject to recall only by the last group to select her/him.
3. Minutes from all levels to be available to all lower levels.
4. All motions passed by all groups to be available to all groups.

Additional Benefits of BASIC Democracy

1. Possibility for involvement by resource groups/special-interest groups.
2. Potential for elimination of nation-states; BASIC Democracy can spread across borders.
3. Eliminates the necessity for municipal governments (notorious for

corruption, especially in real estate transactions) and provincial governments, as governing could take place for any area represented, at any rate, for predetermined and limited matters.

5. Children's representation also possible.

6. Political apathy will be reduced.

7. Minutes of meetings can be distributed without the contaminating effects of money and without the bias existing in the news media owned by the rich. The quantity of information available to the people would be much greater than ever.

Notes

[1] Neither the use of the term "the rich" nor the context it is used in are meant to imply abhorrence of the rich. I agree with those who say the rich are nice people. I am particularly inclined to agree with Stephen Leacock's sentiment when he writes: "I mix a good deal with the millionaires. I like them. I like their faces. I like the way they live. I like the things they eat. The more we mix together, the better I like the things we mix."

[2] BASIC stands for Bowmanville Advisors Starting in Community. Also known as direct, community-based, small group democracy.

[3] On the occasion of his retirement, long-time editor of the *New York Times*, John Swainton, said: "There is no such thing as a free press. You know it and I know it. There is not one of you who would write your honest opinions. The business of a journalist today is to destroy truth, to lie outright, to pervert, to vilify, to fawn at the feet of Mammon, and to sell himself, his country, and his race for daily bread. We are tools and vassals of rich men behind the scenes. We are jumping jacks. They pull the string, we dance. Our talents, our possibilities, and our lives are the property of these men. We are, in short, intellectual prostitutes."

[4] See my article, "Have the Rich Influenced Christian Theology?," *Baptist Peacemaker*, 17:2, Summer 1997, 15.

[5] Canadian Centre for Policy Alternatives, *MONITOR*, July/August 1997, 11.

[6] I am indebted to Ann Hemingway of Grand Prairie, Alberta, for this succinct analysis.

[7] Jack Paar, *The Tonight Show*.
[8] C.B. Macpherson, *The Life and Times of Liberal Democracy*, Oxford University Press, 1977, 108.

Ken Ranney, a retired doctor of medicine, lives in Bowmanville, Ontario where he writes and teaches.

Part Four
Conclusion

The Madness in the Methods of the Common Sense Revolution by Ruth Cohen

This book has attempted to demonstrate that the whole intent, method and consequences of the so-called "Common Sense Revolution" are indicative of a pathological mindset on the part of the current government of Ontario. This is a mindset that must never again be allowed to gain ascendancy. Clearly the whole set of assumptions on which free market ideology is based are going nowhere, because there is no content whatsoever in the abstract concept of 'efficiency' in and of itself. To destroy entire cultures in the name of efficiency is a barbaric intrusion into civil society.

The Harris government is not so much a legitimate political party as it is a dangerous aggressor with the aim of destroying all existing institutions and forcing them into a corporate mould. But the ideology of the business cult must not be allowed to carry everything before it in the twenty-first century. Such an outcome would spell ultimate doom. It is imperative that the ideology of the business cult be clearly understood so that proper planning can begin to reclaim the wholeness and integrity of life on Earth for all people.

It will not be enough to bring about the substitution of one authoritarian regime by another. If we are ever to achieve our rights as citizens to live sane and healthy lives, we must break out of the integuments of the past and forge a new democracy. Because of the enormity of what the Harris regime has visited upon us, it is understandable that many would quail at the thought of resisting so ferocious an onslaught on all our former democratic institutions. There are even those who have given the government some credit as a harbinger of the inevitable.

The day will come when even those who voted this government in for a second term under the mistaken impression that it seemed a good 'manager' will finally understand what the ideology that drives it is all about. Once it becomes clear to these misguided voters that they chose the wrong track, there can be only one course to take, and that is to repudiate the Harris Tories as a force in Canadian politics.

But we must not only rid ourselves of the neo-con Tories who have devised for themselves an illegitimate majority, but we must insist that both remaining provincial political parties pledge to free us from the legislative noose the Tories have put around our necks. Otherwise we will eventually lapse into an acceptance of a third dictatorship that will destroy our health and well-being for generations to come. As this book goes to print, the Tories have introduced mandatory criminal background checks for all teachers in the province, and have been busy fending off allegations of selling public land for a pittance.

All of it must go, from the ominous Omnibus Bill to Bill 160 and beyond. The latest poll by Ipsos Reid released March 15, 2001 reveals that Tory support is now at 31%, the lowest level since the spring of 1995. We may yet see the finale to this occupation sooner rather than later. It will be difficult to reconstruct a province from the shards the Harris Tories have left us, but it must be done, even if it takes decades to accomplish.

Index

education, 69-70, 106-107, 150-152, 153-158, 166-169
Education Relations Commission, 166
Election Act, 22
Elections Canada, 21
Elections Ontario, 20, 21-22, 23
Elliot, Brenda, 58
employment equity, 101
Employment Standards Act. See Bill 49
Energy Act (Bill 35), 109
Enron Corporation, 117
environment, 97-98, 104, 123-129
Environmental Approvals Improvement Act. See Bill 57
Estes, Ralph, 211
Eves, Ernie, 63, 74, 78, 80, 81, 88-89, 91-94
Eyton, Trevor, 47

Family Support Plan, 107
Farkas, Gabriel, 128
Farlinger, Bill, 78
Forbes, Steve, 200
Ford, Henry, 182
Frank magazine, 59, 60, 67
Fraser Institute, 43, 45-49, 150, 159, 160
Freedman, Joe, 152
free market propaganda, 42-44
Friedman, Milton, 33, 34, 43, 185
Frum, David, 157
Fund, John, 48
fundraising, 18-19

Galbraith, John Kenneth, 181

George, Dudley, 54
George, Susan, 27-28
Gibson, William, 181
Giorno, Guy, 53-54, 60, 66, 67-71, 75, 79, 88-89
Glaxo-Wellcome, 72-73, 81
globalization, 173-175, 206-216
Godsoe, Peter, 81
Gordon, Robert, 80
Gramsci, Antonio, 27, 185
Greaves, Bill, 131
"green dowry," 188
Greenspan, Alan, 32
Greyhound bus lines, 72, 76-78
Grossman, Larry, 74
Guthrie, John, 79

Haire, Don, 77
Hammer, Michael, 159
Hampton, Howard, 163
Hargrove, Buzz, 84
Haugh, Gord, 112
Hawken, Paul, 210
Hayek, Friedrich von, 33-34, 56, 175, 185, 186
Health Canada, 126
health care, 47-48, 103-106
Health Services Restructuring Commission, 86, 104
hepatitis, 125
Herbert, Suzanne, 65
Heritage Foundation, 190
Highway 407, 72, 83, 84, 114
Hodgson, Chris, 120
Hogarth, Don, 60
Hotson, John, 45
Houtens, Stephen, 43-44

Walker, Sir David, 202
Walkerton, Ontario, 123-129
Wal-Mart, 101
Water and Sewage Services
    Improvement Act, 124
Waterloo Region, 117
water quality, 123-129
waterworks, privatization of,
    116-118, 125
Watt, Jamie, 53, 61
wealth, upward distribution,
    189-190
Weir, John, 66
welfare, 95, 107-108
Wheel-Trans, 109, 110
Wilson, Jim, 52, 112
Witmer, Elizabeth, 64, 66,
    102-103, 162
womens' shelters, 108
workers' compensation, 102
Workers Health and Safety
    Centre, 100
workfare, 82, 108, 110
Workplace Health and Safety
    Agency, 100
World Bank, 185, 189, 198
World Economic Forum, 206
World Trade Organization
    (WTO), 191, 193, 201, 211,
    215
World Wildlife Fund, 78-79
Worthington, Peter, 69
Wright, John, 113

Young, Bill, 53

THE
SYSTEM

Also by Terry Waghorn

Mission Possible (co-author)

THE
SYSTEM

A Story of Intrigue
and Market Domination

TERRY WAGHORN

With a Foreword and Afterword
by Ken Blanchard

PERSEUS
PUBLISHING

A Member of the Perseus Books Group

Cataloging-in-Publication Data is available from the Library of Congress
ISBN 0-7382-0791-8

Perseus Publishing is a member of the Perseus Books Group.

Find us on the World Wide Web at http://www.perseuspublishing.com.

Perseus Publishing books are available at special discounts for bulk purchases in the United States by corporations, institutions, and other organizations. For more information, please contact the Special Markets Department at the Perseus Books Group, 11 Cambridge Center, Cambridge, MA 02142, or call (617) 252-5298 or e-mail j.mccrary@perseusbooks.com.

Text design by *Brent Wilcox*
Set in 11.5-point Minion by the Perseus Books Group

First printing, October 2002

1 2 3 4 5 6 7 8 9 10—05 04 03 02

To my mother,
Margaret Waghorn, for giving me
the freedom to always be myself,
and to my father,
Gerald Waghorn, for instilling in me at an
early age that where there's a will, there's a way.

FOREWORD

I'VE KNOWN TERRY for almost ten years now, and throughout that period he's never ceased to amaze me in his ability to make gold from straw. As to how he's able to do it, much of that still remains a mystery to me, but what I do know is he's one of the few people I've met who has the uncanny ability to take in all of the noise, hype, and verbal diarrhea that floods our consciousness every day, and then somehow distill from all of that the few basic truths we all need to know. And that's precisely what he's done for you again in this book. After years of listening to the beats and rhythms of the marketplace, and siphoning through reams of data, he has put together what I would argue is his finest work to date. It's a strategy model that is as powerful as it is straightforward.

At its core are three basic concepts: (1) *Focus:* Market domination begins with the need to focus all of your energy and resources on one business and shed all others. And it shouldn't be just any old business, it should be the one in which you have or could have a unique advantage—something that customers value and competitors find difficult to copy. (2) *Fortify:* Choosing a unique position, however, is not enough to guarantee a sustainable competitive advantage. Eventually someone will find a way to imitate it. The challenge, therefore, is to make imitation as difficult as possible for them to do. In short, you need to fortify your position. And, (3) *Foster Futurity*: Regardless of how well you fortify your position, the reality is that eventually your more inspired rivals will find a way to penetrate your defenses. You need to be ready for that day when it arrives, so that when it does, your enemies will arrive only to find that you're no longer there—you've already moved on, leaving nothing but warm ashes in your wake. And the game of catch-up begins anew.

There you have it. If you want to kick the stuffing out of your competitors, or better yet, make them entirely irrelevant, then this is the model to apply. For the simple reason that it works, every time, regardless of setting or circumstance. The only caveats are that you have to follow it meticulously and religiously. You can't be selective in which bits you apply. It's got to be all or nothing, and then you've got to stick to it religiously, and not fall into the trap that awaits you.

The trap: Once you start dominating your market space, profits will follow, just as surely as night follows day. And therein lies the danger. How to invest your newfound wealth? The correct course of action is to use it to further fortify your position and to better prepare for the future; however, that's not what most people do. Most squander it by using it to invest in entirely new businesses, thereby weakening their focus and opening themselves up to entirely new competitive forces. Instead of fighting a single-front war, they suddenly find themselves having to fight on multiple fronts simultaneously. That's a situation few military leaders have ever escaped from.

As an example of this, I refer you to a fictitious company by the name of Quenetics, which you're soon to discover is the centerpiece of Terry's story. Before the story's protagonist—Timothy E. Hunt—enters the scene, Quenetics is in a number of different businesses, and isn't doing very well in any of them. Tim is quick to change that by getting its CEO—David Atkinson—to focus all of his energy on one business and one business only, the temp business. Then, in an effort to help David to differentiate and further fortify his business, Tim comes up with a business model the likes of which the market has never seen before, and one that is certain to be a 'killer app.' The only problem is that there are others who don't want to see that happen and will stop at nothing in their efforts to ensure that it doesn't.

Adding further depth and breadth to the story is the fact that, remaining true to character, Terry has sprinkled it with the latest thinking on many of the issues facing the business community today, issues such as knowledge management, corporate transparency, business performance measurement, human capital measurement, the electronic marketplace, and artificial intelligence. It all adds up to a fascinating read and one that is as entertaining as it is informative. So, sit back and relax, and prepare to begin what is arguably the best management novel ever written.

At least, I thought it was, and I'm quite sure you will too.

Ken Blanchard
Escondido, California

THE
SYSTEM

1

TIMOTHY E. HUNT TOOK a giant stride off the yacht and plunged into the tranquil and turquoise waters of the Caribbean, creating a vortex of rising bubbles. Slowly he descended into the deep, gliding through the brilliant stripes and swirls of a school of multicolored reef fish. His heart raced and his spirit soared. For Tim, few things compared to the joy and exhilaration of diving.

As he continued his descent, he suddenly noticed a green and yellow hawksbill turtle swimming just a few feet away. This could only be seen as a good omen, for the hawksbill, once abundant in these waters, was now an endangered species. So much so that even with over 500 dives to his credit, this was the first hawksbill he'd ever seen. He smiled inwardly and could only wonder what other surprises lay ahead.

Glancing over at his dive companion, David Atkinson, Tim pointed to the hawksbill, then, using his thumbs and index fingers to form a "W," signaled the "Wow" that screamed out in his

1

mind. David nodded in agreement, but didn't seem unduly impressed. Not surprising, as David was the type who was more interested in the large, predatory creatures at the top of the food chain than in those species further down. Tim was completely the opposite. He just loved the little stuff. He could spend an entire dive hovering around a single coral pillar, completely absorbed in the profusion of life and color surrounding it. David, on the other hand, would be bored in an instant.

Another difference between the two men was their respective attitude towards wreck diving. David relished it, Tim did not. As far as Tim was concerned, entering a gloomy, confined structure a hundred or more feet under water typically left him feeling highly claustrophobic. So, not surprisingly, he avoided them whenever possible. However, because of David's obsession for them, he all too often found himself swimming through them, struggling to keep his claustrophobia in check.

The two men had first met eight years earlier while diving off the coast of Cozumel. They had become friends instantly, probably because they had so much in common. They were both highly successful businessmen with a passion for life and the possibility to live it to the fullest.

Over the years they'd get together whenever they could to risk their necks doing one crazy stunt or another—climbing the Vermillion Cliffs in Arizona; para-skiing in Cameron Pass; white-water rafting down the Colorado River. Barbara—an ex-girlfriend of Tim's—used to insist that the two of them had a death wish, but that wasn't it at all. They just liked to feel alive.

This particular dive was David's idea. It was a wreck dive down to the *Wawinet*, a large schooner that had been purposely sunk off the coast of St. Lucia in the mid-1980s in order to create an artificial reef. The *Wawinet* had a reputation throughout the dive community of being one of the most challenging wreck dives in the Caribbean, which meant, of course, that it was something that they just had to do.

Their dive books told them that the wreck lay on its side at a depth of 132 feet, making this a relatively deep dive. That meant that if they wanted to spend much time inside it, they had to get down to it as quickly as possible. David, being the stronger swimmer, led the way.

Tim realized as he continued his descent that this dive was likely to be considerably more exciting than most. Not only were they diving deep, they were also diving in the crease where the cold waters of the Atlantic collided with the warm waters of the Caribbean, often creating rip currents of biblical proportions. And, as though that weren't already enough, there was the added challenge of getting to and from the wreck without getting lost, snagged, or eaten along the way. And then, of course, there was the wreck itself, which Tim still didn't know whether or not he'd enter. He'd decide that once he'd had a good look at it.

The deeper they went, the darker it got. The depth meter on Tim's dive computer indicated that they were nearing the hundred-foot mark, not surprising considering how often Tim had already had to "pop" his ears. Swimming only a few feet ahead, David suddenly pointed off to the right. Just beyond the range of visibility, Tim could barely make out the grayish-blue outline of the sunken vessel nestled against the seabed.

Yes! They'd found her! *And* in record time, which meant they'd have plenty of time to explore her. Better yet, conditions were near perfect. The visibility was good, and the current, though noticeable, was negligible. Tim had heard, however, that that could change in a heartbeat. Apparently, from one minute to the next, a light current could change into a raging torrent, sweeping everything in its path down to unimaginable depths— never to be seen again. Just the mere thought of it was enough to send a shudder rippling through his body. A moment later, the thought had passed, and his pulse quickly returned to normal. They'd be okay. They had Lady Luck on their side. He hoped.

·   ·   ·

With David in the lead, the two men moved alongside the wreck. She lay on her starboard side, her masts and part of her superstructure embedded deep in the soft cover of the ocean floor. She was big, over 300 feet long, and remarkably well pre- served considering the fact that she had spent the last few decades underwater. But it was as a fish magnet where she was most impressive. The resident marine life was both luxuriant and extremely diverse. The surrounding waters were literally teeming with fish, and much of the structure was covered with corals in excellent condition, with broad expanses of staghorn and table corals, plate and lettuce corals, boulder and brain corals, interspersed with large gorgonian sea fans and large barrel sponges. It was a veritable coral garden. It was also sen- sory overkill. But he loved it. As he tried to take it all in, he was reminded yet again why he was so addicted to diving. Here he was floating effortlessly through a kaleidoscope of shapes and colors, hearing nothing but the sound of his own breathing. This is what life was all about.

The two men circumnavigated the vessel, examining every opening, every gouge, every dent in the hull, touching every texture of the metal and steel construction, imagining countless scenes on every part of the now-flooded deck. Then, having covered the ship's outer shell, David indicated that he wanted to go inside. Before Tim could even respond, David swam off in the direction of an open hatch a few yards away. Tim followed reluctantly behind, having already decided that he wasn't going to go in. There was no reason to. With so much yet to see on deck, and with so little time to do so, it made no sense to waste any of it swimming around the darkened, vacuous interior. At least, that was his take on the situation, and as David had already agreed to abide by whatever decision he made, he knew he wouldn't have any problems convincing David not to go inside.

Or at least so he thought, until he suddenly saw David grab the coaming of the open hatch and launch himself through it.

"What the hell is he doing?" Tim wondered. What's this all about? But before he could find out, David had disappeared from sight.

Reaching the hatch a few moments later, Tim grabbed onto the coaming and peered cautiously inside. He could see David, a black silhouette against a charcoal background, swimming away. His flashlight was on, and apparently, his mind was made up. He was going in, with or without Tim at his side.

Tim was utterly dumbfounded. Never before had his friend behaved so strangely. Something was wrong, not as it should be! But what, and how to find out? He had absolutely no interest in going inside. But what else could he do? He couldn't just let David go it alone, for that would mean breaking the cardinal rule of diving—the buddy rule, which stated that a diver should never dive alone. Ever. Not even for a minute or two. There were just too many things that could go wrong. "*But, explain that to David,*" Tim thought to himself, for it was David, and not he who was at fault here.

Tim's face flushed crimson as his temper flared. But, realizing that getting angry wasn't going to resolve anything, he took a series of deep breaths in an effort to calm himself down. Then, while staring into the abyss, a black so complete that it was without dimension, he tried to find the courage to dive in. His heart rate and breathing accelerated immediately, just at the mere thought of it. No, it was clear. He couldn't do it! Not this time. Not at this depth, and especially not with David behaving as he was. It was much too risky. If his claustrophobia were to kick in, which was likely, it was possible that he'd have no one there to help him overcome it. So, no, that was a risk he was just not prepared to take.

Having made his decision, Tim released his grip on the coaming and let the current carry him away. Glancing back at the hatch one last time, he could only hope that David would soon come to his senses and return to his side. In the meantime, he'd try to focus on his surroundings rather than to think too much about it.

With the current quickly propelling him toward the stern of the ship, Tim watched in awe as a school of emperor angelfish swam in formation overhead. Clouds of tropical fish surrounded him, their movements so perfectly coordinated and unified that they gave the impression of being a single, graceful entity moving gently across his path. A small school of surgeonfish darted to his left, fusiliers flitted to his right, a solitary giant barracuda drifted overhead, and everywhere he looked, shoals of jacks and trevallies could be seen hanging in the open water. He took a deep breath and tried to relax. But it didn't help. None of it did. He just couldn't take his mind off David.

Time seemed to telescope, slowing almost to a halt, while the tension built until finally Tim decided he could suppress it no longer. David was still nowhere to be seen, and yet time was running out. A quick glance at his dive computer confirmed what he already knew: they had less than twenty minutes left before they'd have to begin their ascent, if they wanted to make the necessary safety stops along the way.

Feeling a mild sense of panic rush over him, he decided to return to the hatch for one final look around. If David was there, then the two of them could go up together. If not, well . . . *"Well what? Leave him to die? Not possible! But, then again, if trying to find him means possibly killing yourself, then . . . "* He couldn't finish his thought. He didn't want to. Instead, he let go of the railing he'd been holding on to, only to be suddenly pummeled over the side of the ship. The strength of the current had increased—*considerably!*

Fighting its force, he slowly made his way back to the railing and latched on as he tried to catch his breath and flush the terror from his mind. But that was not easily achieved, as he had no idea as to what he was now up against. He could only assume that conditions were likely to get worse before they got better. Not a comforting thought. Now, more than ever, he wished David were at his side. This was something he didn't want to deal with on his own. Suddenly the thought of going inside the wreck didn't seem like such a bad idea after all. At least it would protect him from the force of the current.

With that thought in mind, he started moving along the rail in the direction of the hatch. A few agonizing and thoroughly exhausting minutes later he made it. Then, grasping the coaming with whatever strength he still had left, he willed himself to stick his head inside. Holding his breath, he peered into the stygian blackness.

Nothing! David wasn't there!

Cursing to himself, he pulled himself completely inside. As the adrenaline ebbed, worry and concern gave way to a sense of profound depletion. He badly needed to rest. He needed to refuel, to take stock, to assess his options. *What options?* He didn't have any options. With the current continuing to intensify, he had no options. He'd have to stay inside and wait it out, and hope like hell that the current ran out of steam before he ran out of air! In the meantime, he'd poke around a bit to see if he could find David.

But, before he could even get started, he suddenly felt his head whirl and his stomach knot. For a brief moment, he became light-headed and slightly nauseous. Dizziness stung him. He immediately began to hyperventilate, and for a moment, he felt like he might pass out. Then, just as suddenly, the symptoms passed, and things returned to normal.

Now what was that all about? Was it a claustrophobia-induced attack? No, it couldn't be. He hadn't gone anywhere yet!

Well, if it wasn't claustrophobia, then what else could it be? Maybe he was low on air? No, a quick check of his air gauge told him that he still had plenty of air. So, it had to have been something else. *But what?* He had no idea, nor was this the time to think about it. *Probably just a bad case of nerves,* he decided, and then pumped his fins as he started moving deeper into the ship's interior.

· · ·

Biting hard on his mouthpiece, Tim swam from one compartment to the next, slipping along narrow gangways, slithering through bulkheads, claustrophobia clutching hard at his throat and chest. He needed all his willpower to keep from turning around and trying to find his way back out. But each time, just when he thought he could stand it no longer, he dug deep within himself, and somehow always found the courage to go on.

After almost a full five minutes inside the wreck, Tim was almost a wreck himself. His nerves were frazzled; his breathing labored, and he felt a headache coming on. The tension was starting to get to him. But he couldn't give up. Not yet. He was resolved to keep going for three more minutes. Any longer than that, and he'd be putting his own life at risk.

Knowing that David typically liked spending some time on the bridge, Tim continued moving forwards and upwards, all the while hoping that when the time came, he'd somehow be able to retrace his steps. How, he had no idea. But he didn't want to think about that now. It would only add to his worries—and he already had enough of those.

As he passed from one chamber into another, his heart suddenly skipped a beat. Unless his eyes had deceived him, he could have sworn he'd just seen a flicker of light somewhere ahead. His spirit soared. Kicking furiously, he quickly exited the room he was in and entered another. As he did so, he saw a second flicker of light—this one much brighter than the last. It appeared to be coming from the next room. Galvanized by a fresh surge of adrenaline, he swam for the doorway as quickly as he could. Surging through it, he was met with a sight he'd remember forever. There was David, standing in front of the ship's helm, the wooden-spoke wheel in one hand, his flashlight in the other. It appeared as though he was trying to steer the ship. Not a good sign.

As he swam closer to his friend, Tim's spirit sagged further. It was clear that David was suffering from something. He had the crazed look of a madman. His eyes were wide and wild, seemingly incapable of focusing on anything, not even on Tim who by this point had moved to within a foot of David's face. Tim tapped softly on the front of David's mask, hoping that might help. It did, but the effect was only temporarily. Within seconds, David's eyes had again returned to their drunken drift. Tim shook his head in defeat. David was completely gone.

Tim's mind slipped into overdrive. *"What could possibly be wrong with him?"* he wondered. Because of the depth they were at, nitrogen narcosis was the first thing that came to mind, but then again, they'd gone considerably deeper than they were now on numerous occasions and yet nothing like this had ever happened before. So that probably wasn't it. Which meant that it had to be something else. *But what else could it be?* There was only one other thing that he could think of—maybe he was suffering from contaminated air.

But how was that possible in this day and age, he asked himself. His mind drifted back to the dive shop where they'd filled up their tanks the day before. Had anything seemed out of the ordinary? *"No! Stop this!"* he screamed inwardly. He didn't have time for this. All that mattered now was their immediate survival! He somehow had to get them out of the wreck and back to the surface before their air supply ran out. Otherwise, they would die. It was as simple as that.

What to do? Tim thought for a moment, and then tapped again on David's mask, this time with considerably more force. Not that it seemed to make any difference. For, once again, David's eyes focused in on Tim's but only for a second or two before returning to their drunken drift.

Trying hard to contain his growing fear and frustration, Tim reached for David's dive computer to take a reading. To his amazement, he saw that his friend still had over a third of his tank left. The only problem was that it appeared to be contaminated air. But, reasoning that contaminated air was better than none at all, Tim took that as a point in their favor.

Tim then tried signaling to David that they were in danger and that he was low on air. But, not surprisingly, David showed no signs of comprehension whatsoever. All he seemed interested in was navigating the ship. Nothing else seemed to matter. He was no longer connected to the real world. His world was now only that which existed in his mind.

With his head now throbbing with pain and pulse again quickening, Tim struggled to keep his wits about him, but he knew that it was getting harder by the second. If he was going to do something, he had to do it quickly before he too lost it completely.

And then, just to accentuate the point, Tim was suddenly assaulted by another attack of nausea, this one much worse than the last. Temporarily dazed and disoriented, he had to fight to keep his breathing and emotions in check. Then slowly, ever so slowly, things started to return to normal. As they did, it suddenly dawned on him that maybe he too was inhaling contaminated air. That would explain the attacks he was having, but it wouldn't explain why he was still in much better shape than David was in. The only explanation had to be that, for some reason, the mixture he was breathing was not as toxic as what David was breathing.

Possibly. It all made sense, except for one thing: Where did the contaminated air come from? In all his years of diving, he'd never heard of a single case of contaminated air, and yet here were the two of them, apparently both suffering from it. *"What were the odds on that?"* he wondered. There were no odds. It was all but impossible, unless, of course, it hadn't happened by chance. Sure, anything was possible. But if it hadn't happened by chance, then that could mean only one thing: someone wanted one or both of them dead!

A shiver ran down his spine as his mind filled with questions. Who? Why? How? Feeling slightly overwhelmed by it all, he shook his head in an effort to clear it. He had to stay focused on the task at hand. Survival was their first and only priority. Everything else could wait.

Rechecking his air gauge, he saw that he was now down to fifty pounds per square inch (psi), which meant that at this depth, he only had ten minutes or so of air left. Shuddering involuntarily, Tim realized he didn't have a moment to waste. He had to move quickly—with or without David at his side.

Before setting out, however, he decided to give David one last chance. He grasped his backup respirator in his right hand, while using his left hand to take hold of David's mouthpiece. Then, in one fluid motion, he substituted one for the other, and instructed David to take a few deep breaths. Surprisingly, David did as he was told. A minute later, Tim reversed the exchange, and then grabbing David by his vest, yanked him away from the wheel. Again, surprisingly, David didn't resist. *"Oh, Thank God!"* Tim screamed to himself as he pulled his friend towards the door. They were on their way.

The next challenge was to find their way out of the murky labyrinth. Hastily moving along the narrow passageways, Tim fought back nausea and claustrophobia as he struggled to retrace his path back to the mid-ship hatch, all the while pulling David along with him.

Tim slowed his pace somewhat, taking a moment to recheck his air gauge. He was now down to twenty-five pounds per square inch, which meant that within a few minutes he'd be sucking fumes—while still more than 130 feet down! What a terrifying thought, which was quickly followed up by an almost equally terrifying thought—the thought of having to share air with David. Tim shuddered yet again. No, the best thing to do was to focus on the here and now, and not on what might happen next. He'd just have to take things as they came.

A few moments later, the two men swam into a large compartment faintly lit by a shaft of light from a porthole. It somehow looked vaguely familiar, which could only mean one thing—he'd been here before. Great, they appeared to be heading in the right direction.

Sure enough, less than a minute later, they swam through a bulkhead and reemerged in the compartment under the hatch. Tim breathed a huge sigh of relief. They might still have a chance after all.

It was now all down to the strength of the current. If it was stronger than ever, they were as good as dead. If it had weakened, they had a chance.

And there was only one way to find out. With his arms at his sides and kicking hard, Tim went shooting up through the hatch. To his utter astonishment, David followed close behind. Would wonders never cease!

Before he could even finish that thought, however, renewed spasms of dizziness and nausea assailed his system. Reeling from the effects, he rose slightly in the water, and was immediately captured by the current.

Spinning uncontrollably backwards, he was temporarily frozen. Paralyzed by fear. Until some primitive signal of self-preservation emerged from deep within his hindbrain, propelling him to act.

Flattening himself out, he quickly regained some control over his body. Then, turning to face the current head-on, he suddenly saw David's flailing body hurtling towards him. With no time to think, his reflexes took over. Moving fast and frantically, he quickly angled himself upwards and braced for impact. Two seconds later, the bottom of David's tank hit him full in the chest, knocking the wind out of him. Recovering quickly, he grabbed David's vest and then twisted their bodies around so that they were again facing one another. Then, locking arms and drawing on hidden reserves, Tim kicked hard and didn't stop.

A short time later, and almost numb from exhaustion, Tim glanced down at his dive computer to take a reading. His eyes went wide and his heart skipped a beat. The depth gauge read 94 feet! They were actually going up. *Unbelievable!* Tim breathed a quick sigh of relief. Or more to the point, he tried to breathe a quick sigh of relief. The only problem was, there was nothing left to breathe in. He'd run out of air. His tank was empty! Which meant that he'd now have to share air with David. Bad news, but what else could he do?

Without giving it another thought, he reached over and grabbed David's spare regulator and then quickly exchanged it for his own. Then, continuing their ascent, Tim drew some encouragement from the fact that the current seemed to be weakening the higher they went. But even so, it was still a force to contend with, and tired as he was, he wasn't sure how much longer he'd be able to go before his legs gave out on him completely. For, at this point, he was so now exhausted that he could barely even kick his fins, let alone kick them with much force. He was *so* tired. So very, very tired. If only he could rest for just a few seconds. Nothing more. Just a few seconds, then everything would be all right.

Oh no! he thought. *Must hurry.* David's contaminated air was already starting to poison his mind. He had to breathe less, and kick harder. Otherwise, they'd never make it.

They ascended another ten feet or so before disaster struck again. But this time, with a vengeance. Just as his depth meter was rising above the fifty-foot mark, Tim watched David's eyes close and not reopen. A moment later, David's body went limp, and his head slumped to his chest. He had lost consciousness.

2

A SHAFT OF DIVINE SUNLIGHT peeked through the blinds covering the narrow window of David's hospital room and settled like a white dove on his head. Sitting quietly in a rattan chair by the window, a rather disheveled Tim watched over him as he slept. Not having had much sleep himself the night before, Tim had to work to keep his eyes open. The latest issue of *Time*, bought just a few hours before in the hospital's gift shop, lay open on his lap. But, tired as he was, he just couldn't find the energy to read it. Instead, he spent most of his time just sitting and staring at the walls through half-open eyes.

David also hadn't slept very well. It seemed that every time he'd tried, a nurse would suddenly appear at the side of his bed with either a pill or a needle in her hand. And, oh, how he hated getting needles. Just the mere thought of getting one was enough to keep him awake for hours. Making matters worse, on those few occasions when he had finally nodded off, he'd invariably return to a recurring nightmare. In it, he'd be tumbling in an aquatic freefall into the inky depths of the ocean in full scuba gear. A powerful current would grab him and toss him about like a leaf in a hurricane. In the process, his mask would be torn from his face, his wetsuit shredded, and his air hose severed. Then suddenly, he'd be driven into the seabed, where schools of tiny fish would cluster around him and start nibbling at his face. Not surprisingly, he'd wake up screaming in terror.

This time however, he awoke from what had been a relatively peaceful sleep. Stretching as he yawned, he seemed to sense that he was not alone. Rubbing the sleep from his eyes, he looked over to see Tim seated nearby.

Seeing his friend looking his way, Tim smiled warmly. "Welcome back to the land of the living."

David coughed a few times in an effort to clear his throat. "It's good to be back." Short pause as he lifted his head from the pillow and took in his surroundings. "How long have I been gone?"

"About two days now." The answer came from the other side of the room.

David turned his head in the direction of the unfamiliar voice to see a tall, muscular black man enter the room, closing the door behind him. He strode across the room with the energy of an untamed stallion, taking up position at the end of the bed. Like the voice, the face was unknown to him. "I'm sorry, what did you say?" David asked.

When the stranger spoke, his voice was quick and self-assured. "What I said was that you've been out of it for almost two days now." Shaking his head, he added, "But it could have been worse—much worse. In fact, to be perfectly frank, based on what I've heard you're lucky to even be alive. Had it not been for Tim's courage and tenacity, you wouldn't be here at the moment. You'd still be down there giving guided ghost-tours of the *Wawinet*."

Before David could respond to that, the man asked, "Can you remember much of what happened?"

David fought to clear his mind, his thoughts still blurred, his memory vacant. "Not much, I'm afraid, no. I remember entering the water and starting my descent, but that's about it."

"You don't remember entering the wreck?" Tim asked, trying hard to stifle his astonishment.

David paused as he wracked his brain. "Afraid not. Why? Did I go in?"

"Oh, yeah!" Tim retorted. "And apparently you liked it so much, you decided to stay. Leaving me no choice but to go in after you and haul your ass back out again, which was no cakewalk, let me tell you. Especially with me being as claustrophobic as I am." He appeared to be looking right through David and into his own past. Then, shuddering at the memory, he said, "But hey, that's another story for another day. For the time being, all you should be concerned about is getting well."

"Any idea as to what's wrong with me?"

Tim left his chair, walked over to the bed, and placed a reassuring hand on David's shoulder. "That's a question I've been trying to answer for years now," he replied wryly. "But with respect to why you're in here now, all I've been told is that apparently they can't find anything wrong with you at all."

"Then why am I here?" David's furtive gaze made a quick sweep of the room. "And why am I wearing this?" He asked while pulling on his hospital smock.

"The doctor wants to keep you in here for another day in order to run a few more tests. Apparently it's nothing to worry about. It's just routine stuff." Tim said gently.

David forced a smile, but it failed to reach his eyes. A thought suddenly occurred to him. "How about Kim? Does she know about any of this?"

"Yes, I've spoken to her a lot over the last forty-eight hours. The last time was only about an hour ago, so yeah, she's completely up to speed," Tim replied. "Which means that she also knows that there's nothing to worry about and that Allan and I are here to ensure that it stays that way."

David raised his head a second time. "Allan?"

Tim spoke before Allan could. "Yeah, sorry about that. I should have made the introductions earlier, but hey, you know me, I'm more socially-challenged than most." He flashed a quick smile, and then said, "David, meet Allan Taylor. Allan, meet a friend and fellow adventurer, David Atkinson."

The two men nodded curtly as they shook hands.

Allan spoke first. "It's good to finally get a chance to meet you, David. I've heard so much about you over the years that I feel as though I know you already."

Feeling somewhat uncomfortable accepting adulation from a complete stranger, David said, "I'm happy to hear that, but I'm afraid you've got me at a bit of a disadvantage because I haven't a clue who you are nor do I have any idea as to why you're here."

Tim was quick to cut in. "It's probably best that I explain all of that. To begin with, Allan has been handling all of my security needs for what, at least seven years now I think." He paused to give Allan a chance to respond. Allan simply nodded and then waited for Tim to continue. "And let me tell you, he's great at what he does. Which is not surprising considering his past. He's a former member of Delta Force, which, as you probably know, is one of the toughest and most respected elite special-forces commando units in the world. From there, he moved on to do a stint with the CIA before ultimately deciding to move out west and to go into business for himself. He and his family now live just a few miles away from where I have my beach house in Laguna, California. And he's now got a thriving little business going called Castlerock Security Inc., which specializes in all aspects of the security business." Glancing over at Allan, Tim asked, "Did I leave anything out?"

David answered before Allan could. "Yeah, one rather important detail—like what's he doing here in my hospital room?"

Tim's voice took on a more serious tone. "He's here because I've invited him here. And the reason for that is the highly questionable circumstances surrounding this little 'accident' of ours."

David started to say one thing, and then suddenly switched to something else. "Before asking you to explain whatever the hell it is you just said, let me first ask where it is you're referring to when you say 'here.' Where are we?"

"We're in the hospital run by the British Defense Forces stationed here on Barbados. We were airlifted in from St. Lucia two days ago, as they have the only decompression chamber in the area—which was something that we were both in dire need of by the time we finally surfaced from the wreck."

David frowned as he registered this latest bit of information. "We were *both* in need of?"

Tim nodded. "Yes, both of us. You passed out at about fifty feet, which meant that I had to get you to the surface as quickly as possible. So decompression and safety stops were completely out of the question. Not that they would have been possible anyway as both of us were pretty much out of air by that point. But, what the hell, as Allan just finished saying, things could have been worse."

"How so?" David asked simply.

"Well, for starters, both of us could just as easily have died," Tim replied, with the appropriate level of gravitas. He paused as he thought about how best to explain that. "Both of our tanks were filled with contaminated air, yours, for some reason, more so than mine."

The blood drained from David's face. "Contaminated air! You mean we've both suffered carbon monoxide poisoning?"

Tim nodded.

David stammered and stuttered for a few moments as contradictory thoughts swirled around in his brain, warring with one another until finally he said, "But how's that possible? I thought carbon monoxide poisoning was a thing of the past?"

Allan reentered the conversation. "It is, which is why I'm here. This whole thing may not have been an accident."

"What the hell are you saying?" David snapped.

"I'm saying that both of you went diving with rented tanks and almost died as a consequence. I don't know about you, but that's enough to make me suspicious."

With considerable effort, David sat up in bed, shifting his body so he could lean against the headboard. Though he chose his words carefully, he made no attempt to hide his contempt. "This is utter insanity! Apparently, I was accidentally given some contaminated air. Not a good thing, but, hey, these things can happen. Now, how you can take that and twist it into some sort of conspiracy theory is utterly beyond my comprehension."

With the tension between the two men quickly building, Tim thought it best to intervene. "The problem, David, is that, as you just finished saying, carbon monoxide poisoning in diving is a thing of the past, yet *both* of us were given tanks full of contaminated air. Doesn't that strike you as rather odd?" Not waiting for an answer, he added, "And, what's more, we've had the other tanks on board the boat tested as well, and guess what? They were also filled with contaminated air!" He let his words sink in before continuing. "Now, I don't know what that tells you, but what it tells me is that there's definitely something going on here. And to be honest with you, whatever it is, it's scaring the hell out of me. If I didn't know any better, I'd be tempted to think that there's someone out there who wants one or both of us dead."

David's jaw dropped and his shoulders sagged. "All the tanks were contaminated?"

Tim nodded. "Every single one of them. Sort of makes you wonder, doesn't it? And if so, then maybe you can now understand why I've asked Allan to investigate."

"But if all the tanks were affected, then what makes you think that it was me they were after, and not you?"

"Because, believe it or not, for the past forty-eight hours that's all I've thought about, and yet in all that time, I haven't been able to come up with a single name of someone who I thought was capable of doing something like this. Not one." Significant pause. "But, in your case, however, I would think it would be a very different story."

David snorted. "Oh, you would, would you! And what's that supposed to mean? Are you suggesting you know something I don't?" It was more a challenge than a question.

Tim shrugged. "I only know what I've been told—by you!" Uncomfortable pause. "Like some of the things you've told me about your sister."

"Shannon? Are you nuts?" David looked as though he couldn't decide whether to laugh or cry. "This discussion is getting sillier by the second." Deep sigh. "Granted, she and I give new meaning to the expression 'sibling rivalry,' but that hardly qualifies her as a possible murder suspect."

This time it was Allan's turn to play the role of mediator. "We're not suggesting it does, but on the other hand, it's still early days yet, so I wouldn't want to rule anything out. I'm sure you can understand that."

David shot him a sharp look but said nothing.

"So, with that in mind, I'd greatly appreciate it if you'd tell me more about this sister of yours and the kind of relationship that the two of you have," Allan asked.

"That's none of your bloody business," David objected. "Shannon isn't a suspect nor is our relationship up for discussion, and that's all there is to it. Period!"

Allan persisted. "Maybe she didn't do this herself, but instead, paid someone else to do it for her."

That was the final straw. David finally lost his temper. "What the hell's going on here, Tim? You bring in some guy I've never met before, and then the two of you try to outdo each other at pissing me off. How much more of this do you expect me to take?"

"I can understand your frustration," Tim said softly, "but I'm afraid this is something we can't just brush under the carpet and forget about. It would appear that someone's out to kill you—or possibly me—so for both our sakes, we need to get to the root of this thing as quickly as possible. Because who's to say we'll be quite so lucky next time. So, come on buddy, let's just do this thing and get it over with." Then, in a gentler voice, he added, "All right?"

David took a deep breath in an attempt to calm himself down, then, turning to Allan, he said, "I don't know why you don't believe me in this, but the truth of the matter is, I have absolutely *nothing* to tell you. Shannon and I don't like each other. That's it. That's the full story."

Tim argued, "That's not true, and you know it. For example, how about that little episode that took place up at your cottage about a month ago? Why don't you tell him about that?"

David fell silent for a moment. Then, after throwing Tim a dirty look, he said, "I have no idea what Tim's been telling you, but—"

"Not much at all," Allan replied. "All he told me was that something . . ." short pause, "*odd* happened recently up at your cottage. And that's about it. So, if you could expand on that a bit, I'd appreciate it."

With a deep sigh, David capitulated. "This is utter silliness, but sure, whatever. If it'll make the two of you happy, I'll play along. But, before I do, let me first give you a bit of background."

"I'd appreciate that," Allan said.

"Shannon and I are co-owners of a company called Quenetics, which was started by my grandfather a few years before the outbreak of the First World War. Initially, the company was involved in retail, but has since diversified into real estate and the temporary employment business. When my grandfather died, he passed the company on to my father, Charles, his only son. My father, in turn, passed it on to the two of us—with some strings attached. For example, we were each given 30 percent of the equity—"

"And the other 40 percent?"

"Is publicly traded, yet, having said that, because of the stock's popularity, the vast majority of it has been acquired by a handful of large institutional investors and pension fund managers over the years who don't seem all that keen to sell it."

As soon as David finished, Allan said, "Sorry for interrupting. Before I did, you were saying something about the strings your father attached to your inheritance."

"Oh, yeah. The strings. There were three. The first was that I was to lead the company, and not Shannon. Which made sense, considering the fact that Shannon—a product of my father's second marriage—being thirteen years younger than me, was only twenty-three at the time, and was still in college."

"And when was that?"

David closed his eyes for a contemplative moment. "He died six years and seven months ago, almost to the day."

Allan responded to the undertone of anguish in David's voice by softening his own. "And the second condition?"

"Neither of us could sell any of our shares until we'd reached the age of thirty—don't ask me where he came up with that number because I haven't a clue. But that was my dad for you; he had a mind few could understand—myself included. He was a very complex man. But forgive me, I'm digressing. What was I talking about, oh yeah, we couldn't sell until we were thirty. Obviously, it wasn't a big deal for me as I was already thirty-six when he died. But for Shannon, it's been a different story. She has never been allowed to sell, and still can't, and it's killing her, because it's the one thing she probably wants most at the moment."

"Why's that?" Allan asked.

"Because for the past four months now our share price has fallen dramatically, with no end in sight. So, as you can imagine, she's growing ever more anxious to sell, and thus, is very much looking forward to the twenty-ninth of May."

"Why, what happens then?"

"That's when she turns thirty."

"And what do you think she'll do then?"

"She'll sell immediately. I'm sure of it. Family heritage or not. It doesn't matter to her. All she cares about is wealth and status. Nothing else is of any import."

"But, won't she have a difficult time finding a buyer, in light of what you just finished saying about the current downward pressure on your stock?"

David's response was immediate and laden with contempt. "Are you kidding? You don't know Shannon! She's already found a buyer: Roger Miller, the chairman and CEO of eMaxx—Quenetics' main rival."

Allan digested this and then redirected. "OK, different question. Is there anything that might prevent her from selling?"

David hesitated before answering, as though unsure of what answer to give. "Yes, there is. It's the third condition my father attached to our inheritance. He stipulated that neither of us could sell to a third party without the prior written consent of the other."

Allan looked puzzled. "So what's the problem, then? In order for her to sell, she needs something you're not prepared to give her. So, there's nothing—"

David talked over his words, "True, but if she were somehow able to buy up the other 40 percent, she'd then have 70 percent, and thus, effective control. At which point, the first thing she'd do would be to ask for my resignation. And then once she had that, she'd no longer have any interest in selling. Because as far as she's concerned, I'm the sole reason for the fall in our share price. She thinks the market has lost faith in my leadership capabilities. But, if she were running the show, she assumes that it'd be a different story entirely. It doesn't make any sense, but then again, that's Shannon for you. She rarely makes any sense."

With so many different strands to pick up on, Allan paused for a moment to think about where he wanted to go next. "Go back to what you said about her buying up the other 40 percent. Is that something that she's actually capable of doing— i.e., does she have the money to make it happen?"

David shrugged. "Not personally, but that doesn't mean anything. She's a very resourceful woman. When she wants something, she always finds a way to get it."

Tim cut in. "But, if it's so easy to do, then why haven't you beaten her to the punch and bought *her* out? That way, everybody's happy . . . you retain control and she gets to cash out."

David's voice was inert. "In an ideal world, that's precisely what I would have done. But, because this is anything but an ideal world, I haven't been able to raise the funds necessary to make it happen. And, with my stock in the proverbial toilet, I can't see that situation changing any time soon."

"But if *you're* not able to raise the money, what makes you think she can?" Allan asked.

David flashed a bitter grin. "Because she's not constrained by the same moral, legal, and ethical constraints that I am. That's why. It's as simple as that."

Sensing that it was best to leave that alone for the time being, Allan redirected. "So, let me see if I've got this straight. Shannon sees her net worth going south, and she's understandably anxious to stop the pain. She sees there being only two possible remedies for this: *either* get rid of you and then try to turn things around, *or* sell out as quickly as possible, thereby limiting her losses. Does that about sum it up?"

David flared, flushing crimson, but said nothing.

Allan pressed on. "But you won't let her do either. So, what does she do? The way I see it, her options are limited. She can keep pleading with you to *either* step aside or let her sell, knowing that you'll never agree to do either, *or* she can pay someone to get rid of you in the hope that the board would then ask her to replace you. *Tough choice!* Take the high road, knowing it's going nowhere, or take the low road, and get everything you want."

David couldn't argue with the man's logic, nor did he have the energy to. Instead, dropping his head, he let out a gusty, melancholy sigh, and slowly closed his eyes. He was tiring quickly of this discussion.

Tim and Allan waited in silence.

When David finally spoke, his voice betrayed his exhaustion. "Tell you what, why don't we simply agree to disagree and leave it at that?"

Tim reentered the dialogue. "Because I'm afraid we *can't* leave it at that, David. Our lives are possibly at stake here, so I am afraid we're going to have to resolve this one way or another."

David made no effort to hide his irritation. "Come on Tim, we're talking about my *sister* here. You know as well as I do that she's not capable of—"

Tim interrupted. "Neither of us is suggesting anything at this point. All we're saying is that we have to follow every lead to see where it takes us. And, one of those leads just happens to be Shannon. It's as simple as that."

David, not wanting to argue with his friend, held his hands up defensively, like a parent fending off an overenthusiastic child. Then, after a few more moments of silence, he said, "OK, the cottage incident. What can I tell you? About six weeks ago, Shannon and I met at my home to discuss the future direction of our company. Initially, things went moderately well. For the first time in," short pause as he quickly scrolled though his memory banks, "I don't know, probably at least a year, we actually tried listening to one another. It was great . . . while it lasted. Which regrettably, wasn't for long. In less than an hour things turned ugly, and I mean *really* ugly. She just went completely weird. She started yelling and screaming, and at one point, she actually looked as though she was going to take a swing at me." He shook his head as the memory of it filled his mind. "Thankfully, she didn't, but let me tell you, I've never seen such hatred in her eyes."

"And then what happened?" Allan asked.

David stared off into space for a few moments. When he spoke, his voice was barely audible. "She stormed out of the house screaming that she wished I were dead."

Allan grunted while shaking his head in mock disgust. "Now there's something you don't hear every day. Or, at least, not in my household. I hear a lot of other things, but never death-threats."

David ignored the remark. "Anyway, about two weeks later, I decided I needed some time alone, so I headed up to our family's cottage on Squam Lake. But, since it too is something I share with Shannon, I'd phoned her a few days before, told her of my plans, and then asked that she keep her distance. She agreed, and then hung up on me. And that was the last time we spoke to each other before I headed up to the lake."

Allan eyed him closely. "And then?"

"Come Friday, I decided around lunchtime that I'd try to beat the rush-hour traffic by leaving early—around two, rather than at the end of the day, as I had originally planned. So, telling no one except my secretary and my wife, I slipped out around 2:30, and got to the lake around six. But, as I pulled into the driveway, I was surprised to see that Shannon had left just a short time before."

Allan's brows plunged together. "And how did you know that?"

"It was rather simple, really. It had rained all morning and for much of the afternoon, yet there were fresh tire tracks in the driveway, which could only mean one thing: she had to have been and left since the rain had stopped."

"But how did you know that it was her and not somebody else?"

"I know her tire treads. They have a very distinctive pattern to them which are as recognizable as they are uncommon."

"I'm impressed, David. Or maybe we should start calling you Sherlock," Allan said wryly.

David's response to that was no response at all. He just kept going as though nothing had been said. "Anyway, not thinking any more of it, I got out of the car, grabbed a few things out of the trunk, and went inside. But as soon as I entered, I smelled gas—propane. I immediately dropped what I was carrying and ran into the kitchen to see if I could find out where it was coming from. As I'd suspected, I found one of the elements on the gas range in the open position but without flame. As a result, the place was quickly filling up with gas, which meant that the kitchen had basically become a time bomb, and there I was standing in the middle of it, just waiting for it to go off." His Adam's apple bobbed up and down as he swallowed hard. "They were rather tense moments, let me tell ya. Made all the more tense upon the realization that had I entered later in the evening, as I'd originally planned, I'd have vaporized myself, and the cottage, the moment I'd turned on a light." A shiver suddenly rippled through his body.

Allan leaned forward and asked, "And what do you make of that?"

David lowered his eyes and said nothing.

Allan's question was followed by a period of awkward silence. Then, feeling a degree of sympathy for David, Allan added, "Just to be clear on this, David, what you've just told me doesn't change anything. I'm sticking to what I said earlier. I'm not jumping to any conclusions here. Shannon is a suspect, nothing more. And I'm sure she won't be the only one we investigate before this whole thing is over. But, in the meantime, I guess it goes without saying that you might want to be extra cautious in your dealings with her until you hear me suggest otherwise."

David shrugged as if to say, "Yeah, whatever."

Sensing that that was his cue to wrap things up, Allan turned to Tim and said, "I'm flying down to St. Lucia later this morning to see what else I can dig up. But I'll be back here by this time tomorrow. In plenty of time to escort the two of you back to the States." With that, he shook their hands and then strode quickly out of the room.

Tim moved closer to David's bedside. They looked at each other for a long moment, but with neither able to think of anything to say, David turned away and stared out the open door. "I think I should also get going," Tim said. "I've got a lot to do if we're hoping to get out of here tomorrow. But don't worry, I'll check in on you again later this afternoon."

With his eyes focused on some imaginary spot out in the hallway, David mused aloud, "It really is true, isn't it?"

"What's that?"

"The old adage: it never rains, it pours."

"Oh, I don't know. The way I see it, things could have been a lot worse—"

"Yeah, yeah, I know. But what you don't know is just how bad things already are. Trust me when I say that my life is well and truly in the toilet at the moment. Nothing, and I mean nothing, is going right. My company is in trouble, my personal life is a shambles, and now this, I suddenly learn that my sister may be out to kill me. I don't know about you, but in my books, I have a hard time imagining it getting much worse than that."

Somewhat overwhelmed by David's sudden emotional outpouring, Tim was temporarily at a loss for words. Then, opting to steer clear of the more personal issues, he said, "It's always been my experience that things are never quite as bad as they seem. Take Quenetics, for example. Is it really in trouble or is it simply suffering from this latest downturn in the economy? And if that's all it is, I wouldn't worry about it if I were you because knowing you, I'm sure you'll be able to weather the storm much better than most."

"Yeah, right." David said unconvincingly. "I wish it were that simple. But it's not. The economic cycle is not to blame. But apparently I am. Analysts are now telling me that because Quenetics operates in a variety of different businesses, our stock is now trading at what they call a 'conglomerate discount.' Which I find to be utterly ridiculous, but hey, what do I know? They all seem to think that I'm completely out of touch with this New Economy that we're apparently now a part of."

Tim pursed his lips, again unsure of what to say. But before he could formulate a response, David spoke again. "Then, in addition to that, those same people are now saying that our interim business—which is our core business—is a disaster waiting to happen. They say we've now fallen so far behind our more fleet-footed brethren that it's only a matter of time before we're brought to our knees."

"And how do you respond to that?"

Fleeting facial shrug. "I don't know. Yeah, I guess we were a little slow off the mark when it came to building an Internet presence, but in my view, that's been to our advantage. We've got to learn from the mistakes of others." Short pause as he thought further about what he'd just said, and then added, "Well, that's not entirely true. I guess we've also made a few mistakes of our own, but nevertheless, none of them were as costly as some of those made by our pioneering competitors."

"And as a result of all this, my credibility has now ebbed to an all-time low! Which is bad enough, but then to add insult to injury, Kim has become so fed up with it all, and with the fact that I'm never at home, that she's now talking about getting a divorce." A heavy sigh as he pulled at his smock. "And now this. I'm hospitalized possibly because of my own sister's greed. Unbelievable." A shake of the head.

He had finished, but it took Tim time to understand this, so there was a delay before he said, "Again, we don't know that for certain. All we know is that she has motive and means. Nothing more. So, as Allan pointed out earlier, I think it's far too early for any of us to rush to judgment, particularly with respect to Shannon. After all, as you said yourself, it is hard to imagine that a member of your own family is capable of something like this." He ran a hand across the back of his neck. "Of course, crazier things have been known to happen, but somehow I just don't see Shannon as being the murdering type."

"And how would you know that? How many times have you met her? Was it once or maybe twice?" David said sardonically.

"Twice."

"Need I say more?" Short pause as he cleared his throat, and then in an effort to further strengthen his own suspicions, he added, "And how about the cottage incident? How do you explain that?"

"How can I explain what you couldn't? Like you said earlier, maybe it was just an accident or maybe it wasn't. Who knows? I certainly don't. Hence the reason I think we need to put our faith in Allan and wait to see what he comes up with. Hopefully he'll be able to provide us with the right answers."

David lowered his head and mumbled despondently, "I hope so, too, but in the meantime it looks as though I'm really going to have to start watching my back—both on and off the job. Off the job I've got to watch out for knives and bullets and on the job I've got to remain vigilant that she doesn't pull the rug out from under me."

"As in acquire the other 40 percent of your outstanding stock? Is that what you mean?"

David nodded his head.

"Which is a point I still don't quite understand. You explained earlier that even though you couldn't raise the money to buy her out, you seemed convinced that she'd find a way to buy you out. How's she going to do that?"

David smiled thinly. "Think about it. She's a beautiful twenty-nine-year-old woman who's completely devoid of any sense of morality and is constantly surrounded by men with more money than brains. I'd call that a deadly combination, especially as it pertains to me. Take this Miller guy for example—you know, the head of eMaxx. He's a billionaire playboy who has everything except that which he wants most: a trophy wife. Enter Shannon. Oh, and throw in the fact that the only other thing that he's currently lusting after is my company, and I don't know about you, but I'd say I've got something to worry about."

"Well, when you put it like that, I'd be tempted to agree with you." Short pause for reflection. "So, if there's anything I can do to help, please don't hesitate to ask."

David's response was immediate. "What do you think I've been doing for the last fifteen minutes? I'm not baring my soul for nothing, you know. This is my way of asking for help." Then in a softer voice, he added, "I really need it!"

3

8:22 P.M., Tuesday, April 21   Quenetics stock price: ▼ $98.20

David's home, Wellesley

EXCUSING HIMSELF FROM THE TABLE, Tim pushed in his chair and reached down to gather up his dishes.

Kim's voice made him stop. "Don't worry about it, Tim." Nodding in the direction of her two teenage daughters, Mindy and Sara, she added, "We'll get those. You two can have the night off tonight."

"You're sure?" Tim asked. He felt guilty not helping out in some way, and since he hated to cook, he thought the least he could do was to help with the dishes.

"You two cleaned up last night. Tonight it's our turn."

Before Tim could say another word, David also rose from the table, and said, "Good, that gives us some time to talk. That is, of course, if you don't already have something else planned for this evening."

Tim shook his head. "Nothing that can't wait, so sure, why not." Having just spent the last two days interviewing some of David's people, he could understand his friend's interest in having a chat. He asked, "So, where do you want to do this?"

38

"Why don't we go into my office. It'll be quieter there." Short pause. "But, before I go, I just need to talk to Kim for a minute. Alone. If that's alright with you?"

"Oh, sure. I'll just go in and wait for you." With that, Tim quickly exited the dining room and started down the hallway in the direction of David's office. As he walked, he took the time to reflect on the events of the last few days. He started with the flight from Barbados to Boston which he, David, and Allan had taken together. Then, landing at Logan International they'd been met by two ex-Navy SEALs, whom Allan had hired to watch over them, and Kim and the two girls. Allan had then stayed on at the airport to make a connecting flight back to LA, while the rest of them had driven out to David's ultra-modern and spacious two-story mansion in Wellesley, an upscale suburb of Boston.

Initially, Tim had been reluctant to accept David's invitation to spend "a week or so" with him and his family, for he knew only too well what it would entail: countless hours spent with David and his team discussing strategy, crunching numbers, poring over documents, playing office politics, and generally doing the myriad things executives do. The only problem being, they were all things he no longer had much interest in. He had once, but that was a while ago. At this stage in his life, he now had other things to occupy his time—other passions and pursuits. And managing others wasn't one of them.

Some might have considered that odd, knowing just how good a manager he had once been. Seven years earlier, and with just a few days to go before his thirty-third birthday, both of his parents had died in a mysterious car accident leaving him, their only child, to pick up the pieces. Of which there'd been many. They'd left him two homes, a yacht, a fleet of luxury cars, a $600 million company, and a mountain of debt that was on the verge of collapse.

Within less than a year, however, he'd managed to completely turn things around. The company, which had been called Stabilo at the time, was in some respects much like Quenetics. It had potential but lacked focus. The reason being, his father had initially started out in the consumer electronics industry, but spotting opportunities elsewhere, he'd diversified first into the coaxial cable industry, and then later into the fiber optics industry. Which is the point at which Tim had entered. Quick to realize that the company needed a focus, and equally quick in sensing where the future was headed, he'd sold off the consumer electronics and cable divisions, thereby allowing himself to focus exclusively on the fiber optics business. And he'd done all of this just as the Internet, with its rapacious appetite for bandwidth, had gone ballistic. Two years later, having just turned thirty-five, and already a billionaire, Tim had sold his stake in the company—which he'd since renamed Digitron—and had gone into semi-retirement. But, not wanting to retire completely, he'd set up a small venture capital firm, which had quickly doubled and then tripled in size, before eventually settling into a more manageable 15 to 20 percent growth pattern—which others now managed for him, leaving him ample time for traveling, skiing, rock-climbing, snowboarding, cycling, or diving, and going out with a series of women while fastidiously avoiding settling down with any of them. He loved his freedom too much for that.

But, being free-spirited didn't mean that he was self-centered. In fact, he was anything but. He cared very much for the people in his life, and was quick to put their needs and interests above those of his own. As was evidenced by the fact that he was now here in Boston, lending whatever support he could to David. He just hoped that it wouldn't take much more than a week or so as he was anxious to return home to his normal routine.

Entering David's study, Tim moved briskly across the thickly carpeted floor to one of the leather chairs situated in the middle of the room and dropped wearily into it. Then, sitting back he craned his neck forward, heard the satisfying crack of vertebrae, and then slowly rotated his head in a wide circle allowing his eyes to do a quick sweep of them room as he did so. The first thing they settled on was the large cut-stone fireplace in the middle of the far wall, its mantel at least the height of a standing man. Then, continuing clockwise around the rest of the room, his eyes took in the many photographs arranged on the putty-colored plaster walls—David on skis, on board different sized boats, on holidays with the family, and in a few shots surrounded by people he didn't know. His eyes ended the tour fixed on David, who had just entered the room and was already making a beeline for the bar.

David asked, "Care for a drink?"

"Sure. I'll have whatever you're having."

"Brandy OK?"

"Sure, that's fine."

As he poured, David got straight to the point. "So, what have you learned? Anything of interest?"

"Yes, I think so, but before I get into it, there's something else I'd like to discuss first. If that's OK with you?"

"Oh, sure. Go ahead. What is it?"

"Nothing serious, it's just that I got a call from Allan about an hour ago, which I thought you might want to know something about."

"Oh, sure. Why, what did he have to say?"

"The headline would be that he hasn't come up with anything solid yet; however, he is working on a few promising leads. Though he didn't get into specifics, he promised to let me know as soon as he had something definite."

David didn't comment immediately. Instead, he put down the brandy balloon, picked up the two glasses and walked over to where Tim was sitting. After handing his friend a drink, he then sat down in the chair opposite. Once he'd settled in, he asked, "And that's it? That was his only bit of news?"

"No, not quite. He also told me that he's assembled a small team of experts who'll be flying in here tomorrow to begin upgrading all of your security systems—both here and at the office." Tim hesitated for a moment, and then almost as an afterthought, added, "Oh, and he's apparently put Shannon under twenty-four-hour surveillance."

David bolted forward in his chair, almost spilling his cognac in the process. "He did *what*?" he snapped.

It took Tim almost a quarter of an hour to calm David down and to get him to accept Allan's decision. And even then, he would only do so under one condition: that the surveillance would go on no longer than a week, unless there was a compelling reason for them to extend it further.

Anxious to put the subject to rest, Tim quickly agreed to David's proviso, and then after a long pull from his drink, he said, "OK, with that now out of the way, let's talk Quenetics."

David straightened up immediately. With intensity written all over his face, he replied, "I'm ready when you are."

Before proceeding, Tim took another pull from his drink. Whether it was to bolster his courage or simply to quench a sudden thirst, David couldn't tell. But he knew he'd find out soon enough.

"To begin with," Tim said, "let me just say that everyone I've spoken to so far seems to think very highly of you. They all see you as being honest, open and fair, not to mention very good at what you do. Put otherwise, they all seem to like you."

David cringed at Tim's words. He could only assume that it was his friend's way of preparing him for what was to come next. "Thanks for the accolades, Tim, but let's cut to the chase, shall we?"

Tim smiled benignly. "Sure, but I just thought you should know that, that's all. Anyway, leaving the personal stuff aside, we get into the strategy stuff. And, there, at the top of everybody's list was the issue of *focus*. Everyone seems to think that being in three completely different businesses doesn't make a lot of sense. They felt that you needed to narrow that down to one."

David's reaction was one of mild exasperation. "Yes, we're in three different businesses, granted. But before you start preaching 'focus' too strongly, you might first want to learn a bit more about each of those businesses. Because when you do, what you'll discover is that each of them is a solid business, run by very capable people who've managed, through hard work and perseverance, to create dominant positions within each of their respective markets. In other words, they are all profitable, well-run companies, with a past to be proud of, and a future to look forward to. So, why would I want to get rid of any of them?"

"Well, not that I'm an expert in the matter, but I've always been a strong believer in the notion that *in concentration there is strength; whereas, in diversification there is weakness.* Or in the immortal words of my grandfather, *'man who chases two rabbits catches neither.'* It's the same in war. If you want to win, concentrate on one front at a time. Don't do like Hitler did and try to fight on multiple fronts simultaneously, because if you do, you'll lose. And it's the same in business. If you want to dominate a market, focus all of your energy on it to the exclusion of all else."

David cracked a smile. "Interesting metaphor, the rabbit thing. But I've got one that's even better. Sticking with the animal theme, I'd suggest that 'it's never wise to put all your eggs in one basket.'"

Tim shook his head in disagreement. "I don't agree. Not at all. The way I see it, there are two types of risks in business: 'market risk' and 'competitive risk.'" As he spoke, he pulled out a pen and drew something on the other side of his sheet of paper. When he finished, it resembled the following:

	Market risk	
	low	high
low		**Focused strategy**
high	**Diversified strategy**	

Competitive risk

He showed it to David, who frowned immediately. "This is getting a bit too theoretical for me, I'm afraid. Remember, you're the Harvard grad, not me." David, who'd put attending school right up there with having his teeth pulled, had dropped out of college in his second year at Ohio State, and hadn't gone near a management text since. Theories had never impressed him. They were always too abstract and nonsensical; how could you ever summarize all the complexities of a given situation in a simple equation or two-dimensional chart. Life just wasn't two-dimensional, no matter how you sliced it.

Tim persisted. "Have you ever heard the expression that 'a mind is like a parachute in that it only works when it's open'?"

"Yeah. So, what's your point?" David retorted irritably as he drew the tips of his fingers in a clawing gesture down one side of his face and started scratching.

"My point is that this is simple stuff. Something that anybody could understand, so long as they're open to it." Tim's gaze grew in intensity. "They say the more you know, the more you know you don't know. I find the more you know, the more unsettling it is to come across things you don't know about or fully understand. Call it vanity, or call it caution. Call it whatever you want, but all I know is that I personally like to try to understand what's going on around me, and if a bit of theory is necessary to put it in perspective, then so be it. But, then again, that's just me."

David's jaw muscles flexed, yet he kept his thoughts to himself. When he finally spoke, he said, "Open mind or not, I still don't understand your graph. As far as I'm concerned, market and competitive risk are one and the same, aren't they?"

"No, definitely not," Tim replied gently. "In fact, they're inversely proportional to one another, as the graph shows. The more you have of one, the less you have of the other. Let me explain. 'Market risk,' as its name suggests, is the risk associated with a company's dependence on a particular market. In other words, the more focused the company is on a particular market, the more dependent it is on the whims of that market's customers. If anything deleterious were to happen to that market, the company would likely find itself in a difficult position." Short pause, then, "Take an example. Do you know what a player piano is?"

David's comprehension faltered, then sprang to life. "I think so, yeah. They're the pianos that play themselves, aren't they?"

"More or less. I have one in my home. The playing of famous pianists was mechanically recorded on a cylinder, which, when placed in one of these pianos, reproduced the original performance. It was ingenious, and very popular during its day. And the company that dominated the industry was called Welte & Söhne, which ruled until the phonograph came along, and that was the end of Welte & Söhne and the player piano industry.

"The annals of corporate history are replete with examples like this. Highly focused companies losing out to the forces of change. And that's what I mean when I talk about 'market risk.'

"But, as I alluded to a moment ago, market risk represents only one side of the coin. The other side is what I call 'competitive risk,' which is the risk of getting beaten at your own game by a superior competitor. The likelihood of that increases the more unfocused you become.

"As a simple example of this, just think of a world-class golfer suddenly deciding to divide her time between golf and tennis. Obviously, the more time she spent on one, the less time she'd have to play the other. As a result, her golf game would suffer, leaving her to become average in both sports."

"The same principle holds true for corporations. The more diversified they become, the less competitive they become in each of their individual markets. Over time, regardless of their original market strength, they eventually get knocked down, if not out, by a more focused competitor. Thus, in a nutshell, *competitive risk is the risk of becoming a jack-of-all-trades and master of none.* And regrettably, *the jack-of-all-trades—the generalist—can only compete with other generalists. As soon as a specialist comes along, the generalists usually get knocked out of the ring.*"

"Why's that?" David asked.

"For the simple reason that the focused player is completely dependent on that market, the conglomerate is not. So, it's not surprising that the focused player is more apt to fight harder—they have to, their survival is at stake."

"Well, if that's true, and I'm not necessarily saying that it isn't, then why is it that General Electric—a sprawling conglomerate if there ever was one—is consistently rated one of the world's most successful companies?"

Arrogant shrug, as though he'd been expecting the question. "Ah yes, GE, the one true exception to the rule. You can't imagine how many times I've heard that question."

"Then you must have a very good answer for it," David said impatiently.

"I do. GE is, in a sense, the perfect example of what I've just been talking about. Contrary to what you might believe, they're actually an extremely focused organization. Their mantra is they have to be either number one or number two in each market they compete in or they get out. Put otherwise, GE is little more than a constellation of many different and distinct businesses, each of which is a highly focused organization. And the fact that this constellation has been able to hold itself together for so long is simply the result of exceptional leadership. Full stop!" Tim jabbed the air to further emphasize his point. "And that's my answer on GE. Do you want to try another one?"

David thought about it for a few moments, and then said, "How about Virgin? You know, Richard Branson and his crew."

Tim crooked an eyebrow. "Virgin? Are you talking about the company that's continuously having to sell off its past in order to have a future?" Shake of the head. "You don't really want to go there, do you? You might want to try another example."

David dismissed the rebuttal with a flick of his hand. Rising to his feet, he asked, "I need a refill. How about you?"

Tim hesitated, and then nodded, while holding up his glass.

David fetched the decanter and watched the pale golden liquid swirl into the bottom of the glasses. As he poured, he asked, "I should probably quit while I'm behind, but I'm curious to know, in addition to the focusing thing, is there anything else you think I need to know?"

Tim eyed David steadily. "Yes, there is."

David handed Tim his glass and then returned to his seat. "How did I know you were going to say that?" Quick tug of his drink, then, "Well, don't keep me in suspense. What is it?"

Tim stifled a yawn before proceeding. He was really getting tired at this point. "Well, to me, market domination is not exactly rocket science. In fact, during my stint as head of Digitron,

I used to argue that there are basically only four steps involved. The first of which, the need to focus, we've already covered."

"So, what are the other three?"

"The second would go something like this. Once you've decided what you're going to focus on, you then need to find a way to *differentiate* yourself from everyone else who has decided to focus on that same thing. Then, once you've done that, you're then ready to move on to step three: *fortify* your position, thereby making it as difficult as possible for others to copy whatever it is that you've done. And, finally, step four: be prepared to move on as soon as you see your fortifications starting to give way. In other words, always find a way to *stay one step ahead* of your competitors." Tim paused for breath. "And that's it. That's my four-step process. It couldn't be simpler."

"On paper possibly, but in practice, I'm not so sure. For example, if you were to try to apply it to Quenetics, what would you come up with?"

Tim's response was immediate. "Obviously the first thing you'd have to do would be to focus on one business and sell off the other two."

"And which of the three would you hold on to?"

"Let me throw the same question back at you, but in a slightly different form: of all the businesses you are in, which is the one that you think you have the best chance of becoming the best in the world in?"

David hesitated before answering. "I'd say that that would probably be our temp business."

"Well, that's your answer then. I'd focus on it, and sell off the others."

David digested that, and then moved on. "You said that step two was *differentiation*, wasn't it?"

Tim nodded.

"Then, going with our temp business, how would you differentiate us from our many competitors?"

"To give you a proper answer to that question, I'd first need to do a lot more research. So, I'd prefer not to really get into that at this point."

"That's understandable, but knowing you, you must have something in mind."

Pausing for a moment to marshal his thoughts, Tim took a quick swallow of cognac, and then said, "In my view, *competitive strategy is all about being different. It's about creating new competitive positions that serve to either pull customers away from the competition or pull entirely new customers into the market.* To do this, you basically have only three options. You can try to, one: establish, then 'own,' a word in the minds of all customers; two: establish, and then 'own,' a specific customer segment; or three: if you're operating in cyberspace, you can try to do both at the same time."

David chuckled. "I'm afraid that was just a bit too cryptic for me. Do you want to try it again?"

"Sure. But this time I'll run through them one at a time. I'll start with what is commonly referred to as *category-based positioning*, which is when a company owns the product or service category it competes in. By this, I mean that it owns the word that defines the category in the mind of the customer. For example, when you think cola, the first brand that comes to mind for most of us is 'Coke.' Thus, Coke owns the cola category. When the word 'pizza' is suggested, the first brand name that pops into most people's minds is Pizza Hut—therefore, they own the category. Sports shoes; the first name to mind is typically Nike. Gourmet coffee: the brand is Starbucks. Tissues: it's Kleenex. And so on. These companies all own a word in the minds of *all* customers. They typically don't discriminate between one customer and the next, nor do they have a close connection to any one of them. They might do surveys that give them some idea as to why, *on average,* a customer chooses one product over another or why particular *types* of customers choose one over another, but the one thing they don't know is why any *one particular customer* made a *particular choice* at a *particular moment* in time. They're just not close enough to their customers to know such things."

David interrupted, "And what happens if you want to follow this strategy, but you can never see yourself 'owning' or dominating the category? For example, take Quenetics. Let's say we were to follow your advice and focus all of our efforts on the temp business, but saw no feasible way of ever moving ourselves into a market leadership position. What should we do then? Sell off the temp business as well?"

"No, definitely not. If someone else 'owns' the category, then you simply have to *narrow your focus* to the point where you are able to claim ownership of a piece of the category.* For example, Pizza Hut owns the pizza category; the number two player is Little Caesars, which focuses on 'takeout'; the number

---

*Ries, Al. *Focus: The Future of Your Company Depends On It.* New York: HarperBusiness, 1996, p. 101.

three player is Domino's Pizza, which focuses on 'home delivery.' So, the need to differentiate drove both Little Caesars and Domino's to create entirely new sub-categories, rather than trying to slug it out with Pizza Hut, the category 'owner.'"

David hesitated for a moment, but then his curiosity got the better of him. "And, the second option?"

"Those who choose the second option, what I call *cluster-based positioning,* try to own a particular group of customers. By this, I mean that they try to develop a strong relationship with a targeted set of customers with regards to filling a *specific* need or *set* of needs."

"For example?" David asked.

"Pick a need, and I'll give you an example."

"A need?"

"Yes. Take 'entertainment' as an example. We all like to be entertained, so let's call that a basic consumer need. And the company that's probably best suited to fill that need at the moment is AOL Time Warner. It wants consumers to buy its books, see the movie, buy the CD, or CD-ROM, or the thousand and one other merchandising items that go along with it, and it fuels all of this spending activity by promoting its wares both online and in its different magazines—either in the form of advertisements or more often, in the form of reviews, articles, or newscasts. Or at least that's the theory. However, according to different articles I've read of late, the jury is still out on how successful the company has been in making all of this happen. Yet, still its competitors continue to follow its lead. Take Disney for example. Before launching a film, the Disney people advertise it throughout their theme parks, and on ABC, their television network. Then, as the film makes its way around the globe, they follow it up with countless items of merchandise. A year or so later, as the film makes its way into video, they also turn it into a Broadway show and the story lives on. In the meantime, they go to work on the next lump of content, intent on exploiting it in exactly the same way."

David nodded his head. "I've got the picture, if you'll pardon the pun, but now I've got another question. What happens if another competitor already 'owns' the cluster you're interested in?"

"Same thing I said a few minutes ago. To differentiate yourself, you'd need to either usurp them by delivering something of greater value, or make them irrelevant by carving out your own sub-cluster within the cluster." Tim paused. "Are you still with me?"

"I think so, so keep going before I lose your train of thought."

"OK. Now, because 'a need' is much broader than a specific product or service, a company intent on pursuing this strategy is often forced to think in terms of *solutions* rather than individual products, and thus, is often required to operate across product and industry lines. Put otherwise, more often than not, the companies operate as generalists, whereas, those following a category-based strategy typically operate as specialists.

"Let me give you another example. First Trust Company is a private investment bank where I do all of my banking. It targets individuals with a minimum of $1 million in investable assets, then offers them a wide array of customized services, including investment management and estate administration, oversight of oil and gas investments, and accounting for race-horses and aircraft. In doing so, it tries to meet *all the banking needs* of its targeted customers.

"Companies like First Trust don't focus on a single product or benefit and try to sell it to as many consumers as possible. Instead, they target a select group of customers, then try to sell to each of them individually as much product as possible."

Running a hand through his hair, David said, "I think I pretty well understand the first two options, so why don't we move on to the third?"

"The third option is a child of the Internet," Tim said. "And the reason I say that is because, before the Internet, there was no third option. However, in recent years, companies from across the industrial spectrum have shown that, with one foot in the 'brick' world and the other in the 'click' world, it is possible to *own both a word in the mind of all customers and a customer cluster.*"

"And, an example of such a company would be?" David asked.

Tim fell silent for a few moments as he thought up an answer. "The first name that comes to mind is Charles Schwab, the discount brokerage firm. They created that space in the late 1970s, and then proceeded to dominate it through to the late 1990s, or using the phraseology I've used above, they created and owned a word—discount broker—for more than twenty years. But in the mid- to late '90s, the proliferation of personal computers with modems threatened to change all of that as it allowed for a much richer interface than the twelve keys of the telephone—the cornerstone of Schwab's 24/7 Touch-Tone service. So Schwab had to react, and they did, by creating e.Schwab, an online brokerage firm. Then, as the Internet took off, e.Schwab fought for supremacy of this new medium by offering their clients a whole range of high-quality information services offerings: brand name research reports, personalized advice, portfolio tracking, records management, and the full panoply of cash management services such as money market and checking accounts. And, in so doing, they 'locked-in' all of their new on-line customers. Which, when I translate that into the language I've used above, means that in addition to owning the words 'discount broker,' they were now starting to 'own' all of their customers. Or, in other words, they now did both: they owned a word, and they owned a customer cluster."

David shrugged. "Got it. Now, for the sixty-four thousand dollar question: Which of the three options do you think Quenetics should follow?"

Tim's mouth formed a crooked smile. "How did I know you were going to ask me that. And the answer is, again, I'd need more time to think about it," he replied, "but off the top of my head, I think you should go for option three—trying to own both a word and a customer cluster. It's the option of choice these days, and I think you have as good a chance as anyone of making it happen."

David was suddenly wide-awake again. "How do you figure that? Our current Internet offering is about as low-tech as they come, which would suggest to me that we're in a very weak starting position."

Tim shook his head. "That's true, you are. But so what? Just because you're weak today doesn't preclude you from being strong tomorrow. It just means that you're going to have to try harder."

"But, if it's not a core competence—"

"Again, so what. People *used* to think that the proper way to set strategy was to start by identifying core competencies and then looking for market opportunities. No longer. Out in Silicon Valley, we now do it the other way around. We identify an opportunity, and then we try to figure out what it's going to take to capture it. Once we're clear on what competencies we need, we then either try to get those skills via alliances or develop them internally." Short pause. "You'd have to do the same thing."

David scoffed. "You make it sound so easy when it's not. Because, even if I were to buy in to this argument of yours, which I don't, I'd never make it over the first hurdle, which is the act of identifying a new market opportunity. Believe me, I've been trying to do exactly that for years now and haven't managed to yet. Small wonder. The temp industry is a mature industry. Nothing new ever happens to it. Yes, the Internet came along and stirred things up a bit, but other than bringing a few new faces to the table, we're still doing more or less what we've always done. Matching skills with job requirements. Where's the new market opportunity in that?"

"Well, I'm not one to toot my own horn," Tim replied, "but I think I may have found one. In fact, I think I may have come up with an idea that could *completely* transform your industry. Do you want to hear it?"

4

TONY BERNELLI HAD RETURNED to his room after a quick meal and was now seated at the foot of his bed, staring into a blank television screen. Not in the mood to channel-surf, he put down the remote and flopped onto his back. Here he was, in the posh Ritz-Carlton hotel—a veritable Bostonian institution—and he couldn't even enjoy it. He had too many other things on his mind. Like trying to stay alive.

At forty-four years of age, Tony was a cheap thug whose best years were already behind him. At least, that's what he'd thought up until a few weeks ago when he'd suddenly got a call from an old contact who'd asked if he'd be interested in doing a job. "Easy work; a lot of money." Interested? Hell, yes! Anything was better than stealing car radios for a living, which is what his life had degenerated to. So, twenty-four hours later, the two of them had met, and Tony had been offered the deal of a lifetime—a cool quarter million to waste a businessman while the guy was on holiday down in the Caribbean. There was only one condition attached—he had

57

to make it look like an accident. But hell, how difficult could that be? He watched as much TV as the next guy. He knew that if he really put his mind to it, he'd eventually come up with something.

And then there was the money. Fifty g's up front, the rest on completion. That was a lot of cash. It would buy him a lot of respect, not to mention drugs and alcohol.

So, he'd accepted, without a moment's hesitation.

And oh, how he regretted that now. After screwing up in St. Lucia and not having made any progress since, he knew he was rapidly running out of time. If there was one thing he'd learned during his many years living on the streets and foraging in the shadows, it was that mistakes had a way of catching up to you. You might get away with making one; two, possibly but unlikely; but three, don't even think about it. And he'd already reached his quota, so unless he somehow found a way to turn things around—and fast—he knew he'd soon be living on borrowed time.

Sitting up again, he twisted around and looked at the digital clock by the side of the bed. It blinked 9:26 P.M. Four more minutes to go. Then his cellphone would ring, and he'd answer it. But then what? What was he going to say? He could lie, but what good would that do? It might buy him a few more hours, maybe even an extra day, but then what? They'd find out soon enough that he'd lied, and come after him. It was that simple. So, no, lying was definitely not the wisest of options. But neither was telling the truth, or at least not the whole truth. Because that too could only lead to trouble. Which put him right back where he started—not knowing what to say.

Restless with fear, and frustration, he got up and started pacing the room, desperate to find a solution that might save his miserable life.

Time. He just needed more time.

A few minutes later he shot the clock an unfriendly glance and saw that the moment had arrived. It was now 9:30, and if nothing else, his contact was always punctual. Swallowing hard, he plopped himself down at the foot of the bed and stared into the darkened face of his cellphone. His mind returned to the shadows of his private thoughts.

The room seemed to revolve slowly around him. He clasped his arms around himself and breathed deeply, trying for a moment of calm, a moment of clarity.

Suddenly his reverie was shattered by the insistent sound of his cellphone. Reflexively, he jabbed the receiver button and lifted the phone to his ear, his breath suspended. The voice at the other end of the line was cold and menacing. "This is K-One. Go to scrambler. Now."

"Sure," replied Tony in a voice he barely recognized as his own as he attached an extra piece to his cellphone. "Done."

"Simple question. Can you do this thing or not? And I need to know now—and I mean *right bloody now*! Because if you can't, I'll find someone who can. And, let me tell ya, when I do, I'd sure hate to be you—if you catch my meaning." A pause. "So, what's it going to be? Do you want to continue breathing or what?"

Swallowing hard, Tony stammered, "Course I do. I'll get it done. I swear to you. I'll get it done!"

"When?" It was more an arctic wind than a question.

Tony fell silent for a moment. His mouth continued to move, but no words came out. He had absolutely no idea how to answer that. What would they accept—a day, two days, a week? He had no idea. But he knew that he had to say something.

With his heart racing and his face bathed in sweat, he decided to go with the truth. That way, he'd at least know where he stood. Finding his voice, he replied, "To be honest, I ain't *exactly* sure." He paused, expecting to be interrupted, but heard nothing other than his own troubled breathing. "I just can't get anywhere near the guy. He's got protection 24/7. And both the house and the office are impossible to break into. Believe me, there ain't no way to get inside either of them." Still no response. "So, I'm thinking maybe the best thing for me to do is to lay low for awhile, and just wait for things to die down a bit. When that happens, then maybe they'll lower their guard. And that's when I move in for the kill. Simple." His voice trailed off at the end, as though not even he had faith in what he was saying.

K-One said nothing for a few moments, leaving Tony to fry in his own fear. Then, in a voice laden with contempt and anger, K-One said, "Listen to me, you idiot. What part of this do you not understand? You don't have *any* more time. You've had enough—more than enough. So, let me put this in terms that even you can understand. If you want to live to see another day, I'd recommend you get off your butt, and get out there and do what you've been paid to do. Got it? NOW!"

"Got it!"

The line went dead before Tony could utter another word.

· · ·

Across town, Tim finished outlining his idea to David. Then, eager for feedback, he downed the last of his cognac and sat back in his chair and waited. And waited. And waited. David said nothing. But his body language spoke volumes. He looked like a kid in a toy store—his eyes were wide, his face was flushed, and his whole body seemed to pulsate with nervous energy. It would appear that he liked the idea—a lot.

When he finally spoke, he spoke slowly and with deliberation. "Well, from what I can understand of the idea, I think it's amazing. I really do. I love it. It's original, it's powerful, and it may even be doable." He chuckled, "It would take *a hell* of a lot of time and money, but with sufficient quantities of both, I think it could be done." Then, from one moment to the next, his features darkened and his mood changed. "The only problem is, we don't have any time or money. We've run out of both."

Having anticipated that response, Tim was quick to counter it. "Where there's a will, there's a way, I always say. Or, in the immortal words of Henry Ford, 'If you believe you can do something or if you believe you can't, you'll be right.' It's the law of self-fulfilling prophecies. What you believe in will be yours, so long as you're willing to put in the effort."

"You can also believe in the tooth fairy if you want," David said sarcastically, "but what good's it going to do you? And the same holds true for this. No matter how hard we wish for it, we just don't have what it's going to take to make it happen. Believe me, I know."

"I hear what you're saying, but please do me a favor and just humor me for a few minutes, will you? After all, what have you got to lose?"

David shrugged but otherwise said nothing.

"So, where do I start? Do you want me to go back to the beginning or do you have some specific questions in mind?"

"I'd prefer you go back to the beginning and if I have any questions, I'll just ask them along the way."

"Right." He glanced over his notes. "I began by suggesting that the 'word' you should try to claim ownership of is either 'self-development' or 'personal growth.' That's because the vortal—a *vertical portal**—I see you building would be *the* site people would go to whenever they wanted to further develop themselves. In other words, the vortal would be figuratively just a few feet wide, but many miles deep. Anything and everything one could possibly conceive of relating to the issue of self-development would be there on offer, which would *differentiate* you from your competitors. With them hopefully continuing to limit their role to that of intermediary in the job search process, you would break from the pack by taking on the much more expanded role of continuously developing, informing, nurturing, and educating your clientele. It wouldn't be easy, I grant you that, but it would certainly make you stand out from the competition."

David put up a hand to stop him. "Let me see if I've got this straight. So this vortal, as you call it, would be a site that people would visit frequently throughout their working lives—for career counseling, self-assessment, just-in-time training, general knowledge upgrades, information about prospective schools or employers, and so on; and/or if they wanted to par-

---

*A portal is a front door to the Internet.

ticipate in a labor exchange or learn the latest job-search techniques, and so on, and so forth. Does that about sum it up?"

"More or less. And, yes, I know what you're about to say. It'll require a Herculean effort to pull all of this together, but, again, as far as I'm concerned, it can be done. We obviously wouldn't be able to do it all on our own; we'd need to forge some alliances, but I don't see that being such a problem, do you?"

David nodded, and then said, "OK, let's just say for the sake of argument that you're right, and that it is possible to build such a site. What then? Other companies would see what we're doing and would be quick to follow. And considering the fact that they'd be operating at Internet speed, it wouldn't take them long to catch up. And once they did, then where would we be? We'd be the ones saddled with all of the development costs, and they'd be the ones laughing all the way to the bank. Not an appealing thought."

"I agree. Hence the reason you'd have to take steps to ensure that that didn't happen."

David didn't even try to hide his skepticism. He gave a short nasal snort of amusement. "Yeah, right! And how do you propose we do that?"

"It's too late and I'm too tired to delve into that now. Suffice it to say that each of the steps we'd have to take would play an integral role in *fortifying* your position, thereby *making it as difficult as possible for others to replicate your operating model.*" Significant pause. "Forgive me. You're thinking that I'm being maddeningly elliptical. Of course, you're right, and I apologize for it. It's just it's been a long day and I'm tired, so why don't we pick this up again tomorrow over breakfast?"

David frowned. Tim may have been tired, but he certainly wasn't. He was too wired to be tired. But not wanting to force the issue, he said, "Yeah, it has been a long day, hasn't it? However, before we shut it down for the night, couldn't we just finish up on this one point? You've described the fortification thing in very general terms, but it would be great if you could expand on it just a little bit. Particularly in terms of how you would go about fortifying Quenetics."

Tim smiled despite himself. The man just wouldn't take no for an answer. Stifling a yawn, he asked, "Are you talking about fortifying Quenetics or fortifying iQu?"

David's head lifted sharply. "iQu? What's that?"

"Oh, I'm sorry. I should have mentioned it earlier. iQu is the temporary name I've given to this vortal we've just been discussing."

"What's the iQu stand for?"

Tim shrugged. "Whatever you want it to stand for, I guess. I just like the sound of it, don't you?"

"That doesn't answer my question."

"I don't know. Initially, I'd thought of Intelligence Quotient Unlimited, as in, the more frequently you visit the site, the smarter you'll be. But, it could just as easily stand for IQ University. Or, who knows what else. Again, it's just a temporary name, so let's not get too hung up on it."

"All right. So, let's talk about fortifying iQu. What would that look like?"

"In the broadest of terms, you'd have to do two things. One, you'd have to align both Quenetics and iQu around the 'self-development' concept, thereby ensuring that they complement and reinforce one another. I call that *tightening the fit*. And, two, you'd undoubtedly have to develop and/or acquire a number of proprietary technologies."

"Such as?"

"Oh, I don't know, on the e-learning side you'd probably need to be looking at things like ERP systems, knowledge management systems, collaborative software, interaction hardware, and simulation technologies, and then, on the artificial intelligence side, you'd need to think about thought translation—"

David was quick to interrupt. "Huh? Do you have any idea what you're saying? Do you know how much time and money it would take to start assembling the kind of technology base you're talking about?"

Tim responded with a coy smile.

"I fail to see the humor in what I've just said," David said irritably.

Tim's smile broadened. "That's understandable, because you don't know what I'm thinking."

"Which is what?"

"That I may already be in possession of enough technological firepower to get this thing started."

David was incredulous. "Really?" His voice took on a new sense of urgency as he leaned forward in his chair.

Instinctively lowering his voice, Tim explained, "For the last few years, I've been investing heavily in a company called Celebrix, which, believe it or not, *may* be able to provide you with all the technological wizardry you need. But before I say anything more, I'd first like to discuss the idea with a few of the

Celebrix crew and see what they have to say about it. If that's all right with you?"

"I'd prefer to hear everything now, but if you'd prefer to wait awhile, then so be it. I'll just have to wait." With that, David stood up and waited for Tim to do likewise. To his surprise, Tim didn't move. Mildly perplexed, David looked down at him and asked, "I thought you wanted to go to bed?"

Softly, hesitantly, he replied, "I do, but before I go, there's just one other item I wanted to discuss."

David nodded as he returned to his chair. "And what might that be?"

Tim fidgeted as he struggled to find the right words. "I wanted to talk to you . . . about your sister."

David's eyes narrowed and his voice took on a slightly menacing tone. "Yeah, what about her?"

Tim hesitated as though unsure whether or not to proceed, and then apparently deciding to go for it, he said, "This may come off sounding somewhat strange, but I was just wondering what you thought of the idea of me getting closer to her— befriending her, in a sense. That way I might be able to glean some insight into what she's thinking, and better yet, I might even be able to influence her thinking somewhat."

David, not knowing how to respond, said nothing.

"I realize it's a long shot, but, on the other hand, I think it's worth a try."

David could not believe what he was hearing. "Apparently one of us is nuts, either you for coming up with the idea or me for not being able to see the sense in it. I mean, look at it from my perspective. First, you and Allan try to convince me that she's out to kill me, and now you're talking about trying to climb into bed with her. Am I missing something here? I mean, I know she's a beautiful woman and all, but I thought that you, of all people, would be able to see past that."

Tim squirmed slightly under the intensity of David's glare. "Who said anything about sleeping with her? All I'm talking about is trying to get to know her a bit better and then possibly using that to our advantage. I'm sure you can see the logic in that."

David smirked. "The woman wasn't born yesterday, Tim. She'll see through what you're trying to do, and before you know it, she'll be doing to you what you were hoping to do to her. That is, of course, if she doesn't kill you first."

5

11:18 A.M., Thursday, April 23   Quenetics stock price: ▼ $96.00

Quenetics Headquarters, Boston

DAVID SNATCHED UP THE PHONE as soon as he heard that
it was Matt Baker on the line. Matt was the portfolio manager
of a pension fund that had an 8 percent stake in Quenetics.

For years he and David had gotten along well. Neither
considered the other a friend, yet both had a great deal of respect for the other—David because of Matt's professionalism
and business acumen, and Matt because of David's steward-
ship and consistent performance. Since acquiring the stock
almost five years ago, Matt had seen it more than triple in
value, and, until recently, follow a single trajectory—ever upwards. But that had all ended in late December when the
stock peaked at $125, and had been trending lower ever
since. Hence the reason for the call, David presumed, as he
put the receiver to his ear.

They exchanged perfunctory greetings, and then Matt
quickly got down to business. "Let me just state from the outset that I've been in a moral quandary for a couple of weeks
now about whether or not to make this call."

"Well, now that you've made it, you may as well tell me what's on your mind."

Matt hesitated for a moment, and then blurted out, "I hate to be the purveyor of bad news, but I just thought that you should know that Quenetics is currently in play."

Loud intake of air. "Huh! What do you mean by that? Are you suggesting that we've become a takeover target?"

"That's right."

"A takeover target! But, that's not possible. Shannon and I own a majority of the shares."

Matt's voice dropped. "That's the problem, David. Shannon's one of the parties involved. And the reason that I know is because she and Roger Miller paid me a visit a couple of weeks back to see if I'd be interested in selling my Quenetics shares to them."

David fell silent as he struggled to absorb what he'd just heard. Many seconds later, in a voice just above that of a whisper, he asked, "So, what did they offer you?"

"Strangely enough, they seemed more interested in *getting* information than in *giving* it. Which led me to conclude that they were on a bit of a fishing expedition."

David persisted. "But they must have given you some sort of idea as to what they were prepared to offer."

"Not in so many words, no. But I got the impression that they had the number $110 in mind."

David did a quick mental calculation. "One hundred and ten dollars a share! What are we talking about here? That's less than a 15 percent premium over yesterday's close, which is a joke. You and I both know that the stock is worth a hell of a lot more than that." Pause. "I realize it's taken a bit of a beating of late, but, believe me, that's just a temporary thing. By the third quarter, things will have turned around, and we'll be looking at a very different picture. You can count on it."

Matt nervously cleared his throat. "I agree that your stock is worth more than $110, but that said, if your financial situation doesn't improve soon, I'm afraid I'll be forced to rethink my position. I'm sure you can understand that."

"And what are you talking about when you say '*soon*'?"

"That depends on how your stock performs going forward. If it continues to gather pace on the way down, then 'soon' would be very soon indeed. On the other hand, if it were to stabilize at current levels, then I'll probably be tempted to await your second quarter results before making a decision."

David almost had a cardiac arrest. "But those figures come out in just a few weeks time! You can't expect—"

Matt interrupted. "David, be realistic, will you? The market doesn't remember what you did yesterday. All it cares about is what you're doing today and what it thinks you're likely to do tomorrow. That's reality, and you know it. So, if I were you, I'd do whatever you have to in order to ensure that those numbers meet or exceed market expectations. Because if they don't, I think you're going to be in a bit of trouble."

• • •

About twenty minutes later, David unceremoniously barged into Tim's temporary office, located one floor down and almost directly beneath his own. Tim was still on the phone, possibly the same call he'd been on since David had first tried to get through to him, fifteen minutes earlier.

David sat down in the chair in front of Tim's desk and waited. But after about thirty seconds of that, his patience ran out. Restless with anger, frustration, and despite the mountain of problems before him, boredom, he got up and started pacing the room in ever-expanding circles, his mind clouded with worry. So absorbed was he in his thoughts that he didn't even notice when Tim finally ended his call. Tim had to cough loudly in order to get his attention.

Returning to his seat, he quickly explained the latest turn of events, growing ever more agitated and animated as he did so. He used his hands as visual punctuation marks, stabbing the air or kneading it with his fingers to underscore each point. When he finished, it was in true David style—shoulders and eyebrows rising in unison, elbows tucked in to his sides, palms spread out, lower lip jutting, his voice having reached a crescendo—everything but the feet used to emphasize just how pissed off he really was.

Tim wisely chose not to interrupt until the oration was over, and the frustration spent. Then, in a tentative voice he asked, "So, if I understand correctly, Matt's saying that Shannon and Miller have now approached all three of the pension fund managers, is that right?"

"That's right."

"And all three have turned them down?"

"That depends on how you want to look at it. Yes, all three apparently made it clear they weren't interested in selling at the price Miller seemed to have in mind. But each of them made it equally clear that if either our stock price were to fall much further or if Miller were to raise his bid, they'd be willing to rethink their position."

Tim was silent, trying to determine how receptive David would be to hearing the truth at this point. Feeling his friend's steely glare fixed upon him, he decided to chance it. "That's what you'd expect them to do, isn't it? I mean, after all, these guys are paid to buy low and sell high. They've all had a wonderful run with your stock, but as far as they're concerned, all the evidence seems to suggest that the run is now over. The Internet is fundamentally changing the structure and composition of your industry, and again, as far as Wall Street is concerned, you're not even in the game. So, you'd have to admit, it's only natural that they'd be somewhat concerned at this point about their investment in your company. I certainly would be if I were them."

David colored, but to his credit did not respond. Tim continued, "Then along comes a white knight who offers to solve all of their problems by buying them out at a profit—modest though it may be—and they show interest. Who wouldn't? Again, I certainly would."

David stood up again, his hands flat on the desk as though he were addressing an audience, and barked, "Maybe you would, but I sure as hell wouldn't. I'd stay focused on the big picture, which in this case is the fact that my stock has *consistently* outperformed the market year in and year out for well over a decade now. And believe me, there aren't many companies who can say that about themselves."

"That's true. But, so what? Who cares about yesterday, let alone what happened ten years ago? It's only tomorrow that counts. You know that."

David slowly sat down and started to chew on his lower lip, a clear sign that he was heavily stressed. Looking at his pained expression, Tim decided not to push the issue any further.

It was two or three minutes before David finally spoke again. "So what do we do now? The way I see it, we're basically out of time and out of options. My stock is on a one-way journey to hell, and the barbarians are at the gates—no, correction, one of them, who also just happens to be my sister, is working just a few offices down from mine." He formed a steeple with his hands on Tim's desk, and then sunk his face into them.

Recovering somewhat, David lifted his head out of his hands and said, "There's got to be a way out of this. If only I could figure out what it is."

"I can think of one."

"Is that right." A statement of skepticism, not a question. "And what might that be?"

"Well, you could start by doing what we talked about a couple of nights ago—sell your non-core businesses. Immediately! That would not only boost your cash position, it would also signal the market just how serious you are about turning things around. Then, in addition to that, there's also the iQu concept, which once you've got a better understanding of what it is, you'll be quick to agree that it too could generate a lot of good press."

"I probably would, but I first need to know more. So it's up to you. Are you willing to open up yet?"

"I am. I think that now is as good a time as any to fill you in on some of the details." He paused to clear his throat and to collect his thoughts. "The gist of the idea would be to wed some of the technologies we're developing at Celebrix with this e-learning vortal that we spoke about on Tuesday."

"You mean that *you* spoke about, don't you? After all, it was your idea."

"As a possible solution to *your* problem. Had I not known of the problem, I'd never have come up with the solution. So, in that sense, I see it as 'our' idea, which is why I've already got my lawyers drafting up the articles of incorporation for iQu. Quenetics will own 50 percent, and Celebrix will own 50 percent. Which I think is fair. Don't you?"

David's countenance softened somewhat. "I can't say because I still haven't a clue what it is that we're talking about here."

Tim nodded and then got started. For the next half-hour, Tim fleshed-out the idea in considerable detail, David interrupting every now and again to clarify a point or ask for a fuller explanation.

By the time he'd finished, David's face was flushed with excitement. "Unbelievable! Can you imagine what would happen if we could actually pull this thing off? We'd quite literally become the center of something that's always been thought of as having no center—cyberspace. It's . . . it's . . . wow, what is it? It's pure genius, is what it is!" He took in a long breath. "And everyone you've spoken to about it really believes that it can be done?"

Tim nodded. "They do, and so do I. That means it's now all up to you. Do you want to do this or not?"

"Damn right I do!" David bellowed. "Without a doubt. When can we get started?"

"I'm hoping to get a draft of the articles of incorporation some time tomorrow afternoon, which is about the same time the Celebrix team is scheduled to arrive here in Boston. I've already found space for them here in the building, if that's OK with you, and your secretary is busy making all the necessary arrangements for them—finding accommodations, renting cars, and so on. As you can imagine, it's likely they're going to have to be here for a while—possibly a few months or more."

"And they're OK with that?"

"Absolutely! They're prepared to do whatever it takes to make this thing happen. Don't forget. These people have been working on these technologies for almost fifteen years now, so, as you could imagine, they'd like nothing better than to see them finally leave the lab and go to market in one way or another, and iQu is as good a way as any."

"Can't argue with that. Well, if there's anything I can do to help, just let me know."

Tim smiled. "There is, in fact, something you can do. I'd greatly appreciate it if you'd make five or six of your best people available to work on this on a full-time basis, effective immediately. Is that possible?"

"I can't see why not, after all—" Suddenly David's mouth seized up as he thought about what he was saying. That was followed by a pregnant pause, at the end of which he admitted, "Actually, before I commit to anything I think the first thing I need to do is discuss all of this with the other members of my team. It wouldn't do to be excluding them from the process, especially not if we're going to need their support along the way."

Tim's eyes narrowed. "Does that mean you're going to have to involve Shannon in the process?"

"I'm afraid so. After all, she's both a board member and our VP of marketing, which makes her somewhat difficult to ignore."

Tim's brow furrowed. "Who am I to be commenting on this, but if I were you, I'd keep her out of the loop for as long as possible. Because who knows what she'll do with the information once she gets her hands on it. In fact, I wouldn't be surprised if she were to—"

David interrupted. "Excuse me, but this is coming from the same guy who, not forty-eight hours ago, was talking about wanting to befriend the woman? Come on, Tim, you're not making a whole lot of sense here. You either trust her or you don't. Which is it?"

"Who said anything about trusting her? I was just talking about trying to pump her for information. You know, act like a spy of sorts. Where's the trust inherent in that?"

"Whatever. Look, if I'm going to do this thing, and do it right, I'm going to have to have board approval. It's as simple as that. So, yes, I'm afraid I have no choice but to let Shannon in on what we're doing."

Tim blinked, unsure of how to respond to that. But before he could formulate a response, David spoke again. "But so what. The idea's not even off the ground yet, so what have we got to worry about? How can she destroy, or even damage, that which doesn't exist?"

6

GEORGE BARNETT II SAT IN HIS darkening office, brooding over a cup of lukewarm coffee. Draining the last of it in two loud gulps, he put the cup down, stood up, and walked over to the glass wall to his right. Staring out into the encroaching twilight, he saw that the sun's golden orb was just starting to dip below the tops of the city's concrete canyons, bathing everything in an iridescent symphony of colors. A breathtaking scene, yet it had absolutely no effect on him whatsoever. His mind was elsewhere. In fact, he was so wrapped up in his own thoughts that he failed to notice his secretary, Mrs. Angela Hill—a plump middle-aged woman with a trumpet for a voice—enter his office and move in behind him.

Not wanting to startle him, Angela softly cleared her throat, hoping that would get his attention. Then, when that didn't work, she took two steps forward and tapped him gently on the shoulder. A mistake she'd come to regret immediately.

George was so startled by her touch that he almost jumped out of his customized Fratelli Rossetti's. Then, quick to recover, he spun around and gave her a look that would have sent a grizzly running for cover. "What the hell are you doing?" he snapped. "Are you trying to give me a heart attack?"

She held up her hands in self-defense. "No, not at all," she stammered. "I . . . I just didn't know how else to get your attention."

George eyed her coolly, and then slowly turned to gaze again out the window. The great fireball in the sky was now slipping ever so slowly over the horizon, painting everything in its wake a spectacular array of luminous colors. Temporarily overwhelmed by it all, he stood motionless without uttering a word. After a few moments of meditation, he modified his tone somewhat, and asked, "How come you're still here? I thought you'd already left for the weekend."

Angela shook her head. "No, I've just come from Mary Pitman's office. She was giving me a crash course in that new software program we just got, and I guess we both just lost track of the time. But now I've really got to get going. You know how John hates having to cook for himself."

George nodded.

"Well, I'm off then. Oh, one last thing before I go. Mr. Al-Hassan called a few minutes ago to say that he's going to be late. Apparently he's stuck in traffic and may not get here for another half hour or so. He just wanted to let you know."

George's face clenched in frustration. "How thoughtful of him," he said, his voice heavy with sarcasm.

Not sure how best to respond to that, Angela simply asked, "Is there anything you'd like me to do before I go?"

George waved dismissively. "No, thanks. Please, just go home and enjoy your weekend. I'll see you again Monday morning."

With that, Angela quickly yet quietly exited the room, softly closing the door behind her on her way out, leaving George to return to the shadows of his private thoughts.

George Barnett II was polished, sophisticated, and clever. At the age of fifty-one, he looked like a man whose fortieth birthday was still somewhere in the future—a fact he took advantage of whenever an opportunity presented itself. As a consequence, he was an ardent bachelor and hedonist.

He was lean and wiry in build. His facial features were androgynous, although the years had etched fine lines around his eyes and mouth. His short dark brown hair, laced with silver, was cut stylishly and brushed straight back. His nose was straight and narrow, his clothing, tasteful and refined. His eyes, however, were his most distinctive feature. They were the color of pewter and remained cold and hard even when he smiled. Which was rare.

Though George was often in a foul mood, this one was darker than normal. He'd just received word from his Celebrix informant that not only was the company's highly advanced artificial intelligence software suite almost ready to go to market, but that the company's owner—Timothy E. Hunt—may have found a way to expedite that process even further. According to his source, Celebrix had just sent some of its top people to Boston to join forces with another small team operating out of a company called Quenetics. Their mission, though highly secretive and apparently still poorly defined, was to marry Celebrix's new multi-billion-dollar software suite to a new e-learning concept developed by the Quenetics people. Exactly how they planned to do it, his informer didn't yet know, but had promised to get back to him as soon as he did.

But even without knowing all the details, George already knew enough to be concerned—deeply concerned. Celebrix, the company he'd been lusting after for more than a decade, was now possibly about to move permanently out of reach. That was something he couldn't allow, at any cost. He'd had Celebrix ripped out of his hands once before and he was determined not to let it happen again.

Celebrix was a small Silicon Valley outfit which, in George's view, was on the verge of becoming a modern-day Microsoft. The way he saw it, the company's eclectic mix of behavioral scientists, IT experts, medical psychologists, cyberneticists, and webmasters had developed an artificial intelligence software suite that was so advanced, it was destined to *completely* revolutionize the IT world, and in so doing, it would become the nucleus around which a whole new generation of software companies would emerge.

Celebrix had been formed in the late 1980s as a special unit within the ultra-secretive yet highly advanced research arm of the Pentagon—better known as DARPA, an acronym standing for the Defense Advanced Research Projects Agency. In its first four years of existence, the Celebrix unit had made considerable inroads into the rapidly evolving field of artificial intelligence; however, despite its achievement, time had not been on its side. Within months of the fall of the Berlin Wall, which had signaled the end of the Cold War, DARPA's budget had been slashed to the bone. Any project deemed too risky or too far down the Pentagon's priority list was immediately red-flagged and then subjected to intense scrutiny. Celebrix, with its swollen expense accounts, lofty notions, and rolling deadlines received more attention than any. So much so, that before long, its life-line was severed and the group was set adrift into the uncharted waters of the real world, where they discovered that cash-flow was king, and short-termism prevailed. It was a cruel transition.

Initially, the group had tried to hold itself together, but it didn't take long for cracks to appear. One by one, the group started to disband as reserves dried up and disillusion set in. Yet, try as they might, they just couldn't find a sponsor willing to invest in something with such an indeterminate future. So, before the year was out, the group had already been reduced to half its original size, and was still fraying around the edges. However, though severely weakened, the group—or what was left of it—refused to give up. With considerable courage and unbridled tenacity, they fought on. By connecting up with technology-based think tanks and pioneering organizations and institutions the world over, they somehow managed to scrape by from one year to the next. And that continued for many a year until, as fate would have it, just as their patience had run out, one of them bumped into a business angel by the name of Timothy E. Hunt. Hunt, an avowed technophile and AI enthusiast, immediately recognized their potential and bought in. Initially he'd acquired a 40 percent stake, but that had increased over time to the point where he now owned 92 percent—with the other 8 percent still in the hands of some of the group's top scientists.

And yet, throughout all these changes, one thing had remained constant: George Barnett's obsession to reacquire what had once been his—Celebrix. For it had been he, while head of DARPA, who'd founded the company, and who'd struggled for years to keep it going when everyone else had wanted it shut down. Most saw it as nothing more than an obsession of his to try to accomplish the impossible—to create a machine that was capable of thought and emotion. Pure fantasy, thought some; utter stupidity, thought others. Grand waste of time, talent, and money, thought all. But still George had hung on. Fighting everyone, he'd kept the project alive, until finally the day came when he could fight no more. The forces had aligned themselves against him with such clarity of purpose that not even he could resist any longer. They'd beaten him, and he knew it. Celebrix had to go. But before cutting it loose, he performed one last desperate act: he planted a spy inside the Celebrix organization. That way, he figured that if they ever accomplished what they'd set out to do, he'd be the first to know, and therefore, in the best position to do something about it. The only problem was that what he didn't know was that within the week he'd also be shown the door. He'd become a political liability, and had to go.

Six months later, humbled but not defeated, George had decided to start his own company. A consultancy specializing in applied research and creativity. He called it the Center for Applied Research. Now, almost a decade and a half later, the company had grown into a $100 million enterprise, and he'd amassed considerable wealth. Wealth which should have brought him piece of mind, yet it didn't. Not in the slightest.

As far as he was concerned, those who said that success is the best form of revenge didn't have a clue what they were talking about. Yes, money could buy recognition and respect, but what it could never buy was a plug large enough to fill the hole he felt inside. For he'd lost more than his job when he'd been ousted from DARPA—much, much more. He'd also lost credibility and pride—two things that no amount of money could ever make up for. Thus, the only true way of getting back all that he'd lost—not to mention the billions that were still waiting to be had—was to reacquire Celebrix before its products made their way to market.

This, however, was proving an elusive task, for the simple reason that Timothy E. Hunt was refusing to even meet, let alone discuss selling him his stake in the company. The result: George was now up against the proverbial wall, and it was driving him crazy.

He'd tried everything. He'd begun by offering Hunt obscene amounts of money, but when that hadn't worked, he'd then ratcheted things up a notch or two by bringing in some hired help and paying them to harass, cajole, and on a few occasions even attempt to bribe key Celebrix employees to leave. But, as yet, not one of them had left. It was unbelievable, and extremely frustrating. What was a man to do?

With time running out and his options spent, George realized that there was now only one thing to do: he'd have to raise the stakes yet again. That meant it was time to get serious and to bring in the big guns—hence the imminent arrival of Al-Hassan.

7

Grimaldi's Restaurant, Boston

ROGER MILLER HAD BOLTED from the limo even before it had come to a complete stop. Sprinting around the back of the car, he yanked open the back door, and with exaggerated chivalry, he offered his hand to the woman inside.

Swiveling ever so gracefully in her seat, Shannon Atkinson extended one perfectly sculptured leg, then the other, onto the pavement below. Accepting Roger's outstretched hand, she climbed out of the car and stood for a moment next to him as she smoothed imaginary wrinkles from her Karl Lagerfeld creation. Roger looked on in carnal delight.

Leaving the door to the driver, Roger tucked his arm in hers as he guided her toward the restaurant's entrance. Grimaldi's—the restaurant's name was displayed in coiled neon as well as painted in curlicued script in the window— was reputed to have one of the best kitchens in the city. So said Shannon. And, as this was her city, who was he to argue otherwise? Not that he'd be tempted to anyway. Because if there was one thing that could be said about Shannon, she was a lot more pleasant to be around when she got things her own way. And even then, it was never easy!

Approaching the cozy and quaint colonial-style building, they ducked through the creaky wooden doorway. Once inside, they entered a small, dimly lit anteroom where they were met by the silver-haired, ultra chic, maître d' who introduced himself as Philippe. Philippe led them through another low doorway into a larger, vaulted room lighted by only a few strategically placed candles. Shannon led the way, with Roger, who counted walking behind pretty women as one of the small rewards in life, doing his best to keep his eyes off the undulant hips and the impressive length of her legs. Philippe ushered them to their seats and nodded to the young serving girl standing in the corner.

Once they were settled at their table and had given their drink orders, Roger picked up where they'd left off in the car. "Now then. Let's get back to the issue at hand. Have you decided yet what you're going to do?"

Shannon raised an eyebrow. "No, I haven't, and I don't intend to over dinner. It's as simple as that. I'm here to eat, not conduct business. If you feel different, then maybe you should go and sit with somebody else. Maybe they'll indulge you, but I certainly won't. So, if you want to stay at this table, then I suggest you talk about something else." Short pause. "You are capable of talking about something else, aren't you?" she asked, her voice thick with sarcasm.

Roger really had to fight to contain his emotions. The desire to strike back was almost overwhelming, but somewhere deep within the dark recesses of his mind he seemed to realize that this was neither the time nor the place to get into another verbal fencing match with her. It would just have to wait. He sighed inwardly. Then, sitting back in his chair, he passed a hand through his hair and pondered the question he'd been pondering all evening: How could such a beautiful woman be *so* difficult to get along with? She had to be the most inflexible, intolerant, and demanding woman he'd ever met. Yet, even so, he was still absolutely infatuated with her. She looked like someone who'd just stepped out of the pages of a women's fashion magazine. She stood five foot eight and had the body of an aerobics instructor and the face of a cover girl. She had long, wavy auburn hair that framed finely sculpted features showcasing emerald-green eyes. She walked with elegance and grace, evoking an image of quiet wealth and easy sophistication, qualities that Roger had always dreamed of finding in a partner, as he could never seem to find them in himself.

In a nutshell, at least on the surface, she was everything Roger had ever wanted in a woman, and then some. If only she didn't have such an attitude.

Ironically, while Roger was trying to sort out his feelings towards Shannon, she was doing exactly the same thing, just the other way around. Though somewhat reluctant to do so, she did have to admit that there was an attraction, however slight. For the man certainly had his charms, but physically he just didn't do it for her. He was forty-nine years of age and slightly overweight, although he carried it well. He was tall and burly and had a florid, outdoor complexion. His short black hair, with just a hint of gray at the temples, was parted on the left and carelessly brushed so that a thick black comma fell down over the right eyebrow. The longish straight nose ran down to a short upper lip, below which was a wide and finely drawn but cruel mouth. His pale-blue eyes were the most penetrating she'd ever seen. Staring into them, she was two parts intimidated and one part attracted. Definitely not the ratio she was looking for. That was one strike against him. And then there was the clincher: his personality! The man was an obstinate, narcissistic boor who had about as much sensitivity as a dead toad. So that was it then. Her decision was made. She wouldn't be adding Roger to her list of conquests—at least, not yet. Not unless she had to—which, in this case, meant that if he were to start backing away from his commitment to invest in her, then she'd have no choice but to rethink her position. But until then, she'd keep it strictly professional. It was easier that way. She got his money, he got to expand his empire. Simple.

Roger, as chairman and CEO of eMaxx, a multi-billion-dollar interim company he'd started ten years earlier, was a very wealthy man. As such, he was exactly the type of man that Shannon was looking for. And the fact that they shared a common goal—gaining control of Quenetics—was just an added bonus. It made him the perfect partner. It was just too bad that he wasn't more physically attractive, because then he truly would have been the perfect partner. "Oh well, you can't have it all," she thought to herself.

She was suddenly brought back to the present by the sound of Roger's voice. "Before we move off the subject completely, there's just one other thing I'd like to add." Tenuous pause. "If I may."

Shannon sighed deeply and then produced an artificial smile. "What's that?"

Roger leaned forward and lowered his voice. "My controller has finished crunching the numbers, and I'm afraid they're not quite what I was hoping for."

"And what's that supposed to mean?" Her smile already a distant memory.

"It's simple. eMaxx is a dotcom, and nobody appears willing to invest in dotcoms these days. As a result, my hands are tied when it comes to trying to raise new capital at the moment."

Pause as wide as the Pacific.

Shannon's fingers paid a thoughtful visit to her earring, a sign that her frustration was building. "Do me a favor and get to the point, will you?" Her voice had acquired a serrated edge.

A glint of anger flashed through Roger's eyes, and then was gone. "The point is that my spending is capped at four hundred and fifty million, which roughly translates into about one hundred dollars a share."

Sitting bolt upright, Shannon retorted, "A hundred dollars a share! What are you talking about?" Sensing that she was drawing attention to herself, she immediately lowered her voice. But the aggression was still there. "Nobody's going to sell to you at that price and you know it. So what are we talking about here?"

Roger responded to the edge in her voice by slightly raising the volume of his own. "I disagree. Completely. The way I see it, if your stock continues to tumble, one hundred dollars a share is soon going to start looking rather attractive indeed to most of your shareholders."

She scoffed. "Yeah, right, and if the sky falls, we'll all be wearing blue hats!"

"Huh?"

"Come on, Roger, be realistic, will you?" Shannon said tersely. "There's absolutely no way it's going to go low enough for the pension fund managers, in particular, to accept such a paltry sum. Remember, I was with you when you offered each of them what amounted to a 15 percent premium over market, and where did that get you? Nowhere! None of them were interested. So, if they weren't interested at one hundred ten dollars, what makes you think you can interest them in even less? It doesn't make any sense."

Roger fixed her with his gaze, his brow knit in earnest disbelief. "You just don't get it, do you? You seem to be in a state of denial over this. Your stock has plunged almost 30 percent in four months. What makes you think that it's not going to go lower? I think it will. And when it does, I'll be ready." He caught himself. "Sorry, what I meant to say was that 'we'll' be ready."

She smirked but said nothing.

Not wanting to draw any more attention to his slight slip of the tongue, he quickly proceeded with his argument. "And how do I know that we'll be ready? Because—and this is something that may come as a surprise to you—I've gone back to each of those pension fund guys over the last few days, and do you want to know what I learned?" It was a rhetorical question. "If I were to raise the premium to 25 percent, each of them said that they'd reconsider immediately, which I interpreted to mean that they'd be prepared to sell. Which then leaves us with two possibilities: one, we raise our bid to a hundred and fifteen, which, as I've already said, is not possible; or two, we wait until your stock falls to eighty, and make our move then."

"Eighty!" she parried reflexively. "It'll never go that low. Trust me on this; if you're serious about buying those shares, you're just going to have to find a way to raise more money."

Roger shook his head as if he'd delivered the coming rejoinder a hundred times. "It'll never go that low?" He chuckled. "It started the year at one hundred and twenty-four dollars. And where is it now? Just a hair above ninety-two dollars, which means what, it fell some thirty-two dollars in less than four months and you're telling me that there's no way it can fall another twelve?" He slowly shook his head. "I don't know, Shannon, but I think that if one of us is not making any sense here, it's you."

•   •   •

7:46 P.M., Saturday, April 25
David's home, Wellesley

David was livid. Upon learning that Shannon and Roger were dining together in Boston, right under their noses, he'd slipped immediately into a mild state of panic. The first thing he'd done was to retreat to the safety of his study, pour himself a stiff drink, and take a few big gulps. Thus fortified, he flopped into the nearest chair, bowed his head, and slowly closed his eyes. His heart was pounding, his breath was quickening, and his head felt like it was going to explode. He knew the symptoms well. Apparently he was about to have another anxiety attack. In preparation, he put his glass down on the table beside him, lowered his head onto his chest, and then concentrated on his breathing. A few minutes later it was over and things slowly returned to normal. But, as soon as they did, his mind drifted back to what had caused it in the first place—Shannon!

Something clearly had to be done about her. But what? He had absolutely no idea. "But maybe Tim might," he thought to himself. With that, he decided to give him a call.

Tim answered immediately and explained that he was still at the office sharing a pizza with the other iQu team members. However, hearing the urgency in David's voice he promised to leave immediately.

Half an hour later, David, who was by then on his third drink, heard a car pulling into the driveway. Rushing to the window, he pulled back the curtains and, to his considerable relief, saw Robert—Tim's bodyguard and chauffeur—at the wheel. Good, Tim was finally home. Now at least he had some-one he could commiserate with. Maybe talking about it would help to diminish the vertigo he was undergoing.

It didn't. Ten minutes into the conversation, the sensation was just as strong as ever. No matter how he looked at it, he just saw a bad situation getting progressively worse—and with no solution in sight.

Tim wasn't quite so negative. So, Shannon and Roger were still in contact with one another. Disturbing, yes; shocking, no. He'd expected it.

"So, what do you think we should do about it?" David asked.

Tim hesitated for a moment and then replied, "The way I see it, we have three options at this point."

"And they are?"

Bounding from his chair, Tim began his ritualistic pacing. Moving in fluid circles around the room, he said, "First of all, I suggest we fight fire with fire. If Miller can raise the funds to take you over, then I don't see why we shouldn't be able to do likewise. After all, I probably have as many contacts in the investment world as he does."

David shook his head. "I've already been down that road, and believe me, it's a dead end. Nobody's interested. Everyone is quick to see the logic in fusing Quenetics and eMaxx together as we both dominate completely different parts of the same industry—we the 'brick' side, eMaxx the 'click' side—but that's as far as they're willing to go. None of them, for example, are willing to put any money into it. And for one very simple reason. They all say that with it being a bear market and all, and with dotcoms no longer in fashion, this just isn't the right time to try something like this. Maybe someday in the future, but not now."

Tim could feel his friend's frustration, but wasn't willing to give up so easily. "I hear what you're saying, but I think that before we abandon the idea completely, it might be worthwhile for me to take a shot at it. What do you say?"

"Hey, who am I to tell you what you can or can't do? All I can say is that I think you'd be wasting your time, but again, that's up to you." He cast a sideways glance at his drink, and then thought better of it. He asked, "So, how about your second idea? What's it all about?"

Tim hesitated. "It's something completely different. But, before I get into it, you first need to promise me something."

"What's that?"

"That you'll keep your mind open and your mouth closed until I've finished."

David flashed the feeblest of smiles. "I can't promise that. My reaction will obviously depend on the idea itself. If it has merit, I'll listen. If it doesn't, I won't. It's as simple as that." He cleared his throat. "So, what's the idea?"

"Together, Shannon and Roger pose a formidable threat. But individually, they don't. Do you agree?"

"I do. But so what, it's now become abundantly clear that they're in this together, so your question is a moot point." Slight pause. "Unless, of course, you're suggesting that we too hire an assassin or two. Which, come to think of it, might not be such a bad idea."

Tim assumed that David was joking, but judging by the tone and tenor of his voice, he couldn't be sure. "No, that's certainly not what I had in mind, but it does raise an interesting point." He leaned forward in his chair and spoke with appropriate gravity. "Let's say, just for the sake of argument, that she isn't interested in having you killed, and that therefore, the attempts made on your life weren't attempts at all, but were rather nothing more than random acts of an unfortunate nature."

David scoffed. "Yeah, right, and pigs have lips."

"Just hear me out on this, will you? I'm not saying she's innocent; all I'm suggesting is that in order for us to ensure that we look at this from every angle, we should at least consider the possibility."

"OK, so let's consider the possibility. Let's see now." He paused to scratch his head and to pretend to give it serious consideration. "OK, so she's not out to kill me; so what? In very practical terms, all that would mean is that we're spending money on personal security that could be better spent elsewhere. And that's about it. Everything else remains the same, including the fact that she's still intent on getting rid of me and taking over Quenetics."

"You're right. That's true. Which, for me, raises an interesting question: Why? Why is she so anxious to get rid of you?" Tim asked. But before David had a chance to formulate a response, Tim answered it for him. "I suspect that the answer to that probably has a lot to do with the strategic direction you've set for Quenetics. Apparently, she doesn't agree with it. She wants to go one way, you want to go another."

"Yeah, so?"

"So, what do you think would happen if she were to learn that what I just said is in fact no longer true; that rather than heading in opposite directions, the two of you are now heading in more or less the same direction?" Pause for breath. "I don't know about you, but I think that she'd find that quite useful information, so much so that it might even be enough to give her pause for thought."

David's face scrunched up. "I'm confused. Are you sure we're talking about the same woman here? I thought we were talking about Shannon, you know, the woman who's—"

"Don't be facetious. Yes, I'm well aware of who it is that we're talking about, but at the same time, I don't think that we should underestimate the magnitude of the strategic changes that you're now considering—*selling off non-core businesses; focusing all efforts on the temp industry; and then, within that in-*

dustry, differentiating yourself by laying claim to the word 'self-development.' Then, as though that weren't already enough, you're now talking about turning around and using that platform as a basis upon which to build what could conceivably turn out to be the most powerful Web-based company the world has ever seen."

David was in too dark a mood to get swept up in Tim's enthusiasm. So, rather than building on Tim's words, he concentrated instead on tearing them down. "And you think that that's going to be enough to get Shannon to suddenly switch sides?"

Tim's enthusiasm fizzled. "I realize it's a long shot, but I still think it's worth a try."

David chortled. "My answer to this idea is the same as that I had to your last idea: I think it's nuts! But, hey, if you want to do it, then who am I to suggest otherwise. Just do it, but please, do me a favor, and leave me out of it. I have more important things to do with my time."

Seeing that this line of thinking was also going nowhere fast, Tim quickly moved on to his third, and final, idea. "The other thing we could do is to launch a PR campaign aimed at trying to change your public image."

After a short pull from his drink, David asked, "And, now, why would we want to do that, as in, what's wrong with the public image I have now?"

Tim hesitated, but just for a few seconds. "Nothing major, or at least nothing that a good public relations firm couldn't fix."

"And what's that supposed to mean?" David asked coolly.

"There's no need to get testy about it. I'm just commenting on things that you've been saying to me for almost a week now.

You keep telling me that the market doesn't look all that favorably on you at the moment. You say that many seem to see you as being too staid and conservative to make the changes that they think are necessary to turn this company around."

"Strange. I don't remember ever using those particular words to describe myself," David said. Even to himself, the starchy words sounded too defensive.

"I'm paraphrasing, but I'm sure you catch my meaning."

"I do, but is there a point to all of this?" David asked crisply.

"My point is that I think that we need to cast you in a slightly different light; reposition you, so to speak."

"And just what would this 'new me' look like in your view?"

"He'd be more of a visionary; an industry leader rather than a follower; a rule maker rather than a rule taker; a corporate revolutionary; a man slightly ahead of his time."

"Enough already, I get the point." Lengthy pause. "And even if I were to agree to this, what makes you think that it could actually be done? It's not easy to change public perception, as I'm sure you know."

"I do," Tim said. "But in your case, I think it's possible, particularly in light of the fact that you've got an ace up your sleeve."

"And that is?"

"iQu. Just pump up the volume on iQu and watch what happens next. There'll be fireworks, you can be sure."

"And, by 'pumping up the volume,' do I assume that to mean 'hyping it to the max?'"

Tim nodded.

A short bark of derision from David. "But iQu is little more than a concept at this point. What kind of hype can I build around that? I mean, yeah, maybe in a year or two something's possible, but not now. It's still way too early."

Tim shook his head. "That would be true if Celebrix wasn't in the picture, but that is not the case. So, in my view, I think now is the perfect time to announce iQu to the world."

"What are you talking about, it's still—"

Tim was quick to interrupt. "For once, would you just give me the benefit of the doubt?" As an afterthought, he added, "And even if it were to take us a bit more time than I suspect to get version 1.0 up and running, so what? What's the big deal? That still shouldn't preclude us from trying to get some mileage out of it."

"What on earth are you talking about?" David said curtly. "Are you suggesting we *lie* . . . to everyone?" His voice, though muted, acquired a serrated edge.

"No, absolutely not. Who said anything about lying? All I'm suggesting is that we provide the press with just enough information to get them excited, but not enough to do us any harm, either today or sometime in the future. We can do that. Politicians do it every day, and they get away with it. Why wouldn't we?"

David remained unconvinced. "I don't know, Tim. I just don't see this idea working. I think that if we give them too much information, we'll get ourselves into trouble; if we don't give them enough, they'll ignore us."

"So, we have to strike a balance," Tim said tonelessly.

David shook his head. "I think that would be like trying to balance yourself on the head of a pin, which is a complete impossiblity. So, contrary to what you seem to be thinking, what I think is that we just need to wait awhile. Until this thing is more fully flushed out. Then, we'll see. But going off half-cocked; that to me is a recipe for disaster. Because, don't forget, if I screw this up, whatever credibility I still have left would disappear instantly. And that's something I can't afford. I'm sure you understand."

• • •

9:26 P.M., Saturday, April 25
Grimaldi's Restaurant, Boston

They ate and talked, avoiding any further discussion about the current state of Quenetics, slipping gradually from business gossip into an exchange of likes and dislikes, hopes and ambitions, the small revelations of two people feeling their way towards getting better acquainted with one another. The restaurant was almost empty by the time they finished their coffee and asked for the bill. Shannon paid.

Leaving the restaurant, they went out into the cool night air. Feeling a slight chill, Shannon tucked a hand under Roger's arm as they waited for their limo to arrive. Looking into each other's eyes there was, for the briefest of moments, a tentative, slightly awkward moment. But it quickly passed.

Climbing into the limo behind her, Roger made himself comfortable and then asked, "So, what do you feel like doing now? I'm up for anything."

Shannon hesitated before answering. On the one hand, she didn't want to offend him, but on the other, she also didn't want to lead him on. So, what to do? She turned away and looked out the window as she ruminated. Roger wisely chose not to interrupt.

Staring out the window at the cars speeding by, something suddenly caught her eye. Through a break in the traffic she saw what looked like two guys sitting in a parked car on the opposite side of the street watching them. "Huh? That's not possible," she thought to herself. So she looked again, and sure enough, she saw two faces staring back at her.

"What the hell is going on here?" she screamed to herself. But before she could even attempt an answer, something else suddenly popped into her mind. Staring hard at the guy in the passenger seat, she suddenly remembered having seen him somewhere before—quite recently, in fact. Wracking her brain trying to remember where, it suddenly dawned on her that she'd seen him at her fitness club two nights earlier. He'd been standing at the bulletin board in the reception hall, and had suddenly turned away when she'd looked his way. Out of shyness, she'd assumed then. But now, seeing the guy staring at her through the tinted windows of her limo, a more sinister thought came to mind. *Maybe he'd simply wanted to avoid eye contact. But why would he want to do that? It didn't make any sense, unless . . . unless, he was spying on her!* She shuddered at the thought. *But why? Why the hell would he want to spy on her?* Maybe he was stalking her, or more likely, maybe someone had put him up to it! But who?

Struggling to contain the emotions bubbling up within, she took a few deep breaths in an effort to calm herself down. The thoughts jostled and collided in her mind. *Focus, dammit.*

One by one she considered the different possibilities, but none of them made any sense. So, she threw logic to the wind and listened instead to her intuition. It was almost never wrong. And what it told her was that David almost certainly had a hand in this.

Her anger flared. She felt her stomach climb inside her chest, her breath leave her. The world shrank around her until she heard only the panoply of arguments desperately jockeying for position inside her mind.

Why? Why would he do it? Why would a man put his own sister under surveillance? Questions, questions, questions. Questions to which there were no answers, at least, not initially. But after further thought, the fog started to lift, and things became clearer. The hushed words, the furtive glances, the thinly veiled accusations, everything. Suddenly it all made sense. Not that insanity ever made sense, but at least now she could see method to David's madness.

But what to do about it? That was the next question. And one which drew a very interesting and unexpected response. It was vile, but under the circumstances, perfectly justified. It brought a smile to her face.

Turning to Roger, she said, "Sorry for the delay, but I was just trying to remember what my schedule looks like for tomorrow before deciding how late to make it tonight."

"And?" Roger asked with boyish enthusiasm.

Shannon couldn't help but smile. "I think I can go a few more hours. So, what do you say about going back to my place for a nightcap? Sound good to you?"

8

Shannon's condominium, Boston

SITTING AT THE BREAKFAST TABLE dressed in sweatpants and a loose-fitting T-shirt, Shannon sipped on her cup of decaf and reflected again on the events of last night. After sharing a bottle of wine, she'd asked Roger to stay the night so that they could talk again in the morning. Roger, not surprisingly, had accepted without hesitation, until he'd learned that he'd be spending the night—alone—in one of the guest rooms. He'd found that hard to accept, and had put considerable effort into trying to get her to change her mind. But, to no avail. She'd held her ground and had slept alone. And, quite well, all things considered. She wondered if the same could be said of David. Somehow she doubted it. "How could he?" she mumbled into her coffee. If he really did have her under surveillance, which she was now quite certain that he did, then he would have been aware of the fact that Roger had spent the night at her place. She could only imagine what that had done to his mind. She smiled at the thought of it.

The feeling was short lived, however, because a few moments later she suddenly heard the shower go on in Roger's room. Oh, no. He was awake. She could only hope that he was in a better mood this morning than he was last night. He'd gone to bed one angry man. Maybe if she were to make breakfast for him, that would help to soothe the beast within.

She got up from the table and got started immediately.

•   •   •

Shannon lived in a large and ultra-luxurious five-bedroom condominium in a new high-rise on O Street. The building was less than two years old and was considered to be one of the city's top properties, and for good reason. It was centrally located and had all the amenities money could buy—central air and heat; plush carpeting throughout; marble floors in the kitchen and bathrooms; thick, soundproof walls; a first-class security system; a concierge; indoor and outdoor swimming pools; fitness room; spa; bakery; underground parking; and even a helipad on the roof. As far as she knew, there was no other building like it anywhere along the eastern seaboard.

It had cost her a small fortune to get in, but that was of little concern to her. She had more money than she knew what to do with, which was one of the best things about being an Atkinson. However, that life of privilege came at a price, and the price was high. She was never taken seriously. No matter where she went or what she did, she was always cast in her father's shadow—her achievements, of which there had been many, were simply seen as a natural consequence of his wealth and power. Never once had she received any of the credit. Take university, for example. She'd gotten her MBA at Stanford, and yes, though her father had footed the bill, her top five standing had been of her own doing. In other words, her grades had been earned, and not bought, as most seemed to assume. Likewise, the position she now held within Quenetics was again completely of her doing. Yes, her name had helped her get through the front door, but that was it. From that moment onwards, the rest had been up to her. She'd insisted upon it. And, now, here she was, a mere 29 years of age, and already the VP of Marketing—a position she held for one reason, and one reason only. Because she was the best person for the job. It was as simple as that. The only problem was that nobody else seemed to see it that way. Most assumed that she'd been given the job because of who she was, and not because of what she was capable of. And that absolutely infuriated her! But that was all about to change. Once David was gone, and she was in power, things would be different. Very different. She'd quickly turn the company around, and then maybe, just maybe, she'd get the respect she deserved. At least, that was the plan.

But before that could happen, there was still much to be done. And topping the list of things to do was the need to resolve the Timothy E. Hunt issue. It could be postponed no longer. The man was becoming a menace. The fact that he'd even gotten involved with Quenetics in the first place had been cause enough for concern, yet she'd gone along with it. But now there was the surveillance issue, and that was something she just couldn't accept. Whether it was his idea, or whether he was simply just playing along, it didn't matter to her. He was involved, of that she was certain. And for that he had to go. Which was too bad, because if she was honest with herself, she had to admit that, at least on a physical level, she did find him to be rather attractive.

Then, quickly berating herself for even thinking such thoughts, she flushed them from her mind and returned to the issue at hand—how to get rid of the guy. Thinking while moving, she walked over to the fridge. Opening it up, she peered inside, only to discover what she'd already expected—it was all but empty. Not surprising considering the fact that today was Saturday, and Wednesdays and Saturdays were her shopping days. Undeterred, she bent down and took inventory. There was half a carton of milk, which wasn't looking too healthy—it smelled and looked as if it might hold the cure for HIV. Next to it were some bagels, still in their plastic bag, a few apples and oranges, and half a jar of peanut butter, and that was about it. Then, in the door she found a few eggs—not yet hatched

Staring at them, for some reason, she thought again of Hunt, and suddenly her mood lightened. Beyond her anger and frustration grew an icy confidence, and beyond that a heightened lucidity. A thought was already forming in her mind, racing and developing until she saw clearly what she must do. A smile formed on her lips.

•   •   •

9:07 A.M., Sunday, April 26
David's home, Wellesley

Tim and Robert, his bodyguard, returned from their morning jog to find David standing on the veranda leaning against the railing. Stopping a few yards shy of the front steps, Tim signaled Robert to go on in without him. Then, looking up at

David, he asked, "So, what's the news? Have you heard anything yet?"

"Yeah, I got tired of waiting so I finally just phoned them."

"And?"

"Miller's still there." David hissed.

Tim sighed a gusty, melancholy sigh. "So, apparently this is more serious than we thought. It would appear that they're now sleeping together."

"So it would seem."

"Well, that certainly complicates matters, doesn't it?"

"Now, ain't that the truth," David said tonelessly.

Tim started to say something, then thought better of it. Instead, he asked, "So, what do you think? What should we do now?"

David shrugged. "I haven't got a clue. I really don't. All I know is that this ends any thoughts we may have had to try to separate the two of them. Wouldn't you agree?"

Tim was silent for a moment, and then said. "No, I'm not sure that I would."

David was completely mystified. "And why the hell not? I mean they're probably having sex as we speak. How are we going to compete against that?"

Tim smiled coyly. "I may surprise you."

·   ·   ·

10:42 A.M., Sunday, April 26
....
Shannon's condominium, Boston

Pouring Roger his second cup of decaf, Shannon asked if there was anything else he wanted.

"No, I'm afraid I've really got to get going. My plane leaves in less than two hours, and with security being what it is these days, I should probably have already left. However, before I leave, there's just one other thing I'd like to discuss."

"What's that?"

"Tim Hunt."

Shannon leaned forward, her soft green eyes gone hard. "Yes? What about him?"

"The man makes me nervous. I know that you disagree with me on that, but—"

"But nothing," she exclaimed. "I don't know how many times we have to go through this. This project that he and David are working on is nothing to worry about. It's just another of David's hare-brained, go-nowhere ideas. He has them all the time, like to the tune of maybe one a month, and the story is always the same. From one day to the next, he gets all fired up about something, throws buckets of money at it, until eventually he gets bored with it, and then drops it and moves on to something else. Some might call it 'attention deficit disorder.' I don't. I call it raw, unbridled stupidity, pure and simple."

Roger wasn't convinced. "That may be David's normal pattern of behavior, but this time around, things may be different. Because now he's got Hunt at his side, and Hunt is no quitter. He keeps going until he's won, which is apparently almost always. That concerns me *a lot.*"

Shannon reached across the table and gently rested her hand on his. In her most reassuring voice, she said, "Trust me, you don't need to worry about Hunt. I've got the situation completely under control. You just worry about getting the financing in place, and leave the rest to me."

· · ·

Shortly after showing Roger to the door, Shannon used her cellphone to call someone's beeper. A few minutes later her cellphone rang. Taking the call, she listened, asked a few questions, conveyed some clear instructions, and then hung up, a deep look of satisfaction on her face as she did so. Now, maybe she could enjoy what was left of her weekend.

9

6:12 P.M.,
Wednesday, April 29   Quenetics stock price: ▼ $91.25
David's home, Wellesley

BONE WEARY AND MENTALLY EXHAUSTED, Tim leaned heavily on the banister as he slowly made his way up the stairs to his room. Ever since the iQu project had gotten under way, he and the other members of the team had basically been living at the office, returning to their respective homes or hotel rooms, or whatever the case may be, periodically to get a few hours of sleep and for a change of clothes.

Reaching the head of the stairs, Tim started down the hallway toward his temporary bedroom—one of four guest rooms in the west wing of David's Victorian-style mansion. He wondered if he'd even make it to the bed before his body finally gave out on him. He couldn't remember ever being so physically exhausted and mentally depleted. Yet, the amazing thing was, tired as he was, he knew that the moment his head hit the pillow, his mind would suddenly switch back on, making it once again impossible for him to get a good night's sleep. It was the same thing every night. There he'd be, lying in bed almost paralyzed with fatigue, yet unable to sleep. And it was driving him nuts. If it continued for much longer he knew he'd end up baying at the moon and having to wear white jackets with extra long arms that tied up at the back.

He'd tried sleeping pills, but they'd only made matters worse. They'd made him moody, dehydrated, and lethargic. They were definitely not the answer. Then, upon Kim's advice, he'd tried meditation, but that hadn't worked either. Which left him with but one other option to explore: exercise. Maybe an hour or two atop David's mountain bike would do what a sleeping pill couldn't. Who was to say? But he had to find out. His very sanity depended upon it. So, tired as he was, he resolved to give it a try.

Decision taken, he quickly got himself ready. But as he slipped into the cycling gear he'd bought only a few days before, another thought suddenly occurred to him. Robert—thinking that Tim was going to retire for the night—had taken the rest of the night off. That meant that if Tim were to go cycling, he'd have to go it alone. A thought he didn't relish.

"Ah, what kind of silliness is this?" he mumbled to himself. "Of course I can go alone." Prior to the diving incident he'd never even considered having a bodyguard, and now here he was too frightened to go anywhere without one. Well, enough was enough! The time for living in fear was over—if only for an hour or two. So, yes, he'd go. Alone!

A short time later, feeling tired yet exhilarated, Tim peddled his way towards the forest's edge. So focused was he on what he was doing, he failed to notice a black SUV pull slowly away from the curb and take up pursuit.

Entering the verdant forest less than a minute later, Tim was immediately enveloped in its cool dampness. Breathing it in, Tim stopped for a few seconds to savor the beauty while adjusting his helmet strap. The forest buzzed and chirped and squawked with the frenetic joy of a world gone mad, while shafts of lemon-gold brilliance lanced down to its cushioned floor between bars and pools of brown-green shade; and the light was never still, never constant, because drifting mist floated among the treetops, filtering all the sunlight to a pearly sheen and brushing every pine cone with moisture that glistened when the mist lifted. Sometimes the wetness in the clouds condensed into tiny drops half mist and half rain, which floated downward rather than fell, making a soft rustling patter among the millions of needles.

Clicking the soles of his shoes into place, Tim set off down a path that was serpentine and slick and studded with rocks of every shape and size. Accelerating quickly, he soon found himself racing through a tunnel of green, oblivious to all but his surroundings. All else had ceased to exist; his worries and troubles gone; his fears and phobias banished; his mind empty. Peace at last.

• • •

Tony Bernelli wasn't quite so relaxed. He hated physical exertion of any kind. Even sex had become too much of a chore of late, and as such was performed only on special occasions—like whenever he didn't have to pay for it. And as for running, which is what he had to do now, he hated everything about it. The fire in his chest, the pain in his joints, the sweaty brow, the strained muscles . . . all of it. As far as he was concerned, the sport was a form of modern-day torture designed for fitness junkies with a penchant for spandex and rake-thin bodies. But, if it was a choice between having to do a bit of running or getting shot, it wasn't a difficult decision to make. He'd run, like the wind if he had to. Whatever it took to stay alive.

Having left the SUV at the forest's edge, Tony'd run less than half a mile when he decided to stop for a short rest. His heart was pumping so hard that he could feel it banging against his chest wall, and he had a horrible, dry, rasping sensation in his throat. He had sweat running into his eyes and down the folds of skin at the back of his neck. He flicked his head from side to side in an attempt to rid himself of some of it.

Panting heavily, he leaned forward with his hands on his knees and spit up some mucus. It was clear he'd already gone about as far as he was able to go. But that was no problem, as it had never been his intention to run all that far anyway. All he wanted to do was to get deep enough into the forest to ensure that when the time came to do the dirty deed, no one would see him do it. Looking around he decided that where he was would do just fine. Now all he needed to do was to find a good hiding place, and then wait until Hunt returned. And then hopefully with one well placed shot it would all be over.

•   •   •

Racing past the spot where he normally turned around when jogging, Tim realized he was now heading into unknown territory. Normally that would not have been a problem, but with the forest growing increasingly dark, he had to think twice about whether he should keep going. Braking hard, he brought the bike to a stop and took a swig from his water bottle while surveying the surroundings. Unless he turned around soon, it would be quite dark for much of the return trip. That would make conditions even more hazardous than they already were, but by the same token, it would also make the ride that much more exciting. He decided to go on for a few minutes more.

Sticking the water bottle back into its holder, he got back on the saddle and peddled off. A few minutes later he stopped again. He thought he'd heard traffic off in the distance. Holding his breath, he cocked an ear and listened. Within seconds he heard what sounded like a motorcycle going by. That could only mean one thing—the edge of the forest lay just up ahead. He wondered if he could exit the forest there as well. Assuming that he probably could, and growing increasingly uncomfortable with the encroaching darkness, he decided to go and check it out.

That decision saved his life.

10

TIM SAT ON THE EDGE OF HIS BED and tried to rub the sleep from his eyes. They were swollen and sore to the touch, as he'd just spent another restless night—fitful bouts of sleep, interrupted by a recurring dream of George Barnett squatting over a suitcase filled with cash, his finger beckoning. For some weeks now, Barnett had been trying to poach his top scientists away from Celebrix by waving ridiculously large sums of money in their faces. Thankfully, none had yet accepted, but that couldn't go on forever. Eventually someone would cave in, and when they did, others would surely follow. But, what to do about it, that was the question. To which he had yet to find a satisfactory answer. Though it certainly wasn't for lack of trying. He thought about it constantly. So much so, that the question had apparently now entered his subconscious—hence, the recurring dream.

Rising slowly from the bed, he did a few quick stretching exercises just to limber up a bit, and then shuffled off in the direction of the bathroom.

En route, he passed a mirror attached to the dresser. Stopping for a moment, he glanced at his reflection. Starting with his face, he saw that he looked as tired as he felt. Moving his eyes southward, he took in his chiseled, heavily muscled chest and washboard stomach. But rather than feeling proud, he instead just felt pangs of guilt. Guilt that he hadn't done any resistance training in almost a week, when normally it was something that he did every other day. It was a situation that just couldn't continue. He had to reestablish some sort of balance in his life. But how? iQu wouldn't allow for it. The project demanded his every waking moment, and more. It was exhausting. But, on the other hand, he also had to admit that it was an enormous amount of fun. Never in his life had he been involved in anything quite like it. The team was committed, the challenges were overwhelming, and the potential outcome was beyond comprehension. Just last night alone, for example, they'd put the finishing touches on a report which fleshed out an idea that he felt could conceivably revolutionize the way people, the world over, interacted with, and made use of, computers and other personal communication devices. It was huge beyond compare.

Feeling less guilty, Tim continued on into the bathroom. Twenty minutes later, he made his way downstairs to see what he could find in the kitchen. As he drew near, he could already smell the bacon frying. Maria, David's dependable maid, had obviously heard that he was up.

Upon reaching the kitchen door, Tim flinched at the blare of Sky Radio coming from within—pop music seemingly imprisoned in the seventies and wailing to get out. His efforts to introduce Maria to the strains of Mozart and Brahms had been decisively dismissed. Fallen on deaf ears, so to speak.

Entering the room, Tim was surprised to find that all the kitchen furniture had been moved into the living room, and Maria, on hands and knees, her rump swaying in time to the music, was attacking the already spotless floor tiles with a mixture of water and linseed oil. To her, the mansion was not so much a job as a hobby, a jewel to be scrubbed and polished and waxed and buffed. Dust was forbidden, untidiness a crime. Tim had often thought that if any of them ever stood still long enough, they too would be folded up and tucked neatly into a cupboard.

He yelled over the sound of the radio. "Morning, Maria."

With a grunt, the kneeling figure stood up and turned to inspect him, hands on her hips, a lick of black, silver-streaked hair escaping from the bright yellow Cubs baseball cap she wore for strenuous housework. Maria was what many would gallantly describe as a woman of a certain age, somewhere in that mysterious period between forty and sixty. She matched the furniture in the house: low, heavy-set, and built to last. Her white, seamed face was permanently set in an expression of disapproval.

"Don't come any closer, I've just finished cleaning that section of the floor and I have no intention of doing it again. I'll serve you your breakfast out on the veranda. I've already set everything up for you, so if you'll just—"

She was interrupted by the ringing of Tim's briefcase. Quickly placing it on the counter beside him, he popped it open and reached inside for his cellphone. Glancing at the display, he saw that it was David calling.

"Morning, David, how're things?"

The voice at the other end of the line was terse, almost to the point of being rude. "Bad news. I just got another call from Matt Baker, who said that—"

"Who?"

"Matt Baker, you know, the pension fund guy who first let us in on what Shannon and Roger Miller are up to."

"Oh, yeah, him. So, what'd he have to say this time?"

"It's not good, I'm afraid. But I'd rather not get into it over the phone, so if you could get here as soon as possible, I'd greatly appreciate it."

"I'm on my way."

• • •

9:57 A.M., Tuesday, May 5
Quenetics Headquarters, Boston

Tim entered Quenetics headquarters and went directly up to David's office. Entering the room, he found David and two others sitting around the small conference table—Nancy Lussier, the CFO, and Tom Gibson, the head of corporate communications.

After a quick flurry of "good mornings," Tim took a seat and waited to hear the news. "Thanks for getting here so quickly, Tim," said David. "I much appreciate it."

"No problem." Tim shrugged his shoulders. "So, what's up? What was so urgent that I had to miss my breakfast?"

David took a deep breath before answering. "Apparently someone's trying to talk down our stock."

Tim's eyebrows plunged. "Huh?"

"According to Baker, there's a rumor going round that our second quarter figures are going to come in well below what the market is expecting."

Tim's face scrunched up. "But I thought you were going to meet or possibly even beat market expectations?"

David thundered, "Exactly, that's my point! It's not true. None of this is true, which means that there's someone out there spreading malicious rumors about us. As to why, well, you figure it out. Why would someone want to do something like this? The only reason I can think of is that they're trying to further weaken our stock price. I mean, why else would they do it?" Lengthy pause. His face radiating anger and frustration. Then, in a voice laced with emotion, he added, "And I'm sure we all know who 'they' are!"

Tim ignored the unspoken invitation to state the obvious. Instead, he asked, "So, how much damage have they done?"

David rolled his eyes. "A lot!" Glancing over at his computer screen, he explained, "Our stock dropped to eighty-eight at the opening bell but has recovered a bit since then. It's now hovering around the ninety dollar mark."

Tim looked mildly confused. "Not wanting to add insult to injury, but to be honest, I'm somewhat surprised that it hasn't fallen further."

"That's only because the three of us have been manning the phones all morning trying to convince anyone willing to listen that this whole thing is nothing more than an elaborate hoax perpetrated by someone with an axe to grind."

"And it worked?" Tim asked.

"The fact that our stock has almost halved its losses would certainly suggest that it has."

Tom, who spoke for the first time, was not so quick to agree. "It could also be a 'dead-cat-bounce.'"

David's eyebrows knitted together. "And what's that supposed to mean?"

"I don't know," Tom replied. "I'm just not quite so convinced that the market is listening to us at the moment, and even if they are, I'm not sure they necessarily believe what we're telling them. Most of the people I spoke to this morning seemed barely able to hide their skepticism. In fact, some didn't even bother to try. You could hear it in their voices that they didn't believe a word I was saying. And the harder I tried to convince them, the more skeptical they became." Looking directly at Tim, he added, "Believe me, it wasn't a lot of fun."

Before Tim could respond to that, David turned to Tom and snapped, "What kind of rubbish is that? I must have talked to as many people as you did this morning, and I certainly didn't get that impression at all. Sure, they asked a lot of questions, but that's what they're supposed to do. They're analysts. After all, that's what they're paid to do—to look behind the façade to find out what's really going on inside an organization versus what management tells them is going on. And thank goodness they do, because otherwise, our financial system would be in even more of a mess than it already is."

Tom was not to be swayed. "I've been at this game long enough to know how the system works, and I'm telling you, the reactions I got this morning were completely out of the ordinary. There's healthy skepticism, and then there was what I experienced this morning. And let me tell you, there's no comparison between the two."

Nancy nodded her head in agreement. "Sorry David, but I'm afraid I'm going to have to side with Tom on this one. Things really have turned nasty out there. In fact, I was actually genuinely shocked by some of the reactions I got this morning—they ranged from downright belligerent to mildly offensive, and just about everything in between. The only thing I didn't get was a friendly voice. Not one, and I must have made at least a dozen calls. So, if I were to use that as some kind of barometer of market sentiment, I'd be forced to conclude what I've already said—we don't seem to have a lot of friends out there at the moment. And that scares the hell out of me, because imagine, with that kind of negativity already out there, what would happen if we were to hit them with even one more piece of bad news. I don't think we'd survive it."

· · ·

It was almost one o'clock before the meeting broke up and David and Tim were left to themselves. Holding a hand over his stomach, Tim said, "I don't know about you, but having missed breakfast, I've just got to get something to eat. Otherwise I'm likely to pass out. So, if you don't mind, I think I'm going to run down to the cafeteria. Do you want to join me?"

"Actually, I'd prefer we had lunch in here. That way we can talk more about iQu. Is that all right with you?"

"Sure, whatever. Just so long as I get some food. I don't care where I eat it."

David nodded his head in understanding and then picked up the phone and issued some instructions to his secretary. When he'd finished, he looked over at Tim and said, "OK, iQu. So, what's the latest?"

Tim feigned mild surprise. "I'm surprised that you ask. I thought you weren't all that interested."

"Whatever gave you that idea?"

"Because whenever I brought it up earlier, you'd steam-rolled right over me, which suggested to me that you weren't all that interested."

David scoffed at the remark. "Yeah, right! How could I not be interested? I'm the one who's bankrolling the thing."

Tim threw him a look, which said, "Are you sure about that?"

David was quick to modify his words. "Not all of it, of course, but certainly a major part of it. But that's not the point. The point is that yes, of course, I'm interested to hear what's going on. So, as for my behavior this morning, the only reason I kept brushing the issue aside was because I wanted to keep everyone focused on the problem at hand, and not get side-tracked on issues of secondary importance."

"Of secondary importance? You see iQu to be of secondary importance" Tim asked, more mystified than miffed. "Wow, go figure. I would have said exactly the opposite. In my view, iQu is of critical import. It's precisely what this company needs right now. It's your brighter tomorrow. It's your next generation Quenetics. Meaning, it's not just a slightly modified version of what your company is today; it's a completely new company, built not on the ashes of yesterday but rather on the possibilities and potentialities of tomorrow." He was growing more animated by the second. "So rather than struggling month after month to find ever new ways of squeezing a few more pennies per share out of 'what is,' iQu would be your ticket to step out of all of that and to go after 'what could be.' And, let me tell you, that's precisely the kind of move the market is waiting for right now. It would be their confirmation that you're not just in tune with today, you're actually in touch with tomorrow. Which, I think you'd have to admit, is quite a different image from the one you've got at present. As we've already talked about a number of times now, it appears that there are a lot of people out there at the moment who are questioning your ability to move this company forward. They see the effect the Internet is having on the temp industry—your core business—and then they look at how you've responded to it. And, what do they see?" He paused for effect, but not long enough for David to cut in. "Apparently not much that excites them. They see you tinkering around the edges, but regrettably, that's about it."

"Hogwash!" countered David, calling Tim's tone and raising it a note. "I would hardly call a dedicated team of forty people mere tinkering. Yes, granted, we were a little slow out of the gates, but we've now caught up to the point where, at least as far as I'm concerned, our Internet offering will soon be on par with that of our major competitors. In fact—"

"That's precisely my point. First of all, yes, you were the last of the big interim companies to go digital, and now that you finally have, all that you've managed to do is cobble together a service offering that looks similar to that which many of your competitors have had on offer for a number of years. That doesn't strike me as being very original or inspiring. Nor is it what the analysts are looking for. In my experience, what they want to see is innovation, not imitation, and until they do, they're going to continue hammering your stock. It's as simple as that, and you know it."

Tim paused to see how his message was being received.

David shot Tim a withering glance, but otherwise kept his thoughts to himself.

Tim moved on cautiously. "That's why I think we need to announce iQu to the market sooner rather than later. That way we'd show them just how badly they've misjudged you. That rather than having missed the boat, you're not only onboard, but you're actually steering the damn thing! Now that's what your critics need to hear. So, let them hear it!"

David slowly clapped thrice. "Powerful performance, and convincing argument, but I'm afraid I don't buy it."

"And why the hell not?"

"We've already gone over this, and my answer remains the same. As far as I'm concerned, we're nowhere near ready to announce iQu to the market, and it could be many months before we are."

"You may not have months. In fact, you may not even have weeks to start turning things around. What was it again that Matt said this morning—eighty dollars and he's out? And, what's your stock at now?"

David glanced again at the screen. "Eighty-eight and three quarters," he said reluctantly.

"That's my point. It's down almost fifteen dollars since I arrived here, what, less than three weeks ago." He rubbed the back of his neck. "I don't know, buddy—" He didn't finish his sentence. He didn't need to.

David said nothing for a moment, and when he did his voice had a distinct chill to it. "Is this your way of trying to cheer me up, because, if it is, let me tell ya, it's not working."

Tim shook his head. "Look David, I'm not here to cheer you up, I'm here to try to help you out. Or, more accurately, I'm here to try to help the two of us out, which is precisely what iQu has the potential to do. I'm convinced that it can make us—and, in your case, your other shareholders as well—very wealthy indeed. And the fact of the matter is, everybody involved—either directly or indirectly—needs to know that. The accountants call it full disclosure. Stock market analysts call it increased visibility. I call it just plain common sense."

"Well, I don't," David thundered. "Who do you think you're talking to here—an idiot? I'm well aware of the effect public perception can have on a company's stock price, but I don't see that awareness as giving me the license to lie!"

Not to be outdone, Tim's voice also edged higher. "Who's saying anything about lying? I'm simply suggesting that we present the facts as they are, and then leave it up to everyone else to draw their own conclusions. After all, that's what the free-market system is all about, isn't it?"

"Right, and just what are the facts? The way I see it, the basic fact of the matter is that iQu is a concept and nothing more. It's not a—"

Tim cut him off. "Wrong! iQu is now a *hell* of a lot more than a mere concept. Seventeen of us have been working around the clock on this thing for almost three weeks now, and believe me, we've come a long, long way."

"If that's true, which I don't doubt, then why haven't I been kept abreast of the latest developments?"

"For a number of reasons. First of all, you and I hardly even see each other any more because of the crazy hours we're both keeping. And, second, I wanted to get this thing to a certain point before exposing it to anybody outside of the team."

"And, are you at that point now?" David asked in a grudging, half-conciliatory tone intended to bring the conversation back on a more normal footing.

"More or less, yes. It'd be great if we still had a bit more time, but in light of recent events, it doesn't appear that we do."

"So, please, fill me in." David leaned back in his chair and stretched, trying to release some of the tension from his body. But even as he did, the worm of suspicion was at work in his mind.

Before Tim could gather his thoughts, there was a light rap on the door followed by the sound of Linda's voice. "Lunch." She bustled into the room, dropped off their food, and then left again without saying another word.

There was a bloated moment of silence as Tim and David each waited for the other to make the first choice. Then, his hunger getting the better of him, Tim threw protocol to the wind and reached for a turkey on rye. David was quick to follow, scooping up a thick roast beef sandwich.

After satisfying his immediate hunger, Tim got started. "I think I should begin by making a small confession: I haven't been completely open with you in terms of just how advanced the Celebrix technology really is. And the reason for that was that I didn't want to get bogged down in lengthy theoretical debates over some of the ethical issues involved."

David almost choked on his food. "*Excuse* me?"

Waving his sandwich around as he spoke, Tim replied, "Believe me, it's nothing to worry about. It's just that some of our technologies are *so* advanced, they may cause a bit of a stir when they first come out."

Trying to keep the irritation from his voice, David asked, "And yet you thought that I didn't need to know this?" The worm of suspicion was working overtime.

"Eventually, when the time was right. And that appears to be now. That is, of course, if you've got the time to go into it now."

"Just how long will it take?"

"Probably a good hour. Maybe more. It depends on how much detail you want."

David consulted his diary before answering. "Anxious as I am to hear this, I'm afraid I've got a meeting starting in here in about fifteen minutes."

Tim was not to be deterred. "Well, that should give us enough time to at least get started. And I think the best way to do that is for me to provide you with a quick summary of everything we've talked about so far on the subject of iQu."

David pointed to his watch. "I'm serious, Tim, fifteen minutes. No more."

Tim nodded as he got under way. "So, if you can recall, our original idea was to create a vortal around everything relating to self-development and personal growth. Thus, rather than simply taking your existing business of matching the supply and demand of labor online, we thought we'd broaden and deepen that position by bringing everything from self-assessment tools to just-in-time training; from career counseling to individual mentoring; and from a job clearing house to a labor exchange all under one virtual roof. With the belief that, once completed, the site would then be the most comprehensive career and personal development site on the Web. Right?"

David nodded.

"Then, to ensure that we were able to attract the largest audience possible, we decided to focus initially on the educational or personal development side of the equation, based on the belief that continuous learning is becoming a requirement for just about everybody these days. Then, with that aim in mind, we decided we'd need to build two different sets of educational products and services. One set for individual users, another for multiple users—in other words, organizations of all shapes and sizes. Then, we decided that both sets would need to include both *knowledge acquisition* products, or products designed to increase one's general knowledge level, and *knowledge application* products, or products designed to test one's ability to apply that knowledge."

"Or put more simply," David added, "the acquisition stuff refers to theory, whereas the application stuff refers to practice. Right?"

"Right. Anyway, both user groups would also be provided with an opportunity to earn points as they went along. In other words, each time they consumed another bit of theory or put that theory into practice through use of one of our simulators, they'd earn reward points that they could then later convert into cash and/or cost savings."

David interrupted him again. "Which again, put simply, means that the more they learn, the more they would earn."

Tim allowed himself a weak smile. "How poetic," he said ironically.

David ignored the remark. "None of this is new to me, and I don't see the purpose of going through it all again."

"Just bear with me for a minute and then it all should be clear." He paused to down the last of his sandwich, which he then washed down with a large gulp of milk. "But first, let me just finish up what I was saying. Based on their respective points totals, our idea was to provide both groups with an opportunity to participate in an elaborate ranking system, in which the higher users score, the more marketable they become—either to prospective employers in the case of an individual user or to prospective shareholders and/or creditors in the case of an organization.

"And this is where things begin to get interesting. Once an individual or an organization has entered into our ranking system, we've got them hooked. Because, in addition to ranking them, we'd also be in a position to provide them with a wide assortment of ancillary services—everything from a detailed assessment of their strengths and weaknesses vis-à-vis key competitors, to assistance in eliminating those weaknesses and/or reinforcing their strengths."

"Or e-consulting, for short."

Tim paused, acknowledging David's contribution with a quick smile.

Glancing again at his watch, David said, "Still nothing new."

Tim nodded. "Almost there." He finished off the last of his milk. "Using this model, we'd make money in two ways: one, in selling e-learning products, and two, in selling ancillary services such as coaching, mentoring, and consulting. All of which would undoubtedly make iQu one of the hottest, and most profitable, Websites around. However, that would actually only be the tip of the iceberg."

David suddenly perked up. "Meaning?"

"Meaning that the real gold would lie beneath all of this, which is where we now enter into what will be unfamiliar territory to you."

"Go on!" His eyes fixed on Tim's with unblinking intensity.

"Two words: *intelligent avatar.* That, to me, is what this is all about."

"Huh?"

Tim picked his words with even more than his customary fastidiousness. "Celebrix has developed a sophisticated cocktail of technologies that, when combined with a highly advanced software package that we're now just finishing up, means we'll be in a position to offer the world its first glimpse of an intelligent avatar. Not a lowly digital butler or shopping agent, but rather a thinking machine that, over time, would get to know more about the person using it than that person would know about themselves."

David was incredulous. "That's not possible!"

"Not only is it possible, we've already done it—or almost done it, to be more precise. By bundling together voice recognition, lie detection, thought translation, and biosensory systems, and feeding all of that data into our own artificial intelligence systems, we'll ultimately be in a position to know the physical, mental, and emotional state of a user."

David was completely dumbstruck by what he was hearing. Struggling to make sense of it all, he said, "But I thought you'd told me that Celebrix's core focus these past few years had been developing what you called 'multi-user simulations' aimed at the business market. Or did I misunderstand?"

"No, not at all. You're right, that is what I've been telling you. And it's true, or at least partially true, in that we have been putting an enormous amount of time and money into developing our simulation technology. However, having said that, what I haven't told you—for reasons I'll explain in a minute— is that it's only one of a number of technology fields that we've been investing in heavily. And though we see each of them as being important in its own right, I'd have to say that as far as things stand at the moment, our AI-based technologies are, without doubt, our crown jewels. It's those which will ultimately enable us to construct a technology platform the likes of which the world has never seen." Tim leaned forward in his chair, his eyes ablaze. "*Think about it, a machine that's capable of both thought and emotion!* Can you imagine? A machine that, rather than merely reacting to precise instructions keyed into it by a human, is instead able to use its vast intellectual muscle to think on its own, to problem-solve for us, and to assist us in just about every way possible. It'll completely revolutionize the world, to say nothing of the effect it'll have on your industry. It'll change everything. Like the internal combustion engine did to the era of the horse-drawn carriages, but even more profoundly. Can you imagine the power and potential of this thing?"

"To be honest, not really, no. For the simple reason that I'm not even sure I fully understand it. Let me see if I've got this right. You're saying that whenever users connect up to our Website using this technology set of yours, they'll be providing us with a window into their hearts and minds—whether they like it or not?"

"Oh, they'll like it, otherwise they wouldn't do it. The choice will be theirs to make."

"But I still don't see what the attraction will be. Why would they want to open themselves to such an extent to us, or to anybody for that matter?"

"They wouldn't be opening themselves up to us *per se*. Rather, they'd be opening themselves up to their own personal avatar, and their motivation for doing so would be the same motive that drives all relationships—the more they put in, the more they could expect to get out. In other words, if they wanted their avatar to become a close personal friend, they'd have little choice but to treat it as they would a friend—to tell it everything. Hopes, dreams, desires, fears, opinions, attitudes, feelings—absolutely everything. Then, and only then, would the 'relationship' be worth anything. But once it got to that point, once that threshold had been reached," he paused for effect, "then there would be no stopping it. From then on, the relationship would just continue to deepen and strengthen over time. The two would become one—so to speak."

David sat stone-faced and eyed Tim carefully. Finally, he said, "So what have we got here? We've got an intelligent avatar that would basically sit inside a user's computer, third-generation telephone, or personal digital assistant, and like some sort of giant digital sponge, it would absorb everything that came its way—thoughts, feelings, emotions, the whole kit and caboodle. And then it would use all of that data to gradually, over time, become an indispensable part of the user's life. Does that about sum it up?"

Tim cracked a wry smile. "Couldn't have said it better myself."

David still wasn't convinced. "Okay, so I'm starting to understand the concept, but I still don't see how we'd be able to make any money out of it."

Tim was aghast. "Are you kidding? It would be a veritable gold mine."

"How's that?"

"Probably the best way for me to explain it would be to give you an example. Let's say I'm iQu and you're a financial analyst working for a large investment bank. The bank has just become a client of iQu. I—or your manager, to be more precise—come to you and ask you to register yourself on my system. As you sign in, the first thing you're asked to do is to fill out a detailed personality inventory that assesses you on multiple dimensions: for example, it would rate your 'affiliative style,' your 'competitive style,' your 'oppositional style,' your tolerance for risk, your appetite for knowledge, your drive to succeed, and so on and so forth. There'd be fifteen or so in total."

"This information would then be funneled through to your own personal avatar—which, once equipped with voice recognition, lie detection, thought translation, and biosensory systems, will come to know you possibly better than you know yourself. It'll know your likes and dislikes; your passions and pet peeves; your strengths and weaknesses; your norms and values; and through a rigorous analysis of how you interact with others while online—for example, while using any of our multi-user simulators—it'll also come to learn which personality types you work well with and which you don't. That means, it wouldn't take long before it would be in a position to issue you an extremely detailed assessment—or report card, if you will—of your competencies and capabilities." He paused for a moment to ask, "Still with me?"

David nodded intently.

Tim quickly moved on. "Then, by standardizing that report card, we could follow it up by issuing an itemized analysis of how you compare with other investment analysts either within or outside of your organization. Then, with a bit of help from the headhunters over at Quenetics, we could provide you with an estimate of the compensation range that you could expect if you were to leave the company and put yourself on the market."

For the first time since their conversation began, David showed some signs of life. "Which means that if iQu could establish a market price for each employee, it would then be in a position to add those individual totals in order to come up with a grand total—"

Tim beat him to the punch. *"Which would amount to nothing less than the current market value of the company's human capital!"*

David leaned back in his chair and folded his arms in half until his hands came to rest behind his head. He slowly expelled all of the air from his lungs as he let the magnitude of Tim's idea sink in.

But Tim wasn't finished yet. With a wolfish grin on his face, he said, "And, as if that's not already enough, believe it or not, that's still only half the story."

"You can't be serious!"

"Oh, but I am. And the other half is even more amazing. Once you've established an individual's current market value, there are two things you can do with it. One, as I've already mentioned, you can aggregate it in order to come up with a value for the firm's human capital; or, two, you could capitalize it, and then buy and sell it as you would any other asset."

David hesitated, looking lost. "I'm not sure I follow. When you say 'buy and sell,' are you suggesting we set up some sort of *human capital exchange*—like a stock market for human capital similar to that which we now have for corporate equities?"

"You have to admit, it would be the next logical step."

For a moment, David was genuinely at a loss for words. There was logic in what Tim was saying; it was just the scope of it that left him speechless. "You can't be serious about this, are you?"

"Sure I am. Just think about it. The first phase of this has already happened. A number of rock and movie stars have already converted their royalty streams into bonds and sold them to intrepid investors. Entertainment and sports stars are doing the same thing when they capitalize their future earnings and turn their multiyear contracts into instant, ready cash. As one deal piles onto the next, the financial wrappers and mechanisms will be further refined, the type of packaging will become more standardized, thus bringing more people into the act. To the point where, in a few years time, I could see the asset base expanding beyond superstars to include highly paid professionals and top-notch managers. It's conceivable that it could even evolve to the point where investors bundle risk for lesser-known personalities. For example, this year's Harvard Business School's graduating class could offer themselves as a bundle to the investment community."*

David cut in. "Interesting idea, Tim, but to be honest, I really don't see any of this ever happening. First of all, I don't see there being a market for these types of securities, and I can't see any of the necessary mechanisms in place. For example, who would underwrite these issues; where would they be traded; how would prices be set, and so on?"

"I agree that this will take some time, but again, if you take a closer look at what's going on in the marketplace, we're already moving in that direction. How many people are auctioning off their time every hour of every day on Monster.com? And, as you well know, once there's an auction, there can be futures, and once there are futures, there can be arbitrage. Sounds to me like the makings of a market. As to who'd be willing to buy such an instrument, you need look no further than those investors who are currently holding David Bowie bonds. As to who will

---

*See: Davis, Stan, and Christopher Meyer. *Future Wealth*. Boston: Harvard Business School Press, 2000, pp. 57–65.

do the underwriting, my guess is it'll be the same people who have brought us everything from mortgage-backed securities to junk bonds—the securities industry."

David had his mouth open, ready to ask another question, when they suddenly heard a light knock on the door. A moment later, Linda poked her head inside the room and announced, "Rob Carson and Bill Armstrong are here to see you. What do you want me to tell them?"

David glanced over at Tim and shrugged. "Just give us another minute or two to finish up, and then Tim will be right out."

Linda nodded and then closed the door behind her.

David stretched his arms while stifling a yawn. "Man, am I beat! This little chat of ours has completely fried my brain. But, don't get me wrong. It's been great. I thoroughly enjoyed it, and I'm in love with the idea. Really. I still don't completely understand it yet, but I'm sure that'll come after a few more conversations with you. Like this evening, for starters. Maybe we can talk about it again after dinner. Or are you staying late again tonight?"

Getting to his feet, Tim returned the yawn, and then replied, "No, definitely not. I'm too tired to pull another all-nighter. So yeah, I'm fine with the after-dinner thing." Short pause. "But, before I go, just one final question. Now do you see why I'm so excited about this thing and why I think we need to—?"

David didn't let him finish. "Oh, absolutely. And, as I just finished saying, so am I. I love the idea." But his sour look didn't mesh with what he was saying.

"Then why is it that your mouth is saying one thing while your eyes are saying something else? And you know what they say, the eyes never lie."

David crossed his arms, his face now vacant of any expression. "Trust me, I love the idea. I really do. The only problem is that now that I understand it better, I also see a few more obstacles and hurdles than I did before."

"For instance?"

"Well, for one, now that I see the full magnitude of the thing, I don't see me as having any choice but to involve a lot more people in the process."

"Such as?"

"I think the other members of the board are going to need to know a lot more about this, as will other members of my executive team. And that's just for starters."

Alarm bells began to sound in Tim's head. "Does that list include Shannon?" he asked, concern etched in his voice.

David gave a look as if to say, what kind of silly question is that? He replied, "Well, she is both a member of the board and a senior member of my executive team, so yeah, I can't see how I can tell the others without also telling her. Because, believe me, even if I were to try, she'd just find it out through somebody else anyway. So, I'd rather that she hear it from me. Unless . . . "

Tim took the bait. "Unless what?"

"Unless you wanted to be the one to tell her."

Tim's head lifted sharply. "Me? Why me? I thought you wanted me to stay away from her, not to mention the fact that based on my last few interactions with her I get the distinct impression she's not really a big fan of mine. To put it mildly. I think she simply sees me as an extension of you, and therefore, as someone not to be trusted."

"Maybe so. But at least she's not out gunning for you as she is me—both figuratively and literally. So between the two of us, you probably stand the best chance of possibly getting through to her."

"Yeah, right." Tim gave a short nasal snort of amusement. "Like a snowball's chance in hell."

11

Quenetics Headquarters, Boston

EXITING DAVID'S OFFICE, Tim turned to his left and walked two doors down. He knocked softly on the door and waited for a reply. It came immediately.

"Yes, who is it?" Shannon asked.

Opening the door just enough to pop his head in, Tim replied, "It's me, Tim. I was just wondering if you had a spare minute or two."

She gave a look that was enough to frighten the dead. This was followed by a long and exaggerated sigh. "Not really, no. To be honest, I'm extremely busy at the moment, but if you speak to Lori, I'm sure she can arrange a meeting for sometime early next week."

Tim persisted. "Five minutes, really, no more."

Another exaggerated sigh. "All right, five minutes then. But not a minute more."

Tim stepped reverently inside and quickly closed the door behind him. "Great, thanks."

138

Though this was probably his fifth or sixth visit to Shannon's office, he still couldn't get over how different it was from David's. Compared to David's Spartan interior, this one was so lavishly furnished, one had the impression that they'd just entered the stateroom of a $50 million yacht. It just reeked of wealth and extravagance. As did she. Like usual, she was decked out in an outfit that had probably cost enough to feed a small African nation for a month. She wore a dark blue dress that subtly molded to the contours of her well-proportioned body, and around her neck, a Versace scarf, so resplendent it screamed for attention. Yet, at least in Tim's case, it didn't receive any. He was far too captivated by her beauty to notice much else. Walking towards her, he wondered again how someone so beautiful on the outside could be so ugly on the inside. *"Truly a pity,"* he thought to himself.

Not bothering to get up to welcome him, Shannon simply invited him to have a seat, and then asked, "So, what is it you want to talk to me about?"

Tim explained, and though he spoke at warp speed, it took him a full ten minutes to get everything out. Surprisingly, Shannon had remained silent throughout.

Looking across at her he could almost see the wheels turning in her mind. Though he'd been careful to tell her only the bare minimum, it was clear that it had been enough to get her thinking.

Rolling her Mont Blanc between her fingers, she nodded thoughtfully. "Interesting idea." Short pause. "No, it's more than that. I'd go so far as to say that it's actually a very interesting idea. The only problem with it is that it's about ten years ahead of its time. So, if both of us are still around then, maybe we can discuss it further." She laughed without humor. "But in the meantime—"

"I couldn't disagree with you more. In my opinion—"

"Tim, listen to me. I'm not interested in your opinion," she said tersely. "Look, you asked for five minutes, I've given you fifteen. But that's all the time I can afford. So, let me conclude by stating the following. I think that if anyone was stupid enough to invest the billions required to try to do what you're suggesting, they'd be sunk the moment they tried to bring it to market. Why? Because the market simply wouldn't accept it. It's as simple as that. People would be so intimidated by it that they probably wouldn't use it even if you paid them to. People just won't buy something that's smarter than they are. And that's all there is to it. So, if I were you, I'd abandon the idea before you waste any more time on it. But, of course, that's up to you. Now, if you don't mind, I'd really like to get back to what I was doing." She placed her hands over the top of her keyboard and prepared to begin typing again.

Tim had no intention of giving up so easily. "And if I were to tell you that most, if not all, of the technologies we'd need in order to make this thing happen are already within my grasp?"

Looking at her computer screen rather than at him, she replied, "In the first place, I wouldn't believe you, and in the second place, I'd be forced to repeat what I've already said— the market isn't ready for something like this. Period! Therefore, my answer would remain the same: I'm not interested. Not in the slightest. Now, really, if you don't mind."

"Oh, but I do mind. I mind a lot! This is the type of idea, no, let me word that differently, this is the type of opportunity that comes along *maybe* once in a lifetime, and here it is, an offer, and you're not even willing to take the time to fully discuss it. That just doesn't make any sense to me. None whatsoever. Particularly now, in light of all of Quenetics' current financial concerns, you'd think that—"

Shannon exploded. "Who the hell are you to come in here and tell me how to do my job? This is outrageous! Not to mention ludicrous. I'm not the one driving this company into the ground. That's David's doing. So, if you have any comments on that score, then I'd suggest you direct them at him and not at me." Her voice was an icicle.

Unable to accept defeat even when it was staring him in the face, Tim asked, "Don't you think you're being just a little bit unreasonable here?"

Shannon looked at him with an expression of intense indignation. "I'm the one being unreasonable?!" She laughed artificially. "I don't think so. I think I'm the sanest of the bunch. It's the two of you that I worry about. As you rightfully said just a few moments ago, here we are in the midst of our worst financial crisis ever, and what are the two of you doing? You guys are out chasing rainbows. Now, where's the logic in that?"

Tim's face flushed crimson, but before he could form a rebuttal, she was already off again. "No, tell you what, Tim, what this company needs now is proper leadership. Not a fantasist but a realist. Someone who understands the predicament we're in, and who has the wisdom and strength of character to get us out of it and back on track again. And that someone is not David. I know it. The Board knows it. The workforce knows it. The investment community knows it. And, hopefully, having been here for as long as you have, you now know it. And if so, then I'd suggest that if you really want to be of some service to this company that the best thing you could do would be to sit him down and explain the facts of life to him. Maybe he'll listen to you, because he certainly doesn't appear to be willing to listen to anybody else."

Tim was so taken aback by the things that she'd said that he was temporarily at a loss for words.

She wasn't. Barely missing a beat, she added, "You might want to think a little bit about that, and then maybe we can talk again. But, in the meantime, I really do have to get back to work. So, I'm afraid I'm going to have to ask you to leave."

Realizing that it was pointless to argue further, Tim got up and started moving towards the door. But before he got there, she delivered her final blow. "Oh, and one other thing, Tim, I'd really appreciate it if you'd stop having me followed. It's really starting to get on my nerves."

• • •

Too stunned to do much else, Tim waited in the coffee cove for David's meeting to end. As soon as it had, and the others had left, he re-entered the room.

Seeing the tension in his friend's face, David said, "So, I gather it didn't go all that well."

Tim was seething. "You can't imagine how much I dislike that woman."

"Oh, I bet I probably can." He flashed a crooked smile. "So, what happened?"

"She wasn't at all interested in hearing what I had to say. She pretended to listen for a while, but then from one moment to the next, she just shut me down."

"Yeah, that certainly sounds like Shannon," David mumbled churlishly. "So, what did she say?"

Too energized to sit, Tim started pacing the room—striding up and down its fitted blue carpet, snapping fingers, thrusting elbows, nothing still—while quickly summarizing their conversation. He ended with Shannon's parting remark.

David was incredulous. "She actually said that?"

"Verbatim."

David expelled all the air in his lungs. "Wow, no wonder she's so upset. I would be too if I suddenly found out that a family member had put me under surveillance." He shook his head. "I told you it was a stupid idea."

Tim, not knowing how to respond to that, said nothing.

"So, what do we do now?"

Tim finally stopped pacing and dropped into one of the chairs. "On the surveillance issue, the answer is simple: we'll have to ask Allan to send us another team, and hope that the next one will be a bit more careful. But, as to what to do about iQu, I have no idea. It's clear that she's not going to support it. If anything, she'll probably do everything she can to thwart our efforts. Now, as to how much damage she can do, well, you probably have a better idea about that than I do."

David's eyes narrowed and his facial muscles tensed. "She can try whatever she likes, but let me tell ya, I'll be damned if I'm going to let her destroy all that you've done."

"But how can you possibly stop her?"

"There's only one thing to do—we've got to build so much excitement and enthusiasm around this thing that it basically takes on a life of its own and moves beyond the point where it can be derailed by any one of us. Now, granted, that's easier said than done, but it would appear to be our only option."

"But how can we do that when you won't permit me to expose it to the outside world?" Tim asked.

David shook his head while hoisting a weak smile. "Good question. And you might be surprised at the answer."

"Try me," Tim prompted.

"I've thought a lot about it of late and have decided to come around to your way of thinking."

"Really?"

"Really! So let's do this thing. Let's put together the glossiest, glitziest, presentation package possible, and then let's send it out there and see what happens."

• • •

After several hours spent alone in his office, Tim decided to head up to iQu's temporary nerve center—two adjoining rooms on the same floor as David's office. Entering the larger of the two rooms, Tim immediately spotted the man he was looking for.

Approaching the man from behind, Tim called out, "Hi, Mike. How are things going?"

Mike Warren slowly cranked his bearded head around until he was facing his boss and then sighed as though it was his dying breath. Even before his mouth had a chance to answer, his nonverbal clues said it all for him. Everything about him screamed frustration, tension, and fatigue. His eyes were red and puffy; his face exhausted and gaunt; his shoulders sagged, and he generally looked as if he'd spent the last few days trekking through the jungles of Borneo. Worse yet, he had a body odor to match.

Rubbing the back of his neck in an attempt to work out the kinks, Mike replied, "We keep falling further and further behind schedule, and there doesn't seem to be a damn thing I can do about it."

Mike was one of Celebrix's top scientists and a long-time personal friend of Tim's, so it had come as no surprise to anyone when Tim had asked him to head up the iQu development team. Mike, always on the lookout for a new challenge, had accepted immediately, and basically hadn't slept since.

Mike was an affable, middle-aged man with one of the sharpest minds in the scientific community. When it came to anything relating to the subject of artificial intelligence, he was the man everyone went to see. With two Ph.D.'s and numerous scientific awards to his name, he never seemed to run out of either energy or ideas. Nevertheless, looking at his disheveled appearance, Tim could plainly see that the man was nearing his breaking point.

Trying to mask his concern, Tim asked, "Did you find the ticket I left on your desk this morning?"

Mike's face lit up immediately. "Oh, yeah." He tapped himself lightly on the side of his head in self-reproach. "I meant to thank you for that, but like so many things these days, it just slipped my mind. Sorry about that."

Tim shrugged. "Don't worry about it. I know how preoccupied you are at the moment." Short pause. "So, what do you think—are you going to go to the game?"

In recognition of the many hours of self-sacrifice and hard work Mike had put in over the past few weeks, Tim had given him a ticket to the next Red Sox game. It was a box seat at Fenway for the next afternoon. Pedro Martinez was pitching against the hated Yankees. It was the hottest ticket in New England.

"Absolutely! I wouldn't miss it for the world. You know how much of a Sox fan I am. And to get the opportunity to see them playing the Yankees in their own home park is something I wouldn't miss for the world."

Tim smiled warmly. "Well, that's good to hear." He paused, and then added, "I hope you have a great time tomorrow. And to ensure that you do, you've got to promise me one thing."

"Sure. What's that?"

"When you're there, put your brain on autopilot and just try to enjoy the game, will you? No thinking about work. Deal?"

Mike smiled tightly and gave him a thumb's-up. "Trust me. You needn't worry about that!"

Tim changed tack. "Good, now about the e-mail you sent me."

"Yeah, did you get a chance to read it?"

"Not completely, no; but I skimmed through it. In it, you were saying something about business measurement systems and iQu's need to link up with one of the Big Four auditing firms. What was that all about?"

Before answering, Mike went to his desk and picked up a magazine perched atop a small mountain of paper, computer disks, newspapers, and an assortment of everyday trash. Flipping through its pages, he quickly found what he wanted. "This is the most recent issue of *BusinessWeek*. Inside it is an interesting article entitled, 'The Auditor's Dilemma.' Let me read you the first couple of paragraphs and then see what you think."

Tim signaled for him to go on.

Mike lowered his head and started to read. "'Executives, investors, and regulators alike have been arguing for years now that the traditional model of accounting is becoming ever more antiquated in today's knowledge-based economy. Like the organization chart, and employee handbook, corporate financial documents are increasingly proving themselves too static to keep up with the modern organization, with its fluid structure, spaghetti bowl of alliances, empowered employees, and vital reservoirs of human intellectual capital.'"

Sensing that Mike was just getting warmed up, Tim thought it best to interrupt. "Sounds fascinating, Mike, but what's your point?"

Mike looked slightly miffed, but was quick to recover. "Just bear with me for a few seconds more." Picking up where he'd left off, he read, "'As a result of these deficiencies and distortions, there is currently an unprecedented level of uncertainty and confusion throughout the world's financial markets. Or put otherwise: today's investors are essentially flying blind. *The solution: a better accounting system needs to be built—one that gives investors a better fix on companies' true worth.*'"

Tim looked thoughtful. "Makes sense. But what's that got to do with us?"

Mike seemed genuinely surprised at Tim's question. "Are you serious, you don't know?"

"If I did, I wouldn't ask now, would I?" he retorted irritably.

Shaking his head in amazement, Mike explained. "It's simple. What this article is saying is that *the business community is literally crying out for an accounting system that measures the unmeasurables.*"

"The what?"

"All those New Economy assets that investors consider to be crucial, but don't make it onto today's balance sheets. You know, things like intellectual capital, brand names and trademarks, technological innovations, customer and employee loyalty ratings, and so on."

The puzzled look on Tim's face was starting to give way to one of mild enthusiasm. "Ah, I think I'm finally starting to see where you're going with this. You're saying that in addition to measuring a company's intellectual capital, we could, and probably should, take it a step further and conduct a *full organizational audit* on them—as in, try to measure their intangibles."

Mike brightened. "That's exactly what I'm saying, yes. As far as I'm concerned, once we've tapped into an organization's data stream, all we'd need to do then is send in our intelligent software agents, and presto, we'd have a continuous feed of corporate performance on a multitude of variables. This would then put us in a position to produce comprehensive, real-time, organizational audits, which, in turn, could then be used to rate the company vis-à-vis its key competitors using the same type of scheme we're planning to use for individual users."

Tim rocked back and forth on the balls of his feet as he struggled to digest all of this. Rubbing his forehead, he stopped rocking, and asked, "So, if I understand this correctly, what you're basically talking about here is the establishment of a *rating system for corporate intangibles* along much the same lines as what Standard & Poor's has done for corporate debt. Correct?"

"More or less, yes," said Mike enthusiastically. "Great idea, no?"

"Without a doubt, but to be honest, I don't see it working."

"Huh! Why not?" Mike asked in a voice riddled with uncertainly and confusion.

"Well, to begin with, I don't see us as having the capability to provide a full organizational audit. Yes, we'll be capable of measuring intellectual capital and maybe a few other pieces of the puzzle—for example, things like customer and employee satisfaction levels, customer retention levels, productivity, and maybe even a few metrics relating to corporate development and renewal, but that's about it. So, things like the 'quality' of leadership, brand valuation, and so on would be beyond our purview. Which means that we'd not be in a position to do a *full* and *complete* organizational audit. Or do you see it differently?"

"Very much so! I see iQu as being capable of measuring all of those things, plus much, *much* more." He was away. "Take the leadership issue, for example. We could cover that by incorporating a powerful leadership assessment tool into our user profile questionnaire, which is something the 'leader' would have to fill out when they sign on to the system for the first time." He was flying. "What was the other one you said?

Oh yeah, measuring brand values. For that to be possible, many companies would probably have to put a brand value measurement system in place. But they'd have to do that anyway if they wanted to use live market data in any of our multiuser simulators."

Tim started rocking again, his brow creased in concentration. It was almost a full minute before he spoke again. "Even if we were somehow able to do a full audit, as in we had the software for it, we wouldn't have the hardware. I mean, do you have any idea how much data we'd have to process in order to do what you're suggesting? There isn't a computer big enough to crunch all of the numbers that would come out of even one multibillion dollar company, let alone a couple million of them feeding us all at the same time. Have you factored that into your thinking?"

Mike's response was immediate. "Sure, and believe me, it wouldn't be a problem. We'd simply need to use the same software program that NASA's Jet Propulsion Laboratory uses to track space probes. Which, as you can imagine, is a far more daunting task than what we're talking about here, yet they manage it. Thus, so could we."

Tim's face looked like he'd just swallowed a lemon. "I'm afraid you're going to have to give me a little bit more than that to go on if you hope to convince me of this."

Mike shrugged. "It's really quite simple. Their software is designed to separate the wheat from the chaff—to focus on what's important, and to toss out the rest."

"And how does it know what's important?"

"It looks for anomalies—unusual data points—using complex algorithms, and then it spits out its findings in colorful, multidimensional graphs making it easy for us mere mortals to easily grasp. For example, if a set of errant transactions were to suddenly flow through the system, they would appear as blinking vertical spindles that look like towers sprouting up from the screen. That screen would then get e-mailed to us, or to an auditor, if we ultimately decide to go that route, and then he or she would look into it further. It's as simple as that."

Tim grimaced in concentration as he digested what he'd just been told. Then, shaking his head as though attempting to clear it, he said, "Tell you what, my brain's a little fried at the moment, so if it's OK with you, I'd prefer we leave this discussion for tomorrow morning, when hopefully I'll be a little more alert than I am now."

A long, slow, hesitant shrug, expressing dissatisfaction and false acceptance. Then, looking as mournful as a caged hound, Mike mumbled, "Yeah, whatever."

Suddenly feeling somewhat guilty for not having shown the proper level of enthusiasm for Mike's idea, Tim said, "Don't get me wrong, I think it's a wonderful idea, I really do. But I just need a bit more time to absorb it all. That's all. Then, I'm sure I'll be as excited about it as you are. If not more so." Short pause. "Anyway, now, about tomorrow's game . . . "

Ten minutes later, the two men parted company, with Tim heading for the door, and Mike returning to whatever it was he'd been doing prior to Tim entering the room.

. . .

Trudging down the corridor in the direction of the stairwell, Tim could vaguely hear a woman shouting somewhere off in the distance. As he walked towards the source of the ruckus, he quickly came to realize that it was emanating from Shannon's office. She was apparently in the midst of another temper tantrum. He wondered if it involved David. Anxious to find out, he approached the door with considerable stealth, rolling his shoe from heel to toe, and easing his weight from one step to the next. Then, arriving at the door, he held his breath and strained to hear her opponent's voice. But there was no other voice, leading him to conclude that whoever it was that she was yelling at had to be on the phone rather than there in the room with her.

Feeling somewhat guilty for eavesdropping, he felt an overwhelming urge to move on, but his curiosity kept him riveted to the spot. Listening closely, it appeared that the conversation seemed to hinge around a payment she was to have made, but was refusing to. Her reasoning: in her view the caller hadn't fulfilled the terms of their agreement, and as such, was in no position to demand compensation. When the job was done, she'd pay. But not before.

Hearing this, Tim's imagination went into overdrive. He couldn't help but wonder if perhaps her caller was the guy she'd hired to get rid of David. But, thinking more about it, he quickly dropped the idea for the simple reason that he couldn't imagine her ever making such a call from the office. *But maybe he'd contacted her, as in, he'd just learned of her identity and was now using that knowledge as a means of extracting payment.* Tim had to smile despite himself. It was clear that his imagination had crossed some mental meridian and was now running amuck. Wisely, he spent the next few moments trying to rein it in again.

Then, just when he thought he had it back under control, he heard her yell, "What part of this do you not understand? I'll pay you when you finish, and not before. So, if you want your money, go out and earn it, and stop whining to me about all of your petty little problems. Got it?" With that, she slammed down the receiver.

12

TONY BERNELLI WAS AT WITS' END. Though not the sharpest knife in the drawer, not even he was stupid enough to think that things could go on for much longer. Maybe another day or two, but not longer. After that, if he didn't finish things up, he knew they'd be coming after him, and their guns would be doing the talking. He shuddered at the thought of it.

Berating himself, he went through his usual material. As a practiced self-accuser he tore his hair and called on the heavens to witness his remorse. If only things had worked out differently in the Caribbean. He'd have made his money, got a tan, and then returned to Chicago a happy man. Instead, he'd burned through most of his advance, his reputation was in tatters, and he was soon to become someone else's meal ticket. He swallowed hard.

The only bright spot in all of this: he could still try to make a run for it. Get out while he was still able to. Maybe he could go to Argentina or somewhere like that. But before the thought even had time to take hold, he flushed it from his mind. What sense did it make? Though he was new to the assassination game, he'd been involved in the underworld long enough to know that in a game without rules or borders you can run, but you can never hide. They always get you in the end. Always. So, no. He had no intention of spending the rest of his life on the run. He was going to stay and finish this off. How? He had absolutely *no* idea.

Glancing down at his watch, he saw that it was almost time for his nightly 'progress report.' Oh, how he'd come to dread these calls. Every time the same questions; every time the same answers; nothing ever changed. It was a completely meaningless exercise, which seemed to serve no purpose whatsoever—other than to make him feel even more uncomfortable than he already did. If that was possible. Even the word "progress" itself he'd come to despise. It suggested forward movement, towards a goal or objective, but in this case, how was that possible? How could things move forward? The target was now under twenty-four-hour guard by a team of professionals as good as any he'd ever seen. So trying to get at him was now all but impossible. He lowered his head in self-pity.

His cellphone suddenly interrupted his thoughts.

Now used to the routine, he switched on the scrambler before speaking. Then, struggling to keep his voice as steady as possible, he answered, "Panther here."

The voice at the other end of the line was as inert as ever. "So, what's the story? Do you have anything new to report?"

Already starting to shake, he replied, "Not too much, no." Pause. "However, I may have come up with something that just might work."

"Oh, and what's that?" The voice laden with sarcasm.

Tony nervously cleared his throat. "Well, because of the security around the guy, I've pretty well abandoned any thoughts of trying to get to him directly. But, there may be a slightly more indirect route that I can take."

The voice waited.

Tony quickly went on to explain his plan. When he'd finished there was nothing but silence at the other end of the line. Not a good sign. Swallowing hard, he was about to repeat himself, when the voice finally decided to speak.

"I agree that the time has come for a change in tactics, but before I can decide on what those new tactics should be, I think I need a better sense of what's going on. So, I've decided to come and check out the situation for myself."

Tony suddenly straightened as though someone had just seared him with a branding iron. "Why would you want to do that? Why don't you just ask me whatever it is you want to know? I mean, after all, I'm right—"

He was cut off. "Because you're an idiot, that's why. I should never have hired you in the first place. But, that was my mistake—and now it's time for me to rectify it. So, I'll be flying in tomorrow, and that's all there is to it. So, get a pen and write this down . . . "

Tony grabbed a pen and a notepad off the desk. "Go ahead."

"I'll be coming in on flight number NW 151, which is scheduled to land at 9:25 in the morning. And you'd better be there waiting; otherwise, you'd best find yourself another planet to live on. Got it?"

The line went dead before he could answer.

13

MIKE WARREN CONSIDERED FENWAY PARK to be baseball's most sacred shrine. Yankee Stadium was bigger, Wrigley prettier, but Fenway was holier, more pastoral, more authentic. It paid homage in every brick and girder, in every gruesomely uncomfortable slatted seat, to a tranquil America forever gone. At a summer-long intensive seminar Mike had taught two years ago at Carnegie Mellon University in Pittsburgh, he'd met a software engineer from Manchester who spoke of Old Trafford with the same reverence Mike invoked when he praised the grace and glory of Fenway.

He couldn't believe he was back here for an early May game, just like when he was a student at MIT. In those days he would cross the river with fluttering expectations and sit in the bleachers with the real people. But today he had Tim to thank for putting him in a ground-level box behind the plate and slightly up the third base line, a true VIP perch.

He had come early enough to watch batting practice, like a devotee should, and now in the top of the ninth with two down, he felt as sated as a gourmet aficionado pushing back from the coffee and cognac at a Parisian five-star. Pedro Martinez was putting the final touches on a four-hit, fifteen-strikeout shutout against the Yankees and the turncoat Roger Clemens. When Pedro fanned Paul O'Neill to end it and clock up K number sixteen for a three-nil Sox victory over the loathsome Bronx Bombers, Mike Warren's day was complete. For the first time since he'd been back in Beantown, he felt relaxed and at peace with the world.

He let the crowd shuffle up the aisle before he left his seat. He liked to watch the groundskeepers rolling out the tarpaulin for the infield. He liked to watch the late-afternoon sun shift the shadows on the outfield. He looked at the seat painted red way out in the right centerfield bleachers where Ted Williams had smacked his monster home run years ago, nearly 500 feet from home plate, the ball whacking the seat so hard it broke slats in the backrest. He looked at the Coke bottle sign attached to the light stanchion in left field, above the green monster, and fought from his mind the image of Bucky Dent's feeble pennant-winning home run in the '78 playoff. Instead, he thought of Carleton Fisk and the homer just inside that foul pole that helped the Sox win game six of the '75 World Series. Of course they'd lost game seven that year to Cincinnati's Big Red Machine, just the way they'd lost to the New York Mets in the Series in '86 with the Bill Buckner horror, but they were and always would be his beloved Sox, win or lose.

Mike's reminiscing was suddenly interrupted by the sound of footsteps bearing down on him. More surprised than frightened, he twisted his tubby body around to see what was going on. His concern grew as he watched two well-built men bearing down on him. He stammered, "Wwwhat is it? Have I done something wrong?"

By this point the two men were standing directly behind him waving badges in his face. He took some comfort in the fact that they were both FBI agents rather than lowly thugs interested only in his wallet. On the other hand, what would the FBI be interested in him for? The first thing that popped into his mind was that something must have happened to Tim, as he was the only one who knew his current whereabouts.

But, before he had the chance to say anything, the older of the two agents leaned forward and asked, "Are you Mike Warren?"

Before answering, Mike made a quick study of the man's features. Though he couldn't be certain, he felt that he'd seen the man somewhere before. Even though he wasn't all that good at remembering names and faces, this guy had a face that was hard to forget. Its bones and hollows were deeply pocked, the mark of a rare survivor of the once-dreaded smallpox. His black eyes were hooded, cold, and expressionless, his nose as curved and sharp as a scimitar. His dark brown hair was cropped short and he looked to be of Middle Eastern descent. Still, Mike couldn't place him. Maybe if he were to give it some time, it would come to him.

But time was apparently the one thing he didn't have. The man asked again, urgently, "Are you, or are you not, Mike Warren?"

Mike nodded affirmative.

"Then I'm afraid we're going to have to ask you to come with us, if you don't mind."

Mike did mind. In fact, he minded a lot, but as he stared into the black orbs that were the man's pupils, he found that his voice had suddenly abandoned him. His mouth opened but the words just wouldn't come out.

The second man grabbed his other arm and barked, "Come on, let's get going!" Mike noticed that he spoke with a very faint Italian accent.

As they neared the door to the box, he was finally able to find his voice again. "Am I under arrest?" he asked, thoroughly confused.

The first man glared at him and said, "No, you're not under arrest, but you are very much in danger for reasons I am not at liberty to discuss at the moment. All I can tell you is that we're here at Tim Hunt's request."

That did it. As soon as he heard that Tim was behind all of this, he relaxed immediately and stopped all form of resistance.

That was a mistake, and the last he'd ever make.

14

Quenetics Headquarters, Boston

TIM KNOCKED BEFORE ENTERING. Then peeking his head around the door, he saw that David was waving him in. His friend was still on the phone but a raised finger indicated that he'd be off in a minute.

Walking over to his customary chair in front of David's desk, Tim sat down and waited. Hitching one leg over the other, he picked up a paperweight and started juggling it from one hand to the other. He was clearly nervous about something.

A few seconds later, David ended the call and looked across at his friend. He wore the faintest of smiles, in contrast to the rest of his face, which was etched with worry lines. "Well, that was a much-needed bit of good news—the head of my legal team just phoned to say that the sale of our retail chain is all but complete. She thinks that if there are no sudden last-minute hitches, the deal could be consummated by as early as next week. Not bad, eh?"

Tim feigned interest. "That's very good news indeed." He gave him a thumb's-up. "Congrats." He said all the right

161

things but his words rang hollow, as his heart just wasn't in it.

Sensing that to be the case, David's smile quickly morphed into a frown. "Wow, don't knock yourself out." Short pause. "So what's bothering you? It's clear something is."

"More bad news, I'm afraid." He paused to give David the time to prepare himself. "It would appear that Mike's gone missing."

"What the hell do you mean he's 'gone missing'?"

Tim's features hardened. In a voice riddled with concern, he said, "He hasn't been seen or heard from since he left here early yesterday afternoon en route to the Sox game. We've tried his hotel, his cellphone, and even his wife, Kathy. But nothing. Nobody's seen or heard a word from him. It's as though he's just vanished off the face of the earth."

"Or maybe he's had a bad accident. Have you checked with the police?"

"Of course, but again, they don't know anything either. So then we phoned around to all the major hospitals to see if they had received any John Does matching Mike's description over the past twenty-four hours. But, again nothing. So, at this point we're drawing a complete blank."

"And what are the police doing about it?" David asked pointedly.

Tim shook his head. "They told us that we had to wait a full twenty-four hours from the time of his disappearance before we could officially file a missing person's report and only then would they actively start looking for him. So I've sent Andy down to the station to fill out the report. Maybe that'll get something going. But, I doubt it. Because what they also told me is that they get about fifty of these things a day, most of which later turn out to be false alarms. So, they don't take any of them too seriously until it's clear that the person is well and truly missing. And for them, the key determinant of that is time. If the person has been missing for a day, they don't get too worked up about it; a few days, still not; a week, and then *maybe* they start putting some effort into it. But even then, it depends on—"

David pounded his fist on his desk. "Maybe that's their normal *modus operandi*, but not when I'm involved it isn't, and if Mike's gone missing, then I'm involved. So, don't worry, I'll make a few calls and bang a few heads if I have to, but let me tell ya, within an hour or so, I'll get those hillbillies doing what we're paying them to do."

"Well, that's certainly reassuring to know, but before you make those calls, there's probably one other thing that you should know—I've already phoned Allan and asked him for some help."

"Oh yeah, and what'd he have to say?"

"He's flying in later tonight with a friend of his, who he says is the best in the business when it comes to tracking people down."

Tim's confident tone helped to assuage some of David's fears. As a result, some of the tension lifted from his face. "Well, that's somewhat reassuring." He sat back in his chair and closed his eyes for a moment. Reopening them, he asked, "But I still don't get it. How could the guy just disappear? Do you think it's possible that he just decided to take a couple of days off, and for whatever reason, opted not to tell anyone? I mean, you know the guy a lot better than I do. You must have some theory as to what's going on here."

Tim shook his head. "I wish I did, but no I don't. All I know is this: Mike's not the kind of guy who would just checkout for a day or two without telling anybody where he was going. Definitely not. He's far too responsible to ever do something like that. Which leads me to believe that something's happened to him. And the fact that he hasn't turned up at any of the local hospitals suggests to me that whatever that something is, it wasn't an accident."

David leaned forward in his chair, intensity written all over his face. "No, then what do you think it was?"

"This is just pure speculation on my part, but if I had to guess, my guess would be that he's been either kidnapped or killed." Lengthy pause. "Obviously, I hope I'm wrong in this, but my intuition tells me that I'm not."

David threw his hands up in anger. "Kidnapped or killed! What are we talking about here? Wow! Not even I would have thought Shannon capable of such things! Really, it's beyond comprehension." He looked away for a moment. "Not only that, it doesn't even make any sense. I mean, why the hell would she want to kill Mike? To get to me? Not likely." After a beat of silence, he mused, "Or maybe it was her way of trying to derail iQu, and thereby ensure we can't use it to bolster our stock price? Hmmm. Now, that's a possibility. Maybe there's some method to her madness after all."

"I don't know, David, but I'm not sure I'd go there just yet," Tim said softly.

"Go where?"

"To point the finger of suspicion at Shannon."

"And why the hell not?" David asked heatedly, his face flushed.

"I just don't see her as being capable of doing what we're talking about here."

David was shaking his head even before Tim had finished. "Let me see if I've got this straight. You think she's capable of killing me, her own flesh and blood, but not Mike, a perfect stranger. Is that it?" He waited for an answer, but when he didn't get one immediately, he added, "Come on Tim, now you're the one not making any sense."

Tim looked away while passing a hand over the nape of his neck. In a tentative voice, he said, "None of this makes any sense to me either, but again, it's just a feeling that I have. No, that's not exactly true. There is more to it than that. There's this little voice inside my head that's been getting louder by the day, and—"

"And what's it been telling you?" David asked impatiently.

"It's been telling me that we may actually be focusing all of our attention on the wrong person."

David looked as if someone had just hit him over the head with a two by four. At a temporary loss for words the only sound to escape his mouth was, "Huh?"

Choosing his words carefully, Tim explained, "Up until recently I was so thoroughly convinced that Shannon was behind everything that I basically didn't even consider anybody else. But that all changed a couple of nights ago after I had a very strange dream about George Barnett."

David blinked. "Who?"

"George Barnett. You know. The DARPA guy who set up Celebrix back in the late '80s. I'm sure I've told you about him. He's now running The Center for Applied Research—a high-tech consultancy and research company based out of New York. Do you remember me saying something about him?"

David thought about it for a while, and then said, "Oh, yeah, that guy. Sure, I remember now. But what's he got to do with any of this?"

"The man is utterly *desperate* to regain control of Celebrix, and has been now for quite a while. But up until recently, he'd always gone about it in a very normal and civilized way. He'd call every now and again and want to get together to see if I was any more ready to sell, which, of course, I never was. But he just kept on trying. And it continued like that up until about six months ago, at which point I grew tired of the charade and just stopped taking his calls."

"So, then what did he do?"

"He changed tactics and instead of going after me, he started going after Celebrix's top scientists to see if he couldn't convince them to leave me and to go work for him. And then when that didn't work, he put away the carrot, and pulled out the stick."

"Meaning?"

"He started threatening them. You know, as in, 'either take what I'm offering or don't be surprised if you return home one evening to discover that your wife has just found an envelope in the mail with photographs depicting you and one of your female co-workers in some pretty compromising positions.' That sort of thing."

"But that's blackmail."

Tim snorted delicately. "And that's George Barnett."

David was utterly horrified. "You can't be serious?"

"Oh, but I am. And, as I said earlier, it's been getting worse by the day. In fact, just a few days ago, one of his hired hands went so far as to tell one of my scientists that if she didn't change employers, something unfortunate might happen to her daughter. Can you imagine?!"

Try as he might, David couldn't believe what he was hearing. It was all too shocking. Then, not knowing what else to say, he asked, "But, if all of this has been going on for awhile, then why is this the first time that I'm hearing about it?"

Tim shrugged apologetically. "For the simple reason that you already had enough on your plate. The last thing I wanted to do was to pile on more. That, and the fact that up until now I never really made the connection between Barnett and the things that have been going on around here."

David threw Tim a questioning glance. "And when you say, 'going on around here,' what is it exactly that you're referring to?"

"Everything. First of all, there was the diving—"

David was quick to interrupt. "But what does Barnett have to do with the fact that someone tried to kill me when I was diving down in St. Lucia?"

"Kill *us,* you mean."

"Whatever." Uncomfortable pause. "What are you trying to do here, Tim? First you and Allan try to convince me that Shannon's out to kill me, and now, from one minute to the next, you change your story around completely, and now argue that it's you that they're after—not me—and that it's Barnett that's behind it all, and not Shannon. That's a bit of a switch, wouldn't you say? So, maybe you can understand why I might have a hard time going along with you on this one. Oh, and there's one other little thing that also makes your story somewhat difficult to accept."

"And what's that?" Tim asked tonelessly.

"The cottage incident. How does it fit into this new theory of yours?" David's voice rose both in strength and in intensity. "It doesn't, does it? Of course not, because the whole thing is just pure and unadulterated crap. I mean, don't get me wrong. I'd love to believe it, I really would. Because you can't imagine how painful it is to think that your own sister is out to kill you. Believe me, it hurts like hell, but hey, if that's the way it is, then that's the way it is, and I've no choice but to accept it. And I do—it took me a while, but I do. So please, do me a favor, will you, and drop the Barnett thing, OK? By the sounds of it, he's one very sick puppy, but somehow I just can't see him trying to incinerate my cottage and me in it, nor do I see him feeding destructive rumors about my company to the investment community. Now, Shannon, on the other hand, is another story entirely. For example, why don't you try this out for size: after hearing from you what iQu could mean to Quenetics—and therefore, to me—she panicked and decided to throw a spanner in the works. And by a spanner, I'm referring to the removal of one of us, and as you and I were no longer easy targets, she went after someone who was. And who better to take out than Mike? It wouldn't have taken much digging on her part to find out that he's the most important member of the iQu team, so her choice is easily made. He's the one that's got to go, and so he does. Simple as that." With a philosophical twitch of his eyebrows, he added, "Actually, when you think about it, we should have seen this thing coming."

Tim opened his mouth to say something, but then closed it again. He knew how stubborn David could be when he'd made his mind up on something, and it was clear that on the issue of Mike's disappearance, his mind was well and truly made up. Shannon was the guilty party.

David was silent for a minute. He seemed to be having an internal conflict over something. Eventually, it came out. "At the risk of sounding insensitive, there's just one other thing I need to know. Let's say, hypothetically, that Mike has, in fact, been killed. Where would that leave us? Do you think that we could still get along without him?"

Tim grimaced at the question. Then, trying to put his emotions aside for a moment, he answered, "As you just finished saying yourself, Mike's key to making this whole thing happen. It's been his energy and ideas, more so than mine or anybody else's, that's got us to where we are today. If we were to lose him, then we'd definitely be in a lot of trouble, without a doubt." Feeling the need to temper that somewhat, he added, "That's not to say that we couldn't go on. We could. But it would certainly be at a much slower pace."

David lowered his head and began massaging his temples as he digested this. "So, short term we'd be in deep trouble?"

"Definitely." Tim replied. "But if you don't mind me asking, what are you getting at here?"

David shrugged, a sheepish look souring his face. "I'm just trying to find out how much damage I may have inadvertently inflicted on you and your team."

Tim eyed him carefully. "Why? What have you done?"

David looked away and stared at some imaginary point on the wall. "I've been hinting to people for the last few days now that we had some huge e-deal in the works, and that we'd probably be making an announcement about it any day now."

"Any day now? Why would you have said that? We're still weeks away from being in a position to—"

"Look," David snapped, "you were the one who wanted me to announce it in the first place. So, what the hell are you complaining about?"

"I'm not complaining, I'm just surprised, that's all." Slight pause. "No, that's not true. I am complaining. Yes, I wanted you to make an announcement, but only once we were ready, as in maybe in a week or two. After we've had the chance to put a media package together, among other things."

David waved his hand dismissively. "Sorry, Tim, but with all that's going on at the moment, I just didn't see myself as having any choice in the matter." Then, in a more conciliatory tone, he added, "And furthermore, I didn't really see the harm in it. I was basically just passing on what you were saying to me. I might have used slightly different words, but the message was more or less the same."

Again, Tim wanted to argue with him, but decided against it. What good would it do? he thought to himself. The cat was already out of the bag. What could either of them do about it now? So, not knowing what else to say, he simply got up to leave. But before moving to the door, he said, "Well, let's just hope like hell that Mike shows up before everybody else realizes that he's gone missing. Otherwise, I'm afraid you're going to have a lot of explaining to do."

15

David's home, Boston

DAVID, DRESSED IN HIS BATHROBE and slippers, was picking up the newspaper from the front porch when the telephone rang. Not wanting the noise to wake Tim, he raced back inside and grabbed the phone before it had the chance to ring for the third time. Two minutes later, the call was over. Dropping the handset back into its cradle, David had to lean on the countertop for support. He suddenly felt faint and barely able to remain in an upright position. Closing his eyes, he lowered his head while forcing himself to breathe deeply.

That helped, but only to a degree. The lightheadedness quickly passed, but another, equally powerful, sensation—the need to cry—quickly replaced it. Resting on his elbows, he dropped his head down into the "v" of his shaking hands, and started to weep. A deep, body-quaking cry, the likes of which he'd never experienced before.

The call had signaled the beginning of the end, and he knew it.

· · ·

171

Five minutes later, David woke Tim and told him the news: Mike's body had been found in a Dumpster near the docks, the police having been directed there by an anonymous tip. He'd been shot at point-blank range.

What it all meant Tim couldn't even begin to fathom at this point. Nor did he really care to think about it. The only thing on his mind was the fact that he'd just lost one of his closest and dearest friends. And it hurt. Big time.

Fighting back the tears, his thoughts then turned to the two people who would be even more devastated by the news than he was: Kathy, Mike's wife of twenty years, and Sandy, their teenage daughter. His heart went out to them as he tried to imagine how they'd be feeling at this point. Anxious to offer his condolences and whatever support he could, he leaned over in his bed and reached for the phone. Dialing the number from memory, he got through immediately.

A few minutes later he ended the call and put down the receiver. Then with moisture welling in his eyes he quickly summarized what had been said. "That was Kathy I had on the phone, and—" His voice was starting to break up so he paused for a moment. He took a deep breath and then tried again. "Tough woman. Really. She never ceases to amaze me. She's utterly devastated, but she's somehow holding it together. In fact, she's already started making the funeral arrangements. Can you imagine?"

David nodded in understanding, and then asked, "Why don't you fly out there and see if you can be of some help? I'm sure she'd really appreciate it."

Tim shook his head despondently. "No, on two counts. One, because she's actually coming out this way. She wants to hold the funeral here in the city, as this is where Mike spent most of his youth, and where apparently, many of his relatives are still living. And, two, she just doesn't want any of my help. Whether that's because of her own stubborn nature or because she partially blames me for what has happened, I don't know." He flopped back onto his pillow and screwed his eyes shut in a futile attempt to hold back the tears.

David started to say something, but stopped mid-sentence. Judging by the pained look on Tim's face, it was clear that his friend was in no mood for an argument.

Completely absorbed in their own thoughts, neither man spoke for many minutes. Finally, it was David who broke the silence. "I hate to be the one to bring this up, but the police did ask if one of us would go down to the morgue to identify the body. I promised that we would, but if you'd prefer, I'll go alone, no problem at all."

Tim's eyes popped open. Then, sitting upright in the bed, his face devoid of expression, he replied, "No. No. I'll go. There's no need for both of us to go. You've probably got other things to attend to, and to be honest, I'd just like to spend a few minutes alone with him, if that's all right with you."

"That's fine. Whatever you want."

Tim looked away, and then in a voice seething with hatred, he said, "What I *really* want is to get my hands on whoever did this to him. Because, let me tell you, if I ever do, I'll kill the bastard!"

•   •   •

Fifteen minutes later, both men were dressed and sitting at the kitchen table sipping coffee. Neither had much appetite for food, nor interest in talking. So, both just sat staring at the miniature television perched on a countertop a few feet away. Using the remote, David toggled back and forth between CYNB, the local all-news channel, and CNBC, the financial news network. On CYNB, the discovery of Mike's body was their lead story, while on CNBC, the commentators, having already picked up the story, were keeping a sharp eye on Quenetics' pre-opening share price.

Watching without really listening, Tim tuned in for a moment to hear one of the CNBC commentators saying that Mike was *"a well-known expert in the field of artificial intelligence who'd apparently been heading up a top-secret research project, funded by Quenetics, aimed at finding new ways to apply AI to the rapidly changing world of on-line job selection and recruitment. As to the precise nature of their work, we still don't know for certain; however, according to one source very close to what was going on, it's believed that they're trying to create some sort of digital shadow that will follow its user everywhere, and would always know everything about what the user was thinking, feeling, and saying. Can you imagine?"* she exclaimed as she appeared to shudder on screen. *"Big Brother lives. If only George Orwell had lived to see this day."* She then prattled on about the horrors of modern technology and how, in a world where science fiction was rapidly becoming science fact, nothing was sacred anymore.

David shook his head in amazement. "Where the hell do they come up with this stuff? Do you think they just make it up as they go along?" It was a rhetorical question. "It would certainly appear that way, wouldn't it?"

Not really knowing how to respond to that, or simply not wanting to, Tim just nodded his head and then turned his attention back to the screen. The commentator was now saying, *"But maybe we don't have to worry about all of this just yet, because again according to the same source, the feeling now seems to be that with Mike Bennett no longer there to move the project forward, it's expected that it will soon be shut down."* She, of course, had an opinion about that, but Tim failed to pick up what it was. He'd already tuned her out and was busy thinking about what she'd just said.

His thinking was suddenly interrupted by the sound of David's fist making contact with the breakfast table. "Damn that woman!" Loud expulsion of air. "She doesn't miss a trick, does she?!" His fist slammed the table a second time, this time with such force that coffee drops exploded out of each of their coffee cups. As they fell like black rain all over the table, he cursed her loud and repeatedly. Then, with his anger temporarily spent, he moaned, "Well, what the hell do we do now? She's just trumped the only card we still had left—iQu. So, now, rather than being able to use it to win back support and possibly even to generate some buzz, she's now turned it into some deep, dark mind-control thing that thankfully, due to Mike's death, will never happen." Deep sigh. "Well, so much for iQu helping me climb out of the hole that I'm now in. If anything, it's probably just going to bury me instead."

Tim said nothing. Instead, he got up from the table and went over to the sink in search of something to clean up

David's mess. Returning a few moments later with a dishcloth in hand he busied himself with the coffee stains while allowing himself time to think.

David had his head in his hands, apparently also deep in thought. Then, with his head still lowered, he said, "Well, the way I see it, there's really only one thing I can do at this point, and that is to set up a press conference as quickly as possible and try to set the record straight. I realize that I could be setting myself up to get roasted alive, but what else can I do? She's got me over a barrel and she knows it. I either try to salvage what's left of iQu and my name, or I accept defeat and step down. It's as simple as that." Significant pause. "So, the only question that now remains, is whether I'll even survive long enough to try to make this happen."

"What do you mean by that?" Tim asked.

David finally lifted his head out of his hands, and looking Tim straight in the eye, he replied, "Just as you seem to feel the need every now and again to shelter me from certain realities, I've recently felt the need to do likewise."

Tim didn't like the sound of that. Not at all. "Do you care to elaborate on that?"

David shrugged. "Sure, why not?! You're probably about to find out anyway."

Tim was growing more uncomfortable by the second.

David continued in a voice completely devoid of energy. "Matt Baker phoned a couple of days ago to tell me that if our stock price was to drop below the eighty dollar mark, he'd be forced to sell to Miller, and that he was under the impression that the other pension fund managers would be doing the same thing. So, it looks as though if it goes below eighty, I'm gone."

· · ·

By nine thirty, Tim had left the morgue and was en route to the office. Then, suddenly feeling overcome with emotion, he leaned forward and tapped Robert softly on the shoulder. "Do me a favor and pull into the next parking lot, will you. I'd like to have a few moments to myself, if that's all right with you."

"Sure, Tim, whatever you say."

Less than a minute later, Robert pulled into a Burger King and drove to the back of the lot. Then, turning the engine off, he got out of the car and walked towards the restaurant, leaving Tim to his thoughts.

Remaining in the car, Tim turned his head to look out the window. Then, suddenly, without warning, his breath left his body, his stomach started to quiver, and the tears started to flow. Slowly at first, but before long, they were streaming down his face, and dropping from his chin onto his chest below.

A few minutes later, feeling somewhat dehydrated and light-headed, he wiped the tear tracks from his face, leaned back in his seat and closed his eyes. He had no idea who had done this to his friend, but he was sure as hell going to find out. And, when he did? He left that thought unanswered. He'd cross that bridge when he came to it.

Opening his eyes again, he glanced down at his cellphone, which was lying on his lap. He decided to give David a quick call to tell him where he was and to see how he was making out.

David answered on the second ring. Struggling to conceal his anguish, Tim spoke for a few moments about himself, and then asked, "And how about you? How are you holding up?"

David's voice was terse. "I'm absolutely livid, but I'm trying not to think about it at the moment. Instead, I'm trying to concentrate on preparing myself for the press conference we've got set up for eleven thirty this morning."

"And your stock?" Tim asked. "How's it holding up?"

"It's not! It's still falling. Not as fast as it was earlier this morning, but it's still going down. Which means that I may still be pushed out even before the press conference gets underway. Who knows? We'll just have to wait and see, but let me tell ya, I'm really on pins and needles at the moment."

"I can imagine. But what's the stock at now?"

"It's just slipped under eighty-two and a half."

"And how about Matt and the others, have you spoken to any of them yet?"

"All of them. In fact, that's what I've been doing ever since I got in. Trying to reassure them that everything's going to be fine and to see if I can get any of them to modify their thinking somewhat."

"And?"

David let out a mournful sigh. "Nothing doing. If it goes beneath eighty dollars, they're all going to sell. There's no question about it. In fact, one or two of them may have already sold. They were certainly leaning in that direction the last time I spoke to them. But then again, maybe my arguments were enough to make them think twice before taking action. Who knows? We'll just have to wait and see how this thing plays out.

That is, if I don't die from heart failure in the meantime. Because, let me tell you, I don't think I can handle much more of this. I really don't."

Tim grunted in understanding, and then asked, "And Shannon? Do you think there's any chance of her backing down at the last minute?"

Chortle. "Hardly. I've been trying to get in contact with her, but apparently she's not even coming in today. Her secretary told me that she'd phoned in earlier to say that she wasn't feeling well and therefore, wouldn't be in."

"Did she say what was wrong with her?"

"No, but I wouldn't be surprised if it's simply a bad case of the jitters. Apparently the police have already been out to see her, and Allan just phoned to say that he and a couple of FBI guys were also headed her way. I don't know about you, but that would certainly be enough to get me feeling a bit hot under the collar."

Tim grunted again in agreement, but wasn't really listening. His mind had checked out as soon as he'd heard that the police had been out to visit Shannon. He was growing ever more concerned about the fact that everyone's attention was focused so exclusively on her, and none on Barnett. Yes, she certainly had a motive for killing Mike, but so did Barnett. And, whereas he had a hard time imagining Shannon committing such an act, with Barnett, he had no trouble whatsoever. Barnett had already proven to be a desperate man, capable of just about anything. But, on the other hand, to assume that it was Barnett behind all the murder and mayhem, raised more questions than answers. Questions like: What had happened that day up at

David's cottage? Had Shannon left the gas on intentionally or simply by mistake? And then there was St. Lucia—she'd have known about the holiday well enough in advance to have arranged for the poisoning to take place. With Barnett, he couldn't imagine the same thing holding true. And finally, there was that rather odd telephone conversation he'd overheard a few days back. What had that been all about?

Difficult questions, every one of them. But none of them proved anything. They simply raised the specter of doubt, nothing more. They certainly didn't prove culpability.

So, where did that leave him? In the same state he'd been in for days now: lost in a fog of confusion, unsure of what to believe. Yet, decisions had to be made; people were dying while he dithered.

The only possible solution he could think of was to confront Shannon directly, gauge her reactions, and then draw his own conclusions. Maybe her eyes or the intonation of her voice or body language would give something away, or maybe the opposite would happen. Maybe she'd somehow be able to convince him of her innocence. Who was to say? All he knew was that he had to give it a try—and quickly. Before more time, and possibly another life or two, were lost.

His thinking was suddenly interrupted by the sound of David's voice. "Are you still there?"

Tim cleared his throat. "Yeah, sorry about that, my mind just wandered off for a minute, that's all." Short pause. "I just seem to be having a hard time staying focused at the moment."

David's voice softened immediately. "Which is completely understandable. So, why don't you go for a walk and try to relax a bit before the press conference? It'll probably do you a world of good."

"The press conference?" Tim said hesitantly. "Why do you mention that? What's it got to do with me?"

"I need you to be there, that's why." Slight pause. "Someone's got to talk about iQu, and it sure as hell can't be me, as I hardly know anything about it. So, that someone's got to be you. That is, of course, if you feel up to it."

Tim didn't answer directly. Instead he said, "So if I understand correctly, you want to use the press conference to formally announce iQu to the world?"

"May as well. The story's already out there."

"But don't you think that by moving so quickly, we'll be playing right into Miller's hands? As in, rather than taking the time to put together a really powerful presentation package, we'll instead be going off half-cocked and possibly screw it up as a result."

"That's a risk we're just going to have to take, I'm afraid. Because when you step back and try to take a completely objective view of the situation, you quickly come to realize that we actually no longer have any choice in the matter. It's as simple as that." David's voice left no room for doubt. "With my stock now just above eighty-two dollars, and still going lower, this is it. This is the moment of truth. We either survive this thing or we don't. And if we don't, I think it's curtains for both iQu and yours truly."

16

George Barnett's home, New York

EXITING THE REVOLVING DOOR of his luxury apartment building, George Barnett walked briskly toward the waiting limo. Glaring at the chauffeur as the young man opened the door for him, he snapped, "My plane leaves in less than an hour, so let's get going."

The chauffeur, a new Russian immigrant only too willing to please, heard the command and did as he was told. Within seconds, the limo took off, cut across the nose of a bus and jumped a red light. George quickly recognized that he was in the hands of a sportsman, a cut-and-thruster who saw the streets of Manhattan as a testing ground for man and machine. The driver charged down Fifth Avenue in a series of high-octane lunges and sudden-death swerves.

Feeling slightly nauseous, George yelled, "I would, however, like to get there in one piece, if you don't mind."

The car instantly decelerated. Breathing a quick sigh of relief, George glanced down at his cellphone. Why wasn't the damn thing ringing? Al-Hassan should have called over an hour ago, and yet there'd been no call. Something had obviously gone seriously wrong. But what? If only there was some way he could find out. But there wasn't and he knew it. So, he just had to be patient. Just a little while longer, he hoped.

Suddenly, as though telepathic, his cellphone came to life. Placing it quickly to his ear, he listened for a few moments and then issued a single command: "Do it." With that, he ended the call and turned off the phone. Slipping it inside his suit jacket, he felt a tinge of excitement ripple through his body. Allowing himself the faintest of smiles, he whispered, *"Yes! Finally!"*

·   ·   ·

Shannon was sitting on the couch with her Persian cat when Tim's call came through to her answering machine. She didn't move, as she had absolutely no interest in taking the call. Not now. Not in the mood she was in. She'd already been questioned enough for one day.

But no sooner had Tim left his message and hung up than another call came through. This one was from Andy, her concierge. "What does he want this time?" she mumbled to herself. Placing her cat gingerly on the cushion next to her, she jumped up and strode quickly over to the answering machine. Switching it off, she picked up the receiver and spoke into it. "Yeah, Andy, what is it this time?"

She listened for a moment and then groaned, "You can't be serious! More FBI agents! What the hell's going on here? Haven't I already had my quota for the day?"

She listened to his answer to her rhetorical question, and then said, "Ah, don't worry about it. There's obviously nothing you can do about it." Pause. "Sure, just send them up. Tell them I'll be waiting for them at the elevator."

The time was now 9:39 and the Quenetics stock price had just dipped for the first time below eighty-two dollars.

•   •   •

Arriving at headquarters, Tim went immediately up to David's office only to discover that he wasn't there. Turning to Linda, David's secretary, he asked if she knew where he was.

"Yes, he's in the boardroom at the moment. But that meeting should end just about any minute now."

"And how about Shannon, is she in there as well?" Tim asked.

"No, apparently she's not feeling very well and so has decided not to come in today." Then lowering her voice somewhat, she added, "I was so shocked to hear of Mr. Bennett's death this morning. He was such a wonderful man; why would anyone want to kill him?" When Tim didn't answer immediately, she spoke again. "It's horrible what this world is coming to, isn't it? It's almost getting to the point where a single woman, like myself, is afraid to even venture out of my own home anymore. In fact, about a week ago—"

Knowing how chatty Linda could be once she got started, Tim was quick to interrupt. He had other things to occupy his mind. "Yes, you're right, Linda. It's utterly shocking what has happened to Mike. In fact, even though I've just seen him lying in the morgue, I still can't quite accept the fact that he's gone. It seems that somewhere deep inside me I still keep hoping that he'll suddenly walk up to me and tell me that this is nothing but a bad dream." Letting out a brief sigh, he slowly shook his head. "But, that's obviously not going to happen. Anyway, to be honest, I'd rather not talk about it at the moment, if that's all right with you. Maybe later, but not now, so, if you don't mind, I'm just going to go into David's office and wait for him there."

Linda's features softened immediately. "Oh, I understand completely," she sighed, her silver hair wafting around her face and her dark eyes glittering. "I know how close the two of you were."

"We were," Tim agreed. Then with a slight nod of the head, he turned away and walked quickly into David's office. Closing the door behind him, he made a beeline for David's desk. Dropping himself into the chair, he took a few deep breaths to steady himself. Then, glancing over at the computer screen he saw that Quenetics stock price had now dropped to $81.35, and that an analyst from Goldman Sachs had just downgraded it from a "hold" to a "sell." Things were definitely not looking good. Not at all. In fact, it was difficult to imagine how things could get much worse than they were.

But before he could take that thought a step further, he watched in horror as the stock price dipped again, this time down to $81.10.

Not knowing what else to do, Tim lowered his head, closed his eyes, and said a prayer.

· · ·

At eleven thirty sharp, the press conference got under way. The special room David used for these sorts of events was on the first floor, and though it had a seating capacity of sixty, there was standing room only. The press loved a good drama, and it didn't get any better than this. All the ingredients were there: power, greed, money, murder, and mystery. What more could a reporter ask for? It was the type of story that came along once, maybe twice in a career—if you were lucky. So, quite naturally, everybody wanted to be there.

The atmosphere in the room was electric, the tension almost palpable as the mob waited for the show to begin. Like spectators in an ancient Roman coliseum, this group had come to see blood, and they didn't want to be kept waiting.

David sat, stony-faced, at the table at the front of the room, sandwiched between Tim and Nancy Lussier, the CFO. Tim's laptop was perched on the table off to one side, but still close enough for the three of them to see the screen. Glancing over at it, Tim was relieved to see that the stock price was still holding steady at eighty-one dollars. It appeared that the market had decided to take a breather and await the outcome of the press conference before deciding what to do next. Technical traders had also provided another reason for the temporary respite—they'd suggested that eighty dollars appeared to be the stock's next technical support level, which meant that if the stock fell below it, it was anyone's guess as to just how far it would fall.

That meant that everything hinged on what happened now. If the three of them could convince the mob that Quenetics was in the midst of turning itself around, the stock would likely rebound; if not, all hell was likely to break loose.

The pressure was so intense that Tim was finding it increasingly difficult to breathe. His mouth was dry, his palms wet, his scalp tight, and it felt like his heart had moved up into his throat. He glanced over to see how David was holding up. Surprisingly, he looked to be doing quite well. Other than a glistening forehead, he showed no signs of nervousness whatsoever. *How utterly remarkable,* Tim thought, *particularly in light of the fact that his entire life now hangs in the balance. All he needs to do now is to say the wrong thing or even to say the right thing, but in the wrong way, and he'll lose everything—his career, his name and reputation, much of his own personal wealth, probably his home, and possibly even his marriage.* Who knew where the carnage would end once the destruction got underway? Tim shuddered at the thought.

Peering down at his prepared notes, Tim tried to concentrate. But without success. His brain just refused to register what his eyes were reading. He then tried taking a few deep breaths to see if that would help. It didn't. So, not knowing what else to do, he decided to try one last trick. It was something he'd read in a magazine once. Closing his eyes for a moment, he tried to focus his mind on something else, something pleasant and far away. He tried to picture a beautiful resort he'd stayed at in the Seychelles a few months back, but before he could even remember the resort's name, the image was shattered by the sound of David's voice. Reopening his eyes, he saw that David was now standing and was preparing to address the mob.

David began by thanking everyone for coming, and then quickly moved on to the business at hand. He opened with a short eulogy for Mike in which he gave high praise for the man's honesty, tenacity, and intellect. He talked at length of Mike's many accomplishments, particularly those relating to the creation of iQu, but he was careful not to overdo it. He wanted the mob to understand and appreciate Mike's many talents, but he also wanted them to understand that though the man was gifted, he was not indispensable. His work could and would live on without him. It wouldn't be easy, but it would be done.

When David finally finished his ten-minute oration, he then asked Nancy to spend a few moments discussing Quenetics' current financial situation. Using a computer and a beamer, she put on a performance that left no one in doubt—Quenetics would match or beat "the street's" profit forecasts for the next quarter, and it would do so by shedding non-core businesses, slashing costs, and increasing productivity. By the time she'd finished, not even the most numerically challenged reporter could have misinterpreted her message.

Then, after a brief introduction by David, it was Tim's turn to perform. And perform he did. By the time he'd finished a full twenty-five minutes later, his audience was completely spellbound.

As Tim returned to his seat, David returned to the podium to field any last-minute questions. Ten minutes later, it was over, and the room began to clear. Moving at breakneck speed, the mob exited the room, chattering all the while like school kids freed from detention. The time had come for the jury to cast their votes.

Anxious to escape the few stragglers who'd stayed behind, David, Tim, and Nancy bolted from the room and ducked quickly into a nearby conference room, closing the door behind them. With a calmness belying his true emotions, David walked to the far end of the room, opened a panel in the wall, and hit a series of buttons. Moments later, the central section of the wall slid back, revealing a large screen behind it. He then turned, and with a remote control in his hand, he said, "Well, I guess this is it. The moment of truth has arrived. Either they bought our story or they didn't. If they did, we live to fight another day; if they didn't, well, at least we can take comfort in the fact that we put up a hell of a fight. Especially the two of you. You two were great in there. Both of you were calm, cool, and, at least in my view, thoroughly convincing."

Tim scoffed. "Maybe to you, but were we to them? That's the question now, isn't it? And the only way we're going to learn the answer is by you turning that damn thing on." He pointed to the remote control as he said it.

David nodded his head in agreement, and then after taking a couple of deep breaths to steady his nerves, he activated the TV. Then turning the set to channel five—Quenetics' own internal media channel—they watched as David's image filled the screen. Apparently they were replaying highlights from the press conference. But not wanting to hear himself speak, David quickly muted the sound and then directed his attention to the sidebar down in the bottom right-hand corner of the screen.

The sidebar contained two numbers—the current stock price, and the spread between current and opening, measured in percentage terms. The second number was interesting, but it was the first that they were most interested in. Focusing on it, they saw that the stock price was holding steady around the eighty-one dollar mark. Every now and again it would fluctuate slightly, but generally, it was holding steady.

David breathed a mild sigh of relief. At least it hadn't gone into a freefall. That was encouraging. But the fact that it hadn't made a major move in either direction suggested that the jury was still out. So, anything was still possible.

No one said a word. It was now just down to the waiting. The torturous, nail-biting, oppressive, nerve-wracking waiting. The tension was so thick, one could have cut it with a knife.

The seconds ticked away, minute after agonizing minute, but still there were no major movements. The price held steady. And then it happened. It suddenly dropped dramatically! Down to within a whisker of eighty dollars.

There was a collective suck of air.

David slowly lowered his head in despair.

Tim closed his eyes and offered up another prayer.

Nancy suddenly felt faint and slouched back into her chair.

But then, just as abruptly, the stock bounced back up to eighty-one fifty. And then just kept right on going.

• • •

Half an hour later, with the stock price back above eighty-four dollars and still trending higher, David suggested they go out for a celebratory lunch. Both Tim and Nancy were quick to agree. They arranged to meet in the foyer in five minutes time.

In the meantime Tim went back to his office to check his cellphone for messages. He was amazed to learn his only one was from Shannon. In a voice devoid of energy, she said, "I just wanted to let you know that I got your message on my answering machine here at home, and that yes, I would be interested in meeting with you. And, in light of all that's happened today, I think we should do that as soon as possible. The only problem being that I'm planning to head up for the cottage within the next hour or so, and won't be back in the city again until sometime late Sunday night. Which leaves us with two options: we can wait until Monday, or you can join me up at the cottage. The choice is yours, but please, give me a call back as soon as you can to let me know what you decide." Short pause, then with more feeling, she added, "Oh, and one more thing. If you do decide to come, I'd prefer you make it this evening, as I have a friend coming in on Saturday who'll be staying over until Sunday." Another pause, this one even longer than the last, then in what could be considered almost a seductive tone, she ended with, "Sorry. Two more things. One, depending on when you come, you might want to bring a toothbrush along, as we do have a lot of ground to cover; and, two, it would make me a lot more comfortable if you'd come up on your own, and leave that ridiculous bodyguard of yours behind. Trust me, I won't bite. Anyway, again, the choice is yours. Just let me know what you decide."

Unable to believe his ears, Tim listened to the message a second time. Then, convinced that he'd heard it correctly, he ended the call and slumped into his chair. "What the hell is she up to now?" he mumbled to himself.

·   ·   ·

Two hours later, having failed in his efforts to talk Tim out of going to the cottage alone, David sat down at his desk and made a call. A call that set a whole series of actions into motion.

17

Tim WAS GETTING MORE FRUSTRATED by the minute. He was lost, and had been for some time. Pulling over onto the grass at the side of road, he surveyed the road ahead while pondering his options. "God, why didn't I get a car with GPS in it?" he mumbled to himself. Then, shaking his head in frustration, he hit the redial button on his cellphone and waited to see if Shannon would finally pick up. She didn't. He was again put through to her voice mail, but as he'd already left her two messages, he saw no reason to leave her a third.

He thought about turning back, but that would mean having to accept defeat, which was something that he was loath to do. It just wasn't in his nature. So, no, turning back was not a viable option. He'd find this place, even if it was the last thing he ever did.

With that thought in mind, he slipped the car into gear and set off down the road. Then, a quarter of an hour and many expletives later, he suddenly saw something that gave him hope—a small road sign indicating that there was a waterfall two miles ahead. Could this be the one that David had told him to keep an eye out for? He quickly glanced down at David's directions just to refresh his memory. "Gibson falls" was the name he was looking for. *Oh, please let this be it,* he mumbled to himself.

A few minutes later, he went round a sharp bend in the road, and there on his left was the falls, maybe eighty or so yards from the road. Slowing to a stop in front of the only sign in the vicinity, Tim was greatly relieved to see that it did indeed read "Gibson Falls." Good news, he was getting close. Glancing again at the directions he saw that all he had to do now was to go another quarter of a mile on the road he was now on and then turn off onto the first side road on the right, which was apparently the driveway up to the cottage.

He'd made it, more-or-less! Now the question was whether he wanted to do the last bit by car or on foot. By car would, of course, be a lot quicker and easier, but it would also mean that she'd hear him coming, and he wasn't sure he really wanted that. He had absolutely no idea as to what he was getting himself into and that bothered him. A lot. So, the notion of using the element of surprise to his advantage did have some appeal to it.

It didn't take him long to make a decision. Stealth seemed to be the preferable option. So, now all he needed to do was to find a place to leave the car, and then go the rest of the way on foot.

Scanning the road ahead, he spotted the perfect solution. There was a small parking area—obviously designed as a scenic lookout—fifty or so yards farther up the road, and again on the left. He'd leave the car there.

Pulling into the parking lot he was surprised to find that it was almost full. *That's odd,* he thought to himself, but then wanting to stay focused on the task at hand he pushed the thought from his mind. *It's probably just a group of trampers who have yet to return from an outing. Nothing to be concerned about.*

Finding a space in between two identical SUVs, he parked the car, and then got out. Then, after grabbing his coat out of the back seat, he locked the car and set off down the road.

Fifteen minutes later, he came to a side road on his right. There was a sign posted on either side of it warning, "Private Property: Keep Out!" which is exactly what he'd been told to expect. Good, this was definitely it. Now, all he needed to do was to walk the mile up to the cottage, and he'd be there.

•   •   •

The gunman was in his ghillie suit, a complex overall-type garment made of rags sewn into place on a gridded matrix, whose purpose was to make him appear to be a bush or a pile of leaves or compost, anything but a person with a rifle. The rifle was set up on its bipod, the hinged flaps on the front and back lenses on his telescopic sight flipped up. He'd picked a good place to the east of the cottage that would allow him to cover the entire distance between the lake and the cottage. His laser rangefinder indicated that he was sixty-three yards from the back door of the cottage and twenty-six yards from the edge of the lake. He was lying prone on a dry spot on the forest floor just a few feet from the tree line, and the air brought to him the smell of horses. He thumbed his radio microphone.

"Lead, Rifle Three-One."

"Rifle Three-One, Lead."

"In place and set up. I don't see any movement at this time."

"Lead, Rifle Two-Two, in place and set up. I also see no movement," another voice reported from his spot, two hundred yards away.

The group's leader allowed himself a brief smile. Everything was going according to plan.

. . .

As darkness descended, the forest seemed to come alive. Noises of every conceivable description accosted Tim's ears and stoked his imagination, further fueling his growing fear. He couldn't help but wonder if he was walking into a trap. A trap set by the same person or persons who'd already committed one murder in the last 48 hours. What was to stop her or them or whatever the case may be from committing a second? He had no gun; no bodyguard; no police back up; nothing, other than the knowledge that she knew that David knew that he was going to see her. He'd been sure to make that clear in his message to her. And knowing that she knew that, he couldn't imagine her doing anything crazy. But, then again, if she really had tried to kill David twice, and both times tried to make it look like an accident, then who knew what surprises she now had in store for him? And it was that thought that worried him most. That, combined with the growing darkness, the noises, the isolation, the sinister outlines of bushes and rocks, and generally, the fear of the unknown all played havoc on his mind. He started seeing things that weren't really there—or were they? He heard noises that didn't seem to fit into the forest's natural symphony of sounds, or again, was it simply his imagination playing with his mind? It was impossible to tell.

He stopped for a few moments to gauge his progress and, for the umpteenth time, to check to see if he were being followed. He stared long and hard back in the direction from which he had come, but didn't see anything unusual. Not that that meant there was nobody there. It simply meant that if they were there, they were better at this than he was, which wasn't saying much.

Leaning against a poplar, he glanced up and down the road but was still not able to see or hear anything out of the ordinary. Yes, there was the stream between the rocks, the wind among the needles of the pine branches, the chatter of insects and the cries of small arboreal mammals, as well as the birdsong; and from time to time a stronger gust of wind would make one of the branches of a cedar or a fir move against another and groan like a cello. But otherwise, there was nothing.

Breathing a mild sigh of relief, he continued on his way.

Five minutes later, he rounded a sharp bend in the road and breathed another sigh of relief. The cottage was now directly ahead, probably no more than sixty yards away.

His sense of relief quickly morphed, however, into an acute sense of foreboding. The cottage was in almost complete darkness. There was one light on, in what appeared to be the kitchen, but otherwise, there was nothing. Even the porch lights were off. Again, how odd. Hadn't she received his messages telling her that he was coming?

Shannon was obviously there, because her BMW was parked out front. But then, why were all the lights out? It was only 9:30, so it was unlikely that she'd already gone to bed. And even if she had, then why would she have left the light on in the kitchen? It didn't make sense. Unless, of course, she was having a late dinner in the kitchen and had simply forgotten to leave a light on over the porch. *That's possible,* he thought. Not very likely, but it was possible.

Clinging to that thought, Tim started moving forward again. Still not wanting to be seen, he veered off the road and then started walking parallel to it through the forest. Before long, he was standing beneath the window. The challenge facing him now was to find a way to see inside, for the bottom sill looked to be a good eight to ten inches over his head. Looking around for something to stand on, he saw a large chunk of wood that might do the trick a couple of yards away. But, just as he was about to move towards it, the silence was suddenly shattered by the shrill sound of a ringing tone. He froze immediately to the spot as his heart jumped into his throat and his pulse went through the ozone layer. Eyes wide, he looked frantically around to see if he could detect where the sound was coming from until it suddenly dawned on him that it was emanating from his own jacket pocket. It was his damn cellphone! He'd forgotten to switch it off.

Jabbing his hand into his pocket, he fumbled to disconnect the phone's battery. Within seconds it was done. But, was it too late? Had the damage already been done? Time would tell.

Holding his breath, he remained motionless for a good half-minute. With sweat streaming down his face, and his heart pounding in his chest, he watched the window for any sign of movement within. There was nothing. Then, just as he was starting to think that he was in the clear, he suddenly heard a twig snap over to his left.

Crouching down immediately, he again held his breath and cocked an ear. Silence. Then a very faint "clunk," like the sound of metal brushing against stone. And then again silence.

Staring into the darkness in the direction of the sound, he felt his body tense and his stomach knot. Reflexively, he quickly looked around to see if he could find something that he could use as a weapon if necessary. A broken limb, a rock, anything. But there was nothing to be had, at least not within reach. He cursed himself again for not having brought a gun along, not to mention someone to shoot it.

Then suddenly, his ears registered more movement, this time a little to the right of where he'd heard something a few moments before. Staring hard, he struggled to keep his breathing in check. But it wasn't working. He was teetering on the edge of terror, and he knew it.

Shape, shine, shadow, silhouette, spacing, and movement— he knew what to look for. But the problem was that now wherever he looked, objects were taking on the shape of imaginary enemies. Was that a boulder over to his right or the head of someone lying spread-eagle on the ground? Likewise, was that a broken tree branch a little to the left of it, or was it the shoulder of someone hiding behind the tree? Taking a deep breath, he closed his eyes for a few moments, hoping that that might squelch his anxieties.

It didn't. For no sooner did he reopen them than he saw a reflective object off in the distance, maybe twenty or twenty-five feet away. Fixing his gaze on it, he grew ever more convinced that he was staring down the barrel of a gun!

No, it couldn't be. It had to be his imagination playing tricks on him again. Or so he thought until he suddenly heard the muted spit of a silenced bullet. He was about to die!

But, before that thought even had time to register, he felt the searing pain of a bullet passing through his body. Looking down at the source of the pain, he saw a neat little hole in his shirt, parallel with, and maybe five or six inches to the right of, his belly button. Staring at it in complete amazement, he watched as a bright red blob slowly spread out in all directions.

Wide-eyed, and in a complete state of shock, he slowly lifted his head and rotated it in the direction of the killer. Amazingly, the man was now clearly visible and moving swiftly towards him, and yet he didn't feel any fear whatsoever. In fact, come to think of it, he wasn't feeling anything at all. Maybe he was already dead. He had no idea. All he knew was that the guy who'd shot him was now standing directly over him, with the gun now pointed directly at his head. And then it dawned on him: if he wasn't already dead, he would be soon!

He took a deep breath, and then he heard it. *Crack!* A gunshot. Followed by another.

The assassin's head seemed to disintegrate before his eyes.

A few seconds later, the forest erupted with ghostly apparitions rising from the floor and moving swiftly toward him. That was the last thing he saw before everything went black.

18

WHEN HE CAME TO, TIM FOUND himself in an unfamiliar setting. Rubbing his eyes in an attempt to get them to focus, he winced as his bullet wound reminded him of its presence. Cursing aloud, he screwed his eyes shut until the pain had subsided somewhat.

Reopening them a few moments later, he slowly took in his surroundings. He was in a large bed in the middle of a country-style room in which just about everything appeared to be made of wood—the floor, the walls, the ceiling, the furniture, and even many of the little knick-knacks which were scattered around the room. On either side of him were bedside tables with a lamp on each. The lamps were on, and cast a soft glow throughout the room.

While trying to figure out where he was, another jolt of pain shot through his body, causing him to cry out in agony. He closed his eyes and clenched his teeth, desperately hoping that it would pass quickly.

It didn't. This time around, it seemed to go on forever as wave after wave of mind-numbing agony rippled through his body. Then, just as he was about to scream out for help, it suddenly disappeared. He opened his eyes to see that in the meantime the room had filled with people. David and Allan were approaching on one side of the bed, and Shannon on the other. Another man, whom he didn't recognize, stood by the door, a grim look on his face and an automatic weapon strapped across his chest.

David spoke first. "Sorry we weren't here when you awoke, Tim. But we were gone for just a few minutes. There's an FBI agent in the room across the hall who's been shot-up pretty bad. We just went over to see if we could be of any help, but apparently not. The doctor threw us out."

Tim's eyebrows knitted together. "FBI agent? Would someone mind telling me what the hell is going on here? Where am I and how did I get in here? And better yet, why is there a wounded FBI agent in the room next to me?"

Allan glanced over at David, and whispered, "He's obviously suffering from temporary amnesia. Give me a minute while I talk to him." With that, Allan sat down on the edge of the bed, and then quickly filled Tim in on all the details.

"And how about me? What did the doc say about me?" He prodded the swath of bandages wrapped around his torso and winced.

"You're going to be fine. You've just got a flesh wound. Worst case, the bullet may have grazed your liver, but he doesn't think so."

"How can he be so sure?"

Allan shrugged. "Apparently, had the bullet hit something solid on its way through, it would have changed direction, which it didn't. It came out almost exactly opposite to where it went in. So as I said, you were extremely lucky."

Swallowing hard as another jolt of pain surged through him, Tim caught his breath and asked, "Well, let me tell you, I certainly don't feel very lucky at the moment. I'm in serious pain here. Can't the guy give me a painkiller or something?"

"I'm sure he will once he finishes with the other guy. But that may take awhile, because as I just finished saying, he's been shot up pretty badly."

Tim's watery eyes brimmed with concern. "How badly is 'badly'?"

Allan frowned. "I think it's quite touch and go at the moment. He caught two slugs at almost point-blank range—one to the side of the neck, and the other to the side of the head. So, he's lost a lot of blood and appears to have now slipped into a coma. The doc's doing all he can, but considering what little he has to work with—"

"But there's still hope, right?" Tim asked, his brow a sea of creases.

There is as long as we're able to get him to a hospital before his condition gets any worse. There's a helicopter on its way now, so hopefully he should be on his way within the next ten or fifteen minutes."

"And how about the guy responsible for all this carnage? Whatever happened to him?"

Allan's eyes narrowed and his features grew grim. "He's dead! Very dead!"

"Any idea who it was?"

Allan looked at Tim as though trying to assess whether or not he was ready for the truth. Apparently he decided that he was. "It was your old friend, George Barnett. First he took a shot at you, but before he could finish you off, the agent blew out his left kneecap. But before the agent could get to him to disarm him, Barnett got off two more shots. Bad luck for the agent, but a fatal mistake for Barnett, because before he could get off a third shot, the other members of the S.W.A.T. team literally blew his brains out."

Tim's mouth dropped and his eyes bulged. In a voice just above a whisper, he repeated, "George Barnett. Now, why am I not surprised? I knew the guy was a psycho!" Short pause. "And Mike? Do you think that was Barnett as well?"

Shannon answered before Allan could. "Yes and no. No, he wasn't the one who actually pulled the trigger, but yes, he was the one ultimately responsible."

Tim turned to look at Shannon, his face registering both anger and confusion. "And how the hell would you know that?"

"Because he told me, that's why," she replied genially. "After his goons kidnapped me from my condo, they—"

"Kidnapped? You were kidnapped?"

"That's what I said, didn't I?"

"How the hell did they manage that? We had a surveillance team on you 24/7, not to mention the fact that, at least according to David, your condo is supposed to be as difficult to get into as Alcatraz was to get out of. So, with all of that security around, how could they have pulled something like that off?"

"It was quite simple really. They posed as FBI agents." She pushed a hand through her hair. "And, I don't know about you, but I'm not in the habit of saying no to those guys. And, apparently, neither was Mike."

"Meaning?"

"That's how they got him as well. Apparently they went to Fenway Park posing as Feds and convinced him that they'd been sent by you to pick him up. A couple of hours later, they brought him to an abandoned warehouse and . . ." she lowered her eyes, "and you know the rest."

"But why?" There was considerable anguish in his voice. "Why did they do it?"

She shrugged. "To be honest, I don't really know. All they told me was that Barnett had simply run out of patience with you. Apparently he'd been trying to get you to sell Celebrix back to him for quite some time, but he wasn't having any luck. So, more out of desperation than anything else, he shot Mike, presumably thinking that maybe, just maybe, that might get your attention and possibly even get you to change your mind."

Tim's head sank further into the pillow as if retreating from reality. Through half-closed eyes, he mumbled, "What a sick, sick man. Unbelievable." Turning to Allan, he added, "It's a damn good thing you killed him, because otherwise, I'd have had to do it myself. Animals like him just don't deserve to live!"

"You'd have killed him? How about me?" asked Shannon. "I'm the one he kidnapped."

"And I'm the one with a dead friend and a bullet hole in my side!"

"That's true."

"But I still don't see the connection between Celebrix and you." Tim asked, "Why would he want to kidnap you? That doesn't make any sense to me. You're against us, and therefore, you'd think that he'd have been more interested in partnering with you than in kidnapping you. Or am I missing something here?"

"You are, because believe it or not, the answer is actually quite obvious when you think about it. He used me as bait in order to get to you. And as you can see, it worked."

"But, where would he have even come up with the idea?" Tim asked.

"I don't know. I can only assume that he must have had someone working on the inside—maybe someone who was working on either the iQu team or at Celebrix."

Before Tim could respond to that, another shot of pain flooded through his body. Gritting his teeth, he took short, sharp breaths, his face contorted.

It was almost a full minute before he spoke again. He glanced briefly up at Shannon, and then looked away. "As to coming up here to see you, I didn't see myself as having much choice in the matter. With one friend already lying in the morgue, and with others possibly to follow, I felt that I had to do something. Anything. And the only thing that came to mind was to talk to you to see if I could determine your innocence or guilt. Don't ask me how I was going to do that, because I had no idea. All I knew was that I had to give it a try."

His voice tailed off at the end as Shannon's eyes bore into him.

She was furious, and it showed. In a voice brimming with anger, she said, "So, what you're saying is that you thought that I'd killed Mike, is that it?"

Unable to hold her stare, Tim looked away. "Or possibly paid someone else to do it, yes."

Shannon's anger continued to escalate. "And your diving accident. You thought that I was behind that as well, didn't you?"

"I wasn't sure, but to be honest, yes, the thought did cross my mind."

"Which is why *you* put me under twenty-four hour surveillance, correct?"

"Well, for that, and for other reasons."

Shannon's eyes narrowed. Placing her hands on her hips, she asked, "And, what might they be?"

Tim hesitated, so David quickly moved in. He brought up the gas-leak incident, and ended by saying, "Now, as to whether or not you did it intentionally, that's something I'll never know. But, in light of the current state of our relationship, I'm sure you can understand my suspicions."

Shannon was either genuinely shocked or was putting on the performance of her life. She looked deeply hurt, and for a moment seemed to be suffering from an inconvenient clotting of the voice. "It's good to hear that you think so highly of me."

The room fell silent as the two of them glared at one another until the fires died down. It was Shannon who finally broke the silence. Trying her best to keep her emotions in check, she explained, "Well, dear brother, I hate to disappoint you, but I'm afraid that once again, your perception of reality is not at all accurate. No, I most certainly did not intentionally leave the gas on in an attempt to blow up *our* cottage." Sour look; a shake of the head. "Really! Where do you come up with this stuff? I really do have to wonder about your sanity sometimes. You might want to go and have it checked out. I know a wonderful shrink back in the city who specializes in this sort of thing."

David ignored her remarks. "Well, what were you doing up here then? I thought I'd asked you not to—"

"If you must know, I drove up here that day to pick up some documents that I'd forgotten the weekend before, and was not all that anxious to have you see. I'd gotten here around noon and had planned to spend the afternoon, but then changed my mind when my secretary phoned about an hour later to say that you were already on your way up. As soon as I heard that, I quickly gathered up my things, had a quick cup of coffee—hence my use of the stove—and got out as quick as I could, apparently forgetting to turn the stove off in the process. Believe me, it was just an accident. Nothing more." She eyed him sharply. "Really. I can't believe this. You actually thought I was trying to kill you?" She shook her head in disgust. "You're even nuttier than I thought you were."

Once again the room fell silent. Tim considered asking her about the phone call he'd overheard a few days back, but decided against it. He'd already heard enough to convince him that her only sin had been one of poor judgment in choosing Miller over David. The real culprit was clearly Barnett, and not her.

Growing increasingly uncomfortable with the silence, Tim said to her, "I'd appreciate it if we could go back to the kidnapping story. I still don't understand how they were able to smuggle you past our surveillance team."

Allan answered for her. "They used chloroform to knock my guys out before they went into the building."

"Chloroform? Are they OK?" asked Tim with a hint of a smile creasing his face.

Allan chuckled. "Yeah, other than bruised egos, they're fine."

Returning his attention to Shannon, Tim asked, "So, once they got you out of the building, what did they do next?"

"They brought me to an old abandoned warehouse—apparently the same one in which they'd shot Mike—and after tying me to an old wooden chair, they told me that someone else was coming to deal with me. I was only to learn later that that someone was Barnett. Anyway, in the meantime, I pretended to sleep while they sat in front of an old television set and watched—of all things—your press conference from beginning to end. And liked it, I might add."

"How do you know that?" Tim asked.

"Because they talked about it afterwards. There were two of them: an Iranian by the name of al-Hassan, who was the smarter of the two, and a short pudgy Italian by the name of Tony. And Tony was a talker; in fact, the man rarely shut up. He talked about everything. He talked about the two of you," she nodded first at Tim and then at David, "about Mike, about what he'd done down in St. Lucia, about his life back in Chicago, about what he was going to do with all of his new-found wealth, and so on, and so on, and so on. Really, the guy just wouldn't shut up. And, the fact that the Iranian didn't force him to told me that as far as he was concerned I'd soon be dead anyway, so it made no difference to him as to how much I knew."

Tim continued to ask her about her ordeal for another ten minutes or so, and then suddenly changed tack. "Well, now that that's all been cleared up, I guess there's just one other thing I'd like to know."

"And that is?"

"What happens now between the three of us? Where do we go from here? Do we continue battling one another or do we try a different tack?"

David answered before Shannon could. "She doesn't have much choice in the matter considering the fact that our stock has now become too rich for Miller's blood!"

Shannon ignored David completely and continued looking directly at Tim. "I can't speak for the two of you, but as far as I'm concerned, I'm ready to bury the hatchet and see if we can't start trying to work together." She paused to gauge their reactions, but as both men were too stunned to speak, she spoke again. "It'll be tough, I realize, but I'm willing to give it a shot."

All David could manage out of his mouth was one word, "Why?"

"Two reasons. One, I also watched the press conference this morning, and though I'm loath to admit it, I have to say that the three of you put on a hell of a show. It was extremely convincing, especially the part about iQu. Which is not to say that I've been converted over completely, but it is to say that I'm now more receptive to the idea than I was before."

"Well, that's a start," Tim acknowledged. "And the second reason?" he asked. But before she had a chance to answer, Tim was again overcome by an attack of acute pain. This time, worse than ever.

Hating to see his friend in such pain, David said, "I'll see if I can get the doctor in here for a minute," and then quickly left the room.

Shannon also sprang into action. Moving closer to Tim, she took his hand in hers, and then bending over him, she whispered words of comfort in his ear.

When Tim finally reopened his eyes, they were moist and red-rimmed. He nodded to Shannon for her kind words, and then taking back his hand, he turned to Allan and said, "Before I pass out completely, there's just one other little thing I'd like to know."

Allan approached the bed. "What's that?"

"How did you get involved in all of this? And better yet, since you were involved, how did I end up with a bullet-hole in the side? Couldn't you have prevented this somehow?"

Allan nervously cleared his throat. "To answer your first question, I first learned of your intention to come up here from David, who called the moment you left his office early this afternoon. And, not surprisingly, as soon as I heard what you were planning, I put a call through to a friend of mine to see how I could get a S.W.A.T. team up here before you arrived." Short pause. "Purely as a precautionary measure, because obviously at that point I still had no reason to suspect anything, yet I was highly suspicious. The whole thing seemed just a little too contrived. But then, a short time later, when I received word from Shannon's surveillance team as to what had happened to them, that changed everything. And that's when I decided that I needed to get up here as well. So I took a private plane into Moultonborough, which is only about an hour from here, and then drove the rest of the way on my own."

"That's an answer to the first question, now how about the second—couldn't you have prevented this from happening? For example, why didn't you just phone me and tell me what was going on? Believe me, I would have been too keen to turn around."

Allan shook his head. "I thought about doing that, but in the end, decided against it for one simple reason: I didn't have proof of anything. All I had was two drowsy field agents, a missing suspect, and a strange feeling in my gut. Not enough to convict anybody of anything. So what I really needed was to catch the perpetrators in the act. And in order to do that, I needed to play this thing out."

Tim frowned. "But, again, couldn't you have done that in a way that avoided shots getting fired?"

"Afraid not." Allan replied. "Believe me, I tried. I took every precaution that I could think of, but in the end, I needed Barnett to make the first move."

"Barnett?" Tim repeated with more than a hint of confusion in his voice. "But what led you to suddenly conclude that it was Barnett who was behind it all? Because last time I spoke to you, you still had Shannon as your key suspect. Or am I mistaken?"

"No, you're not mistaken. Not at all. But a lot has happened since we last spoke to one another. First of all, there was my discussion with Shannon this morning. I went into it pretty well convinced that she was the guilty party. But by the time it was over, I wasn't so certain anymore. And then there was the chloroform incident. That really sent me for a loop, until I thought back over some of the things that you'd said about

Barnett. That really got me thinking. So I made a few calls, which led me to make a few more, until before I knew it, all the pieces started to fit together—and at the center of the puzzle was one man—Barnett. Why I hadn't seen it earlier, I'll never know, but it just goes to show, none of us are infallible. Not even me."

Tim wanted to ask another question, but before he could get the chance David suddenly barged back into the room with the doctor in tow. The doctor was a youngish man—Tim thought no more than forty—with what appeared to be a permanent scowl on his face. He was wearing blue jeans and a light sweater over a light yellow polo shirt. He had smatterings of blood everywhere—on his pants, sweater, hands and face. He looked utterly gruesome.

Wanting to give them their privacy, David did a quick u-turn just inside the door and then asked Allan and Shannon to join him out in the hallway. Allan, only too anxious to escape Tim's questions, pivoted on his heels and quickly followed David out. Shannon started to do likewise, but then suddenly turned back around and returned to the side of Tim's bed. Leaning down she cupped a hand over her mouth and whispered something in his ear.

Tim's eyes widened and his throat suddenly went dry. "Really?"

"Oh, absolutely, I wouldn't have it otherwise." With that she gave him a quick peck on the cheek and then straightened up before turning and heading for the door.

Tim turned his head and watched her go. He sighed inwardly and, for a brief moment, completely forgot about the pain.

EPILOGUE

7:47 P.M., Tuesday, June 30   Quenetics stock price: ▲ $98.50
Shannon's condominium, Boston

LISTENING TO THE THUNDER ROLL off into the distance, Tim left the sofa and moved towards the sliding glass doors leading out to the balcony as though wanting to wish the storm a final farewell. Peering through the glass, he saw that the rain had all but stopped, with just a light drizzle now coming down. Unlocking the door, he slid it open and stepped outside. The air was hot and muggy, yet lightly scented with the smells of luscious flowers. Taking in the view he watched the lights swimming in the rainy mist and glimpsed through fitful clouds neighboring towers as they faded in and out of view. He marveled at the beauty of it all, and not for the first time since he'd been shot, he offered up a silent prayer in thanks for still being able to bear witness to God's handiwork.

Much had happened since that fateful day in early May when a bullet had almost taken his life. The wound had healed, and the bandages were gone, but the scars—both mental and physical—would remain always. The only consolation was that at least Barnett had gotten his just rewards. He drew some comfort from that.

He also drew comfort from the fact that he and Shannon were now getting along so well. He was now spending at least three nights a week at her place, and they'd just spent a long weekend together back out in California. They were even talking about going on a diving holiday together in late August down in the Caymans. Who would ever have expected it? "God really does work in mysterious ways," Tim mumbled to himself. Then, suddenly hearing something behind him, he quickly turned to see if it was Shannon having finally returned from her aerobics class. It wasn't. There was nobody there. "*Must have been the cat,*" he thought to himself.

Returning his gaze to the glimmering lights of the city and the dark corpulent clouds drifting by overhead, Tim's mind turned to Quenetics and iQu. Both companies were doing well—extremely well, in fact. Quenetics stock was now trading in the high nineties, and still edging higher, in large part due to the strategic changes David had made, but also in part because of the buzz building around iQu. Nary a day went by when it wasn't making headlines somewhere. In fact, it had received so much attention of late that David and he had been asked to make a presentation about it and Quenetics' miraculous turnaround to the U.S. Chamber of Commerce in a week's time.

Though he was never all that keen to get up on stage, if he was honest with himself, he had to admit that he was looking forward to this event. And with just cause. The organizers had told them that over 50,000 executives were expected at the event, either live or via satellite link-up. But, just the mere thought of having to stand in front of so many people was enough to make Tim's mouth go dry and his stomach knot. The only remedy for that: meticulous preparation.

With that thought in mind, Tim headed back inside, where the sofa and his trusty laptop were waiting. Placing the computer on his lap, he scrolled up to the top of the document and started to read what he'd gotten down so far. Knowing how nervous he'd be in the opening minutes, he decided to start things off with a personal anecdote:

My father grew up in a small community of 2,200 people on the northern shores of Lake Superior in Ontario. The town was quite isolated, to put it mildly. In fact, from the edge of my town to the edge of the next town was nothing but thousands of square miles of rugged wilderness. In that "protected" business environment, my grandfather owned and operated a small pharmacy in which he sold everything from jewelry to cutlery, from paper products to candy bars. In other words, he sold a little of everything. And, quite successfully, I might add. In fact, so much so, he was able to retire young, a wealthy man. And why not; having a virtual monopoly on many of the products he sold, he could charge what he wanted, confident in the knowledge that his customers would be only too willing to pay.

Now, imagine for a moment what would have happened had he chosen to move his business, lock, stock, and barrel, to the center of New York City. What do you think would have happened to his thriving little enterprise?

216 · *Terry Waghorn*

It would have gone bankrupt in a heartbeat. Why? For the simple reason that he wouldn't have been able to compete. He'd have been surrounded by specialty stores and category killers undercutting him on everything he sold. Even the Internet would have played a part in quickening his financial demise.

The moral of the story: *the more competitive a market becomes, the more focused you have to be.* Which, in the context of today's global marketplace where everybody is able to sell to everybody else, means that the more focused you become, the more successful you are likely to be.

Moderately satisfied with that, Tim continued scrolling down until he came to the next section: his three-step strategy model—*focus, fortify, and foster futurity.* He read on:

If you agree with the maxims presented above, you're then left with a decision to make: What is it you're going to focus on? And, believe it or not, your choices are limited. In fact, there are only three. One: you can focus on a specific product or service category. Two: you can focus on a particular customer cluster. Or three, you can attempt to do both. What is not a viable option is to choose not to choose.

Now, if all that sounds rather cryptic then let me explain it otherwise. Your options are: you can set your sights on trying to "own a word" in the mind of all customers; you can try to "own a specific customer cluster," or you can attempt to do both.

The text then went on to explain each option in greater detail. As he'd already memorized the material, he skipped over it (if you, however, would like to read more about it, I'd refer you to the Supplementary Material), and then stopped when he came to the next section.

With the distinctions now clear, we can return to the original question: *What is it you are going to focus on*—a word (if so, which one?), a customer cluster (if so, which one?), or both (if so, which word and which cluster)? It's got to be one of the three, otherwise you'll find yourself in with the vast majority of organizations, not owning anything, and as a result, struggling to make yourself heard above the market din, yet never quite managing to do so.

To assist you in making your decision, you may find the following chart to be of some use. It lays out the different options available to you and provides you with a few thoughts on how each can be achieved.

Options	Own a Word	Own the Customer
Create an entirely new market	• Unearth latent customer needs • Wed new technologies to create new products/services • Core-competency creep	
Replace existing market leader	• Value innovation (break compromises / create a new and superior value curve) • Value improvement (offer more for less)	• Remove all layers of interference • Offer solutions rather than products • Offer personalized products / services
Subdivide the market	*Types of differentiation* • Price differentiation • Image differentiation • Support differentiation • Quality differentiation • Design differentiation	*Types of segmentation* • Geographic segmentation • Demographic segmentation • Behavioral segmentation • Psychographic segmentation • Combinations

Following the chart were fifteen to twenty lines of text beginning with the words, "David to discuss how he focused Quenetics," followed by a few simple bullet points. They read:

- He's focusing the company on the interim business and getting out of everything else.
- Within the interim business, he's decided to differentiate himself from his competitors by broadening and deepening his service offering to encompass everything that has to do with "personal growth" and "self-development." His ultimate aim is to own these words in the minds of all customers.
- iQu will ultimately play an essential role in helping him to achieve that aim.

With the issue of *focus* out of the way, Tim moved on to the next step in his model: the *fortification process*. As he did so, his stomach growled, reminding him that he hadn't eaten anything in over seven hours. Glancing down at his watch he wondered again what could possibly be taking Shannon so long. Her class finished at seven, and she was normally home by seven-thirty, which was now over half an hour ago. With the memory of Mike's death still weighing heavy on his mind, he couldn't help but wonder if something might have happened to her. Otherwise, he assumed, she'd have called by now.

He returned to his speech material, hoping that that would take his mind off his worries. But when he stared at the screen, the words failed to register. It was useless. His mind was still firmly fixed on Shannon. Maybe some coffee would help. Quickly making himself a cup, he lingered a moment in the kitchen, savoring the novelty of his impatience to be with somebody. It had been a long time since he'd felt the tug of a human magnet, and he had to admit, he liked the feeling.

Returning to the sofa, he got started rereading what he'd put down for step two—*fortifying your position*. It read:

Choosing a unique position, however, is not enough to guarantee a sustainable advantage. A valuable position will eventually attract the interest of others, who, in turn, will then try to imitate it. In some industries, value innovators may not face a credible challenge for many years; in others, the competitive response time may be much quicker. In an effort to fend off these copycat competitors, a number of actions must be taken. There are eight in total, and again, they all relate back to the question: *How can you defend yourself against those who are intent on imitating you?*

The set of actions you need to take is somewhat contingent upon whether you're competing in a digital or a non-digital domain, as you can see on the following chart. But regardless of which you choose, the essential ingredients remain the same: you begin with value creation measures (steps 1–4), followed by loyalty-building measures (steps 5–7) and disciplined-growth initiatives. (For more details on each, please refer to the Supplementary Material.)

Step	Non-Digital	Digital
1	• Fine-tune your focus	• Outsource to the customer
2	• Make trade-offs	• Personalize your offering
3	• Tighten the fit	• Create communities of value
4	• Continuously improve the activities that are left	• Open all systems to customers and give away as much information as possible for the lowest possible price.
5		• Build customer loyalty
6		• Build employee loyalty
7		• Learn to coopete (cooperate with competitors)
8	• Maximize volume advantages	• Expand your offerings

Tim's thinking was to then turn the floor over again to David so that he could say a few words about how he'd adapted the model to suit his own strategic requirements. To assist David's thinking on this, Tim had made some notes. They read as follows:

On the Quenetics side:
- *Fine-tuning his focus:* He had two smaller subsidiaries within Quenetics that didn't mesh with his new full-service self-development concept. One was a specialty headhunter business focused on the IT industry; the other, a low-budget, no-frills organization focused on seasonal labor. Both had already been sold off.
- *Making trade-offs/eliminating inconsistencies:* Quenetics had outsourced all of its training work to third parties. No longer. It had also been continuously reducing its spending on employee training as a way of saving money. That trend had been reversed.
- *Tightening the fit:* Too many to mention. A more sophisticated sales force, better interviewing techniques, a more

comprehensive hiring process, a more integrated IT infrastructure, to list but a few.

- *Continuous improvement:* TQM teams were being set up and equipped with the proper tools and training.

On the iQu side:

- *Technological advantage:* First and foremost, we have such highly advanced proprietary technology that it'll take those intent on imitating us a great many years, not to mention huge sums of money, to do so (and by then, we'll long since have moved on, but more on that later!).

- *Outsourcing to our customer:* Once connected to our system, we will assist all users in creating their own Web page, tentatively called 'MeInc,' which would then serve as their own personal learning portal.

- *Mass customization:* Users would be given the opportunity to customize everything from the look and feel of their avatar to the level of intimacy they have with it, and from the design and structure of their own personalized training scheme to the specifics as to how, when, and where they received it.

- *Create communities of value:* In addition to the ubiquitous chat rooms, community bulletin boards, virtual classrooms, and the like, one of iQu's most appealing features will be its highly advanced multi-user simulation games. Not only would the games give the user the opportunity to apply—in a perfectly safe, and highly entertaining way— the principles and theories they'd acquired throughout other parts of the program, they also have the added attraction of being able to play these games anytime, any-where, and with anybody.

- *Pricing model:* I'm afraid I'm going to have to keep that a competitive secret for the time being. Suffice it to say, how-ever, that like Henry Ford and his Model T, we're committed to ensuring that our products will be affordable to all. Put otherwise, we're keen to do our part to eliminate the grow-ing digital divide.

- *Building loyalties:* We'll, of course, be tracking customer flows, and will be going to great pains to built loyalty and minimize defections. We'll be doing the same with our employees.

- *Building an entire business ecosystem:* In order for us to accomplish all that we've set out to do, which, by the way, includes establishing a rating system for corporate intan-gibles, setting up a human capital exchange, and creating an AI platform upon which anyone who wants to sell any of our users any form of learning material—whether it be on the subject of needlework, automotive maintenance, or Kamasutra—will have to do it through us, we realize that we're going to have to partner up with a myriad of different companies. We're in the process of doing that now.

- *Expanding our offerings:* We expect that once the connection between user and avatar has been properly established, the avatar will then become a digital gateway to that customer. Any other Web-based firm wanting to sell products and ser-vices—especially those that are knowledge-based—will find that they'll have to do so through us. Once we arrive at that point, it will be very difficult indeed for a competitor to ever steal that customer away from us.

On the combined enterprise:

David to spend a few minutes summarizing the efforts under way designed to ensure a seamless integration between "brick" and "click" (Quenetics and iQu).

Before moving on to the third, and final, section of the speech material—that relating to the issue of *fostering futurity*—Tim did a quick time check. He was surprised to see that it was now 8:22. And still he'd heard nothing from Shannon. This was definitely not normal at all.

He reached for his cellphone and hit the redial button. Placing the phone to his ear, he waited tentatively for the connection to be made. But as soon as it had, he was put through to her voice-mail. Not wanting to leave a message, he ended the call, and then just sat there staring at his own reflection in his telephone screen. A thousand different thoughts whirled around in his head, some more disturbing then others. He could feel his anxiety level starting to ratchet up. In an attempt to head it off, he decided to give David a call. Maybe she was at his place. It was on the way home from the club, and with the two of them now getting along moderately well, she was spending ever more time over there.

It was David who picked up. "No, she's not here, Tim. Sorry. In fact, I haven't seen her since she left the office shortly after five."

"Five? So early?" Tim asked.

"Yeah, apparently she had something going on this evening."

"Really? How come I haven't heard anything about it?" Trying to keep the irritation out of his voice, he asked, "Any idea as to what it is?"

"No, she didn't say, nor did I ask, to be honest. I didn't have the time to. We just passed each other in the hallway, she heading for the elevator, I for a meeting that I was already late for. But, I wouldn't worry about it if I were you. She probably just wanted to meet a friend for a drink or something."

"But, if that were true, then the least she could have done was to give me a call. She knew I'd be here tonight."

"Ah, again, I wouldn't worry about it. As we both know, she's not the most conscientious person on the planet. She'll call when she gets around to it."

"When she gets around to it! It's now almost 8:30!"

Loud sigh. "That's Shannon, Tim. I don't know what else to say. Just relax. I'm sure she'll be home soon, and I'm sure she'll have a good reason for being late." Anxious to move off the subject, he asked, "The speech material—how's it coming along?"

Tim paused for a moment as he tried to change gears. "I'm almost finished. In fact, I'd say I'm about 90 percent of the way there."

"Yeah, I read what you e-mailed me just before I left the office. It's good stuff, but I missed the *foster futurity* bit. You obviously haven't gotten to that part yet."

"I have now; in fact, I'm almost finished with it. Do you want to hear what I've got?"

A few moments of hesitation, then, "Ah, sure. I was just about to run to the store for some ice cream, but I guess that can wait a few minutes. So, yeah, go ahead."

Transferring the phone to his left hand so that he could operate the cursor with his right, Tim read:

In today's hypercompetitive world, it seems that regardless of how well you fortify your position, your more inspired rivals will eventually find a way to penetrate your defenses. You need to be ready for that day when it arrives, so that when it does, your enemies arrive only to discover that you're no longer there—you've already moved on, leaving nothing but warm ashes in your wake. And the game of catch-up begins anew.

Tim paused, waiting for feedback.

"That's great," David said enthusiastically. "Short, and to the point. But I'm curious as to what comes next. You make it sound as though you're about to unveil the greatest corporate secret of all time—the secret to eternal growth and profitability."

Tim laughed. "I don't know about that, but what I would say is that, yes, by preparing for tomorrow today, you not only stand a much better chance of surviving today, you're also more likely to ensure that tomorrow evolves in a way that suits you."

"Compelling argument, but let's move on, I want to get to the shop before it closes. So, you were saying something about staying one step ahead of both customer and competitor. How's it done?"

Tim resumed reading.

Three things need to be done. They are, in no particular order:

(a) *Create a new value curve*: If others have evolved to the point where their value curves are converging on your own, you have little choice but to create a new and improved value curve.

(b) *Manage innovation as a portfolio of options*: Being able to produce a new value curve on demand requires always having something up your sleeve. This is not easily achieved, yet it can be so long as you're willing to stick to a simple piece of advice: manage innovation as a portfolio of options. Look at your corporate investments much as you would a stock portfolio. Rather than putting all your eggs in one basket and exposing yourself to high levels of risk, invest small amounts in a diverse basket of opportunities, thereby spreading the money around, and in so doing, lessening the underlying risk. Put otherwise, you need to invest in a plethora of promising technologies and developments, never with the intention of becoming an owner, but rather with the aim of being an active stakeholder. You might even go so far as to set up a small venture capital firm within your own firm.

The reasons for investing in this way are manifold. First and foremost, investing in this way is a cost-effective way to learn about the future. Direct, hands-on experience is gained at minimal expense, and therefore, at minimal risk.

Your portfolio of investments can also prove valuable because they can be used in creating options for the future. When the future does arrive, you should have a number of different responses ready at your disposal.

Experimentation is also valuable for defensive reasons. It lowers the probability of being blindsided by unanticipated futures. By probing all four corners of the competitive landscape, you're more likely to uncover threats, such as new competitors or emerging technologies.

(c) *Align your company with its new future*: When the time comes to roll out your new value curve, you're then left with the question of how best to do this. You have five options.* You can place:

- a foot in both camps;
- both feet in the new camp;
- both feet in the old camp;
- both feet in the new camp with a new name;
- two separate camps, two separate names.

David cleared his throat. "I was with you right up until that last bit. Those five options—could you go through them again, and this time, maybe slow down a bit, and provide a few more details along the way?"

Tim said, "Sure." He was just about to get started when he suddenly heard a key scraping in the lock. "David, just a sec, I think I hear Shannon at the door. Let me just go and find out." With that, he dropped everything and ran to the door. By the time he got there, Shannon was already inside, sporting a big smile.

She spoke before he had a chance to. "If you're not doing anything, do you want to come out in the hallway for a few seconds? There's something I want to show you."

---

*Ries, Al. *Focus: The Future of Your Company Depends On It*. New York: HarperBusiness, 1996, p. 149.

"In the hallway?"

"Yes, in the hallway. Come on, it'll just take a second."

Trying to decide whether to be angry or glad, he hesitated for a few moments, then asked, "What is it?"

"If I were to tell you that, it wouldn't be a surprise now, would it? So, are you coming or not?"

Leaving his anxieties, and his telephone, behind, Tim followed her out the door. There, standing across the hall, was a new Cannondale mountain bike. The Jekyll 3000. It was the undisputed "king of the trails," and truly a thing of beauty.

His emotional barometer went through the roof. Never before had a woman given him such an awesome gift. And it wasn't even Christmas or his birthday. Amazing!

Temporarily at a loss for words, Tim turned to her and, scooping her up in his arms, kissed her passionately and repeatedly. When they'd finished, Tim said in a voice laden with emotion, "Tell you what, now you're really going to have a tough time trying to keep up to me."

Her eyes lit up as she flashed another smile. "Oh, I wouldn't be too sure about that if I were you."

"And why not?"

"Because I also bought one for myself."

AFTERWORD

There you have it. Terry Waghorn's Strategic Model: focus, fortify, and foster futurity. Having read the story and seen it being applied, I trust that many of you will be quick to agree that it is a powerful model. So much so, in fact, that once I had fully come to terms with it, I decided to apply it to my own enterprise, The Ken Blanchard Companies, a medium-sized firm currently employing over three hundred people.

Prior to being exposed to the model, our company was a collection of disparate business units, each operating within the field of human resources management. One unit concentrated on selling learning materials such as books, workbooks, assessments, videos, and inspirational speeches. Another unit sold a variety of training programs and change management processes. And still another unit provided services and products to the international market through both direct sales and through licensees. Each of these units was doing fine, but I knew they could do much better. The question was how to make that happen. That's where Terry's Strategic Model came into play.

In applying it to Blanchard, we pulled a cross-section of people together to do some self-diagnosis—and it didn't take us long to uncover some powerful lessons. We were missing the focus necessary to maximize our success. We didn't own a concept or a word, and by no means did we own a customer cluster. For example, while Situational Leadership was the concept that launched our business—and, in many ways, had become a recognized brand—we didn't technically own it. We had to share the concept with my co-developer, Paul

Hersey, and his Center for Leadership Studies. While several of my co-authored books, including *The One Minute Manager*, *Raving Fans*, *Gung Ho!*, and *Whale Done!*, had essentially gained brand status in the marketplace, focusing our energy on any of those brands seemed too limiting, too focused.

After much soul searching, we realized that we were a serious contender in each of the markets in which we were competing, but we were not the dominant player in a single one of them.

What to do about it?

We began by thinking a lot about which service category or customer cluster we had the potential of dominating. Regardless of how we segmented the market nothing popped out at us. This suggested that going after a customer cluster was probably not a viable option. That left owning a word or concept. But which word or concept? The words "empowerment" or "people power" came to mind but were quickly dismissed as being far too broad for any company, let alone ours, to lay claim to. The words "performance improvement" or "management" also held considerable appeal. Upon further reflection, however, we decided that they might be too limiting and wouldn't get at the heart of who we are and what we can do. We were known first and foremost for our ability to help people think differently about the *potential of people*. In fact, in recent years we had declared that our purpose was "to unleash the power and potential of people and organizations for the common good." As a rallying call we had contended that we were "The World's #1 Advocate for Human Worth in Organizations." So maybe we were the "relationships" company. But that seemed too broad, too.

After discussing all these possibilities, we were struck by a blinding flash of the obvious. We are in the *leadership and performance business*. For thirty years I have been studying, writing about, and teaching about leadership. Any problem an organization has is a leadership problem. If your customers are dissatisfied that's a leadership problem. If the morale of your people is low that's a leadership problem. If you are not accomplishing your goals and are financially unstable that's a leadership problem. Time after time I have seen a single individual or high-performance team come in and turn an organization around because they are effective leaders. We felt so strongly about this that we have started a joint Master of Science Degree Program in Executive Leadership with the University of San Diego. In addition, I have co-founded the Center for *FaithWalk* Leadership, a non-profit organization dedicated to helping leaders of faith walk their faith in the marketplace.

When we talk about leadership what do we mean? Leadership is an influence process. Any time you attempt to influence the behavior of someone else to accomplish a goal, that is leadership. In other words, leadership is about going somewhere: if you don't know where you are going and what you want to accomplish, your leadership doesn't matter.

And that's what performance is all about. In *The One Minute Manager* we wrote that "people who feel good about themselves produce good results." And that's true. If you feel good about yourself, you work hard. But after that book came out I realized that I might have been caught in the old human relations trap because you can't try to make people feel good in a vacuum. So in *Putting the One Minute Manager to Work,* I updated that phrase to read, "people who produce good results feel good about themselves." The best way to enhance the self-esteem and satisfaction of your people is to help them produce good results, and the best way you can help organizations win is to focus leadership on performance. I am now convinced that this is the concept that we should own. Every speech I give, every book I write, every product we sell, every intervention we make, all hinges around that core concept.

Amen and Hallelujah! We found our words! We found our concepts: *Leadership and Performance.* That was a market space we could definitely define and dominate. All we would need to do was commit ourselves to serve as a one-stop shop for people who want to help themselves and others to perform better through effective leadership. Simple enough—the only problem was that we would probably not be the only ones moving in that direction. Market research confirmed our suspicion.

The solution: we would have to further differentiate ourselves. That's what "fortify" is all about.

How would we differentiate ourselves from others competing in our space? How would we prevent others from replicating what we do or imitating our processes? We decided we would do three things. First, in the learning materials and speakers area we established a Blanchard Leadership book series. This would permit me to not only co-author books in the area of leadership but also sponsor and write forewords to books by other leading thinkers. Not only would this give us more leadership exposure but it would provide more books and other materials that could be sold in the leadership and performance area.

Second, in our training area we developed what we call Blended Solutions. This involves combining the best of technology with up-front, face-to-face training. Our Blended Solutions involve four elements:

- Setting the stage (engaging top management)
- Teaching the concept (collaborating with the best technology partners)
- Application and use (employing the best consulting partners and facilitators)
- Sustainability (making the learnings part of the culture)

Third, to reinforce our commitment to sustainability, we have developed an intervention strategy through which we offer a guarantee to companies who help us set up their leadership and performance systems: if they don't return to their bottom line four times the amount they pay us, we return the fees. We believe that this sustainability area will give us a competitive edge and be tough for others to invade.

And finally, we were ready to foster futurity. We already had a head start in this area because my wife Margie had stepped down as president of the company to head up the Office of the Future. This was an outgrowth of Terry's and my book, *Mission Possible*, in which we argued that things are moving so fast today you have to manage the present and create the future simultaneously. Yet we felt it was not appropriate to have the same people doing both jobs. Having people with present-time operational responsibilities planning your future will kill your future. People with present responsibilities are already overwhelmed as it is, and generally not as open to new ideas. None of the people in the Office of the Future have present-time responsibilities. Their focus is to look out there and find out what our competition is doing, what's happening in technology, and to keep us on the cutting edge. (In fact, the Office of the Future has played a significant role in developing our Blended Solutions.)

That's what happened when we started to look at Terry's Strategy Model and apply it to our organization. I got more than I bargained for in agreeing to write the Foreword for *The System*. I got a way of looking at our organization that is going to make us a tough competitor for anybody who wants to come into our leadership and performance space. Thanks, Terry.

Ken Blanchard
Escondido, California

SUPPLEMENTARY MATERIAL FOR TIM AND DAVID'S UPCOMING SPEECH TO THE U.S. CHAMBER OF COMMERCE

STEP 1

Focus

Step	Non-Digital	Digital
1	• *Fine-tune your focus* (Don't try to straddle different strategic positions—it can blur or degrade your focus)[1]	• *Outsource to the customer* (Build an interface into your information sources and give customers the tools they need to navigate and customize it)
2	• *Make trade-offs* (Eliminate any activity that is inconsistent with the image you're trying to project in the marketplace)[2]	• *Personalize your offering* (Customers like the appearance of a personalized product, especially when they have done the personalizing themselves)
3	• *Tighten the fit* (Ensure all activities complement one another in ways that create real economic value)[3]	• *Create communities of value* (The more like-minded individuals you attract, and the more opportunities you provide for these people to interact with one another, the more valuable your network becomes)
4	• *Continuously improve* the activities that are left (Strike a balance between process improvement and process innovation, using economic value added [EVA] as a baseline measure for everything)	• *Open all systems to customers* and give away as much information as possible for the lowest possible price (continued on p. 237)

STEP 1

Focus

Step	Non-Digital	Digital
5	• *Build customer loyalty:* Measure customer flows (both additions and defections) and then search for the root causes of each individual's decision to alter his or her buying behavior. Reward loyalty and try to reduce defections.	
6	• *Build employee loyalty:* Measure employee defections and conduct exit interviews to find out what needs to be fixed. The challenge: to identify and eliminate any policy that discourages or destroys employee loyalty. Reward loyalty and reduce defections.	
7	• *Learn to coopete (cooperate with competitors):* You need to have a plan not only for your own product or service, but also one for your entire business ecosystem. This requires being expert in identifying potential partners quickly, determining the appropriate level of intimacy, securing the corresponding level of commitment, and leading the group's evolution.	
8	• *Maximize volume advantages:* To make imitation as costly as possible, it's vital that you maximize economies of scale. Growth is best achieved through geographic expansion and possibly by further product-line rationalization.	• *Expand your offerings* (Customers go to the sites that give them what they want for the fewest clicks of a mouse. Convenience is crucial.)

---

[1] Porter, Michael E. "What Is Strategy?" *Harvard Business Review,* November-December, 1996, p. 68.
[2] Ibid., p. 68.
[3] Ibid., p. 70.

STEP 2

Fortify

Options	Own a Word	Own the Customer
Create an entirely new market	• *Technology as competitor:* Most companies use technology as an "essential enabler." They begin with existing ideas—products or services—tweak them, and then throw them over to the IT department and ask them to design the systems components required to bring their new creation to market. Revolutionaries turn this process on its head. They begin with technology, and then build out from there. Thus, to them technology is looked upon as being the essential disrupter of the status quo and its underlying assumptions. They see technology as being the problem rather than the solution.	

• *Latent needs:* Say's Law: supply can create its own demand. People don't know they want something until they see that they can have it; then they feel they can't live without it. One way of unearthing these latent needs is to mix and match, to blend attributes of one product with those of another. (Think of the Sony Walkman. By combining the sound quality of boom boxes with the low price and the convenient size and weight of transistor radios, Sony created the personal portable-stereo market.)

• *Convergence:* Rule-breakers have been known to blur the boundaries between industries. This is currently popular within the rapidly changing media sector, which is quickly becoming the product of the convergence of the computing, communications, and content industries.

• *Competency Creep:* Innovative companies have taken talents learned in one arena and directed them into others, and have created whole new industries as a result (night vision in cars would be an example of this).

(continued on page 239)

STEP 2

Fortify

Options	Own a Word	Own the Customer
Replace existing market leader	• *Value innovation:* Rather than trying to beat their rivals, value innovators seek to make them irrelevant by creating something that is completely different from the rest. One way to do this is to look across the conventionally defined boundaries of competition—across substitute industries, across strategic groups, and across buyer groups. Another is to question existing orthodoxies and/or break customer compromises with the aim of creating next generation products. • *Value improvement:* In every industry, there is a ratio that relates price to performance: X units of cash for Y units of value. The challenge is to improve that value ratio and to do so radically—200%, rather than 10% or 20%. Put otherwise, the trick is to increase one's margins by creating disequilibria between the perceived value offered and the price asked by either significantly increasing the former or by significantly reducing the latter.	• *Disintermediation:* Middleman functions between producers and consumers are being eliminated through digital networks. Thus, power is shifting down the distribution chain to those who own the customer. Consequence: middlemen need to create new value or risk being eliminated. • *Offer solutions:* In many industries product complexity is outstripping customer sophistication. In this situation some revolutionaries have come to realize that their customers want solutions rather than products. They realize that their true value no longer resides in the product itself. Instead, their real source of utility is an entire problem-solving system, a system in which the product is only an element. • *Mass customization:* No one wants to be part of a mass market. We'll all buy the same things—but only if we have to. Deep in our need to be ourselves, to be unique, are the seeds of industry revolution.

STEP 3

Foster Futurity

Option	Description	Examples
One foot in both camps[1]	One foot in the old business, one in the new. Highly popular, yet extremely ineffective. Tragically, when companies try to straddle both the past and the future, they typically succeed in going nowhere. Why? Because the market sees you for who you were, not for who you want to become.	• Xerox was a powerhouse in copiers when it saw a mad rush to computers taking place. So it tried to get into the computer business with a copier name. The media asked, "What does a copier company know about the computer business?" Xerox exited shortly thereafter.
Both feet in the new camp[2]	If you're really sure that the new will completely replace the old, it's best to go in with both feet. Somewhat understandably, there aren't all that many companies that have actually done this.	• When Intel faced devastating competition from Japan in the memory chip business, it stopped making memory chips and diverted all of its energy into making microprocessors.
Both feet in the old camp[3]	One way to develop a unique position is to go in the opposite direction of everybody else. If they're all running after the next big thing, you could opt not to follow. You may end up with an old-fashioned product, but there are always those who want exactly that.	• Jack Daniel's bourbon • White Castle hamburgers • Levi's 501 jeans • Zippo lighter • Bic pens
Both feet in the new camp with a new name[4]	This is rare, yet it has been known to happen. When it does, it's typically because the previous name has been tarnished or has become redundant.	• The Haloid Company, a manufacturer of photographic paper that bought the rights to Chester Carlson's electro-photography invention, subsequently changed its name to Xerox Corp.
Two separate camps, two separate names[5]	If a company can't or doesn't want to exit its current business, but at the same time, wants very much to have a foot in the new business, the best course of action is to launch the new company under a new name. That way, there is no confusion in the marketplace.	• Levi Strauss is the world's largest producer of brand-name clothing. Thus, it is loath to discard its name, yet when it saw the trend developing towards casual wear, it knew it had to do something. It responded by setting up a separate company—Dockers.

[1] Ries, p. 150
[2] Ries, p. 158
[3] Ries, p. 160
[4] Ries, p. 163
[5] Ries, p. 165

AUTHOR'S NOTE

For additional information on Terry Waghorn's thoughts and activities, please contact:

KPMG
Burgemeester Rijnderslaan 10
1185 MC Amstelveen
telephone + 31 20 656 7567
mobile + 31 65 582 2464
email: waghorn.terry@kpmg.nl

For additional information on Ken Blanchard's activities and programs, please contact:

The Ken Blanchard Companies
125 State Place
Escondido, CA 92025
Telephone: (800) 728-6000 or (760) 489-5005
Fax: (760) 489-8407
or visit the website at www.kenblanchard.com